Studies on the Chinese Economy

General Editors: **Peter Nolan**, Sinyi Professor of Chinese Management, Judge Institute of Management Studies, University of Cambridge, and Fellow of Jesus College, Cambridge, England; and **Dong Fureng**, Professor, Chinese Academy of Social Sciences, Beijing, China

This series analyses issues in China's current economic development, and sheds light upon that process by examining China's economic history. It contains a wide range of books on the Chinese economy past and present, and includes not only studies written by leading Western authorities, but also translations of the most important works on the Chinese economy produced within China. It intends to make a major contribution towards understanding this immensely important part of the world economy.

Titles include:

Thomas Chan, Noel Tracy and Zhu Wenhui
CHINA'S EXPORT MIRACLE

Sarah Cook, Shujie Yao and Juzhong Zhuang (*editors*)
THE CHINESE ECONOMY UNDER TRANSITION

Xu Dixin and Wu Chengming (*editors*)
CHINESE CAPITALISM, 1522–1840

Christopher Findlay and Andrew Watson (*editors*)
FOOD SECURITY AND ECONOMIC REFORM

Samuel P. S. Ho and Y. Y. Kueh
SUSTAINABLE ECONOMIC DEVELOPMENT IN SOUTH CHINA

Kali P. Kalirajan and Yanrui Wu (*editors*)
PRODUCTIVITY AND GROWTH IN CHINESE AGRICULTURE

Bozhong Li
AGRICULTURAL DEVELOPMENT IN JIANGNAN, 1620–1850

Alfred H. Y. Lin
THE RURAL ECONOMY OF GUANGDONG, 1870–1937

Dic Lo
MARKET AND INSTITUTIONAL REGULATION IN CHINESE INDUSTRIALIZATION

Jun Ma
THE CHINESE ECONOMY IN THE 1990s

Guo Rongxing
HOW THE CHINESE ECONOMY WORKS

Sally Sargeson
REWORKING CHINA'S PROLETARIAT

Ng Sek Hong and Malcolm Warner
CHINA'S TRADE UNIONS AND MANAGEMENT

Michael Twohey
AUTHORITY AND WELFARE IN CHINA

Wang Xiao-qiang
CHINA'S PRICE AND ENTERPRISE REFORM

Xiaoping Xu
CHINA'S FINANCIAL SYSTEM UNDER TRANSITION

Yanni Yan
INTERNATIONAL JOINT VENTURES IN CHINA

Wei-Wei Zhang
TRANSFORMING CHINA

Xiao-guang Zhang
CHINA'S TRADE PATTERNS AND INTERNATIONAL COMPARATIVE
ADVANTAGE

Studies on the Chinese Economy
Series Standing Order ISBN 0–333–71502–0
(*outside North America only*)

You can receive future titles in this series as they are published by placing a standing order.
Please contact your bookseller or, in case of difficulty, write to us at the address below with
your name and address, the title of the series and the ISBN quoted above.

Customer Services Department, Macmillan Distribution Ltd, Houndmills, Basingstoke,
Hampshire RG21 6XS, England

The Chinese Economy under Transition

Edited by

Sarah Cook
Fellow
Institute of Development Studies
University of Sussex

Shujie Yao
Professor of Development Economics
University of Portsmouth

and

Juzhong Zhuang
Economist
Asian Development Bank

First published in Great Britain 2000 by
MACMILLAN PRESS LTD
Houndmills, Basingstoke, Hampshire RG21 6XS and London
Companies and representatives throughout the world

A catalogue record for this book is available from the British Library.

ISBN 0–333–71675–2

First published in the United States of America 2000 by
ST. MARTIN'S PRESS, INC.,
Scholarly and Reference Division,
175 Fifth Avenue, New York, N.Y. 10010

ISBN 0–312–22621–7

Library of Congress Cataloging-in-Publication Data
The Chinese economy under transition / edited by Sarah Cook, Shujie
Yao, Juzhong Zhuang.
    p.   cm. — (Studies on the Chinese Economy.)
"This volume includes a selection of papers presented to the
Chinese Economic Association annual conferences in 1995 and 1996"–
–Preface.
Includes bibliographical references and index.
ISBN 0–312–22621–7 (cloth)
1. China—Economic conditions—1976–   2. China—Economic
policy—1976–   3. Industries—China.   4. Rural industries—China.
I. Cook, Sarah.   II. Yao, Shujie.   III. Zhuang, Juzhong.   IV. Chung
-kuo ching chi hsüeh hui.   V. Series.
HC427.92.C4672168   1999
338.951—dc21   99–33850
                                                                      CIP

This book is printed on paper suitable for recycling and made from fully managed and sustained
forest sources.

10   9   8   7   6   5   4   3   2   1
09   08   07   06   05   04   03   02   01   00

Printed and bound in Great Britain by Antony Rowe Ltd, Chippenham, Wiltshire

Contents

List of Figures

List of Tables

Preface

China's transition from a centrally planned economy to a market-oriented one provides important lessons and experiences for other similar economies in the world. Rapid economic growth has helped reduce poverty and raise people's living standards. However, income growth has been accompanied by rising inequality. Economic growth has led to unbalanced development between regions. Moreover, the reforms have not so far established a free and democratic market system similar to that in the advanced industrial countries. There are still serious structural problems within the national economy. Market imperfections persist, especially in the financial and banking sectors. The agricultural sector is still weak and unstable. In addition, rural industrialization has led to severe degradation of the natural environment caused by air and water pollution. Despite a long period of income growth it is still difficult to eliminate rural poverty. The most recent reforms of the state-owned enterprises have caused significant urban unemployment, which may have serious social, economic and political implications. All these transitional problems require urgent research and analysis.

This volume includes a selection of papers presented to the Chinese Economic Association (CEA(UK)) annual conferences in 1995 and 1996. They cover a wide range of issues on the Chinese economy under transition, including the urban industrial sector and state-owned enterprise restructuring, a set of questions relating to the rural (both agricultural and rural industries) sector, and theoretical and empirical approaches to the modelling of transition and structural change. The CEA (UK) was established in 1988 by overseas Chinese students and scholars living in the UK. It has now become the leading academic organization in the UK for research into the Chinese economy. This volume is part of its efforts to disseminate research results of its members both within the UK and elsewhere throughout the world. It does not attempt to be comprehensive in its coverage; nor does it aim to provide a coherent perspective on the transition process. Instead, it presents a selection of papers representing important theoretical and empirical contributions to our understanding of China's reform experience, the policies adopted and their impacts.

Acknowledgements

The papers included in this book are selected from the Chinese Economic Association (UK) annual conferences in 1995 and 1996. The conferences were generously sponsored by the following institutions and organizations: the Department for International Development, the Education Section of the Chinese Embassy, ESRC, the Royal Economic Society, the London School of Economics, the Prudential Corporation plc, BP, BT, the HSBC Midland Bank, Eagle Star Holdings plc, the Mar Tian Group Ltd, Martin Clarke Asia Ltd and the MTM Partnership Ltd. The editors are grateful for the generosity of these organizations. They are also indebted to the CEA advisors, the board of directors and all CEA members for their support to and participation in the CEA conferences and other academic activities. They are particularly grateful to Professor Peter Nolan for his encouragement to publish this manuscript.

The editors and publishers also acknowledge with thanks permission from the following to produce copyright material in the tables in this volume: Coricelli *et al.* (1997); Lo (1997); Alfandari and Schaffer (1998); Fan (1996); Hofman (1996); Woo (1996); Cornelli *et al.* (1996); Schaffer (1996); Troner and Miller (1995); Hendry (1989); Bell *et al.* (1993). Full details are provided on the relevant pages.

Notes on the Contributors

Philip Andrews-Speed is Assistant Director of the Centre for Energy, Petroleum and Mineral Law and Policy at the University of Dundee. He leads the China Programme which focuses on the natural resources and energy sector in China, and is currently managing a European Commission, Synergy Programme project on Energy Structure and Policy in China. He has published widely on the reform of China's energy sector, as well as on wider issues of energy policies in Asia and investment in the former communist states of Europe and Asia.

Fiona Carmichael is a Lecturer in Economics at the Department of Economics, University of Salford. Her research interests include multinational corporations, industrial organization, minority labour markets and health economics. She has published in a number of academic journals including the *Scottish Journal of Political Economy*, the *International Journal of Manpower*, *Applied Economics*, *Applied Economics Letters*, *Renewal*, *International Review of Applied Economics* and *Journal of Health Economics*.

Sarah Cook is a Research Fellow at the Institute of Development Studies, University of Sussex. Her research focuses on the social and micro-level impact of economic reform in China, and includes work on labour markets and employment in rural China, rural social welfare reform, poverty and gender. Publications include articles in *Journal of Development Studies* and *Oxford Development Studies*.

John Davis is Director of the Centre for Rural Studies and Head of Agricultural and Food Economics in The Queen's University of Belfast. One of his main research interests in recent years has been the effects of the reform process on rural economic change in China. He is co-author of two books and a number of articles on the Chinese grain sector. He is a regular visitor to China and is co-ordinator of a link with South China Agricultural University.

Meibing Fu is a Lecturer in Economics at the Department of International Economics at Renmin University of China. Between 1994 and 1995 she was a visiting academic at the Department of Economics, University of Salford. She is currently a PhD candidate in industrial organization at the University of Ontario, Canada.

Shumei Gao is a Lecturer in Economics in the School of Management, Heriot-Watt University. Research interests include international trade policy with particular reference to the Multi-fibre Arrangement (MFA) and the impact of trade liberalization between the EU and Central and Eastern European (CEE) countries.

Chaodong Huang is currently a Research Officer working on the Pacific Asia programme at the National Institute of Economic and Social Research (NIESR) in London. He received his undergraduate and postgraduate education from South China University of Technology in Guangzhou, China, and holds a PhD in economics from the University of London. His current research interests include trade and foreign direct investment (FDI), Britain's economic relationship with Hong Kong and economic modelling of the Chinese economy in transition. Prior to joining NIESR he worked at the University of Leicester.

Athar Hussain is a Senior Research Fellow, London School of Economics. He has published extensively on the Chinese economy. He has worked as a consultant for many different international organizations, including the World Bank, the European Union and the Chinese government. He has published widely in different economic journals.

Aying Liu is a Lecturer in the Business School, Middlesex University. He was previously research officer in the University of Oxford and the University of Portsmouth. He has published extensively in refereed journals, including *Environmental and Resource Economics, Journal of Agricultural Economics, Economics of Planning, Economic Systems Research, Development Policy Review, Applied Economics Letters* and *Regional Studies*. His current research interests include applied economic modelling, environmental and resources economics and trade and employment.

Xiaming Liu is a Lecturer in Aston Business School, University of Aston. His research interests include foreign direct investments (FDI) in China and emerging financial markets. He has published in *Journal of Applied Econometrics, Applied Economics, Weltwirtschaftliches Archiv, International Review of Applied Economics* and *Applied Economics Letters*.

Feng Lu is an Associate Professor at the China Centre for Economic Research of Beijing University. His publications appear in *World Development* and the *Journal of International Development*.

Minquan Liu is a Lecturer in Economics at the University of Leicester. A micro and development economist, his research interests include Chinese agriculture, enterprise and financial reforms, and foreign direct investment. He has recently led and completed a major UK DFID-funded project on Chinese and Taiwanese agriculture and is currently undertaking another collaborative research project on FDI in Guangdong Province, China. As well as Chinese economic development, he has also taught economic development in East Asia. He has published papers in the *Journal of Comparative Economics, International Review of Applied Economics* and *International Journal of Economic Development and Trade.*

Peter Nolan is Sinyi Professor of Chinese Management and Fellow of Jesus College, University of Cambridge. He is author (or co-author) of *Big Business in China* (with Xiaoqiang Wang, 1998), *China's Rise, Russia's Fall: Politics and Economics in the Transition from Stalinism* (1995), *State and Market in the Chinese Economy: Essays on Controversial Issues* (1993), *The Political Economy of Collective Farms: An Analysis of China's Post-Mao Rural Economic Reforms* (1988), *Inequality: India and China Compared,* 1950–1970 (1976, with T. J. Byres) and editor or co-editor of many other books.

Duo Qin is a Lecturer in Economics, Queen Mary and Westfield College, University of London. She was previously Research fellow at Oriel College, University of Oxford. She entered economics in 1982 by taking a three-year MA course in economics at the Graduate School of the Chinese Academy of Social Sciences. Special interests are macroeconometric studies of transitional economies and developing economies; and history and methodology of econometrics. She has published articles in *Oxford Economics Papers, Journal of Comparative Economics, Journal of Asian Economics* and *Econometric Theory.*

Peter Romilly is a Lecturer in the School of Social and Health Sciences, University of Abertay, Dundee. He has published in the *Journal of Applied Econometrics, Applied Economics, Weltwirtschaftliches Archiv, International Review of Applied Economics, Economics of Planning* and *Applied Economics Letters.*

Mark E. Schaffer is Professor of Economics and Director of the Centre for Economic Reform and Transformation (CERT) in the Department of Economics, School of Management, Heriot-Watt University. He has written widely on the economics of transition in Central and Eastern Europe (CEE), the former Soviet Union and China, and has worked as a consultant for a number of international organizations, including the World Bank, the International Monetary Fund, the European Bank for Construction and Development and the European Commission. He currently serves on the editorial board of the *Journal of Comparative Economics* and the *Journal of Post-Soviet Geography and Economics.* Professor Schaffer's current research interests include enterprise and financial sector reforms and labour markets in transition economies.

Haiyan Song is a Lecturer in Economics at the School of Management Studies, University of Surrey. His research interests include the Chinese consumption function and emerging financial markets. He has published in a number of academic journals, including *Journal of Applied Econometrics, Applied Economics, Economic Modelling, Weltwirtschaftliches Archiv, International Review of Applied Economics, Economics of Planning, Journal of Transport Economics* and *Policy,* and *Applied Economics Letters.*

Hui Tan is a Lecturer in Economics at the Department of International Economics at Renmin University of China. Between 1994 and 1995 he was a visiting academic at the Department of Economics, University of Salford. He is currently engaged in research on emerging markets and international trade in the School of Management at the University of Bath.

Liming Wang is a Research Fellow in the Centre for Rural Studies, The Queen's University of Belfast. He worked as Division Director in the Ministry of Commerce of the People's Republic of China in Beijing (1982–8). His PhD thesis *An Economic Analysis of Supply and Demand in China's Grain Sector* (1995), developed both theoretical and empirical models for China's grain economy. He has recently co-authored *China's Grain Supply and Demand: The Challenge of Feeding a Billion* (1998). Main fields of interests are China's rural development, the Chinese grain economy and economies in transition.

Xiaoqiang Wang is a Research Fellow in the Research Institute for Economic System and Management, State Commission for Restructuring the Economic System (China) and Research Fellow in the China Business Centre, Hong Kong Polytechnic University. He is author (or co-author) of *Groping for Stones to Cross the River – The Way of Chinese Reforms* (1990), *The Poverty of Plenty,* with Bai Nanfeng and translated by Angela Knox (1991) and *Big Business in China* (with Peter Nolan, 1998).

Shujie Yao is Professor and Director of Development Economics Research, University of Portsmouth (UK). He has worked as a consultant for a number of international organizations, including the World Bank, the European Union, and the Food and Agriculture Organization of the United Nations in many different countries of Asia and Africa. He is author of *Agricultural Reforms and Grain Production in China* and co-author of *Economic Reforms and State-Owned Enterprises in China, 1981–87.* He has published papers in many economics journals, including the *Journal of Political Economy, Economic Development and Cultural Change,* the *Journal of Development Studies,* the *Journal of Comparative Economics, Applied Economics,* the *Journal of Agricultural Economics, Food Policy, Environmental and Resource Economics, Regional Studies,* the *Journal of Environmental Management.* He is also a member of the international editorial board of *Food Policy.*

Qiren Zhou is a Research Fellow in the China Centre for Economic Reform, Beijing University. His main research interests include agricultural and rural development in China.

Juzhong Zhuang is Economist in the Asian Development Bank. While working on this volume, he was Research Officer at the London School of Economics. He has published articles in *Economica, Economics of Planning*, the *International Review of Applied Economics*, and the *Asian Pacific Business Review*. He edited and co-edited two special issues for *Economics of Planning* and the *International Review of Applied Economics*. His current research interests include corporate governance and financing in Asia, reform of state-owned enterprises, and privatization.

List of Abbreviations and Acronyms

ADF	Augmented Dickey–Fuller
ADL	autoregressive distributed-lag model
APC	average propensity to consume
BOT	build–operate–transfer
CEE	Central and eastern Europe
CEEFSU	Central and East European States of the Former Soviet Union
CIS	Commonwealth of Independent States
CMEA	former Soviet satellite states' economic group
CNCOFEIC	China National Cereals, Oils and Foodstuffs Export and Import Corporation
CNOOC	offshore national oil company
CNPC	onshore national oil company
CPE	centrally planned economy
CSO	Central Statistical Office
CV	coefficient of variation
DF	Dickey–Fuller
ECM	error-correction mechanism
FDI	foreign direct investment
FSU	Former Soviet Union
GDP	gross domestic product
GMM	generalized method of moments
GVIO	gross value of industrial output
HPEC	Harbin Power Equipment Company
HRS	Household Responsibility System
JV	joint venture
LDC	less developed country
LRMC	long-run marginal cost
MEAS	macroeconomic analysis system
MGMR	Ministry of Geology and Mineral Resources
MIT	Ministry of Internal Trade
MNC	multinational corporation
MOA	Ministry of Agriculture
MOC	Ministry of Commerce
MOFERT	Ministry of Foreign Economic Relations and Trade
MOFT	Ministry of Foreign Trade
MPC	marginal propensity to consume
NBF	net bank financing
NI	national income
NIC	newly industrializing country

NID	normally and independently distributed
NRC	net relative change
NTB	non-tariff barrier
OECD	Organization for Economic Co-operation and Development
OLS	ordinary least square
PBC	People's Bank of China
PCIV	possible co-integrating vector
POI	public ownership institution
PPP	purchasing power parity
PRC	People's Republic of China
R&D	research and development
RLS	recursive least square
RNIA	real national income available
RPC	real personal consumption
RTVE	rural township and village enterprise
SEZ	Special Enterprise Zone
SOE	state-owned enterprise
SPC	State Planning Commission
SSB	State Statistical Bureau
STB	State Tax Bureau
SUR	seemingly unrelated regression
TFP	total factor productivity
TVAPV	time-varying average propensity to consume
TVE	township and village enterprise
TVMPC	time-varying marginal propensity to consume
TVP	time-varying parameter
VAR	vector autoregression
WTO	World Trade Organization

Introduction

Sarah Cook, Shujie Yao and Juzhong Zhuang

After two decades of economic reform, China's transition path continues to attract keen academic interest and debate, and to produce new challenges and innovative policy responses. The reform process has been gradual in comparison with the more 'orthodox' model followed by most other former socialist economies, but it has often involved relatively rapid adjustments in particular sectors while reform in other areas has been held back. Thus, for example, the swift decollectivization of agriculture in the early 1980s was followed by the dramatic emergence of a rural industrial sector in the mid-1980s and the phenomenal movement of labour out of agriculture; by contrast, the state-owned enterprise (SOE) sector has undergone only marginal restructuring. Twenty years on, the transition process appears to have maintained its momentum, accompanied as it is by sustained annual growth rates of over 8 per cent, with recently appointed leaders adopting new and radical reforms in specific areas. The latest examples are the renewed impetus for SOE reform, related initiatives to establish a social welfare system, and major reform and retrenchment of the state bureaucracy.

A number of the key issues and challenges posed by China's reforms are addressed by the authors in this collection of papers, all of which were presented at the Chinese Economic Association (UK) Annual Conferences of 1995 and 1996. Established in 1989 by overseas Chinese students and scholars, the CEA is the leading academic organization in the UK for research into the Chinese economy. This volume does not attempt to be comprehensive in its coverage, nor does it aim to provide a coherent perspective on the reform process. Instead, it presents a selection of papers by Chinese and British economists representing important theoretical and empirical contributions to our understanding of China's transition experience, the policies adopted and their impacts. While these are primarily economic studies of themes which have been prominent in debates over the past two decades, some of the authors have been closely associated with the policy-making process, and these papers also speak to broader questions of the institutional and political environment which shapes policy choices.

The topics covered range from the perennial development debates of rural growth, agricultural productivity and employment, to the more pressing issues of the mid-1990s – SOE restructuring, related issues of urban unemployment and welfare provision and financial sector reform. The volume is organized in three main parts. Part I focuses on the urban industrial sector and SOE restructuring; chapters in Part II address a set of questions relating to the rural (both agricultural and industrial) sector; finally, the four chapters in Part III speak to broader macroeconomic issues, focusing in particular on theoretical and empirical approaches to the modelling of transition and structural change.

Industrial restructuring and enterprise reform

Reforms affecting the state enterprise sector have been piecemeal but have led to significant changes in the price and wage system and an increase in the autonomy of enterprise managers. Nonetheless many loss-making enterprises remain dependent on the state banking system for financial support. The complexity of SOE reform lies in the social and political role of the enterprise as the basis of the urban social welfare system; enterprise restructuring thus needs to be accompanied by the establishment of alternative mechanisms of social welfare. China has recently embarked on a new stage in its ongoing efforts to reform the SOE sector. Setting itself an ambitious three-year target (1998–2000), the government aims to eradicate loss-making firms through mergers and bankruptcy, and to establish a social welfare system complemented by schemes for the reemployment of labour and the development of unemployment insurance.

Part I starts with a provocative chapter by Nolan and Wang (Chapter 1) which raises an important issue for international political economy and one which is critical for China's future position in the global order – the rise and structure of big business and its relationship with multinational corporations. Through a comparison of how big business developed in the industrial economies, particularly the USA, and the role of the state in this process, the authors argue that – contrary to dominant neo-liberal ideology – the Chinese government must play an important role in creating indigenous big business in order to compete with global giants.

The following two chapters are concerned with issues related to enterprise ownership and financial discipline, or the soft budget constraint. Liu in Chapter 2 explores the political dimensions of privatization programmes, focusing on the nature and causes of the 'soft budget constraint' characteristically associated with public enterprises. He argues that the soft budget constraint has a political logic to it which lies in a state-dependent mentality arising from previous policies; this heightens the political risks involved in privatization, for example, where the public sees the state renouncing its perceived social obligations towards the labour force. This 'state-dependent' mentality may suggest alternative paths towards privatization based on the principle of delegation. Gao and Schaffer's Chapter provides a comparative analysis of financial discipline and the soft budget constraint in China and the transitional economies of Central and Eastern Europe and the Former Soviet Union (CEEFSU). They find some differences between the two regions in the sources of financing for poorly performing enterprises: for example, in China new finance comes primarily from banks whereas in CEEFSU countries tax arrears have emerged as an important financial source.

The extent to which enterprise performance has been affected by the wage and management reforms is explored by Hussain and Zhuang in Chapter 4, who analyze the relationship between employment and wages using industrial survey data from 1986 to 1991. They find that regular wages and bonuses are lower in loss-making than profit-making enterprises, implying that employment did depend on enterprise performance. Results also show a lower output elasticity of employment than is the case in market economies, supporting other evidence on the presence of surplus labour in state enterprises.

Focusing on one strategic sector – energy – Andrews-Speed in Chapter 5 shows that reforms leading to an increase in productivity in other sectors have not affected the energy industry. This is due to lack of competition caused by high barriers to entry and the absence of effective regulation as state enterprises act as both operator and regulator. He argues that if the government fails to reform the energy sector, it will require considerable financial support to meet the growing demand for energy.

The rural sector – agriculture and industry

The on-going restructuring of the urban industrial sector will inevitably have repercussions for the rural sector – for example, through its effect on prices, employment and industrial competitiveness. The success of rural and agricultural reforms over the past twenty years has been well documented. The initial focus on incentive and institutional change led to rapid productivity gains in agriculture. This was followed by diversification and industrialization of the rural economy, with the surplus labour released from agriculture being absorbed by rural non-farm enterprises – the so-called 'township and village enterprise' (TVE) sector – which provided an important engine of growth in the late 1980s. Successful development of TVEs, particularly in the coastal regions, has transformed local economies and dramatically improved rural living standards; however, this process of rural industrialization has not been so successful in some inland areas.

In the context of this transformation from a predominantly agrarian economy to one where an increasing share of the labour force is engaged in non-agricultural activities, an important question concerns the contribution of agriculture to overall economic development and growth. Chapter 6 by Yao first reviews the evidence on this question, and then uses co-integration analysis to show the extent to which agriculture remains a driving force behind growth in other sectors of the economy, while the reverse relationship does not hold. He provides a convincing argument that government policies remain biased against agriculture and that many of the benefits from agricultural development are experienced by the urban sector.

The longer-term development of the agricultural sector nonetheless remains a policy concern for the government. In an insightful discussion of agricultural marketing channels in both China and the Former Soviet Union, Zhou in Chapter 7 makes the case that the privatization of production alone is insufficient for the emergence of an efficient market-oriented economy. The development of efficient large-scale trading institutions will be critical for the longer-term agricultural development of a large country such as China. This development is hindered by state control, through powers of procurement and regulation, over major trading institutions which thus operate as 'profitable bureaucracies'.

Who benefits from growth in the rural economy largely depends on access to more remunerative employment. Through an analysis of household survey data, Cook in Chapter 8 explores the relationship between employment and income distribution, and thus who gains or loses in the process of transition. She examines the contribution of different income sources to inequality – the principal sources being agricultural income, which is most equitably distributed, non-agricultural wage income generated from collectively or privately owned enterprises and non-wage income from self-employment, the latter being the least equally distributed. This pattern is found to vary, however, for households at different points along the income distribution.

A major concern within China, and more recently in international debates, is whether China has the capacity to continue to feed its growing population. Two chapters on China's grain economy address complementary aspects of this question, highlighting the political and economic importance of the grain sector in China. Lu's Chapter undertakes an institutional analysis of China's grain trade policy and domestic grain production. He argues that the grain import policy has traditionally been driven by a desire for self-sufficiency irrespective of economic efficiency. With changes in the economic environment, more emphasis has been placed on principles of economic efficiency and comparative advantage; however, there remains an important role for the state in planning imports in order to stabilize domestic supply. Chapter 10 by Davis and Wang examines the impact of the continuing dual-track system of quotas and staple crop pricing in the grain sector, modelling the response of grain producers to changing government policies. Their empirical analysis suggests that economic reforms have brought about more market-like behaviour especially in relation to sown acreage decisions but that non-price policies, particularly quotas, continue to influence supply decisions.

The final chapter on the rural sector focuses on TVEs, particularly those producing for export. Carmichael, Tan and Fu in Chapter 11 provide additional evidence that TVE development has been spatially uneven, with the eastern provinces reaping most of the benefits both in terms of domestic and international markets. They then identify the main determinants of labour productivity among those enterprises producing primarily for export.

Modelling transition and structural change

The Chapters in Part III illustrate different approaches to modelling aspects of macroeconomic transition and structural change in China's economy. While a considerable number of excellent studies of transitional economies have been published in recent years, Qin in Chapter 12 argues that the macroeconomic modelling of transitional economies remains very much an uncharted area. Through a review of recent theoretical and methodological approaches to the analysis of transitional economies, she argues that theoretical modelling has been based on an assumption of equilibrium while empirical studies focus on short-run dynamics. Hence she emphasizes the need to separate out the transitional features from long-run information. In addition, she stresses the importance of understanding the behavioural adjustments to policy change by heterogeneous actors, and how these affect aggregate macroeconomic dynamics. Her analysis thus points to the need for greater interaction between theorists and applied modellers, between macro and micro economists, and between academics and country specialists and policy makers.

The second chapter in this section analyzes structural change in employment and investment in China over the period 1985–94 using the shift-share method. Liu in Chapter 13 decomposes the structural changes in each regional economy into parts which can be explained by national trends, local industrial mix and locational competitiveness.

The remaining two chapters in this section provide examples of the application of co-integration techniques to the analysis of macroeconomic issues. Huang's Chapter investigates the implications of economic reforms for money demand. His major finding is that the long-run demand for money exhibited considerable instability during the period 1952–93. This instability resulted from the economic reforms since the late 1970s which led to an observed structural break in the demand for money. Song, Liu and Romilly in Chapter 15 apply a similar technique to investigate the long-run relationship between aggregate consumption and income. Although no constant long-run equilibrium can be identified, there is evidence of a gradually changing long-run relationship between consumption and income, a pattern which is closely associated with political, economic and social changes occurring during transition.

Analysing transition: theory, method and policy

In addition to the valuable analyses of specific issues in China's transition provided by individual chapters, themes recurring in several studies contribute to broader theoretical, empirical and policy literatures. First, the collection contributes to the comparative literature on transition economies through a number of studies which explicitly examine China's experience in the light of Eastern European and Former Soviet Union (FSU) experience; this includes studies on subjects from agricultural reform (Zhou) to state enterprise finance (Gao and Schaffer), as well as the theoretical modelling of transition (Qin).

Second, several of the chapters apply new methodologies to the analysis of economic issues raised by China's reforms. These include studies using co-integration techniques (Huang, Song *et al.* and Yao) and other methods for modelling structural change such as the shift-share method (Liu). Third, and most important from a policy perspective, many of the chapters supplement their economic analyses with insightful discussion of policy processes, illuminating the institutional contexts within which reforms are designed and implemented in particular sectors.

China's experience provides valuable material for examining the processes of reform, and for analyzing the political economy and institutional dynamics of policy implementation and outcomes. Ultimately, analyses of these processes have the potential for contributing both to economic theory and methodology, as well as to better policy formulation which integrates the theoretical concerns of economists with the political and institutional factors which determine a country's transition path. Taken together, these chapters thus provide not only an illuminating commentary on China's reform path and on the consequences of policies pursued, but also present analyses which should be of relevance in resolving some of the reform dilemmas currently facing China's new leadership.

We would like to express our sincere thanks to the ESRC (UK), the Education Section of the Chinese Embassy in London, the Department for International Development (UK), the Great Britain–China Centre, Commercial Union, Eagle Star Holdings Plc, the MTM Partnership, the London School of Economics and the University of Middlesex for their generous support.

Part I

Industrial Restructuring and Enterprise Reform

1
Reorganizing Amid Turbulence: China's Large-scale Industry

Peter Nolan and Wang Xiaoqiang

Introduction

The transformation of Chinese big business stands at a crossroads. China's explosive economic growth since the early 1980s has been accompanied by major change in the nature of China's big businesses. This has occurred alongside the institutional transformation of big business in OECD countries, especially the USA, a rapid increase in multinational investment in emerging markets, particularly in China, and a transformation of international politico–economic relationships. Moreover, China's rise poses large challenges for international politics. The future pattern of the relationship between multi-national business and emerging big businesses in China will be powerfully shaped by international relationships, especially that between China and the USA.

In the mid-1990s, the world's biggest capitalist businesses are rapidly penetrating the 'commanding heights' of the Chinese economy through joint ventures (JVs) with large, formerly state-owned enterprises (SOEs). Two systems in the midst of colossal system change are coming into ever-closer contact. The world's big businesses are massive institutions; the Chinese state has a long tradition of unity and cultural distinctiveness. The rapid locking together of these two systems is a central – perhaps the most important – issue in the global political economy. While China has made progress in reforming its large-scale industry, the country's planners face major challenges in responding to rapidly changing circumstances in their attempt to create powerful indigenous big businesses that can compete with the global giants.

Changing international relations

China's growth and the increase in foreign direct investment

China's average annual GDP growth rate in 1980–90 was 10.2 per cent, accelerating to 12.8 per cent in 1990–5 (World Bank, 1997, p. 234). This is the most sustained period of explosive growth seen by any economy, let alone one of China's size, and has significant consequences for international relations. China's international ranking in the production of steel rose from fifth in 1980 to first in 1996; in coal, from third in 1980 to first in 1995; in electricity consumption, from sixth to second; in cement, from fourth to first; in fertilizers, from third to second; in chemical fibres, from fifth to second; and in TV sets, from fifth to first (SSB, 1996, p. 821). China's exports grew at 11.5 per cent per annum in 1980–90, and at 15.6 per cent per annum in 1990–5 (World Bank, 1997, p. 234). Sino–US trade surged from $2.5 billion in 1979 to $42.8 billion in 1995 (State Council Information Office, 1997, p. 21). Official US data show that China's trade surplus with the USA rose from $8.4 billion in 1991 to $23.1 billion in 1995, with China overtaking Japan as the country with which the USA had the largest trade deficit (*Financial Times*, 13 March 1997).[1]

China's huge size and sustained growth stimulated a massive capital inflow: for three successive years, in 1994–6, China was the second largest recipient of foreign direct investment (FDI) after the USA (*Financial Times*, 9 January 1997). From 1991 to 1995, US direct investment in China increased tenfold from $0.3 billion to $3.1 billion (SSB, 1993, p. 648–9, and 1996, p. 598–9) (Table 1.1).

By 1996, around 200 of the world's largest 500 companies had invested in China (*Business Weekly*, June 29 1997) and the share of large foreign companies in the Chinese economy was rising fast. By 1997 Coca-Cola had 23 plants, and accounted for around 26 per cent of total soft drinks sales in China (Coca-Cola, 1997).[2] By 1996 Volkswagen's giant JV in Shanghai accounted for around 52 per cent of China's total sales of sedan cars (*Business Weekly*, January 5 1997). Until the 1990s, government policy restrictions and

Table 1.1   FDI inflows, 1984–95 (billion dollars, % in brackets)

Inflows by regions	1984–9	1990	1991	1992	1993	1994	1995
Total inflows	115.4	203.8	157.8	168.1	207.9	225.7	314.9
Developed countries	93.1	169.8	114.0	114.0	129.3	132.8	203.2
Share of total (%)	*80.7*	*83.6*	*72.2*	*67.8*	*62.2*	*58.8*	*64.5*
Developing countries	22.2	33.7	41.3	50.4	73.1	87.0	99.7
Share of total (%)	*19.2*	*16.5*	*26.2*	*30.0*	*35.2*	*38.5*	*31.7*
Central and Eastern Europe	neg	0.3	2.4	3.7	5.5	5.9	12.1
Share of total (%)	*neg*	*0.1*	*1.5*	*2.2*	*2.6*	*2.8*	*3.8*
Developing countries							
minus China	19.9	30.2	37.0	39.2	45.6	53.2	62.2
Share of total (%)	*17.2*	*14.8*	*23.4*	*23.3*	*21.9*	*23.6*	*19.8*
Asia	11.5	22.1	22.7	29.1	50.0	56.3	68.1
Share of total (%)	*10.0*	*10.8*	*14.4*	*17.3*	*24.1*	*24.9*	*21.6*
China	2.3	3.5	4.4	11.2	27.5	33.8	37.5
Share of total (%)	*2.0*	*1.7*	*2.8*	*6.7*	*13.2*	*15.0*	*11.9*

Notes: The figures for 1984–9 are average averages.
Sources: UNCTAD, (1996), pp. 227–31.

caution on the part of large international firms limited investment in 'upstream' sectors. However, with the apparently stable political situation in the wake of Tiananmen, and a significant relaxation of Chinese government policy, multinational direct investment began to flow in large amounts into upstream industry.

For example, by the end of 1996 in the petrochemical sector four large JVs for the construction of ethylene plants had been concluded, with Dow (US), BP (UK), BASF (Germany) and Exxon (USA), and a further two were close to completion. If all these plants are completed, they will account for around three-quarters of China's estimated ethylene demand in the year 2000. In the power-generating equipment sector, three indigenous firms, Harbin, Deyang (Sichuan) and Shanghai, account for around 80 per cent of total output. By late 1996 two of these were JVs with large multinational companies. In Shanghai, Westinghouse (USA) had established JVs with the steam turbine and thermal generator plants, and Voith with the hydro generator plant. In Deyang, Siemens had established a JV with the thermal generator plant, Hitachi with the boiler plant and GE (Canada) with the hydro generator plant.[3]

The response within and outside China

Within China the response to the huge inflow of foreign capital has ranged from 'Boxer Revolution'-type xenophobia, symbolized by the best-selling Chinese book *China Can Say 'No'* (Song Qiang *et al.*, 1996), to the neo-liberal approach which argues that the Chinese state should allow the inflow of capital to be governed by market forces. Much policy discussion falls between these two extremes, recognizing the necessity of deep involvement in the world economy but reiterating the need to do so cautiously and in a planned fashion:

> As the Chinese economy has opened up to the outside world, the national and non-national industries have become interwoven and begun to evolve together. National industry is now facing a very complex and serious situation in terms of global competition and both the opportunities for and the risks involved in expanding national industry have increased considerably. It is therefore important that we urgently adopt effective measures to enable the national industry to grow faster and in a sounder manner.
>
> (Research Group, 1997, p. 66)

China's rapid emergence as a potential superpower has had a profound effect on popular consciousness, and on US foreign policy thinking. There are calm voices which argue for 'constructive engagement', and believe that China is essentially a force for international stability (Ross, 1997). However, a powerful coalition of interests favours a policy of limiting China's economic rise or 'destructive engagement' (*Financial Times*, 13 March 1997). These interests embrace US trade unions and employers in industries, typically labour-intensive ones, threatened by imports from China, human rights lobbyists, and political groups fearful of China's threat to US global dominance. Mirroring the best-selling status in China of *China Can Say 'No'* has been Bernstein and Munro's *The Coming Conflict With China* (summarized in Bernstein and Munro, 1997). They argue that the primary US objective in Asia should be 'to prevent China's size, power, and ambition from making it a regional hegemon'. This, they suggest can be accomplished only by 'maintaining the American military presence in Asia and keeping it vastly more powerful and effective than China's armed forces' (1997, p. 31). Japan's rapid rise to global power caused a similar response in the USA. However, the potential size of the Chinese economy is vastly greater than that of Japan and even of the USA. China's growth rate is faster even than that of the Asian NICs, and the speed with which China's trade surplus with the USA has overtaken that of Japan has frightened many people.

Sino–US relations

When the USA bargains with China over economic matters, it is against a backdrop of hugely unequal military power. China is still a poor country. Its national product (in purchasing power dollars) is still only 44 per cent of the USA's (World Bank, 1996). Its military capability is far behind that of the USA, with a defence budget in the mid-1990s that is only around 3 per cent of that of the USA.[4] The Gulf War demonstrated graphically how far behind the USA China was in military terms:

> [W]ell into the [next] century, the West, meaning primarily the United States with some supplements from Britain and France, will alone be able to intervene militarily in almost any part of the world. And only the United States will have the air power capable of bombing virtually any place in the world (Huntington, 1996, p. 186).

The importance of Sino–US relations in the global political economy has become even more marked by the sharp change in economic fortunes of different parts of the advanced capitalist system in the 1990s. During this decade, corporate America has experienced a far-reaching restructuring, much of it learned from Japan: 'Displaying remarkable flexibility, many US industries have regained their competitive edge . . . and this has helped power an extraordinary bull market in equities' (*Financial Times*, 24 January 1997). The USA has the lion's share of those corporations equipped to exploit global markets and supplies the bulk of the technology that 'knits those markets together' (*Financial Times*, 14 June 1997). A study by Morgan Stanley (reported in *Financial Times*, 21 November 1996) identified a total of 238 companies that were 'world leaders', of which no less than 125 were American. The increased competitive strength of US big business has been closely related to a surge in US foreign investment: American FDI outflows rose from an annual average of \$17 billion in 1984–9 to \$70 billion in 1993–5 (UNCTAD, 1996, p. 233), and the USA's share of total world FDI outflows rose from 14 per cent in 1984–9 to 30 per cent in 1993–5 (UNCTAD, 1996, p. 233).

Reorganization of big business in advanced capitalist economies

Big businesses still occupy centre stage in the advanced capitalist economies. Huge corporations with tens or even hundreds of thousands of employees stand at the centre of the capitalist system. In the USA in 1990, the100 largest manufacturing companies accounted for 24 per cent of GNP and 42.3 per cent of employment. From 1978 to 1990 in Japan the share of the top 100 manufacturing firms rose from 22.1 per cent of GNP to 29.7 per cent and their share of employment rose from 17.4 per cent to 22.4 per cent, while in Europe the share of the top 100 manufacturing firms in GNP rose from 18.1 per cent to 19.5 per cent and the share of employment rose from 25.1 per cent to 28.2 per cent (Ruigrok and van Tulder, 1995, p. 155).

The 1990s have witnessed a massive process of asset reorganization within giant capitalist firms. The 'core' of the world's most powerful firms is growing fast, despite outsourcing and disposal of 'non-core' business. In the 1990s the rapid liberalization of world markets has led to a powerful tendency towards concentration of ownership. In industry after industry there has been a rise in the global market share of a small number of firms expanding through organic growth, merger and acquisition within their core competence as the size of competitive global markets has massively increased. Hardly a sector has not seen this process, with a powerful trend towards concentration in activities as diverse as automobile components, aerospace, defence equipment, power equipment, farm machinery, pharmaceuticals, soft drinks, snack foods, household goods (from detergents to shampoo and toothpaste), telecommunications, chemical fertilizers, advertising, power generation, investment finance and legal practices.

Power-generating equipment

This industry was already highly concentrated at a global level by the 1980s, and has become more so. There are now just five main integrated producers of power plants worldwide – General Electric, ABB, Westinghouse, GEC Alsthom, and Siemens. General Electric alone has around one-half of the word's gas turbine market. It is likely that the already small number of firms will grow even smaller alongside growing world demands for power-generating equipment:

> The all-round skills needed to compete simultaneously in building, alliance making, financial investment and servicing gives enormous advantage to the big integrated companies. The time when this battle of the giants is resolved is fast approaching.

Civilian aircraft

Twenty years ago there were three significant makers of 100-seater-plus aircraft in North America – McDonnell Douglas, Boeing and Lockheed. By 1996, Lockheed had given up making civilian aircraft entirely and was taken over by Boeing. The merged company is a colossus with $48 billion in annual revenues, 200 000 employees and 75 per cent of the global civilian aircraft market. Moreover, the merged company has a greatly enlarged defence business, enabling it to withstand the downturns on the civilian side, and to benefit from government subsidies to R & D on the defence side.

Defence

Revolutionary changes have affected the defence industry since the 1980s, driving a rapid process of merger and acquisition in the USA. In the 1980s there were over twenty sizeable defence industry producers in the USA. Soon there will just three – Boeing, Raytheon and Lockheed Martin. The chairman of Lockheed Martin admitted that the Pentagon had 'pushed American defence contractors to join together into a few strong companies "to encourage efficiency"' (Quoted in *International Herald Tribune*, July 4 1997). With the large fall in defence spending there was a high risk that the US defence industry would be weakened; instead, the Pentagon appears to have actively supported the process of concentration in order that a small number of giants would emerge with the financial and technological capability to develop a new generation of military equipment that would sustain the USA's global military superiority. The main elements in this extraordinary process have been:

- *Boeing* In 1996 Boeing bought Rockwell's defence subsidiary for $3 billion, and announced the agreement to merge with McDonnell Douglas, itself a giant in the defence sector.
- *Raytheon* Raytheon began the 1990s as a diversified industrial group with strong defence interests. In subsequent years it bought Hughes from General Motors for $9.5 billion, E-Systems for $2.3 billion and TI's defence business for $3.0 billion.
- *Lockheed Martin* In the early 1990s Lockheed bought the Fort Worth fighter plane business for $1.5 billion. Martin Marietta bought General Electric's aerospace business for $3.1 billion, and General Dynamics space launch business. In 1995 Martin Marietta and Lockheed agreed to a $10 billion merger. After 1988 Loral bought the defence businesses of Honeywell, Ford, Unisys and LTV Missiles, and in 1996 Lockheed Martin bought Loral for $9.1 billion (*Financial Times*, 18 January 1997). In 1992 Northrop and Grumman undertook a $2.2 billion merger, which in turn purchased the defence subsidiary of Westinghouse for $3 billion. In 1997, Lockheed Martin agreed to buy Northrop Grumman for $8.2 billion, to

form a company that will have around $35 billion in annual sales and 235 000 employees (*Financial Times*, 4 July 1997).

Lockheed Martin's purchase of Northrop Grumman appears to signal the end of one of the most remarkable epochs in concentration of economic power that capitalism has ever witnessed.

Automobile components

In the 1990s a very rapid consolidation of component makers has occurred: 'in the biggest change in its history the once diversified components business is being rationalised as large specialists gobble up the minnows' (*Financial Times*, 28 October 1996). Over the next decade it is thought likely that the number of leading components companies will be reduced from around 150–200 to just 15–20 global groups (*Financial Times*, 28 October 1996). By the mid-1990s a small group of players with global sales of over $3 billion was emerging, each able to spend large amounts on R & D and each with a global reach. Of the 26 firms in the sector with annual sales of over $3 billion, half were American (*Financial Times*, 21 May 1996).

However, 'auto components' is a broad category, containing several sub-markets, each with its own specialist technologies. Within each sub-market consolidation is already well advanced. The chief executive of Tenneco believes that 'the number of suppliers for many key parts will be whittled down to two players, maybe three ' (quoted in *Financial Times*, 28 October 1996). Indeed, in many branches, the consolidation is already close to this position. The size and growth rate of the global market for specialist automobile components is so large that narrowly focused firms can enjoy global sales much greater in real terms than those of even a relatively large, but nationally-based, automobile firm of a decade or so ago.

Tyres

Fifteen years ago, Bridgestone was a relatively small Japanese producer. Since then it has grown fast, initially as the main supplier to the indigenous motor industry, and subsequently with a leap into the USA alongside the rapid growth of North American production by Japanese vehicle makers. In 1988 it purchased the giant Firestone (US) company. By the mid-1990s, Bridgestone had risen to the position of Number One tyre maker globally in terms of value of sales. In the 1950s, Michelin was a relatively small firm, based mainly around the French market. Between 1960 and 1990 it opened or bought an average of one new plant every nine months, which culminated in the Uniroyal Goodrich (USA) purchase in 1989. By the early 1990s it had risen to Number One position globally in terms of unit sales, and Number Two in terms of value of sales. Although no longer the single most important global tyre producer, Goodyear remains a powerful force. By the mid-1990s, these top three firms accounted for over 46 per cent of the value of global tyre sales (*Financial Times*, 29 January 1996, 14 March 1997).

Chemicals

Chemical producers are among the world's largest corporations. The traditional industry was characterized by large plant-level economies of scale, and by economies of scope which were exploited 'more effectively than in any other industry' (Chandler, 1990, p. 170). The traditional petrochemical industry had many of the world's largest companies, mostly characterized by a high degree of horizontal, and often vertical, integration. In the early 1990s, twelve of the world's top fifty companies, ranked by value of sales, were petrochemical producers (Drewry Shipping Consultants, 1994, p. 23; DRC, 1993, pp. 476–7).

After many decades of relative stability, the 1990s have seen dramatic changes in the structure of leading firms in the chemical industry. The impetus has come from rapidly growing global markets, ageing, out-of-patent technology in basic processes, rapid growth of low-cost bulk production in developing countries and over-capacity in advanced economies. Maintaining global technological leadership across a complete range of products is increasingly regarded as unfeasible for a single company, however large it may be. In the 1990s the chemical industry is rapidly moving towards a situation in which there is a small number of globally dominant players in each segment of the high-margin, high-R & D, high-profit parts of the industry:

> The critical mass for success is becoming larger as the industrial complexity rises and the participants themselves are becoming more global with the change in the boundaries of competition.

As the global giants regroup, they are each developing a focus on a small number of core competencies in which they aspire to become one of a small number of dominant global players.[5]

Pharmaceuticals

An important part of the unravelling of the old integrated petrochemical companies, was separation of the pharmaceutical from the chemical business, through flotation, merger or acquisition. In the early 1990s the pharmaceutical industry was considered to be 'extraordinarily fragmented compared to other global industries' (*Financial Times*, 10 November 1995). In 1994 the top ten companies held 28 per cent of the total global market, and top twenty companies held 46 per cent (*Financial Times*, 12 March 1995).[6]

In two and a half years in the mid-1990s, from 1994 to mid-1997, there were more than twenty large take-overs in the pharmaceutical sector and two massive mergers. Of these no less than five of the take-overs were at a cost of over $5 billion. By 1996, the global market share of the top ten pharmaceutical companies had risen to 34 per cent, and share of the top twenty companies had risen to 50 per cent (*Financial Times*, 24 April 1997). Industry analysts believe that the process of concentration still has a long way to run, with further restructuring 'continuing for years' (*Financial Times*, 25 March 1996). Most drug industry chiefs have a common vision of the future of the healthcare industry: 'within five to ten years the business will be dominated by just a dozen or so companies' (*Financial Times*, 22 August 1995).

Soft drinks

In the early days of the soft drinks industry there was a 'sea of small local companies' (Sutton, 1991, p. 220). Over a long period, the giants steadily reduced the market share held by smaller companies. By the early 1980s, Coca-Cola and Pepsico between them accounted for the lion's share of the soft drink market in the advanced economies; however, large parts of the world did not permit the product to be sold and in much of the developing world *per capita* consumption was negligible.

Coca-Cola and Pepsico's sales prospects have been transformed compared to a decade or so ago as they are faced with the potential for enormous long-term growth in liberalizing emerging markets. In the battle to position themselves in these markets, Coca-Cola has taken a decisive lead over Pepsico, with currently reported global market shares for soft drinks of 47 per cent and 22 per cent, respectively (*Financial Times*, 28 September 1996). Coca-Cola's huge investments placed it in an extraordinarily powerful position at the critical juncture at which markets were opening up, so that it is poised to ride a virtuous circle of profits and reinvestment, maintaining its leading position over a long period as total volume grows steadily. There are huge advantages to the 'first mover' in this situation.

Implications

The disparity in the size, research capability, financial resources and business skills between the leading firms in the advanced economies and those in emerging markets has rapidly widened as a result of the reorganization within advanced capitalist big business. Big business, especially that based in the USA, is now much 'leaner and stronger'. Liberalization of markets in developing countries, of which China is much the most important, is occurring in the face of a more powerful business opponent than was the case a decade ago. The decade ahead presents a unique opportunity for accelerated growth of output and profits for the existing giant corporations. Today may be the dawn of a new 'Golden Age' for already established big businesses.

The state and big business

Active functions of the state

The activities of national governments have been central to the explanation of successful growth in developing countries. The state has been central to the rise of most of the world's giant corporations. Far from emerging from the free market, the normal path through which the world's leading corporations developed was through extensive government support (Ruigrok and van Tulder, 1995, p. 221). Britain's Industrial Revolution took place under an explicitly mercantilist philosophy of high protection and export promotion. The USA in the nineteenth century unashamedly industrialized behind high protectionist barriers, 'free riding on free trade'. In Asia, there is a common current of economic thinking which stretched from Meiji Japan through to Sun Yatsen and the Kuomintang (initially on mainland China, and subsequently in Taiwan), through to South Korea and Singapore since the 1950s. This approach pragmatically regarded the best arrangement as that which would more rapidly produce national prosperity in a world of hostile international competition. The free market and the Stalinist command system were regarded as equally irrelevant.

Government procurement has been widely used as a source of support for national businesses. Associated with this has been extensive use of government support for R & D especially, but not exclusively, in the military sector.[7] The big businesses in Europe and the USA that now benefit from the fast-being-established 'level playing field' of international competition, have benefited massively over a long period of time from a hugely 'uneven playing field' in terms of government support. Moreover, the beneficiaries of government expenditures are relatively limited in number, concentrated especially in the high-technology and military-related spheres. Further, under the present high-speed concentration of production occurring in these sectors, the beneficiaries from these colossal outlays will be even fewer.

Subsidized export credit (e.g. from the US Export–Import Bank) and subsidized investment insurance (e.g. through the US Overseas Investment Corporation) has been a powerful weapon of government support for 'national firms' in all the advanced capitalist countries. Moreover, owing to their dominant position in international economic activity, the benefits from these subsidies are disproportionately captured by big business (*Financial Times*, 8 May, 1997).

A further channel of assistance for big business in the advanced economies has been government support for the ideology of globalization and for the struggle to change international regulations governing trade and capital movements. The USA has been at the forefront of this movement, with large sums spent supporting and influencing international institutions. The most important of these are the GATT and, currently, the WTO. The salary of Charlene Barshevsky, the US Trade Representative, and her large support staff, for example, constitutes a large subsidy to big US business, the benefits from which hugely outweigh the expenditure by the US government. It may well be the case that, ultimately, globalization and liberalization will on balance benefit developing countries. Eventually the benefits of this may well trickle down to benefit poor people in poor countries. However, for at least a long period ahead, the 'distribution of the gains' will be highly uneven.

Consider, for example, the most important recent milestone in liberalization, the WTO-negotiated telecoms agreement of February 1997. US government effort over three years of 'gruelling negotiations' was put into brokering this complex deal. The historic agreement was signed by almost seventy countries, the notable exceptions being China and Russia. It will usher in 'an era of free competition, low prices and cross-border investment' (*Financial Times*, 18 February 1997). Undoubtedly, poor developing countries will benefit from access to capital with which to construct telecommunications facilities, which will in turn have powerful positive externalities in stimulating market development.

However, the gains for a small number of competitive telecommunications companies in the advanced economies, especially those in Britain and the USA, are likely to be vast. The telecommunications market is huge.[8] Charlene Barshevsky, then US trade representative designate, commented that this was 'a triumph for the American way . . . US companies are the most competitive telecommunications providers in the world; they are in the position to compete and win under this agreement' (quoted in the *Financial Times*, 18 February 1997). The British and US negotiators 'know that their countries have the advantage of the experience of more than a decade of competition – and are best placed to benefit from liberalization' (*Financial Times*, 18 February 1997). The establishment of the 'level playing field' in telecommunications will work massively to the advantage of already powerful firms, which especially means a tiny number of US and British companies and their shareholders.

Passive functions of the state

It is rare that national governments in capitalist countries have strictly applied free market principles to monopolies and mergers. If they had it would have been impossible for a small number of giant corporations to occupy such a large share of the market in industry after industry. However, in recent years, as the imperatives of global competition have become ever more intense, so the formal approach towards market power adopted by regulatory bodies in the advanced capitalist countries has shifted. An explicit recognition has emerged that without powerful national champions, the national economy may be severely handicapped in the global battle.

The grounds on which the US anti-trust authorities – the Justice Department and the Federal Trade Commission (FTC) – approve a merger are flexible and are being radically reinterpreted in the light of the current rapid move towards globalization. In the 1990s in the USA, alongside a period of record mergers and acquisitions and spiralling market power for a small number of firms, the FTC has initiated hardly any significant anti-monopoly actions (*Financial Times*, 11 March 1997). Moreover, the very definition of 'the market' adopted by the anti-trust authorities has undergone a sharp alteration:

[T]he FTC has looked at large regions or even at market share worldwide, reflecting the shift towards global competition in many industries . . . That has enabled greater concentration of market share among US companies than would otherwise have been the case.

(Financial Times, 11 March 1997)

It appears that almost any merger will be approved by the US government as long as it increases the international competitive power of the firm concerned.

Big business in China under economic reform

Building modern big business under new circumstances

In sharp contrast to the transition orthodoxy, the Chinese government has attempted to support the growth of powerful, autonomous big businesses that can compete with the global giants. Large enterprises, initially purely state-owned, maintained their leading role throughout the reform process. In this strategy, China's planners have proceeded experimentally, making important institutional innovations in respect to the large-scale, no less than the TVE sector.

China's situation is in many ways different from that of other East Asian countries. China is reforming a comprehensively state-administered industrial system. China is much larger than any of its East Asian neighbours, making it more difficult for the Chinese state to control economic activity as closely as they do, and also making the Chinese market and production level potentially vastly more important. If China wishes to benefit from the large trade opportunities available in the advanced economies, and from the transfer of capital and technology, it will be obliged to conform to the rules of the advanced capitalist countries much more closely than its predecessors did. In particular, it will have to conform to the rules of the WTO, including 'the removal of tariffs, quotas, subsidies, investment restrictions and other barriers, and acceptance of the core WTO principles and disciplines' *(Financial Times,* 3 March 1997). The key advanced capitalist countries – the USA, the EU and Japan – disagree strongly with China over the length of time it should be allowed to take to conform to WTO rules:

That is really the guts of it. The closer to five-year transitional periods, the happier we will be. But for the Chinese, the closer to 15 years, the more satisfied they will be.

(Western official, quoted in *Financial Times*, 3 March 1997)

Protecting and supporting emerging big businesses

During the reform period the Chinese leadership realized that deeper integration with the world economy was essential for modernization.

However, it was acutely aware of the possibility that hasty, unplanned integration could lead to major problems. Instead of the 'close' integration[9] recommended by the reform orthodoxy with free trade and free movement of capital, the government's intention was planned, 'strategic' integration. An important component of this was a policy of support for emerging indigenous big business while simultaneously attempting to benefit from capital and technology transfer from multinational companies (MNCs).

As we have seen, after the cautious growth of FDI in the early 1980s, the pace accelerated remarkably, especially from the early 1990s onwards. The Chinese government was confident that, in strategic sectors, it could ensure that FDI went mainly to JVs in which the Chinese side was a majority owner. Cash-short SOEs with large welfare payments and high levels of over-manning, were desperate for access to capital. A significant shift also occurred in government ideology, with much ground in the continuing policy battle gained by the neo-liberal orthodoxy.

In the late 1970s, the Chinese large-scale state industrial sector had resembled an 'infant industry', both institutionally and technically. Under these circumstances, China's large enterprises could not compete on a level playing field with the world's leading MNCs. In sharp contrast to the prevailing conventional wisdom in the Bretton Woods institutions, China's attitude towards international trade was mercantilist: 'In foreign trade our principle is to encourage exports and organize imports according to needs' (*Beijing Review*, 33(44), 1990).

The reforming government employed a wide array of import restrictions. In 1995 the simple average tariff on China's imports still stood at 36 per cent. In addition, China adopted non-tariff barriers (NTBs) such as requiring rigorous inspection procedures for selected imports. Government procurement policy, especially for infrastructure investment, also constituted an important form of support for emerging indigenous large businesses. In the mid-1990s, the situation began to change, as China sought to gain admission to WTO, and as pressure for reduced protection increased from the USA especially owing to the large size of its trade deficit with China. In 1996 the government agreed to a large reduction in tariffs, the simple average falling to 23 per cent. However, China still maintained important NTBs – and, indeed, evolved new forms of NTB in the 1990s.[10] Intense international pressure to liberalize China's trade and foreign investment laws developed as China's exports continued their high-speed growth and the trade surplus with the USA grew rapidly.

Redrawing the boundaries between state and non-state sectors: 'grasp the large, let go of the small'

Size structure

During the reform period, the government began gradually to 'give up' the myriad of small SOEs, contracting them out, leasing or selling them, and increasingly allowing them to go bankrupt (*Project Group*, 1996, pp. 18–19). Individually run small businesses were allowed to start up. The share of industrial output produced by SOEs plummeted from 78 per cent at current prices in 1978 to 48 per cent in 1992 (SSB, 1993, p. 412).

Within the state sector the central government increasingly focused its planning efforts on the relatively small number of large firms. Its policy was 'grasp the large and let go of the small' (*zhua da, fang xiao*). 'The dominant role of the state-owned enterprises should be brought into play mainly through the large and super-large enterprises' (Project Group, 1996, pp. 16–17). Large SOEs actually raised their share of total industrial output from 25 per cent in 1980 to over 28 per cent in 1991 (gross value of industrial output at current prices; SSB, 1981, p. 212, SSB, 1992, p. 70). Within the 'formal' sector (i.e. township level and above) their share of industrial output value rose from around one-quarter in 1980 to over 38 per cent in the mid 1990s[12]. In the state sector in the mid-1990s, the 500 largest enterprises accounted for 37 per cent of total assets, 46 per cent of sales value and 63 per cent of total profits (Project Group, 1996, p. 17).

Sectoral structure

State industry increasingly concentrated on large-scale 'upstream' activities, leaving the small-scale 'downstream' activities to other ownership forms. The main arena of state ownership and direct planning in the coming period will be: (1) natural monopolies; (2) industries related to energy resources and basic raw materials (petroleum and natural gas, iron and steel, non-ferrous metals and basic raw materials); (3) 'pillar' industries that play a leading role in the national economy (petrochemicals, heavy machinery, electricity generating equipment, automobiles and construction); and (4) industries 'playing an important role in national defence and national strength' (defence, aerospace, atomic energy, high and new technology industries) (Project Group, 1996, pp. 16–17).

From 1978 to 1992 light industrial growth (real GVIO) accelerated to almost 15 per cent per annum (SSB, 1993, p. 58). In a relatively closed economy such as China's this required simultaneous rapid growth of output from 'upstream' heavy industry: from 1978 to 1992 the real average annual growth rate of GVIO in heavy industry was almost 11 per cent (SSB, 1993, p. 58). SOEs were hugely dominant in these sectors. They typically require much larger amounts of capital per unit of output, need larger plant size, rely much more on technical skills than pure entrepreneurship (e.g. marketing, product choice, skills in distribution) and have much longer gestation periods than does light industry.

Managerial autonomy

China's large SOEs have not been viewed by the Chinese government as objects to be closed down but, rather, as institutions with 'great strength and potential' (Project Group, 1996, p. 6) whose performance can be improved with careful, experimental reform. The central focus of reform of large SOEs has been to grope towards ways of enlarging managerial autonomy – in other words towards the 'separation of ownership from control'.

Decline of the material supply system

Over the course of the reform years, the central authorities engineered a gradual decline in resource allocation through the material balance planning system. By the early 1990s, less than 10 per cent of total industrial output value was directly controlled by planners and even in the largest of upstream industries, managers decided most key issues. They needed to co-ordinate input supplies through the market, to evaluate the capability of different suppliers and to bargain about price and delivery. They had to decide the product mix and product price, and to compete for markets. Accountancy and marketing departments grew rapidly. In large SOEs producing complex engineering products such as power equipment, product reliability and after-sales service became significant elements in inter-firm competition.

Contract responsibility system

The contract system was experimented with from the late 1970s and became generalized in the mid-1980s, with innumerable local variations. Enterprises were required to hand over agreed amounts of profits and taxes to the state, in return for which the management was given extensive autonomy and large responsibility for raising investment funds from retained profits, bank loans and eventually other sources such as JVs, stock market flotations and bonds. By the late 1980s, over two-fifths of fixed investment undertaken by state enterprises was financed from enterprise 'self-raised funds'.

The contract system established a strong link between the performance of the firm and the prosperity of the local government or other 'principal' to which 'hand-overs' were made. A substantial share of contracted profit and tax 'hand-overs', even for large SOEs, was typically handed over to the local authorities. The 'contract responsibility system' turned large SOEs toward profit-seeking, establishing a strong link between profits and both retained earnings and capacity expansion (Jefferson and Rawski, 1994). Simultaneously, there was 'a considerable reduction' in the 'softness' of the budget constraint (Jefferson and Rawski, 1994). Many fast-growing and fast-modernizing large SOEs emerged under the contract system, with strong managers allowed a high degree of autonomy in return for fulfilment of the contracted 'hand-overs' (Byrd, 1992; Nolan, 1995).

In one variant or another, the contract system was the dominant form of relationship between large SOEs and their administrative superiors until at least the mid-1990s. It technically ended in 1994. The goal was to replace it with a system of joint-stock companies (see below) with 'hand-overs' decided by a combination of dividends from share ownership and a new structure of corporation tax and value-added tax. In practice, there were substantial continuities, with negotiation of both sorts of 'hand-overs' between 'principal' and 'agent'.

The joint-stock company

The joint-stock company played an important role in the separation of ownership and control in large capitalist firms. By the mid-1990s in China, the joint-stock company had become a powerful weapon for transcending the limits of the previous form of ownership and operation. SOEs themselves welcomed the introduction of this form of ownership, partly because of the flexibility provided by the corporate share-holding structure, but more importantly because it gave a separate identity to the secured corporation.[12] The joint venture, by introducing foreign investors, signalled the start of ownership reform. In the 1980s most of these were small-value JVs with 'downstream' firms. However, as we have seen, in the 1990s there was a rapid growth of FDI in the strategic 'upstream' industries such as power equipment and petrochemicals.

Beginning in 1993, the Chinese government allowed selected large SOEs to issue shares on 'foreign' stock markets, the vast majority of which were in Hong Kong and a small number in New York. By June 1997, twenty-nine Chinese mainland SOEs had been listed in Hong Kong and a similar number was planned for future listing (*Financial Times*, 16 June 1997). The companies allowed to list abroad are mostly at the forefront in terms of performance and prospects, and from key upstream sectors including the petrochemical sector (five firms), and the power generation equipment, iron and steel, glass, heavy machinery and shipbuilding sectors. Prior to their international flotation, these companies went through a thorough process of institutional restructuring. In each case, the original SOE separated off the social service component from the main company, to which fees were to be paid, and established a new joint stock company in which the original SOE was a majority shareholder, with a minority share-ownership floated abroad. The flotation provided an important source of capital. At least as important, it helped to promote the idea of the joint-stock company as a suitable path for large SOEs to follow. A further development in April 1997 was the report that leading industrial companies would be allowed to raise capital on international markets through the issuance of bonds (*Financial Times*, 8 May 1997). Through this channel, the increasingly autonomous large industrial enterprises would be able to increase their capital without diluting ownership.

In 1994, the government unveiled a plan to transform SOEs, other than those 'producing special products and military industrial enterprises', into joint-stock companies with managerial independence from government control. The majority of large and medium-sized SOEs were to become limited liability companies (Project Group, 1996, p. 12). Consistent with the policy of 'grasping the big and letting go of the small', after the reorganization of large and medium-sized SOEs, the state intends through state holding companies to maintain a controlling ownership share in the 'pillar industries' and 'key enterprises in the basic industries'. As for 'general enterprises where non-state owned capital will be absorbed as much as possible', the state will have equity participation, 'not a controlling interest' (Project Group, 1996, p. 12).

One hundred large SOEs were selected as the first batch formally to put into practice the 'modern enterprise system' with joint-stock companies as the basis. Behind each of the emerging large joint-stock SOEs lay a multiplicity of institutions. Under this 'pluralized institutional ownership' each part-owner had an interest in the firm's performance mainly, but not exclusively, attributable to their share in the firm's ownership. These might include:

- the local authority who benefited from dividend payments to the state holding company and tax hand-overs, as well as from the income and employment generated by the firm[13]
- the relevant central ministry or quasi-ministerial body (e.g. Sinopec) which benefited from either the forwarding of some portion of the contracted profit payment or from the direct hand-over of contracted profits
- other domestic institutional shareholders, including giant, quasi-governmental investment institutions, such as CITIC or Everbright Holdings, as well as smaller ones, such as other local authorities
- a foreign JV partner, which benefited from the dividend payments from the JV
- foreign shareholders (mainly institutions) which received dividend payments.

This was a potentially powerful network of institutions, each of which had some common interest in promoting the firm's performance, none of which had the interest or capability to run it directly, and all of whom perceived that their best interest was served by having a strong management team running the firm. The joint-stock company route to property rights transformation is highly flexible:

> There could be any desired mix of public and private ownership, including ownership by various kinds of financial intermediaries. The mixture could also be quite easily changed in the light of experience and the development of China's financial sector. (Wood, 1994, p. 39).[14]

From state factories to large multi-plant firms

The emergence of the multi-plant firm formed another avenue for the development of managers' autonomy relative to state owners.

Enterprise groups

The construction of industrial groups became a central plank of government policy for enterprise reform. The concept helped to legitimate a widespread process of expansion of large SOEs into multi-plant firms, in which the core firm was 'connected through capital' with a network of smaller firms. At the centre of most of them was a large SOE 'core company'. A typical large SOE by the mid-1990s had investments in numerous 'second-tier' companies, mainly supplier firms. The core firm typically had an incentive to upgrade the technology and control the quality of supplies from 'second-tier' companies. It typically appointed the managers of the subsidiary company, reorganized their production structure, shifted workers and equipment to other locations and set contract targets for profits to be achieved and 'hand-overs' to be made to the core firm.

Mergers and acquisitions

A large process of mergers and acquisitions developed in China during the transitional process, typically with the state as the mediator. The state often required large SOEs to absorb and reorganize loss-making enterprises; frequently, mergers were initiated by large firms themselves. Often, the superior authority of loss-making firms sought out more powerful firms in order to initiate a take-over, in the hope that they would be relieved of the burden of the loss-making enterprise. When a large firm voluntarily took over a weaker, loss-making firm, they usually did so in order to 'dig out' hidden value, involving careful calculation of the prospects for turning around the performance of the firm being taken over, with tough insistence on the conditions necessary to bring about this goal. To some degree, acquisitions by large firms are a 'positioning' process in anticipation of a possible future privatization. Through merger, a large firm can acquire assets of great potential value, including the site, from which the employees may gain at some future point.

Mergers may be an especially powerful process for advancing business capabilities in a transitional economy where business and technical skills are not so widely available as in advanced economies. The merger process, led by capable firms with advanced technological and management skills, can have a powerful positive externality effect, spreading business capability more rapidly than would be the case otherwise. Moreover, the pressure for mergers is reinforced in a poor transitional economy such as China where the undeveloped state of market institutions inhibits the capacity to obtain needed inputs easily and reliably through market mechanisms.

The limitations of China's big business in international perspective

We have seen that during China's reforms a powerful group of fast-growing and modernizing large indigenous firms, mainly former large SOEs, has emerged which are gradually becoming competitive businesses with growing managerial autonomy. However, these firms have serious limitations in relation to the global competition which they increasingly face.

In China, the 'merger' boom has involved large SOEs 'merging' with small ones, or small ones merging among themselves; not one merger between large SOEs has occurred. For example, in 1996 China took over as the world's Number One steel producer. However, its leading enterprises, such as Shougang, Angang and Baogang, still had a far smaller steel capacity than the world's leading firms, such as Posco, New Japan Steel, British Steel, and Usinor Sacilor (France). Under the contract system, each of China's large steel enterprises merged with a large number of smaller enterprises.[15] However, by the mid-1990s not a single merger had occurred among any of the top ten steel enterprises. Nor, indeed, had any of the largest enterprises in any other sector merged with another within that sector, let alone with one of the largest enterprises in a different sector. By contrast, when New Japan Steel was formed in 1970 it was from just such a super-merger between large firms. New Japan Steel consisted of four major plants, Kimitsu (10.5 million tonnes crude steel capacity in 1977/8), Yawata (9.7 million tonnes), Oita (9.3 million tonnes) and Nagoya (8.3 million tonnes), with a combined capacity of 38 million tonnes (Yonekura, 1994, p. 7), each of which would rank among the top ten steel enterprises in China today.

Up to the mid-1990s, the Chinese government had not apparently given active thought to the possibility of mergers among China's leading enterprises in order to create firms that could challenge the world's largest. Moreover, managers were jealous of their newly won autonomy and still regarded such a move as outside their scope. The locality, as well as the superior ministry in which the large enterprise was situated, was typically reluctant to allow ownership to pass to 'outsiders', jealously protecting their right to the stream of revenue from 'their' large SOE.

In the mid-1990s, despite changes in their behaviour, even the largest SOEs were still small compared to the global giants in all aspects other than employment. For example, Harbin Power Equipment Company (HPEC) is the leading firm in this key 'upstream' sector, and the state's 'national champion'. However, in 1996, despite large changes in its operational methods and its growth in size, HPEC was still far from being able to compete directly with the leading multinational power equipment makers (Table 1.2). It has mainly to concentrate on catching up through acquiring existing technology from the world's leading multinational firms. However, as it cannot afford to purchase the necessary technology, this has to be acquired through some form of co-operation with MNCs.

There is a danger that, in their competition with each other, increasingly autonomous Chinese firms may be prepared to improve their own firm's short-term position through JVs that do not extract the maximum possible technical transfer from the multinationals. This may leave them in the position of dependent sub-contractors for the multinational firm, but technically a 'domestic firm' as far as the supply of equipment is concerned. The essential obstacle to Chinese industrial integration is the conflict of

Table 1.2   Size of HPEC and leading firms in the world's power-equipment industry, 1995

Companies	Employees (000)	Turnover ($ million)	Assets ($ million)	Profits ($ million)	R and D ($ million)
HPEC	27 000	310	898	14	3[d]
General Electric	216 000	59 316	252 000[b]	5915	1280
of which power division	25 000[a]	5900[a]	–	1200[a]	–
Westinghouse	84 400	8848	10 398[c]	77	–
of which power division	–	3000	–	–	–
GEC Alsthom	–	11 108	–	–	444
of which power division	–	4000	–	–	–
Siemens	393 000	57 948	58 400[a]	1445	5008
ABB	207 557	29 718	24 900[a]	1447	2589
of which power division	–	–	–	870	–

Notes:
a   1994
b   1993
c   1992
d   Even if one made the heroic assumption that all of the 1500 staff involved in R & D at HPEC ought to be re-valued at the average wage levels of US scientific personnel, then the total expenditure on R & D at HPEC would still be a maximum of around $70 million, and may, properly adjusted for technical levels, be substantially less than this.
Sources: HPEC (1995) *Financial Times,* 1 January 1996, 27 June 1996, 15 May 1996; DRC (1993) pp. 478–9.

interest among different personnel, departments and regions. This phenomenon is especially pronounced owing to the greatly enhanced autonomy that the reforms have permitted to firms and local authorities. For example, within the city of Nanjing, four petrochemical firms were unable to merge, and have instead each formed separate JVs with different MNCs.

There are some similarities between the current situation in China and that in Europe. In Europe, national political interests after the Second World War led each country to have its own 'national champion', typically state-owned, in such sectors as defence, aerospace, steel, oil, petrochemicals and telecommunications. Despite extensive privatization, even by the mid-1990, there were still substantial barriers to cross-country mergers in these sectors owing to state intervention to retain domestic control of 'national champions'.

While Chinese indigenous large enterprises are suspicious of each other, a new wave of MNCs investing in China are rapidly forming an integrated business system within China by constructing JVs with different indigenous partners. This contrasts with the typically small-scale, non-integrated enterprises formerly established by Hong Kong and Taiwanese investors. For example, Samsung (South Korea) already has sixteen JVs within China, producing video cassette recorders, colour televisions, audio equipment, semiconductors, washing machines, cameras, TV tubes, microwave ovens, monitors and other electronic components (*Business Weekly*, 5 January 1997). By the year 2000 it plans to have invested $4 billion, when it will employ 40 000 people, compared to 15 000 in 1996. Samsung's stated aim is to diversify its investments in order to 'build integrated industries, making its products more competitive within China'. Siemens already has 30 plants in China, and plans to invest US$1 billion to open 20 more new plants, increasing the number of employees from 6000 to 30 000 by the year 2000. LG (Lucky Group), South Korea's largest *chaebol*, which produces 10 per cent of the country's GDP, already has more than one-third of its total number of plants in China, and plans to invest $10 billion in China by 2005 (*Business Weekly*, 29 July 1997).

Not only do the MNCs each form an integrated system of multiplant investment, but large MNC investments stimulate further investments by other MNCs. For example, there are the 180 foreign-funded or JVs enterprises providing components for the Volkswagen Santana JV in Shanghai. Delphi, the world's biggest automobile component manufacturer, has three plants in Shanghai, as well as many elsewhere in China, and plans to start another two or three in Shanghai in 1997 (*Business Weekly*, 5 January 1997).

One of the motives for MNC investment in China is to integrate the domestic partner into the international division of labour within the multinational firm. For example, in the power equipment industry, the JVs established with Dongfang and Shanghai involve different parts of the business, each with a different foreign partner, thus slicing the formerly integrated companies into segments. This process threatens China's capability to build complete power equipment units in the future. In effect, the local enterprises are becoming sub-contractors for the respective multinational companies. Large Chinese SOEs may find that they have struggled to gain autonomy from the Chinese state, only to give it up to the MNCs.

Conclusion: co-ordinated or unco-ordinated restructuring?

China is attempting to restructure its industrial institutions in a turbulent and rapidly changing world. This presents great challenges for industrial policy, much greater than those faced by previous late-comer countries such as Japan and South Korea. China's vast size means that its rapid growth engenders great international hostility and renders the task of internal co-ordination of policy immensely difficult. Its restructuring is occurring amid unprecedentedly rapid globalization and technical change, especially in information technology (IT). It is also a time of resurgence in the economic power of the USA, which is itself in the throes of transforming its big business institutions.

China has made immense strides in gradually developing effective large-scale business institutions. However, it has reached a new stage in the challenge of restructuring the old industrial system, with increasing pressure to move towards closer international economic integration and a sharp acceleration of MNC investment in the strategic 'upstream' sectors of the economy. Unco-ordinated formation of JVs with MNCs is not the way to develop Chinese industry. Nor was this the way in which the large firms of the capitalist world emerged. The most recent and striking example of the role of government in restructuring large-scale capitalist big business has been the explosive reorganization of the US aerospace industry in the 1990s, falling from twenty-odd large firms, to three giants in less than ten years, with the co-ordination of the Pentagon ('America's MITI') behind the process.

Many Chinese scholars consider that the most effective way to develop Chinese industries is to allow them to compete freely in the global market economy. However, as this chapter has argued, the market in the real world is far removed from the textbook picture of perfect competition. The dramatic changes in the institutional structure of capitalism in the past decade have resulted in a new and even more powerful form of oligopolistic capitalism than was the case a decade ago. American big business has emerged as much the strongest component of this process, it is in potentially the strongest position to benefit from globalization and liberalization, in which China is a key building block.

Despite big advances in output and institutional structure, China's big business remains weak. China faces significant barriers to the rapid construction of powerful businesses. Many of these have paradoxically emerged from the reform path chosen, and the devolution of rights to large plants and local authorities, because of the vested interests thereby created. It remains to be seen how the Chinese state responds to this immense planning challenge. At the time of writing, significant thought is being given to the function of the holding company in this epoch. The aerospace, non-ferrous metals, and petrochemical industries have already established semi-autonomous, commercially interested central holding companies to effectively replace the old ministries, and it has been announced that the steel industry will shortly have such a body.

China's big businesses stand at the crossroads. When asked what the shape of the petrochemical industry will be in five or ten years time, one industry expert in China answered that it might well take the form of comprehensive reorganization into three massive, vertically integrated regionally based companies. Each might be organized around one of China's major sources of oil or natural gas, and each would integrate upstream and downstream through to high value-added final products. In other words, from today's semi-autonomous petrochemical plants, with separate semi-autonomous oil extraction companies, each conducting its own negotiations with the MNCs, China might have established three mighty equivalents of Shell, the world's second largest company by market capitalization. On the other hand, the expert answered, it was possible that Sinopec may by then be disbanded and the industry be almost entirely a sequence of branch plants of the MNCs.

In a time of intense turbulence, the function of the state becomes more, not less, important. The interaction between the national government, international organization and MNCs will be the key to politico-economic development in China and in the world in the coming decade).

Notes

* The research for this paper was funded by the ESRC (grant number R00055235) for the project 'The emergence of the modern industrial corporation in China since the 1970s' based in the Department of Applied Economics, Cambridge University. Unless otherwise indicated, information in this article is from field trips to China undertaken between 1994 and 1997.

1. In fact, there is considerable ground for debate about the true figure. For a careful refutation of the official US view see State Council Information Office (1997).
2. Coca-Cola's share of carbonated soft drinks is even higher.
3. Moreover, in the Ninth Five-Year Plan (1996–2000) it is estimated that around 60 per cent of China's power equipment will be imported. Twelve of the first batch of fourteen Three Gorge Dam turbines will be imported, with only a possibility of the second tranche of twelve being supplied from 'domestic' sources, much of which may be from the JVs.
4. Even heroic attempts at upward revaluation of the Chinese defence budget suggest that it is no more than one-third of the size of the US defence budget (Bernstein and Munro, 1997).
5. A representative example of this was the decision taken by ICI and Du Pont to swap important parts of their businesses. ICI concluded that 'for technical and financial reasons' it could not become a global player in nylon. Du Pont had come to the same conclusion for acrylics, and the two businesses were swapped. As a result of the transaction, ICI became the world's largest producer of acrylics and Du Pont became the world's largest producer of nylons (Hampel, 1992).
6. It should be noted, that to describe as 'extraordinarily fragmented' an industry in which only twenty firms accounted for 46 per cent of the total world market, which is today vastly greater than it was twenty or thirty years ago, is a reflection of the degree to which control of world markets has passed into the hands of a small number of companies, and concentration of economic power is taken to be a fact of life.
7. In 1970, the share of R & D funded by the government stood at 64 per cent in France, 58 per cent in the USA, 45 per cent in Germany, and 28 per cent in Japan (Fransmann, 1995, p. 107). Despite a gradual decline, in 1990, the share of R & D funded by the national governments stood at 49 per cent in France, 46 per cent in the USA, 33 per cent in Germany and 19 per cent in Japan (Fransmann, 1995, p. 107).
8. Worldwide industry revenue has grown from around 440 billion dollars in 1990, to around 830 billion in 1996, and is predicted to rise to over 1200 billion in 2000 (*Financial Times*, 18 February, 1997).
9. For an extensive evaluation of the Chinese government's approach towards integration with the world economy in terms of 'close' versus 'strategic' integration.
10. In the case of the steel industry, although the simple average tariff on imported iron and steel had fallen to just 9.1 per cent in 1996, and the licensing system was ended, powerful new WTBs were erected in the mid-1990s. These included import 'registration', which could be withheld if there was felt to be a 'market need', and

'canalization' of steel imports through selected state importing companies. China's barriers to steel imports have been 'strengthened and reformulated' since 1993, despite apparent liberalization.

11. The share of large enterprises in gross industrial output value (at current prices) of enterprises at township (*xiang*) level and above rose from 25.1 per cent in 1980 to 38.0 per cent in 1994 (SSB, CEY,1981, p. 212, SSB, ZGTJNJ, 1996, p. 388).

12. The board of directors and shareholders could cushion the enterprise against government intervention, which has always been the biggest problem of state-owned firms.

13. For example, Yulin Yuchai in Guangxi Province is the largest medium-duty diesel engine manufacturer in China. Yulin City obtains around 80 per cent of its tax revenue from Yuchai, and the local Yulin City's Assets Management Bureau obtains 40 per cent of the dividends handed over to the state holding company. Similarly, Harbin City in Heilongjiang Province is heavily dependent on HPEC. Dividends from HPEC are handed over to the majority owner, the state holding company, and help to directly sustain the life of the city. In addition, tax payments from HPEC account for around 60 per cent of the total industrial tax revenue of Harbin City.

14. For example, the head of the Shanghai Petrochemical Company, Wu Yixin, interviewed by us in March 1996, said he could easily foresee the day when the state's ownership share in the firm could fall from its present majority position, to around 30 per cent, as other sources of capital were invested in the business. However, he found it hard to imagine in the foreseeable future that it would be allowed to fall below this level.

15. Interviews with Ministry of Metallurgy (*Ye Jin Bu*).

Bibliography

Amsden, A. A. (1989) *Asia's Next Giant: South Korea and Late Industrialization* (New York and Oxford: Oxford University Press.

Bernstein, R. and R. Munro (1997) 'The Coming Conflict with America', *Foreign Affairs*, 76(2) March–April.

Byrd, W. (ed.) (192) *Chinese Industrial Firms under Reform* (Washington, DC: Oxford University Press).

Caves, E. R. (1996) *Multinational Enterprise and Economic Analysis* (Cambridge: Cambridge University Press).

Chandler, A. D. (1990) *Scale and Scope: The Dynamics of Industrial Capitalism* (Cambridge Mass: Harvard University Press).

Coca-Cola Company (1997) *Annual Report.*

Development Research Centre (DRC) (1993) *Listing of China's Largest Enterprises* (Zhongguo daxing qiye paixu), (Beijing: Management World Editorial Department).

Drewry Shipping Consultants (1994) *Petrochemicals East of Suez: The Outlook for Chemical Trade and Shipping in Asia to 2000* (London: Drewry Shipping).

Dunning, J. H. (1993) *Multinational Enterprises and the Global Economy* (Wokingham: Addison-Wesley).

Dunning, J. H. and N. Sauvant (1994)

Fransmann, M. (1995) 'Is National Technology Policy Obsolete in a Globalised World? The Japanese Response', *Cambridge Journal of Economics* (1 February).

Gray, F. (1996) 'The Most Ambitious Target', *Financial Times*, 26 June.

Hampel, R. (1992) 'Directing a Global Chemical Operation in the Nineties', *Financial Times Conference*, 8–9 December.

Harbin Power Equipment Company (HPEC) (1995) *Annual Report* (Harbin).

Hsieh, T. Y. (1996) 'Prospering Through Relationships in Asia', *McKinsey Quarterly*, 4.
Huntington, S. P. (1996) *The Clash of Civilizations* (New York: Simon & Schuster).
Jefferson, G. H. and T. G. Rawski (1994) 'Enterprise Reform in Chinese Industry', *World Bank Research Paper Series, China.*
Johnson, C. A. (1982) *MITI and the Japanese Miracle* (Stanford: Stanford University Press).
Krugman, P. (1995) 'Does Third World Growth Hurt First World Prosperity?', in K. Ohmae (ed.), *The Evolving Global Economy – Making Sense of the New World Order,* (Boston, Man: Harvard Business School Publishing,), pp. 113–27.
Krugman, P. (1996) *Pop Internationalism* (Cambridge, Man: MIT Press).
Lall, S. (1990) *Building Industrial Competitiveness in Developing Countries* (Paris: OECD).
Luesby, J. (1995) 'The Future Lies in Asia', *Financial Times*, 27 October.
Nolan, P. (1995) 'Joint Venture and Economic Reform in China: A Case Study of the Coca-Cola Business System, with Particular Reference to the Tianjin Coca-Cola Plant', *Working Paper Series of ESRC Center for Business Research*, WP 24, December (University of Cambridge).
Ohmae, K. (1995) 'Putting Global Logic First', in K. Ohmae (ed.), *The Evolving Global Economy – Making Sense of the New World Order* (Boston, Man: Harvard Business School Publishing) pp. 129–37.
Overholt, W. C. (1993) China: *The Next Economic Superpower* (London: Wiedenfeld & Nicolson).
Petit, R. (1992) 'Restructuring and Rationalising: An Industry Appraizal', *Financial Times Conference*, 8–9 December.
Porter, M. E. (1990) *The Competitive Advantage of Nations* (London: Macmillan).
Project Group for the Establishment of a Modern Enterprise System, the Industrial Economy Institute, Chinese Academy of Social Sciences (1996) 'Several Problems Related to the Establishment of a Modern Enterprise System', *Social Sciences in China*, Winter.
Reich, R. (1995a) 'Who is Us?', in K. Ohmae (ed.), *The Evolving Global Economy – Making Sense of the New World Order* (Boston, Man: Harvard Business School Publishing), pp. 141–60.
Reich, R. (1995b) 'Who is Them?' in K. Ohmae (ed.), *The Evolving Global Economy – Making Sense of the New World Order* (Boston, Man: Harvard Business School Publishing), pp. 161–81.
Research Group for 'A Comparative Study of the International Competitiveness of Chinese Manufactured Goods' (1997), 'The International Competition Facing Domestically Produced and the Nation's Industry', *Social Sciences in China*, 18(1), Spring.
Ridding, J. and A. Gowers (1995) 'Michelin Men Make Their Mark', *Financial Times*, 5 October.
Ross, R. S. (1997) 'Beijing as a Conservative Power', *Foreign Affairs*, ( ) March–April.
Ruigrok, W. and R. Van Tulder (1995) *The Logic of International Restructuring* (London and New York: Routledge).
Schwab, K. and C. Smadia (1995) 'Power and Policy: The New Economic World Order', in K. Ohmae (ed.), *The Evolving Global Economy – Making Sense of the New World Order* (Boston, Man: Harvard Business School Publishing), pp. 99–111.
Singh, A. (1993) 'The Plan, the Market and Evolutionary Economic Reform in China' *UNCTAD Discussion Paper*, 76.
Song, Q., B. Qiao and C. Zhang (1996) *China Can Say 'No'* (Zhongguo keyi shuo bu) (Beijing, Zhongguo gongshang lianhe Publishing House).
State Council Information Office (1997) 'On Sino–US Trade Balance', *Beijing Review*, 40(14), 7–13 April.

State Statistical Bureau (SSB) (1981) *Chinese Economic Yearbook* (CEY, English) (Hong Kong: Economic Information Agency).

State Statistical Bureau, (SSB) (1992, 1993, 1996) *Chinese Statistical Yearbook* (Beijing: Tongji chubanshe).

Sutton, J. (1991) *Sunk Costs and Market Structure: Price Competition, Advertising and the Evolution of Concentration* (Cambridge Mass: MIT Press).

United Nations Conference on Trade and Development (UNCTAD) (1993) *World Investment Report 1993* (New York: UNCTAD).

United Nations Conference on Trade and Development (UNCTAD), *World Investment Report 1994* (New York: UNCTAD).

United Nations Conference on Trade and Development (UNCTAD) (1996) *World Investment Report 1996* (New York: UNCTAD).

Wood, A. (1994) 'China's Economic System: A Brief Description, With Some Suggestions For Further Reform', Programme of Research into the Reform of Pricing and Market, London School of Economics, CP 12, mimeo: revised and republished in Nolan and Fan Qimiao, (eds), *China's Economic Reforms: Achievements and Problems* (London: Macmillan).

World Bank (1996), *World Development Report* (Washington, DC: Oxford University Press).

World Bank (1997), *World Development Report* (Washington: Oxford University Press).

Yonekura, S. (1994) *The Japanese Iron and Steel Industry, 1850–1990* (London: Macmillan).

Young, P. 'Current Chemical Industry Restructuring and Financing Trends', *Financial Times, Conference*, 22–23 November 1993.

2
Capitalist Firms, Public Enterprises: Ownership Reform and Privatization of Chinese State-owned Enterprises

Minquan Liu

Introduction

Privatization has been a policy programme designed, as it was often put in Britain by Conservative Party politicians, to 'roll back the frontiers of the state'. It has characterized government policies in much of the 1980s and early 1990s from the developed to developing, and from the Western mixed to formerly socialist economies. The issue has also figured prominently in debates on Chinese economic reforms, and many are convinced that this is a dose of medicine the Chinese economy simply has to take.[1]

This chapter consists of four main parts. We review issues surrounding the efficiency of the modern capitalist firm, focusing in particular on the market for corporate control, or take-overs. The objective is to argue that even in the case of modern capitalist corporations, full internal efficiency is by no means guaranteed.[2] Recognition of this fact is important for allaying unrealistic hopes of what ownership reform can achieve. We then briefly consider one of the main themes in current debates – namely, the relative importance of competition and privatization – and argue that without simultaneously emphasizing, if not giving precedence to, competition policies, the goal of privatization of fundamentally improving public enterprises' performance is unlikely to be achieved. It is widely accepted that public enterprises' poor efficiency was caused by the 'soft budget' constraint they faced. We then examine the cause of the soft budget constraint, emphasizing its political origin and exploring the political implications such a diagnosis has. The principle of delegation is discussed in and is applied to ownership reform of Chinese state owned enterprises (SOEs), and a final section concludes.

The first two sections are essentially a review of some well known propositions. The reason for revisiting them is that in the current consensus on privatization, many extremely important points have too often been neglected. A review of them also helps to point to the need to address the vital question of the politics of privatization and ownership reform, an issue thus far largely eschewed in the literature.

Efficiency of the modern capitalist firm

Ever since the diffuseness of ownership and separation of ownership and control were studied by early economists such as Robertson (1923) and Berle and Means (1933),[3] the efficiency of the modern capitalist firm has been called into question. It was recognized that these factors could render owners, the numerous small shareholders, powerless to control professional management. Management may be able to pursue their own goals, which need not and in general do not coincide with those of owners. The goal of profit maximization could be sacrificed, with all the efficiency implications. Managers could work at expanding the empire they run, or pursue a quiet life, etc.[4]

This view is by no means agreed by all. Nevertheless both empirical and *a priori* theoretical support for the argument seems strong. It has also long been contended, however, that shareholder meetings and capital market disciplining would render these cases unlikely, if not entirely eliminate them. We review the underlying arguments below. The discussion closely follows Stiglitz (1985), Shleifer and Vishny (1988) and Singh (1992).[5]

Corporate control

Shareholder meetings and internal corporate control

It has often been argued that shareholder meetings can, in a strictly formal legal sense, provide a forum whereby shareholders control the management, for they can replace managers who fail to act in their interest, which is to maximize the stock market value (long-run profit stream) of the firm.[6] However, there are good reasons why shareholder meetings may not actually fulfil this role. Theoretical considerations suggest that good management (value-maximizing management) is a public good. When ownership is diffused and each shareholder owns no more than a fraction of a firm's shares, a single shareholder would receive no more than a fraction of the benefits from her personal supervision of the management, while she has to incur all the necessary costs of information collection (she has to collect the necessary information to vote intelligently). So no rational shareholder would supervise the management.

Although the evidence remains conflicting, there is a substantial body confirming the above view. In any case, as Stiglitz (1985, p. 136) points out, what ought to cause surprise in practice is 'not that shareholder meetings generally fail to exercise effective control over management, but that there are instances in which shareholder meetings have had an effect'.

Shareholder meetings are one form of internal corporate control. Another is the supervisory role of the board of directors (the non-executive directors). The board has a range of power from blocking major managerial decisions to hiring and firing chief executives, and determining managerial compensations. However, as Shleifer and Vishny (1988) note, for a number of reasons, including a lack of information regarding performance of the firm made available to non-executive directors, and the possibility of these directors being co-opted by the management, the potency of this form of disciplining is also seriously suspect.[7]

The take-over mechanism

Take-overs, especially hostile ones, through the operation of the stock market provide another form of disciplining.[8] It is often reasoned theoretically that in the event of a firm not maximizing value, any individual or another firm could come along and purchase the firm, reorient its policy towards value maximization, and make a profit when the firm's value subsequently rises. However, again there are reasons why this form of discipline may not work.

The first is the argument put forward by Grossman and Hart (1980). We have just noted the public good phenomenon displayed by shareholders with regard to voting. However, in the event of a take-over bid, the same shareholders may reason thus: 'if the take-over is successful and, as a result, the company value rises, it is better that I stay with the company.' If each shareholder thinks in this way, then the expected take-over would not take place.[9] In this view, in fact, as Stiglitz (1985) points out, it can take place only if all or the majority of shareholders expect the post-take-over value of the firm to fall.[10]

Grossman and Hart's argument relies on the assumption of small shareholders such that any single shareholder's decision not to sell her shares would not affect another's decision to sell. However, even with significantly large shareholders, Stiglitz (1985) presents two information-related factors that may again render the take-over mechanism ineffective. One stems from the information asymmetry between the insiders and outsiders of a firm. The insiders, the managers, are likely to know better about the performance of the firm. Thus, as Stiglitz (1985, p. 137) notes:

> when those who have a controlling interest in the firm are willing to sell their shares, it indicates that the individual or firm attempting the take-over has paid too much; if they refuse to sell, it indicates that the individual or firm attempting the take-over has paid too little: take-overs will only be successful when the firm taking over pays too much.[11]

The other information-related factor is of a somewhat opposite nature – the inability to keep information secret. It is costly to ascertain which firms are not well managed and hence taking over may yield a capital gain. The discovery firm would have to spend a great deal of resources. However, when it eventually makes a take-over bid, this would provide a signal to other firms to look at whether the bid represents an under-valuation of the target firm. These firms may then bid against the discovery firm, driving the expected profits to zero, but this means that the discovery firm, which had initially expended resources sifting through a large set of firms, would make a negative expected profit.[12]

Finally, aside from the above-mentioned problems, there are measures the incumbent managers could take to discourage potential raiders. For example, firms could commit themselves to long-term contracts with severe penalties for breach, thus making post-take-over policy changes difficult and less profitable, thereby deterring would-be raiders. Malatesta (1992) discusses possible take-over defences in more detail.

On account of the above considerations, it would seem that take-overs are generally unlikely to take place in practice. However, available evidence shows that take-overs do actually often take place in practice, and in waves (Jensen, 1992; Singh, 1992). At the same time, it is also quite widely agreed that take-overs in fact occur for a variety of reasons – including for synergic reasons, pursuit of monopoly power, empire-building, tax motives and for certain defensive and strategic reasons. For example, there is evidence that size, along with profitability, is a principal explanatory factor of take-overs, such that an inefficient large-sized firm may take over an efficient small-sized firm (Singh, 1992). There is in particular an accumulated body of evidence that while take-overs may serve to discipline the management of a target firm, they themselves can be major instances of non-value-maximization by the acquiring firms' management (Shleifer and Vishny, 1988; Scherer, 1988).[13]

The above provides only a sketchy review of the take-over controversy. The literature is vast, and growing, and many issues are as yet unsettled. Our intention is to emphasize the fact that there are great uncertainties about the efficiency of the capitalist firm, and it is by no means the case that modern capitalist firms are all free from inefficiency problems.

Voting with dollars

There is yet a third form of disciplining related to a firm's ability to raise additional capital. It may be argued that inefficient firms would not be able to raise new capital through issuing new shares. However, for a start this form of disciplining is effective only if a firm does need to raise new capital; managers of many firms may actually have considerable discretion over their own cash flow. And even when they do need to raise new capital, with good investment opportunities banks provide an alternative source. Indeed, as Stiglitz (1985) points out, for various reasons when firms do need to raise new capital, they mostly turn to banks.[14]

Managerial slack, market competition and efficiency

So far we have considered various forms of corporate control and their possible role in ensuring internal efficiency of the modern capitalist firm. Product market competition is another mechanism to enhance efficiency, and is the one that has been recognized ever since the classical economists. We look further at this below.[15]

Consider a textbook-type perfectly competitive product market in which numerous firms compete to sell the same product using identical production processes (i.e. there are no firm-specific demand and production advantages). Competition in the product market alone would then ensure a manager maximize profits and achieve efficiency, for otherwise her own firm would go under.

But once we move away from the textbook perfect competition model, the situation immediately changes. For example, suppose there exists some firm-specific factor on the production side, other things being equal. Suppose that as a result of, say, innovation, one firm gains a cost advantage. Then product market competition alone is not enough to ensure that managers of the firm maximize profits. Without a proper corporate control device, it is hard to see how managerial slack could be eliminated.

The introduction of a firm-specific cost factor is only a mild relaxation of the perfect competition assumption. Turning to the demand side and to cases of monopoly, duopoly and monopolistic competition, cases that are more typical in today's capitalist economies, possibilities of managerial slack abound. Without some proper internal or external corporate control device, it does not seem that such slack could be reduced significantly, let one eliminated.

The above points to the potential for managerial slack under a variety of market conditions. At the same time, it indicates that the extent of managerial slack is likely to be related to product market conditions. Thus in the textbook perfect competition model, managerial slack is absent. Similarly, if we compare a monopoly and, say, a firm with independent cost advantages but nevertheless competing with many firms in the same product market (i.e. still under somewhat competitive market conditions), we would expect the potential for managerial slack to be much greater with the former firm. The latter has its cost advantage, but the former enjoys the seclusion of an entire market. It can raise prices so long as doing so serves its interest, something which the latter firm is not able to do.

In general, one would expect the potential of managerial slack to depend sensitively on product market conditions. Indeed, one of the recurring themes in current debates about privatization concerns precisely the relative role played by policies to enhance product market competition and privatization.

Public enterprises and privatization

We now turn to public enterprises. In principle, public enterprises could take many ownership and governance forms, including the one proposed by Wood (1991, 1993) in the context of reforming China's state sector, at which we shall look closely below. Until then, by a 'public enterprise' we shall mean the historically dominant form, whereby an enterprise is directly owned by a central or local government, and may also be directly controlled by them with respect to production, investment, labour-hiring, personnel and other matters, as was the case in the former socialist countries.[16]

In turning to issues of privatizing public enterprises, we shall argue, first, that as far as its economics is concerned, what privatization does is essentially to impose an *ultimate* bankruptcy constraint on an enterprise. Secondly, privatization can be expected to enhance efficiency, primarily in those cases where reasonably competitive product markets exist, and where the textbook perfect competition model predicts that efficiency of a modern capitalist firm would be high. The implication is that privatization ought, then, to be coupled with, and even preceded by, measures to improve product market competition. In developing countries, it is relatively easy to improve *product* rather than factor market competition. Questions concerning the rationale for public enterprises are also discussed in order to put the issues surrounding privatization in a better perspective.

Public enterprises, market competition and the 'soft budget' constraint

No one would dispute the statement that the efficiency of many public enterprises in both the developing and developed countries leaves much to be desired, and there are good reasons for that (although this is not to say that public enterprises are necessarily less efficient than private firms).[17] For purposes of discussion, let us first consider a public enterprise operating in a competitive market environment (but not necessarily one of perfect competition). Needless to say, this was hardly true of the situation in the former socialist economies, nor is it true of China today.

The immediate question that arises is whether this enterprise is subject to a *bankruptcy* constraint. For if it is, then there is no reason why it would operate any differently from, and be less efficient than, a capitalist firm. With perfect competition, any inefficient practice would mean the enterprise going under. If there are particular cost advantages or market power specific to it, there could then exist a degree of managerial slack, but the same would be true of a capitalist firm with diffused ownership.

However, save for a few exceptions, the experience of public enterprises in socialist and mixed economies alike in the past decades has not borne this out. The principal problem has to do with what Kornai (1986) calls the 'soft budget constraint'. We will further examine what in turn causes the soft budget constraint. Meanwhile, the fact of the matter is that soft budget constraints have been what most public enterprises operate by. Government subsidies were almost automatic to cover losses; there was no threat of bankruptcy, and there was of course no take-over.[18]

A further problem is that in most cases there were in fact no competitive markets for these enterprises. In the mixed economies, public enterprises were often monopolistic and were not subject to stringent competition. In the former socialist countries, the economies were by and large centrally planned, and consequently there could be no markets for these enterprises.

Competition and privatization

Depending on product market conditions, even private sector firms may not fully face an effective bankruptcy threat. If a private monopoly can freely raise prices without ever being seriously exposed to the prospect of closure, then it is effectively not subject to a bankruptcy constraint. With this possible exception, however, when comparing the operation of private firms and public enterprises, we see that the main difference lies in the presence of an ultimate bankruptcy constraint in the former and its absence in the latter. What privatization may be expected to achieve is to remove the automatic subsidies and to harden the budget constraint to that extent – that is, to impose an *ultimate* bankruptcy constraint.[19] The bankruptcy constraint is only 'ultimate' since there could exist large scope for managerial slack depending on market conditions. (It may be argued that privatization could impose extra capital market disciplining as well, but in view of our early argument, such disciplining may not be substantial.)

It is important to stress that the efficacy of privatization in promoting efficiency, in fact, critically depends on product market conditions. Where product market competition is high, privatization can be expected to improve efficiency significantly by imposing a tighter and more tangible bankruptcy constraint. On the other hand, as Kay and Thompson (1986, p. 22) point out,

> '[i]f . . . there is little competition in the product market, if the risk of bankruptcy is slight, and if the risk of take-over is also minimal, the pressures of the market affect a private sector manager no more than his public counterpart.

In their view, '[i]t is not ownership as such, but the interaction of ownership and competition that promotes efficiency'.

It may be argued that since even a private monopoly will ultimately face closure if it does extremely poorly, in a way a public monopoly does not, simply turning an existing public monopoly private could increase efficiency. This is true. Nevertheless, the fact of the matter is that in the absence of strong product market competition, even private sector managers will have large margins of discretion, and there does not seem to be any effective corrective mechanism.

From the viewpoint of policy dynamic, there is also a case for simultaneous emphasis on, if not prior measures of, competition policies. As Kay and Thompson (1986, p. 29) correctly warn in relation to the British privatization programmes, a single-pronged attack on ownership may actually turn out to be damaging 'because privatization makes it more difficult to introduce further competitive incentives in the future'. For example, 'fragmenting into smaller operating units is harder to impose on a private firm than a public one' (p. 29). This touches on the wider question of the sequencing of different reform measures, which we cannot go into here.

We have questioned the wisdom of an exclusive emphasis on privatization. At the same time, we also appear to have conceded the necessity of it. For if it is true that private firms and public enterprises do differ in their exposure to an 'ultimate' bankruptcy constraint, and since introducing an ultimate bankruptcy constraint would be the first step to improve an enterprise's efficiency, privatization would be necessary. However, this need not follow. It remains to be established whether alternative forms of public ownership could not significantly mitigate against, if not completely remove, the soft budget constraint. This issue is discussed below.[20]

Some arguments for public enterprises

In the current popular wisdom accepting the superiority of private firms, the question is seldom raised why many industries were nationalized and public enterprises were set up in the first place a few decades back in both the developing and developed economies. Some firms were placed under public ownership because they were making huge losses in private hands. It may appear like an act of folly to keep an inefficient firm going; however, it is not clear how many in Britain would wish Rolls Royce had been wiped off the map and believe that Britain would have been better for it.[21] The case of Rolls Royce is but one example of how market valuations of a firm might at times fail to reflect its real social worth (however defined), or indeed real long-term market worth.

In the above, we considered only the likely managerial slack present in both private firms and public enterprises, and discussed the issue of privatization on that basis. However, there are other factors of importance. The case of Rolls Royce serves to show the possible short-term nature of market valuation. There are other limitations with market valuations, for example, involving externalities. Coase (1960) has argued that given any private property rights, generating and receiving parties to an externality could be expected to solve the problem between them. However, often the real difficulty is precisely that of establishing and enforcing private property rights in these cases. In such circumstances, there is a case for setting up public enterprises – or, for that matter, for subsidizing private firms to carry out particular activities.

A second major reason for setting up public enterprises was the concern over natural monopolies. The allocative inefficiency and welfare implications of private monopolies, apart from the managerial slack problem discussed above, are well known.[22]

A third important reason, certainly insofar as many developing nations are concerned, was the absence of a well functioning capital market, including a lack of a tradition for equity investment and a preference for family businesses, in these countries. For a long while after the Second World War, the state in many developing countries was actually a reluctant entrepreneur, being forced to sponsor new ventures in capital-intensive sectors which the private sector would not and could not undertake. And, as Aylen (1987, pp. 22–3) points out,

> [e]ven now most developing economies lack financial markets of sufficient size and sophistication and companies with managerial capacity to marshall the two to three billion US dollars needed to build a small integrated steelworks from scratch on a greenfield site.

In these cases governments have been forced to step in, and Aylen discusses these issues more fully.[23]

There are further arguments to be advanced for public enterprises, which we omit here (Streeton, 1983, provides a fairly comprehensive list). Our purpose in discussing the above is to stress that the issue is complex. Aside from managerial slack, other factors will need to be taken into account when assessing whether the case is for or against public enterprises, and in many instances, especially in developing countries, private firms may not be a realistic alternative, whether in respect of setting up a new large venture, or taking over and running an existing public one.[24]

Politics of privatization and ownership reform

We have so far considered the issue of privatization only in economic terms, and have been casting doubts on pursuing it single-mindedly, without a simultaneous emphasis on – and, indeed, prior measures for – making markets more competitive. However, privatization also has a political side to it. Even if the economic case for privatization is established, its political acceptability, or the likely political risks associated with it, need also to be addressed. No leadership of a country is likely to attempt it if it is deemed to carry too high a political risk.

Below we first consider the real underlying differences in the constraints facing private firms and public enterprises, which we argue are very much political in origin. These differences have sometimes been alluded to in the literature, but they have seldom been clearly spelled out. A clear spelling out will improve our understanding of the full complexity of a drastic privatization programme. Implications of the analysis both in terms of undertaking privatization and of reforming public ownership more generally are now drawn.[25]

The cause of the soft budget constraint

We return to Kornai's soft budget constraint characterization of the behaviour of public enterprises. It has generally been accepted as self-evident. However, the question needs to be posed why the state across countries did not impose a 'hard budget constraint' on these enterprises and let them go bankrupt if need be (although bail-outs in such cases themselves are not necessarily inefficient, *expectations* of them are). The state could simply operate steadfastly by the financial rules it lays down (the state may of course make inefficient allocation decisions, but that is a separate matter).

It is sometimes argued that in the case of public enterprises there lacks a performance monitor who is also a residual claimant. According to this view, government officials, seeing that it is not their own interest being sacrificed, do not have incentives to perform monitoring. However, while this may be true, we noted above that private shareholders may not be better motivated to monitor their managers.

Private firms and public enterprises are said to be subject to different constraints in another way. Managers of the latter may be thought to enjoy a certain 'moral-hazard advantage'. Even if the right monitoring incentives are there, when a public enterprise makes a loss, the authority concerned has to determine the cause, and that is not always easy. In the absence of any hard evidence that the management is to blame, the authority has to cover the loss.[26] In contrast, a private firm manager cannot, or at least is not supposed to, expect a similar recourse from the shareholders when the firm makes a loss, should the loss threaten the long-term profitability of the firm. It is, however, puzzling why private firm managers generally cannot seek a bail-out from their shareholders, and why public enterprise managers usually can from the government.[27]

The principal reason for the soft nature of budget constraints facing public enterprises lies, it is suggested, in the political constraint these enterprises and the government face. Consider a private firm faced with closure whose workers and managers are to lose jobs. What might they do? They may not like it, but they could hardly resist it. They could hardly ask the firm's owners, the shareholders, for a bail-out. A private firm is in the business to make a profit and that is how things are! If a private firm is due for closure because of loss-making, one hardly has a case to resist it and to insist on the firm staying in business so that one keeps one's employment.

However, as soon as a public enterprise is threatened with closure, the situation rapidly changes. For some reason, our standards regarding public enterprises are different. Calls will soon be heard for the state to provide subsidies and to launch rescue packages. The workers will feel an injustice if the enterprise is closed and they lose jobs. If they are thrown onto the dole queue, it will not be perceived as an act by a commercial concern doing what it is entitled to do, but the treachery of a government. Somehow, we expect the government to be caring, and above purely commercial objectives. Indeed, however people dislike the excessive power of the state, most have a kind of 'state-dependent mentality'. Rightly or wrongly, they expect the state, and hence public enterprises, not to operate by the same commercial principle which private firms operate by. Job losses owing to the closure of a private firm are acceptable, but job losses as a result of the closure of a public enterprise are not.[28]

Of course, even the threatened closure of a private firm might in certain cases cause its employees to demand government assistance, but this precisely confirms the kind of state-dependent mentality people have.

Such a mentality is quite universal. It is undoubtedly present in many countries (e.g. Britain), but it is especially strong in China. This probably has to do with the ideology with which the present generations in China were brought up with. For decades, people were taught that they were 'masters' of the country, and although many have seldom acted as true masters should in terms of carrying out responsibilities, they expected to enjoy the rights and privileges conferred on a master. This has become an accepted phenomenon. However, it implies enormous political risks should the state decide to renounce its obligation.

Kornai (1986) attributed the soft budget constraint largely to the 'paternalistic' disposition of the state. For some time, the state in China and in other former socialist countries did indeed appear to display strong paternalistic tendencies. The state attempted to preside over and provide for nearly every aspect of people's lives, from employment to housing, health and general livelihood. But if the phenomenon is simply a matter of the paternalistic dispositions of the state, then one expects that when the state decides to off-load its responsibilities, the general public would feel relieved (assuming that they do not prefer to be patronized). This, however, has not usually been the case in countries from developed to developing and from the East to West where privatization has been practised.[29]

There is no doubt that the sometimes paternalistic actions of the state did contribute to the citizens' expectation of it to provide jobs and livelihood. But it also seems that the expectation itself is a cause, and perhaps is the principal one. This may have been due to socialist education, as in China, or to what many view as simply an ideological shift, as in the West.[30] In the case of China, however, its culture and tradition may also have played a part. For even before decades-long socialist education, similar expectations had already existed, and were powerful. In the history of China, a succession of dynasties fell because in the eyes of the population at large they were unable to ensure them an essential livelihood. In other countries, such dynastic changes have been relatively rare.

Whatever role the Chinese history may have played, the foregoing indicates that the 'state-dependent mentality', rather than the paternalistic dispositions of the government, may be the chief cause of the soft budget constraint; the latter may have contributed to the former. However, one would admit that the matter needs more study.[31]

Privatization and political constraints

As noted, the state-dependent mentality need not apply to public enterprises only. There may be cases where even the closure of a private firm may force a government to act. However, in general there do seem to be major differences in the public's view of the acceptable behaviour of public enterprises and private firms, and the government may want to capitalize on this. Specifically, the government may want to privatize its existing public enterprises. Below, we consider this and other implications of a diagnosis of the cause of the soft budget constraint that is based on the public's state-dependent mentality.

While private firms are thus politically 'convenient' to the government, privatization could entail political risks, since in doing so the state could be seen as abdicating its responsibilities. In the case of China, such risks could be high, and they ought to be considered carefully before a radical privatization programme is embarked upon. What are possible risks? Since the public's perception of the role of the state in ensuring them a livelihood is at the heart of the matter, the public's tolerance of economic hardship needs to be considered. The tolerance level could be different in different countries.

Among the enterprises destined to be privatized will of course be large state corporations concentrated in the urban areas. If privatization is to be followed by immediate job losses, as experience from many countries demonstrates, will the sacked workers feel forsaken by the state? Will they demand the state provide them with new jobs? Will there be urban unrest if the state fails to do so? And what are the implications for the country if there is unrest?

It is not possible to provide definite answers to these questions. In practice, broad judgements, based on a careful reading of available evidence, would have to be made. In this respect, the cautious approach taken by Taiwan to privatizing its public enterprises may be worth noting. In much of the 1980s and early 1990s, the Taiwanese authorities had considered a privatization programme (Lee, 1993). Compared with mainland China, Taiwan had had a much smaller state sector. However, it took the Taiwanese authorities close to a decade to come up with a policy package that it reckoned would be acceptable to the incumbent state sector employees. The authorities were mindful of possible political implications of a radical privatization programme, and they designed, with great care, schemes of post-privatization protection for state sector employees with respect to pension, medical insurance, and unemployment benefits. What Taiwan was mindful of clearly indicates of what mainland China perhaps also needs to be, if only because the two parts of China have a common culture.

Ideally, one would welcome changes in the public's state-dependent mentality. However, such changes are likely to take time; there is some evidence that after nearly two decades of reform, the public's tolerance of economic hardship and adversity associated with the reforms has increased.[32] However, in the crucial aspect of the public's attitude towards the state's obligation as a job provider, there does not appear to be a significant change. Perhaps because the government recognizes this, while in recent years a great many loss-making SOEs have been permitted to lay off workers, few have actually been closed. The laid-off workers have continued to expect the state, and the state has continued to affirm its obligation, to provide them with new jobs.[33]

In the absence of marked shifts in the public's attitudes towards the role of the state in this regard in the near future, are there ways of reforming China's SOEs? We turn to this now.

Delegation, public ownership reform and privatization

We explore a line of thought that centres on the principle of *delegation*. After first briefly describing the principle, we then look at a proposal advanced by Wood (1991, 1993).[34] We also comment on recent developments in enterprise reforms in China from the viewpoint of Wood's proposal.

Delegation is a widespread phenomenon in today's world, the separation of ownership and control characteristic of the modern capitalist firm being one instance. The agency problem, which delegation almost always entails, has been much studied in the recent economic literature, as has been the 'information advantage' associated with it (this refers to the fact that delegates – e.g. firm managers – rather than the source of power – firm owners – know better how to make certain decisions). However, delegation has another useful function to those who delegate the power. In his well-known book *The Strategy of Conflict*, Schelling (1960, pp. 142–3) speaks of

> (t)he use of thugs or sadists for the collection of extortion or the guarding of prisoners, or the conspicuous delegation of authority to a military commander of known motivation ...

to carry out acts which the original source of the power may find it difficult or profitless to do. To put it simply, if a principal finds it difficult to carry out a certain act, it may hire some agent to do it.

Applied to matters of our concern, it means that should a government find it difficult to undertake privatization itself given the associated political risks, it might hire certain agencies to do the work. Similarly, within the domain of public ownership, if a government is burdened with social responsibilities and expectations other than pursuit of profits, while pursuit of profits is arguably best for efficiency, then it might delegate that task to some agency. In both these cases the question, however, is how.[35]

Delegation and public ownership reform

We explore the latter possibility first. The crucial task here is to find an arrangement under which the new agency would not become yet another government department burdened with the same responsibilities and expectations from society. Such an arrangement is essentially what the Wood proposal aims to provide. To summarize briefly, the proposal first of all calls for creating a series of special public ownership institutions (POIs), which would be made up of such existing or new institutions as the central and local state asset management bureaus, banks, insurance companies and pension funds (Wood, 1991, 1993). At the same time, existing public enterprises would be converted into joint-stock companies, whose shares would then be divided and vested in the new POIs. To ensure that the POIs would be interested only in their constituent enterprises' profits, and would not be dissuaded from this by pressures from the public, a system of cross-region ownership is advocated, with each POI regionally based and responsible to its local authority but owning shares of enterprises from across regions in the country. As Wood (1993, p. 2) explains, this is because

> the government of locality A, B and C, as owners of an enterprise in locality D, would be less concerned than the government of locality D about wages, jobs and output in locality D, and more concerned about the enterprise's profitability.

In addition, the fact that ownership is dispersed among several POIs should also help a POI to resist the pressure to pursue objectives other than profits: local government may want greater output, and workers secure employment and higher wages.

Several points need clarification. Although ownership dispersion is envisaged, to ensure that owners have adequate incentives to monitor their enterprises, and to avoid escalating co-ordination costs, dispersion should be controlled (Wood recommends it to be around two–eight per enterprise depending on size). Secondly, an enterprise from a given locality need not be entirely owned by POIs from other localities; it may be partly owned by POIs from its own locality, and that means by its local government. In the case of certain enterprises (e.g. local utilities), because of the social nature of the services they provide, there may even be a case for a local POI to be the sole or majority owner. Exactly how ownership of an enterprise should be geographically dispersed would, therefore, depend on factors in addition to the need for safeguarding the enterprise's profit orientation. Thirdly, POIs need not all be regionally based; central-level POIs are also consistent with the basic thrust of the Wood proposal. However, it may then be added that, except in special cases, it would probably be wise for central-level POIs not to become the sole or majority owner of an enterprise.

Below we consider the relationship between a local (or the central) government and its POI, between a local government and the enterprises from its jurisdiction and between enterprises and the POIs owning them, and the nature of ownership, under Wood's proposed system. First, an enterprise would clearly remain publicly owned under the new system, since the ownership institutions owning it are still public. The ownership institutions would only be *agencies* of the central or local governments which create them, and as such they would be 'answerable' to these authorities. On the other hand, their responsibility should probably not go beyond the efficient and profitable management of the assets entrusted in them. Specifically, their responsibility should not go beyond providing the highest financial returns on the entrusted assets.

Secondly, while remaining public in ownership, generally under the proposed system an enterprise from the jurisdiction of a local authority would no longer, at least not wholly, be 'owned' by that authority, since it is likely to be simultaneously owned by POIs from several localities. Consequently, the decision to close an enterprise, or to carry out other restructuring that substantially affects the welfare of the workers, would no longer rest with the local authority alone, if at all. This fact is likely to be recognized by the workers. The new owners, not burdened with the same social responsibilities as the local government-cum-owner, are likely to make decisions purely on a profit-seeking basis. Although the affected workers might still expect and demand their local government to offer financial help when their enterprise is, say, being closed, they are less likely to hold their local government responsible for any eventual outcome. And even if the authority does consider providing financial help, it would have to negotiate the terms with the new owners, which could turn out to be financially too costly for it to bear (the authority would at least have to cover for the new owners the opportunity cost of the resources tied up).

Thirdly, except where a local POI is a sole or majority owner of an enterprise, relationship between an enterprise and its new owners would be relatively straightforward, and is expected to resemble that between a private corporation and their owners. Where a local POI is a majority owner, the profit motive might be compromised with efficiency losses, because of the social pressures that may be placed on it. However, even in this case there are likely to be demands from other minority owners to reorient an enterprise's policy towards profit-seeking.

We now turn to a brief overview of Chinese enterprise reforms before focusing on some more important developments. Noted for its gradual approach, Chinese enterprise reforms have taken only fairly modest steps in recent years. The government has resisted the temptation of mass-privatizing its SOEs, and consequently ownership reform has proceeded in only very small steps (as we will see shortly). However, a range of other measures have been adopted which have in the main involved giving enterprises more autonomy in output, input and investment decisions; greater choice of incentive payments (e.g. bonuses) and flexible labour-hiring practices (e.g. more contract workers); and greater pay-related managerial responsibility (e.g. the asset responsibility system). In addition, product markets have been made more competitive following various price liberalization measures and competition from the non-state sector. Largely for these reasons, SOEs have, aggregately but especially in certain sectors, shown significant productivity gains over the reform years. On the other hand, they have also been making growing financial losses, with many having been persistent loss-makers. In the case of loss-makers, the state has almost always continued to prop them up with direct subsidies or directed bank loans. And, as noted earlier, while in recent years some SOEs have stopped production and laid off workers, few have actually been closed down.[36]

There are a number of factors explaining the government's resistance to mass-privatizing the SOEs. It is not possible to go into them here; suffice it to say that the most important one is likely to be the perceived political risks.[37] However, from the viewpoint developed in this chapter and Wood's proposal, important moves have been made, which centre on the emergence of stock companies.

Even in the early years when the focus of enterprise reform was on giving more decision-making power to enterprises, China had its first 'stock experiment'.[38] In 1986 the central government authorized the first small group of SOEs to engage in stock experiments with a view to restructuring and leveraging the inefficient medium and large-scale SOEs. Subsequently, the number of firms that engaged in the experiment grew. At the end of 1991, the total number of stock experiment enterprises was estimated to be from 3600 to 6000. By early 1994, the number was reported to be between 11 560 and over 13 000. Since 1995, the state has launched a new round of reform programmes involving more widespread stock experiment.

The stock companies that have emerged have taken diverse forms, depending on how shares are distributed. Shares may be distributed to an enterprise's own staff, may be held by other state enterprises or state sector units, or may be distributed on the basis of factor contributions (labour, capital and technology) of the parties concerned, or indeed publicly issued to individuals. Any enterprise's shares may be distributed on the basis of one or a mix of these. The higher authorities typically also hold some of an enterprise's shares, on behalf of the state. While shares may be issued to individuals, known as individual shares, there have been ceilings on the proportion of individual-held shares of an enterprise (the current ceiling is 20 per cent). The remaining 80 per cent or over shares are to be held by institutions such as state sector enterprises or units (institutional shares), or the higher authorities (state shares). Individual shares may be either A shares, issued to Chinese nationals, or B shares, issued to foreign nationals.

Under the rules in force at present, state shares cannot be traded; institutional shares are tradable but only on an 'Electronic Network System' between institutions. A and B shares are permitted to be traded on the nation's fledgling stock markets in Shanghai and Shenzhen, with A shares traded only among Chinese nationals, and B shares foreign nationals. Recent years have seen frenzied trading in A shares.[39]

Institutional shares are of special importance to us. Exactly how an enterprise's shares are dispersed among institutional shareholders largely depends on circumstances surrounding the enterprise's conversion into a stock company. A typical case is as follows. Enterprise *A* might have been a supplier of a certain intermediate good to *C* and *B*, a purchaser of *C*'s product. Then *C* might experience some financial difficulty, or might plan to technically upgrade its product, or to undertake various other investment and restructuring, and needed funding or technical know-how from *A* and *B*. In exchange for such funding and know-how, and with the consent of the relevant authority, *C* might then decide to become a stock company with portions of shares to be distributed to *A* and *B*.

In this example, *A* and *B* are upstream and downstream enterprises. But this need not be so. *A* and *B* may be related to *C* horizontally, or provide a product complementary to *C*'s, or may be related to *C* in a variety of other ways.

In recent years, with the encouragement of the central government, merger-type acquisitions by a large SOE of one or more smaller SOEs has become common. In particular, the central government has recently permitted some 'especially large' enterprises each to take over a number of medium and small enterprises to form a large enterprise group. In the process the latter enterprises are converted into stock companies, whose shares may be split between the central and local authorities. Shares of the central authority are then given over to the enterprise group.[40]

From the viewpoint of our foregoing analysis and Wood's proposal, the currently evolving stock system in China signals certain important positive developments and limitations. On the positive side, first, there is emerging a system of cross-region ownership among institutional shareholders. This is what was explicitly called for in Wood's proposal, and is in line with our delegation principle. To return to an early example, even though enterprises *A* and *B* are only traditional SOEs, and not POIs as proposed by Wood, compared with the local or central government that used to 'own' *C*, they are much more likely to be interested in *C*'s profits.

Secondly, where individual shares are issued, setting a low ceiling to these shares seems appropriate given that such shares are likely to be highly dispersed and rapidly traded, as attested by the recent high levels of activity on China's stock markets. Owners of these shares are unlikely to take a keen interest in monitoring an enterprise's real performance.

On the limitation side, first, the fact that state shares may take up a substantial proportion of an enterprise's total shares is not welcome. The 80 per cent minimum rule regarding the shares owned by institutions and the state in principle allows a higher authority to hold the majority of an enterprise's shares. The danger of this is that, being the majority owner, the authority may again find itself being forced to satisfy diverse demands, especially if the newly converted stock company similarly finds itself in financial difficulty. To avoid this danger, it is important that the authority in question should reduce its holding of an enterprise's shares to no more than a minority. Given the current rule that state shares cannot be traded, and in the absence of proper POIs proposed by Wood, the government may consider divesting its shares to still other SOEs, preferably not those from its own jurisdiction – say, in exchange for a negotiated financial yield.

The fact that institutional shareholders are not POIs as recommended by Wood, but are themselves enterprises and are often technologically or in other ways related to the enterprise they own, is likely to be another limitation. It means that these shareholders could be interested in things in addition to the profits of the enterprise they own. To return to the early example, in addition to *C*'s profits, enterprise *B* may also be interested in *C*'s output, and *A* in *C*'s use of its output. In these cases, *A* and *B*'s interest in *C* seeking the highest profits could be compromised. However, it should also be recognized that such inter-enterprise ownership may enable externalities to be harnessed; the issue is thus even more complex.

Delegation and privatization

We now turn to considering the possibility of 'delegated privatization'. Rather than look for every possible arrangement, we shall consider the matter only in relation to Wood's proposal and the practical developments of Chinese enterprise reforms. Given our account above, our discussion only needs to be brief.

The scope of privatization within Wood's proposal is easy to see. Obviously, the creation of special POIs vested with the ownership of SOEs should allow for subsequent sale of the shares to private agents. As for the recent practical developments in China, in one sense private ownership rights have already arisen, as shown by the individual shares issued. Under the present rules, however, private shares are severely restricted, but a process could be envisaged in which these restrictions are gradually lifted. For example, the 20 per cent ceiling on individual shares could over time be relaxed, and more companies could be authorized to issue individual shares, and perhaps even to become listed (not all stock companies have been listed).

It is important to see why privatization in such a manner differs in implication from an immediate sale of enterprises to private capital, and why the prior public ownership reform phase can make a difference. Principally, as we discussed above, in such a phase central or local governments are removed from their position of being the sole owner of an enterprise, and new owners are created. It is true that the new owners, be they the special POIs as proposed by Wood, or some other enterprises as is the practice in China, are still a public entity. However, cross-region ownership, if and when it becomes a strong feature of the system, would mean that these owners and the enterprises they own do not belong to the same local government. This, along with a fair degree of ownership dispersion, should help ensure that if, one day, an enterprise does become privatized and this is followed by closure or large-scale job losses, its workers may not hold their local government as ultimately responsible. The decision to privatize in such a case is likely to be seen as the rightful decision of the owner, and not the treachery of the government. This may help to reduce the political risks of privatization.

Limits to ownership reform and privatization

While we have considered the scope of delegated public ownership reform and privatization, it is also important to recognize that there may be limits to these reforms, in that they may fail to deliver the intended effect. There are two cases where this can be true. The first is the quite widely known case where an existing public enterprise is of vital importance to the national economy (a strategic or targeted growth industry). Its closure might consequently not be acceptable to the government even after it is in private hands. The other is the possibility given rise to by our early diagnosis of the cause of the soft budget constraint. The public's state-dependent mentality may be so strong that, even when a private company is faced with closure, the public likewise expect the government to provide financial assistance and bail-out.[41]

The government may well make prior announcements that it would never bail out a privatized enterprise, but such announcements would not be credible if there are clear incentives for the government to so act *ex post*.

Cases of governments bailing out an already privatized company are not uncommon. In Chile, where massive privatization took place in the mid-1970s after a military coup, the early 1980s then saw a 're-socialization' of many large, debt-ridden privatized corporations (Yotopoulos, 1989). These corporations were considered by the Chilean government as simply too important to the national economy to be closed (they included some privatized banks). So the government bailed them out and took them back to the public sector.

A government may bail out an already privatized company because it thinks it is in the country's economic interest to do so. It may also bail out such a company because of public pressure, owing to the public's state-dependent mentality. In these cases, public ownership reform or privatization are unlikely to realize their intended effect of hardening the budget constraint and substantially reducing or even eliminating managerial slack. Our earlier argument for delegated ownership reform and privatization was based on the premise that the public holds differential standards regarding the acceptable behaviour of public and private enterprises. If this in fact is not the case, then privatization or other forms of ownership reform are unlikely to make a material impact on managerial behaviour. However, we expect that in most cases the public do hold such differential standards.

Conclusion

To summarize the main points argued in the chapter, we began by examining issues concerning the internal efficiency of the modern capitalist firm, and we found that because of a lack of effective internal and external corporate controls, managerial slack is likely to be pronounced. A major source of the slack may be the imperfect or non-competitive product market. So improving product market competition can increase the internal efficiency of a capitalist firm.

Compared with public enterprises, a capitalist firm generally faces an 'ultimate' bankruptcy constraint. The constraint is ultimate only because managers often enjoy a large margin of managerial discretion without exposing the firm to closure. A public enterprise, however, in most cases faces a soft budget constraint; government subsidies are almost automatic to cover losses, and there is no threat of bankruptcy. What this implies is that privatization, turning a public enterprise private, may not fundamentally improve an enterprise's internal efficiency without taking the necessary parallel, if not prior, measures to improve product market competition.

Public enterprises have by no means all been inefficient, or less efficient. Empirical studies generally give inconclusive evidence regarding the comparative efficiency of public and private enterprises. It also needs to be borne in mind that aside from managerial slack and internal efficiency, there are other factors to consider in determining the choice and continued presence of a public enterprise, which have largely to do with capital market failures common in developing but also in developed countries.

The soft budget constraint is generally accepted as a self-evident characterization of the behaviour of public enterprises, resulting in widespread inefficiency. From this it would appear to follow that privatization is the solution, if not a sufficient then at least a necessary measure. Two questions, however, arise. First, need all forms of public enterprises be inefficient? Secondly, if privatization is the correct policy goal, need it imply an immediate mass-privatization of the existing public enterprises in an economy?

In addressing these questions, it is necessary to start by examining the cause of the soft budget constraint. That cause, we argued, lies with the differential standards generally held by the public regarding the acceptable behaviour of public and private enterprises. For various reasons, the public generally expect the state, and hence public enterprises, to be above commercial concerns, while they would usually accept a private firm's right to be profit-seeking and to operate by commercial criteria only. We called this the 'state-dependent mentality' of the public.

Two implications follow. First, while private firms may be politically convenient to a government (in that the government does not then have to deal with the conflict between the efficiency goal and its social responsibilities), privatization could entail political risks since the public may view it as the renunciation by their government of its proper social responsibilities, especially if privatization is to be followed by large-scale job losses and welfare cuts. It is important that these risks are assessed before a radical privatization programme is embarked upon.

Secondly, and more generally, the state-dependent mentality diagnosis of the cause of the soft budget constraint suggests possible middle roads of reform – and, indeed, politically less risky ways to undertake privatization. These centre on the principle of delegation. If a party, the principal, is unable or finds it unprofitable to carry out a particular act itself, it may appoint an agent to do the work. Applying the principle to reforming public enterprises, it means that if the state finds it difficult to seek the efficiency goal, it may delegate that responsibility to an agent.

We explored this idea in the context of China's reform of SOEs. An embodiment of that idea is an early proposal by Wood, and we examined this proposal and practical developments in Chinese SOE reforms. Chinese enterprise reform has been characterized by its gradual approach. However, from the viewpoint of Wood's proposal and our analysis, important moves have been made. An increasing number of enterprises have been undergoing the 'stock experiment', which involves converting an existing SOE into a stock company whose shares may then be held not only by its higher authority but also, more importantly, by other state sector institutions and sometimes individuals. In particular, there is the beginning of a system of cross-region ownership, whereby one state sector institution from a region becomes a part-owner of an enterprise from another region. A system of cross-region ownership similar to this but involving regionally based special public ownership institutions (POIs) owning SOEs's shares was proposed by Wood. The reason why cross-region ownership is important is that it may then remove local governments – which means removing the government as such – from their former position of the owner of an enterprise. Local governments would still carry out their range of social responsibilities, but under cross-region ownership owners would be left to seek profits. In addition, the fact that ownership is dispersed among several owners should also help an owner to pursue profits.

Under a public ownership system both as proposed by Wood and as is emerging in China, it is also easy to see how privatization, if this indeed is the stage-two target, could proceed next. Under Wood's proposal, POIs may then divest their shares in a given enterprise to individuals. Under the current practice in China, the proportion of the individually held shares in a given enterprise, currently restricted to no more than 20 per cent, may be raised. However, after the public ownership reform phase, privatization is likely to be associated with less political risks. Being no longer the owner of an enterprise, the decision to privatize is unlikely, or less likely, to be seen by the public as an act of treachery by the government, but the rightful decision of the owner.

Chinese enterprise reform is evolving, and the contours of the future system are far from clear. It has not been an aim of this chapter to discuss these matters in detail. But the state-dependent mentality analysis has been useful to our thinking about both the direction and practical measure of enterprise reform in China. By looking behind the soft budget constraint characterization of the behaviour of public enterprises, the analysis provides a richer set of possibilities for reforming SOEs in China, and hopefully it will help inform practical reform measures as well.

Notes

1. 'Privatization' has been a term used to refer to a number of distinct means of changing the boundaries between the state and the private sector. In Britain, it has been used to refer to policies of denationalization, contracting out and deregula-

tion. What it is most commonly associated with is, however, denationalization, the sale of publicly owned assets. We use the term in this sense.

2. By 'internal efficiency' is meant the productive efficiency of a firm or enterprise – that is, the cost-minimizing production of a given output. This is to be distinguished from external or allocative efficiency, which concerns the balance of outputs. See Kay and Thompson (1986); Yarrow (1986); Vickers and Yarrow (1988). In this chapter we are primarily concerned with a firm or enterprise's internal efficiency.

3. I am grateful to Maurice Howard for drawing my attention to the earlier writing by Robertson.

4. On modern ownership structures of firms and their efficiency implications see, among many others, papers from the June 1983 issue of the *Journal of Law and Economics*, and Demsetz and Lehn (1985); Stiglitz (1985); Cosh and Hughes (1987).

5. Two broadly distinct corporate finance and control systems exist, the capital market-based system (the Anglo-Saxon model) and the bank-based system (the German–Japanese model). We shall consider the market-based system only. For comparison of the two and views of their relative superiority, see Aoki (1990); Cosh, Hughes and Singh (1990); Franks and Mayer (1990); Prowse (1992); and papers from the Autumn 1992 issue of *Oxford Review of Economic Policy*.

6. See, however, Vickers and Yarrow (1988) on unanimity of shareholders' preferences.

7. The issue of internal corporate control is but part of the more general subject of the economics of organizations. See the symposia of papers in *Journal of Economic Perspectives* (Spring 1991); *Journal of Comparative Economics* (June 1993). Jensen (1993) provides an evaluation of internal corporate control in the USA.

8. Take-overs are but one form of corporate acquisition. See Singh (1992).

9. The 'raider' may offer share prices above those commensurate with the expected post-take-over profit stream, but this would make the 'raid' unprofitable.

10. Grossman and Hart (1980) discuss a possible solution to their type of public good phenomenon, which is to exclude minority shareholders from sharing post-take-over gains (dilution) See Yarrow (1985) on the UK experience.

11. Shleifer and Vishny (1986) show that the presence of large shareholders could help overcome the Grossman-Hart-type free-rider problem. See Shleifer and Vishny (1988) and Morck, Shleifer and Vishny (1990) for discussion and evidence of 'over-payment' by acquiring firms in take-overs. Scharfstein (1988) argues that take-overs can take place only when raiders are informed and shareholders not.

12. Jarrell, Brickley and Netter (1988) discuss multiple-bidding and report evidence on the effect on returns to bidders.

13. There is the important view that even if take-overs effectively fulfil their disciplining role, the behaviour this generates may be short-termist in nature, in that managers are then motivated to maximize the firm's short-term stock market value, at the expense of its long-run profitability, insofar as these differ, and these do often differ (Stein, 1988, 1989).

14. See Jensen (1986), Griffin and Wiggins (1992) on firms' own 'free cash flow' and its agency cost. When firms turn to banks for capital, it raises the question whether and how they are subject to banks' monitoring. See no. 5 above.

15. For modern literature on the role of market competition in promoting efficiency see, among others, Hart (1983) and Hermalin (1992).

16. See Ayub and Hegstad (1987) on alternative forms of public ownership in practice.

17. Comparing efficiency in the two cases is fraught with difficulties (Vickers and Yarrow, 1988, Chapter 2). However, a large number of empirical studies do exist. See Yarrow (1986); Millward (1988); Boardman and Vining (1989); Willner (1994); for some surveys.

18. Kornai (1986) defines the soft budget constraint as including cases of soft subsidies, soft taxation, soft credit, soft prices, and more. Although this helps to emphasize how ubiquitous soft financial constraints had become in both the mixed and former socialist economies, the definition glosses over important differences (e.g. that between a government providing subsidies to rescue a bankrupt enterprise and soft prices enjoyed by a monopolistic firm when it has some price-setting power). While endorsing Kornai's notion of a soft budget constraint, in this chapter we shall primarily mean by it a direct bailing-out by the government to rescue a bankrupt enterprise – i.e. the opposite of a bankruptcy constraint. (Kornai does stress the softness and hardness of a budget constraint as points on a 'stringency scale'.)

19. See, however, the qualification made on p. 42.

20. Lin, Cai and Zhou (1995) maintain that the soft budget constraint facing public enterprises in China is due to an uncompetitive market environment rather than ownership *per se*. We do not agree with this view. It appears quite clear that the soft budget constraint has had to do with the character of the ownership system of Chinese SOEs. However, does it then follow that it must take private ownership to tackle the problem? We argue that it need not. See also Chen, Jefferson and Singh (1992); McMillan and Naughton (1992); Naughton (1994) on the relative importance of competition policy and ownership reform in the context of Chinese enterprise reform.

21. For an account of the nationalization of Rolls Royce in Britain and its subsequent reprivatization see Vickers and Yarrow (1988).

22. Demsetz (1968) advances a market solution to natural monopolies involving franchising. However, as Newbery points out in his comments on Demsetz's paper, this will inevitably call for much regulation, which is one reason for having public enterprises.

23. A response may be that such investments are inefficient anyway, since private agents were reluctant to make them. However, how many would consider all government investments in East Asian countries as inefficient or unwise? See World Bank (1993).

24. Aylen (1987) calls for a comprehensive range of measures to set up a capital market and other related institutions in developing countries. See also Newbery (1992).

25. Many have considered the political process of privatization, which it inevitably is (see, for example, Bienen and Waterbury, 1989). We are here considering the matter from a somewhat different angle – namely, the likely political repercussions of a radical privatization programme in the specific context of China.

26. Government may cover the loss anyway, but where there are clear sanctions against mismanagement, it obviously makes a huge difference to a public enterprise manager whether she is held responsible for the loss, and this fact influences her behaviour.

27. In his comments on this chapter Maurice Howard points out that private firm managers may issue 'rescue rights' shares although at high cost, a recourse frequently used. However, to avoid such issues being shunned the managers must show that the problems causing the loss have been solved and changes made.

28. We shall refrain from giving a rigorous definition of the 'state-dependent mentality', but a loose one may be that it is 'the expectation by the public of the

state to be above commercial criteria and to provide essential livelihood for them, which may include a job guarantee'.

29. Kornai (1986, p. 26) also speaks of 'the increasing, and often overloading demand of society on the State to become a 'protector', responsible for welfare, growth and national economic interest.' However, a close reading of his work leaves one with no doubt that to him the 'paternalistic' disposition of the state is the principal, if not the only, cause of the soft budget constraint. (In fact, when reading Kornai, one gets a distinct impression that the above quoted remark was added very much as an afterthought.)

30. See Crozier, Huntington and Watanuki (1975) on ideological shifts in the West in the post-war decades. They speak of 'an overloading of government', a powerful trend for citizens to expect the state to take up ever more responsibilities in meeting their needs. See also Kornai (1986); Brett (1988); Twight (1993).

31. A small literature exists exploring the reasons behind the soft budget constraint (Bardhan and Roemer, 1992; Stiglitz, 1991; Vickers and Yarrow, 1991; Prager, 1992). Schaffer (1989) models the soft constraint as a case of incredible commitments from the centre in a centre–enterprise game. See also Kornai (1993).

32. Thus the sharp price rises in 1992–3 did not appear to lead to the same panic buying and public outcry as they had in 1988 and 1989. There is also evidence of an increased acceptance of economic disparity by the population in recent years.

33. Some SOEs have been made bankrupt but they are almost entirely 'small-scale' ones, owned and managed by county- or city-level government. *Beijing Review* (3–9 March 1997, p. 20) reports that in the first nine months of 1996, 518 of the nation's 240 000 or so small-scale enterprises were closed in a recent pilot city programme aimed to reform and rejuvenate small-scale SOEs. Even in these cases, however, the local governments concerned have continued to affirm their commitment to finding alternative employment for the unemployed workers.

34. The Wood proposal first appeared in World Bank (1985) and was subsequently elaborated in Wood (1991, 1993). Morris (1995) proposes a similar 'transitional model' for reforming China's SOEs, which we shall not, however, discuss below.

35. Vickers (1985) applies the delegation principle to industrial organization, generating some interesting results.

36. See Jefferson and Xu (1991); Jefferson, Rawski and Zheng (1992); Hay *et al.* (1994), Groves *et al.* (1994), Wu (1995); Jefferson, Rawski and Zheng (1996), Liu and Liu (1996), Yao (1997); Lo (1997) on productivity gains by SOEs over the reform years. These studies also attribute the gains to particular reform measures. Naughton (1995) gives an account of the rise of the non-state sector, and its growing share of output in each of the major industrial sectors. However, although achieving marked productive gains, SOEs generally compare unfavourably with non-state enterprises in efficiency.

    At the end of 1996, about 65 per cent of SOEs made losses, which are disproportionately concentrated in textile, coal, machinery, forestry and military industries (*Beijing Review*, 9–15 June 1997, p. 15). Hussain and Zhuang (1996) analyze the pattern of SOE loss-making using a sample annual panel data from 1986 to 1991. It also needs to be borne in mind that SOEs have been burdened by their social responsibilities in areas of housing, health, and pension, towards workers. See Lin, Cai and Zhou (1995); Hu (1997).

37. Other factors include: a belief in the fundamental value of public ownership; the worry that, if privatized, many of the enterprises would be made bankrupt and

forced to close, with widespread output and productive resource losses (a worry that is to some extent supported by the experience of mass-privatization in other transitional economies); and other arguments commonly advanced in support of public enterprises.

38. The first enterprise publicly to issue equities was the Tianqiao Department Store Company in Beijing in 1984, followed by a small number of other enterprises issuing either equities or bonds. In these early cases, stock issuing was purely a means of raising capital. For details of the history of China's emerging stock system, stock markets, and the rapidly growing number of stock companies until 1994 see Karmel (1994); Brooks (1995); Mookerjee and Yu (1995).

39. There are also shares issued and traded on foreign capital markets, namely, the H shares in Hongkong, and N and L shares in New York and London (see *Beijing Review*, 11–17 August 1997, pp. 12–14). These are not subject to the 20 per cent ceiling. Note that in spite of the strict partition into individual, institutional and state shares, there are ways of transferring the latter two types of shares to individuals, so that the total privately held shares of an enterprise may exceed 20 per cent. However, these transferred shares are not permitted to be traded on stock markets under the present rules.

40. At the time of writing, several parallel enterprise reform programmes are running in China, each involving a varying mix of industrial restructuring and enterprise governance change, including ownership change. Two relate to large and medium-scale enterprises: (1) the bank-led reform aimed at greater supervision by banks of their client enterprises, and (2) the so-called 'large enterprise group programme', involving the setting up of 100 or so large trans-sector, trans-region enterprise groups which are given the special role as 'managers' of the state assets of their subsidiary enterprises. In addition there is the pilot city programme, initially in 58 and subsequently extended to 110 cities (1997), which aims to 'optimize the capital structure' of enterprises through industrial reorganization and restructuring (merger, establishment of enterprise associations and bankruptcy). In recent years, the state has given the reign of small-scale enterprises to their responsible local governments, granting local authorities a greater freedom in their choice of reform measures, including reorganization, forming enterprise associations and joint-stock partnerships, merger, leasing, contract operation and ultimately sell-off. Except for the bank-led programme, all the other reform measures have involved a varying degree of stock experimentation.

41. The reason why public ownership reform or the more radical privatization option may not produce the intended effect in both cases is that if, even after ownership reform or privatization, the government is still compelled to act when a given enterprise is due for closure, then this generates expectations on the part of an enterprise's managers for automatic government financial handouts in the event of financial losses, and such expectations result in managerial slack.

Bibliography

Aoki, M. (1990) 'Toward an Economic Model of the Japanese Firm', *Journal of Economic Literature*, 28, pp. 1–27.

Aylen, J. (1987) 'Privatization in Developing Countries', *Lloyds Bank Review*, January, pp. 15–30.

Ayub, M. A. and S. O. Hegstad (1987) 'Management of Public Industrial Enterprises', *World Bank Research Observer*, 2, pp. 79–101.

Bardhan, P. and J. E. Roemer (1992) 'Market Socialism: A Case for Rejuvenation', *Journal of Economic Perspectives*, 6 (3), pp. 101–16.

Beijing Review (1997) 3–9 March, 9–15 June, 11–17 August.

Berle, A. A. and C. C. Means (1933) *The Modern Corporation and Private Property* (New York: Macmillan).

Bienen, H. and J. Waterbury (1989) 'The Political Economy of Privatization in Developing Countries', *World Development*, 17 (5), pp. 617–32.

Boardman, A. E. and A. R. Vining (1989) 'Ownership and Performance in Competitive Environments: A Comparison of the Performance of Private, Mixed, and State-owned Enterprises', *Journal of Law and Economics*, 32, pp. 1–33.

Brett, E. A. (1988) 'State, Markets and Private Power: Problems and Possibilities', in P. Cook and C. Kirkpatrick (eds), *Privatization in Less Developed Countries* (London: Harvester Wheatsheaf).

Brooks, J. (1995) 'China's Stock Markets', in K. Cao (ed.), *The Changing Capital Markets of East Asia* (London: Routledge).

Chen, K., G. H. Jefferson and A. Singh (1992) 'Lessons from China's Economic Reform', *Journal of Comparative Economics*, 16, pp. 201–25.

Coase, R. H. (1960) 'The Problems of Social Cost', *Journal of Law and Economics*, 3, pp. 1–31.

Cosh, A. D. and A. Hughes (1987) 'The Anatomy of Corporate Control: Directors, Shareholders and Executive Remuneration in Giant US and UK Corporations', *Cambridge Journal of Economics*, 11, pp. 285–313.

Cosh, A. D., A. Hughes and I. Singh (1990) 'Take-overs and Short-termism: Analytical and Policy Issues in the UK Economy', in *Take-overs and Short-termism in the UK*, Industrial Policy Paper 3 (London: Institute of Public Policy Research).

Crozier, M., S. P. Huntington, and J. Watanuki (1975) *The Crisis of Democracy* (New York: New York University Press).

Demsetz, H. (1968), 'Why Regulate Utilities?', *Journal of Law and Economics*, 11, pp. 55–66.

Demsetz, H. and K. Lehn (1985) 'The Structure of Corporate Ownership: Causes and Consequences', *Journal of Political Economy*, 93(6), pp. 1155–77.

Franks, J. and C. Mayer (1990) 'Capital Markets and Corporate Control: A Study of France, Germany and the UK', *Economic Policy*, April, pp. 191–231.

Griffin, J. M. and S. N. Wiggins (1992) 'Take-overs: Managerial Incompetence or Managerial Shirking?', *Economic Inquiry*, 30, pp. 355–70.

Grossman, S. J. and O. D. Hart (1980) 'Take-over Bids, the Free-rider Problem, and the Theory of the Corporation', *Bell Journal of Economics*, 11(1), pp. 42–64.

Groves, T., Y. Hong, J. McMillan, and B. Naughton (1994) 'Autonomy and Incentives in Chinese State Enterprises', *Quarterly Journal of Economics*, February, pp. 183–209.

Hart, O. D. (1983) 'The Market Mechanism as an Incentive Scheme', *Bell Journal of Economics*, 14, pp. 366–82.

Hay, D., D. Morris, G. Liu, and S. Yao (1994) *Economic Reform and State-owned Enterprises in China, 1979–1987* (Oxford: Clarendon).

Hermalin, B. E. (1992) 'The Effects of Competition on Executive Behaviour', *Rand Journal of Economics*, 23(3), pp. 350–65.

Hu, Zuliu (1997) 'Social Protection and Enterprise Reform: The Case of China', in M. Rein, B. L. Friedman, and A. Worgotter (eds), *Enterprise and Social Benefits after Communism* (Cambridge: Cambridge University Press).

Hussain, A. and J. Zhuang (1996) 'Pattern and Causes of Loss-making in Chinese State Enterprises', *Development Economics Research Discussion Paper Series*, CP 31, STICHERD (London School of Economics).

Jarrell, G. A., J. A. Brickley and J. M. Netter (1988) 'The Market for Corporate Control: The Evidence Since 1980', *Journal of Economic Perspectives*, 2(1), pp. 49–63.

Jefferson, G. H. and W. Xu (1991) 'The Impact of Reform on Socialist Enterprises in Transition: Structure, Conduct, and Performance in Chinese Industries', *Journal of Comparative Economics*, 15, pp. 45–64.

Jefferson, G. H., G. T. Rawski and Y. Zheng (1992) 'Growth, Efficiency, and Convergence in China's State and Collective Industry', *Economic Development and Cultural Change*, 40(2), pp. 239–66.

Jefferson, G. H., G. T. Rawski and Y. Zheng (1996) 'Chinese Industrial Productivity: Trends, Measurement Issues, and Recent Developments', *Journal of Comparative Economics*, 23, pp. 146–80.

Jensen, M. C. (1986) 'Agency Costs of Free Cash Flow, Corporate Finance, and Takeovers', *American Economic Review*, 76(2), pp. 323–29.

Jensen, M. C. (1992) 'Market for Corporate Control', in (ed.), *New Palgrave Dictionary of Money and Finance*, 2, (London: Macmillan), pp. 657–66.

Jensen, M. C. (1993) 'The Modern Industrial Revolution, Exit, and the Failure of Internal Control Systems', *Journal of Finance*, 48(3), pp. 831–80.

Journal of Comparative Economics (1993) Symposium on 'The Structure and Behaviour of Economic Organizations: Theoretical and Empirical Perspectives', 17(2).

Journal of Economic Perspectives (1991) symposium on 'Organizations and Economics', 5(2).

Journal of Law and Economics (1983) symposium on 'Corporations and Private Property', 26(2).

Karmel, S. M. (1994), 'Emerging Security Markets in China: Capitalism with Chinese Characteristics', *China Quarterly*, 140: 1105–1120.

Kay, J. A. and D. J. Thompson (1986) 'Privatization: A Policy in Search of a Rationale', *Economic Journal*, 96, pp. 18–32.

Kornai, J. (1986) 'The Soft Budget Constraint', *Kyklos*, 39, pp. 3–30.

Kornai, J. (1993) 'The Evolution of Financial Discipline under the Postsocialist System', *Kyklos*, 46, pp. 315–36.

Lee, C. J. (1993) 'An Assessment of Taiwan's Privatization of Public Enterprises and Development of Small and Medium Enterprises', paper presented at the Seminar on the Reform of State-owned Enterprises: Privatization and Experiences of Asian Countries (Vietnam) (27–8 May).

Lin, J. Y., F. Cai and L. Zhou (1995) 'The Core Task in Reforming China's State Owned Enterprises Is to Create an Competitive Environment', *Xin Hua Wen Zhai*, September, pp. 42–47 (in Chinese).

Liu, Z. and G. S. Liu (1996) 'The Efficiency Impact of Chinese Industrial Reform in the 1980s', *Journal of Comparative Economics*, 23, pp. 237–55.

Lo, D. (1997) 'Re-appraising China's State-owned Industrial Enterprises', *Working Paper Series*, 67, Department of Economics, School of Oriental and African Studies, University of London.

Malatesta, P. H. (1992) 'Takeover Defences', in (eds), *New Palgrave Dictionary of Money and Finance*, 3 (London: Macmillan), pp. 633–6.

McMillan, J. and B. Naughton (1992) 'How to Reform a Planned Economy: Lessons from China', *Oxford Review of Economic Policy*, 8(1), pp. 130–43.

Millward, R. (1988) 'Measured Sources of Inefficiency in the Performance of Private and Public Enterprises', in P. Cook and C. Kirkpatrick (eds), *Privatization in Less Developed Countries* (London: Harvester Wheatsheaf).

Mookerjee, R. and Q. Yu (1995) 'Capital Market Reform on the Road to a Market-Oriented Economy: The Case of Stock Markets in China', *Journal of Developing Areas*, 30, pp. 23–40.

Morck, R., A. Shleifer and R. W. Vishny (1990) 'Do Managerial Objectives Drive Bad Acquisitions?', *Journal of Finance*, 45 (1), pp. 31–48.

Morris, D. (1995) 'The Reform of State-owned Enterprises in China: The Art of the Possible', *Oxford Review of Economic Policy*, 11 (4), pp. 54–69.

Naughton, B. (1994) 'What is Distinctive about China's Economic Transition? State Enterprise Reform and Overall System Transformation', *Journal of Comparative Economics*, 18, pp. 470–490.

Naughton, B. (1995) 'China's Macroeconomy in Transition', *China Quarterly*, 144, pp. 1083–1104.

Newbery, D. (1992) 'The Role of Public Enterprises in the National Economy', *Asian Economic Review*, 10 (2), pp. 1–34.

Oxford Economic Policy Review (1992) Symposium on 'Corporate Governance and Corporate Control', 8 (3).

Prager, J. (1992) 'Is Privatization a Panacea for LDCs? Market Failure versus Public Sector Failure', *Journal of Developing Areas*, 26, pp. 301–22.

Prowse, S. D. (1992) 'The Structure of Corporate Ownership in Japan', *Journal of Finance*, 47 (3), pp. 1121–40.

Robertson, D. H. (1923) *The Control of Industry* (Cambridge: Cambridge University Press).

Schaffer, M. E. (1989) 'The Credible-commitment Problem in the Centre–Enterprise Relationship', *Journal of Comparative Economics*, 13, pp. 359–82.

Scharfstein, D. (1988) 'The Disciplinary Role of Takeovers', *Review of Economic Studies*, 55, pp. 185–99.

Schelling, T. C. (1960) *The Strategy of Conflict* (Cambridge, Mass.: Harvard University Press).

Scherer, F. M. (1988) 'Corporate Take-overs: The Efficiency Argument', *Journal of Economic Perspectives*, 2 (1), pp. 69–82.

Shleifer, A. and R. W. Vishny (1986) 'Large Shareholders and Corporate Control', *Journal of Political Economy*, 94 (3) pp. 461–88.

Shleifer, A. and R. W. Vishny (1988) 'Value Maximization and the Acquisition Process', *Journal of Economic Perspectives*, 2 (1), pp. 7–20.

Singh, A. (1992) 'Corporate Takeovers: A Review', *Discussion Paper*, 9206, Department of Applied Economics, University of Cambridge.

Stein, J. C. (1988) 'Takeover Threats and Managerial Myopia', *Journal of Political Economy*, 96 (1), pp. 61–80.

Stein, J. C. (1989) 'Efficient Capital Markets, Inefficient Firms: A Model of Myopic Corporate Behaviour', *Quarterly Journal of Economics*, 104, pp. 655–69.

Stiglitz, J. E. (1985) 'Credit Markets and the Control of Capital', *Journal of Money, Credit, and Banking*, 17 (2), pp. 133–52.

Stiglitz, J. E. (1991) 'Symposium on Organizations and Economics', *Journal of Economic Perspectives*, 5 (2), pp. 15–24.

Streeton, P. (1983) 'Twenty-one Arguments for Public Enterprise', in K. Haq (ed.), *Global Development: Issues and Choices* (Washington DC: North-South Roundtable of the Society for International Development).

Twight, C. (1993) 'Channelling Ideology Change: The Political Economy of Dependence on Government', *Kyklos*, 46 (4), pp. 497–527.

Vickers, J. S. (1985) 'Delegation and the Theory of the Firm', *Economic Journal Conference Supplement*, 95, pp. 138–47.

Vickers, J. S. and G. K. Yarrow (1988) *Privatization: An Economic Analysis* (Cambridge, Mass.: MIT Press).

Vickers, J. S. and G. K. Yarrow (1991) 'Economic Perspectives on Privatization', *Journal of Economic Perspectives*, 5 (2), pp. 111–32.

Willner, J. (1994) 'Efficiency under Public and Private Ownership Reform: A Survey', *Economics Paper Series*, A. 422, Department of Economics, Abo Akademi University, Finland.

Wood, A. (1991) 'Joint Stock Companies with Rearranged Public Ownership: Invigoration of China's State Enterprises Further Considered', *Discussion Paper*, CP 11, The Development Economics Research Programme, London School of Economics.

Wood, A. (1993) 'Joint Stock Companies with Rearranged Public Ownership: What Can we Learn from Recent Chinese and East European Experience with State Enterprises?', *China Economic Review*, 41 (2), pp. 181–94.

World Bank (1985) *China: Long-Term Development Issues and Options* (Baltimore and London: Johns Hopkins University Press).

World Bank (1993) *The East Asian Miracle* (Oxford: Oxford University Press).

Wu, Yanrui (1995) 'Productivity Growth, Technical Progress, and Technical Efficiency Change in China: A Three Sector Analysis', *Journal of Comparative Economics*, 21, pp. 207–29.

Yao, Shujie (1997) 'Profit Sharing, Bonus Payment, and Productivity: A Case Study of Chinese State-owned Enterprises', *Journal of Comparative Economics*, 24, pp. 281–96.

Yarrow, G. K. (1985) 'Shareholder Protection, Compulsory Acquisition and the Efficiency of the Take-over Process', *Journal of Industrial Economics*, 34 (1), pp. 3–16.

Yarrow, G. K. (1986) 'Privatization in Theory and Practice', *Economic Policy*, 2, pp. 325–77.

Yotopoulos, P. A. (1989) 'The (Rip)Tide of Privatization: Lessons from Chile', *World Development*, 17 (5).

3
Financial Discipline in the Enterprise Sector in Transition Countries: How Does China Compare?*

Shumei Gao and Mark E. Schaffer

Introduction

The aim of this chapter is to make some selective comparisons of the empirical evidence relating to financial discipline and soft budget constraints[1] in the enterprise sector in China and the transition countries of Central and Eastern Europe and the former Soviet Union (CEEFSU). We divide the evidence into four categories: budgetary subsidies, trade credit, the banking system and tax arrears. The reasons for this division include the following.

First, government budgetary subsidies to enterprises are the most frequently cited as evidence of traditional soft budget constraints in centrally planned economies, and are therefore a natural starting point for our analysis. We find that in both CEEFSU countries and China, budgetary subsidies have fallen as prices have been liberalized, and the budgetary subsidies which remain are not clear evidence of soft budget constraints. Secondly, the appearance of overdue trade credit or 'inter-enterprise arrears' is a relatively new phenomenon in transition economies and has often been considered as a particularly important and typical source of soft budget constraints. Our analysis suggests, however, this is not usually the case: firms in both CEEFSU countries and China typically impose hard budget constraints on each other. We estimate that the level of total trade credit in China was roughly constant in 1994–6 at about 20–25 per cent of GDP. A constant stock implies that inflows approximately equal outflows – i.e. inter-enterprise debts are being paid. Moreover, the volume of trade credit in China is comparable to that observed not only in CEEFSU countries but also in developed Western economies. We suggest that when overdue trade credit does appear to be a cause of soft budget constraints, it is because it leads the government, in response to lobbying by firms, to bail them out. Thirdly, we investigate whether soft budget constraints in the enterprise sector occur via the banking sector by using enterprise-level data from China and Hungary to see if poorly performing firms were receiving positive net bank financing. We find that in China, banks were providing poorly performing firms with new financing, whereas in Hungary, banks were reducing their exposure to bad firms. Finally, tax arrears in CEEFSU economies have emerged as a major source of soft budget constraints in recent years. We consider the evidence and explanations for this, and use enterprise-level data for China to show that, as of the early 1990s, tax arrears were not an important source of financing for loss-making Chinese firms.

Budgetary subsidies

Budgetary subsidies in most CEEFSU transition economies were cut very substantially early in the transition, and have stayed much lower than pre-transition. Table 3.1 shows that budgetary subsidies in both rapid and slow reforming transition economies in CEEFSU fell from about 10–25 per cent of GDP prior to the start of transition to about 3–5 per cent of GDP by the early 1990s. In the case of China, budgetary subsidies have also declined in recent years, from 8.6 per cent of GDP in 1985 to 1.2 per cent in 1995 (Table 3.1). Why such a big fall?

The explanation for the declining budgetary subsidies in CEEFSU countries and China is primarily price liberalization. Under central planning, a state-owned enterprise (SOE) was a passive production unit. The state set all the prices and quantities of its inputs and outputs. Budgetary subsidies to enterprises were used as a device to adjust for the effects of comprehensive price and quantity control. When the controlled price of a good was low relative to the costs of its inputs, a product-specific subsidy was used to compensate. Price liberalization means that firms are now free to decide the level of their output and prices, and in particular they are free to raise prices to

Table 3.1   Budgetary subsidies as a percentage of GDP, CEEFSU countries and China, 1985–95

Country	1985	1989	1990	1991	1992	1993	1994	1995
Bulgaria		15.5	14.9	4.1	1.8	2.2	1 .3	
Former Czechoslovakia		25.0	16.2	7.7	5.0			
Czech Republic					4.9	4.1	3.6	3.4
Slovak Republic					5.2	5.1	4.9	4.8
Hungary		12.0	9.5	7.4	5.5	4.3	4.5	3.5
Poland		10.6	7.7	5.1	3.3	3.9	4.1	1.8
Romania		5.7	7.9	8.1	12.9	5.5	3.8	
Russia					14.2	7.3		
China	8.6	5.7	5.2	4.1	2.9	2.1	1.5	1.2

Sources: IMF, *World Economic Outlook* (October 1994), pp. 82–3 (former CSFR, Russia); IMF, *World Economic Outlook* (May 1996), p. 81 (Bulgaria, Romania); Coricelli, D' browski and Kosterna (1997), p. 29 (Czech Republic, Slovak Republic, Hungary, Poland); Lo (1997), Table 3 (China).

cover costs. Firms' losses resulting from price controls were eliminated and hence the corresponding product-specific budgetary subsidies were no longer needed.

Are the observed remaining budgetary subsidies obviously evidence of soft budget constraints? The answer to this question depends on how and why these subsidies are used. If they are used to bail out inefficient and otherwise loss-making enterprises, then there is clearly evidence of soft budget constraints. If they are used to subsidize firms whose losses derive simply from government price controls and which are actually operating efficiently, then this is not a case of soft budget constraints. Unfortunately, we can not readily empirically separate these two cases. There is evidence, however, suggesting that the remaining subsidies in both CEEFSU countries and China are closely related to their remaining price control practices.

Schaffer (1995) shows that the remaining budgetary subsidies in the leading transition economies of CEEFSU are highly sector-specific, and typically, though not exclusively, related to the price controls still remaining in these countries. The sectors receiving subsidies in these countries are mainly public transportation, especially railway transportation; the energy sector, especially coal; housing subsidies; and agriculture.[2] Budgetary subsidies in the slower reforming transition economies of CEEFSU are larger than in the leading reformers, and more often relate to both soft budget constraints – outright grants to ailing firms or sectors – or to other forms of financial indiscipline and weak government.

China's price liberalization has been much more gradual than that of the CEEFSU countries. This is why the reduction in budgetary subsidies in the former appears less dramatic than in the latter. Budgetary subsidies to SOEs in China can be broken down into two categories: loss subsidies and price subsidies. As a per centage of GDP, enterprise loss subsidies declined from 5.7 per cent in 1985 to 0.6 per cent in 1995, while price subsidies fell from 2.9 per cent to 0.6 per cent during the same period.[3] This clearly indicates that subsidies to compensate for enterprise losses have been reduced much more substantially than price subsidies; by 1995 budgetary subsidies were small and equally divided between the two categories. However, SOE losses might still be price-related, and therefore the existing loss subsidies could well be due to existing price controls – indeed, several studies suggest that this is the case. Lo (1997) and Broadman (1994) show that the main loss-making SOEs are concentrated in price-controlled sectors – e.g. grain, coal, oil, electricity and wool sectors, though they also existed in other sectors – e.g. textiles, machinery and food processing. Nevertheless the point here is that the remaining budgetary subsidies in China are at least in part price-related and hence are not clear evidence of continuing soft budget constraints.

Another significant source of SOE losses in China is the social and public obligations imposed on them by the government. Chinese SOEs are burdened with the support of an excessive workforce by keeping redundant workers on their payroll and the provision of public services such as housing, health care, pensions and childcare for their employees. Even if a firm is profitable in terms of its operating costs and revenues, its social and public obligations may still cause it to be in the red. The remaining subsidies may therefore be justified if they are also used to compensate for SOEs' losses owing to their social safety net obligations. The World Bank (1997) reports that the most recent practice in China is to provide direct fiscal subsidies to SOEs only for 'policy losses' (e.g. in the coal sector where prices are controlled below costs) and for 'operational losses' when there are extenuating circumstances and only on a temporary basis (e.g. when a loss-making SOE cannot meet its employee medical expenses). These practices further suggest that budgetary subsidies do not seem to be an obvious source of soft budget constraints.

It therefore appears that the situation we observe in China is similar to that in the leading CEEFSU countries: the bulk of remaining budgetary subsidies are used to compensate for the remaining price controls, which are typically concentrated in a relatively small number of sectors and are not clearly related to soft budget constraints. It is also interesting to note that the current level of budgetary subsidies as a percentage of GDP in leading CEEFSU transition countries and in China is also comparable to that observed in developed Western economies – typically of the order of a few per cent of GDP.

Trade credit and 'inter-enterprise arrears'

'Trade credit' refers to the credit extended by one firm to another as part of sales and purchases of inputs and outputs. It arises from the period between the time goods are delivered and services performed and time payment for these goods and services takes place. A time period is normally specified (e.g. 4 weeks), by the end of which the customer is supposed to pay. If a payment is delayed beyond this deadline, the trade credit is 'in arrears'. Under strict central planning, levels of total trade credit were low, reflecting only the time taken by the banking system to clear payments between firms, and overdue trade credit – 'inter-enterprise arrears'- in principle did not exist at all. In transition economies, firms become responsible for paying for goods and services themselves; the result has been the emergence of large volumes of total trade credit and overdue trade credit.

It has been observed that stocks of total trade credit, and of overdue trade credit, have increased very substantially in CEEFSU countries. This is sometimes put forward as evidence of soft budget constraints, financial indiscipline, etc. We argue instead that the presence of inter-enterprise arrears in CEEFSU countries is not necessarily evidence of soft budget constraints and, when it is, it is the government that has been 'soft', and not firms.

The most straightforward way to establish that the presence of trade credit and inter-enterprise arrears in CEEFSU countries is not necessarily evidence of financial indiscipline is to compare the levels of trade credit with those

Table 3.2   Trade credit and overdue trade credit (receivables), selected Western and CEEFSU transition countries, 1988–94

	Total trade credit		Overdue trade credit		
	Payment period (months)	*% of annualized GDP*	*% overdue*	*Payment period (months)*	*% of annualized GDP*
Western countries					
Finland	1.8	20	45	0.8	9
France	3.5	38	44	1.6	17
Germany	1.6		38	0.6	
Japan		59			
Sweden	1.6	21	38	0.6	8
UK	2.6	20	62	1.6	12
USA		17			
Transition countries					
Czech Republic 1994	2.5	50	37	0.9	18
Hungary					
1988	1.4	37			
1989	1.3	35			
1990	1.5	36			
1991	1.7	35	47	0.8	17
1992		27			
Poland					
1988	1.4	30			
1989	1.3	24			
1990	1.2	20			
1991	1.5	22			
1992	1.3	19			
1993	1.4	19	51	0.7	10
Russia					
1990	0.6	10			
1991	0.6	12			
1992	2.5	22	46	1.1	10
1993	1.6	15	44	0.7	7
1994	1.4	17	56	0.8	9

Source: Alfandari and Schaffer (1996).

observed in developed Western countries, and to observe the levels of trade credit over time.

Table 3.2 shows that the stock of trade credit in most Western and CEEFSU countries falls in the range of 10–50 per cent of GDP; if anything, trade credit in CEEFSU transition economies is relatively low compared to the West. The figures in Table 3.2 also show that both in the West and in CEEFSU, typically about half of the stock of trade credit is overdue. Consequently, the stock of overdue trade credit ('inter-enterprise arrears') in CEEFSU countries, amounting to around 7–18 per cent of GDP, is also comparable to that observed in Western economies.

Finally, the level of trade credit in CEEFSU countries has been roughly stable in the transition period, meaning that the average total payment periods of the stocks of trade credit have remained at about two months or so in CEEFSU countries. This means that if the average firm paid its suppliers with a delay of two months, these are the stocks we would observe. The stocks of overdue trade credit translate into an average delay period of one month. In other words, the average CEEFSU firm has one month to pay its suppliers, but actually pays after two months. These periods fluctuate, but in a relatively small range of up to a few months. Over five or more years – 60-plus months – of transition, the total stock of outstanding trade credit is still only a few months: simplifying somewhat, almost everything sold has been paid for. What we observe in CEEFSU countries is what we observe in Western countries – firms pay late, but most firms eventually pay. In terms of stocks and flows, the inflow of overdue trade credit is matched by an outflow of payment of debts in arrears, and hence the stock is stable.

'Inter-enterprise arrears' have not been a problem in the CEEFSU transition countries because firms have learned to apply hard budget constraints towards each other. In particular, they adopt simple credit control mechanisms such as requiring partial or full payment in advance or on delivery, stopping shipments of supplies to customers who are too far behind in their payments, and so forth.[4] Both firms in CEEFSU countries and firms in Western economies tolerate late payment by customers because if they insisted on strict payment discipline they would lose their customers to competitors that offered more relaxed payment terms. It is interesting to note that firms in CEEFSU countries were able to impose financial discipline on each other in spite of the absence of a well functioning system of bankruptcy law and actual low numbers of bankruptcies – the simple credit control mechanisms identified above appear to have been sufficient.

It is well known, however, that inter-enterprise arrears crises in CEEFSU countries have in some cases caused governments to inject funds in an attempt to clear them.[5] This bring us to our second point, namely that government may be 'soft' in the presence of inter-enterprise arrears. If the government is soft, firms may collude in non-payment to each other, anticipating that the state will bail them out.[6] In all cases of government clearance of inter-enterprise arrears in CEEFSU countries, the arrears reappeared – not surprisingly, given that late payment is a normal feature of market economies. Experience from CEEFSU countries suggests the policy which is more likely to be successful is for the government to do nothing: if firms are left alone, the inter-enterprise arrears problem disappears because firms are not soft and apply hard budget constraints towards each other.

The case of China is very similar to that of the CEEFSU transition economies. The level (stock) of trade credit in China has grown considerably over recent years, and is now comparable to levels observed in both the CEEFSU countries and developed Western economies. The stock of trade credit has, moreover, stabilized in recent years – inflows now more or less match outflows. Furthermore, in common with some of the slower-reforming CEEFSU countries, China has attempted several times – like the CEEFSU countries, without success – to clear the inter-enterprise arrears.

Table 3.3 shows that in 1985, the level of trade credit in China was very low by Western standards, and comparable to that observed in a planned economy – the average payment period was about two weeks, the same as that in Russia prior to the start of transition (see Table 3.2). The level of trade credit began to increase in the late 1980s, and we estimate that by 1994 the volume of total trade credit in the non-agricultural economy was the equivalent of 22 per cent of GDP, corresponding to an average payment period of two months. Since 1994, the level of trade credit has remained at these levels. A comparison with Table 3.2 shows that the current levels of trade credit in China are comparable to those observed in both CEEFSU and developed market economies. Unfortunately information on overdue trade credit in China is not available, and therefore a comparison can not be made here.

It has often been argued that in China, SOEs face soft budget constraints whereas collectively owned enterprises (e.g. township and village enterprises, TVEs) and private firms face hard budget constraints. Are SOEs capable of imposing hard budget constraints on their customers? Table 3.4 shows that in 1996, trade credit extended to customers by Chinese SOEs was somewhat larger than that extended by TVEs in particular (average payment period of 2.3 months for SOEs versus 1.3 for TVEs), but about the same as that extended by private firms and non-TVE collective firms. We saw, moreover, from Table 3.3 that the volume of trade credit extended by SOEs was the equivalent of about two months of sales over the period 1995–6, again implying that on average SOEs have been collecting payment for their sales; inflows have been roughly equal to outflows as old goods are paid for and new goods are shipped. It is often observed that currently many SOEs are in financial difficulties, and this is evident from the low profitability rates and the large proportion of loss-making firms (Table 3.4), but an inability to impose hard budget constraints on their customers does not appear to be a major source of financial problems of SOEs.

In sum, after 11 years of economic reform, 1985–96 – 132 months of reform – total trade credit outstanding amounts to perhaps two months' transactions overall. It therefore seems that, as in the CEEFSU countries, almost everything has been paid for in China as well. However, as discussed above, trade credit has been an indirect source of soft budget constraints in China. Between 1990 and 1992 the People's Bank of China (PBC, the central bank) attempted to clear inter-enterprise debts by injecting three tranches of credit amounting to a

Table 3.3   Trade credit (receivables) in China, 1985–96

Year	Receivables of 370 000 industrial firms (billion yuan)[a]	Total receivables in the non-agricultural economy as % of GDP[b]	Average payment period in industry (months)	
			All firms[c]	Large SOEs only[d]
	(1)	(2)	(3)	(4)
1985				0.4
...				
1988				0.5
1989				0.8
1990	90.1	7.7	0.6	1.0
1991	124.4	9.5	0.6	1.0
1992	161.3	10.1	0.8	0.9
1993	345.7	16.2	1.2	
1994	631.4	21.5	1.9	
1995	799.6	21.5	2.0	2.1
1996	927.0	22.0	2.1	2.3

Notes:

a Data on receivables cover approximately 370 000 industrial enterprises (including non-SOEs).
Source: Fan (1996), Table 2; *Chinese Statistical Bulletin* (1996).

b Estimates cover non-agricultural non-financial enterprises (industry, construction, trade, transportation, communications). The coverage of data in the *Chinese Statistical Yearbook* for all firms in industry with self-accounting status is somewhat wider than the data in column (1) covering approximately 500 000 enterprises. Sales of the 370 000 firms account for approximately 90% of sales of the 500 000 firms. To estimate total trade credit in the economy in non-agricultural firms, the receivables data in column (1) is scaled up, first to cover the missing 10% of industrial sales, and then using weights from sectoral GDP to estimate receivables in the sectors other than industry.

c Figures on payment period are based on the data in column (1) and are calculated as the ratio of end-year receivables to average monthly sales.
Source: column (1), *Chinese Statistical Bulletin*, various years, *Chinese Statistical Yearbook*, various years; own calculations.

d Figures for 1985–92 are based on data from 40 000 industrial enterprises subordinated to the budget.
Source: Fan (1996), Table 1 (receivables); *Chinese Statistical Bulletin*, various years (sales); own calculations. Figures for 1995–6 are based on data on 15 000 large industrial SOEs.
Source: *Chinese Statistical Bulletin* (1996); own calculations. Average payment period in months is defined as in c above.
Source: Fan (1996), Table 2, and *Chinese Statistical Bulletin*, 1996.

total of 46.6 billion yuan (the equivalent of 2 per cent of GDP); in addition, 3.9 billion yuan of government spending was used for the same purpose (Fan, 1996). Although this programme resulted in the clearing of a substantial volume of trade credit, amounting to 201.8 billion yuan or 10 per cent of GDP, it was clearly ineffective in stopping the increase in trade credit in China, as we saw in Table 3.3.

Table 3.4   Trade credit and profitability, Chinese enterprises, 1996[a]

Enterprise	Average payment period (months)[b]	After-tax profit as % of sales	Share of total industrial sales (%)	Percentage of firms which are loss-making
	(1)	(2)	(3)[c]	(4)
All	2.1	2.6	100.0	23.0
State-owned	2.3	1.6	48.3	37.7
Medium and large	2.3	2.1	40.2	39.9
Small	2.4	−1.1	8.2	37.1
Collective	1.6	3.1	29.7	17.9
TVEs	1.3	4.1	20.4	13.5
Other collective	2.2	0.7	9.3	26.3
Other (incl. private)	2.2	4.3	22.0	34.2

Notes:
a Data based on survey of 390 000 industrial firms.
b Average payment period calculated as ratio of end-year receivables to average monthly industrial sales.
c Column (3) may not sum to 100 owing to rounding.
Source: Chinese Statistical Bulletin 1996; own calculations.

The Chinese experience is thus similar in a number of respects to what has been observed in some CEEFSU countries: the state appears to be soft, and arrears reappear following the attempted clearing operations. The CEEFSU experience suggests that Chinese policy-makers should consider the alternative policy of letting market forces take care of the inter-enterprise arrears 'problem' – if Chinese firms are left alone, the level of trade credit should stabilize. Indeed, Fan (1996) reports that since 1993 the policy of the PBC has been that loans to clear inter-enterprise arrears should not be granted in any circumstances, and as levels of trade credit in 1994–6 stabilized at levels comparable to those observed in developed Western economies (as well as in CEEFSU economies), it appears this policy has been successful.

We note here that the relative weakness of the bankruptcy law framework in China is sometimes cited as an obstacle to solving the arrears problem, but the experience of the CEEFSU countries suggests this is not a major one – the CEEFSU countries also had weak bankruptcy law frameworks, and despite this, firms were able to impose hard budget constraints on each other, and volumes of trade credit stabilized at levels observed in Western economies. The fact that the level of trade credit in China in 1994–6 also stabilized at these levels suggests that weak bankruptcy laws have not been an obstacle there either.

Bad debts and banks

The bank–enterprise relationship in transition economies is very complex, with a considerable degree of variation between countries. Roughly speaking, the evidence suggests that banks in the leading transition countries are fairly hard and are not a source of soft budget constraints; the debate there is how long it has taken for this behaviour to emerge. In the slower reformers, governments have used the banking sector to channel soft credits to loss-making or politically influential firms; this is a case of the soft budget constraint, though it is the government rather than the banks which is the source of the softness. In this section we first use the experience of CEEFSU countries to illustrate some of the measurement problems involved in assessing whether the banking sector contributes to the soft budget constraints of firms. We will concentrate in particular on the large and growing volume of 'bad debts' in the enterprise sector and try to assess whether they constitute evidence of soft budget constraints. We then turn to evidence on bank behaviour in China.

The first measurement problem relates to what is meant by 'bad debts'. Typically, when statistics on the 'bad debts' of the banking sector are cited, the figures come from the banks themselves and refer to loans which have been qualified as substandard, overdue, non-performing, etc. by the banks. If bad debts thus measured are increasing it means that banks are classifying increasing volumes of their loans as 'bad'. This does not necessarily imply they are actually making bad loans at that time. The increase in bad debts may instead arise either because firms which received loans in the past have only now entered economic difficulties and are not servicing their debts, or because loans became non-performing in the past but the bank temporarily delayed formally qualifying them as non-performing by capitalizing the interest due and rescheduling the principal.[7] Put another way, increases in bad debts observed today may not indicate the existence today of bad lending practices and soft budget constraints; it may simply result from recognition by the banks of their pre-existing stock problems.

The second measurement problem is that when firms that are in financial difficulties do not service their bank debt, the bank debt will grow in nominal (real) terms so long as the bank charges a positive nominal (real) interest rate on the overdue debt. So long as bad debts are not being worked out and firms are not being liquidated and their debts actually written down or written off, the amounts owned by the debtors will continue to grow even if banks are not soft and are not making new loans to their problem debtors. This will be true even if banks are trying to avoid declaring bad loans as bad and are capitalizing the interest and rescheduling the debts; the banks will still not be providing the firms with soft budget constraints so long as they are not making new loans on top of the old, 'bad' loans to these customers. This suggests that where possible, we should look at the flow of credit provided by banks to firms net of interest payments – i.e. net bank financing. If net bank financing of problem firms is positive, banks are in effect 'throwing good money after bad' and we have evidence of soft budget constraints.

In the case of CEEFSU, most economies started transition with a deep recession – on the order of a 20–50 per cent fall in GDP. In any economy with output declines of such depth we would expect many firms to experience financial difficulties, and in particular to be unable to service the bank debts they had at the start of the period. We should therefore expect large volumes of non-performing bank loans to emerge eventually, when the banks finally recognize and formally qualify them.

In addition to these 'inherited bad debt stock' problems, we would also expect to observe some initial bad debt 'flow' problems to firms. At the start of transition, many firms in CEEFSU countries continued to borrow even though credits were expensive because of their expectation that the recession would only be temporary and their investment would be paid off once the recession was over. At the same time, banks in early stages of transition lacked the necessary experience and expertise to evaluate their true portfolio positions. Loans made even with the best of intentions in early transition may also turn bad owing to similar factors such as lack of experience and expertise.

Hungary provides a nice example of these measurement problems. In 1992–3, the volume of bad loans grew tremendously, by a factor of about 5 in real terms, the increase being equivalent to about 10 per cent of GDP. Some observers concluded from this that the Hungarian banking sector was very soft and that firms had soft budget constraints. Bonin and Schaffer (1995) and Schaffer (1998), however, use enterprise data to argue that Hungarian banks were not injecting new funds into unprofitable firms: on the contrary, they were apparently trying to reduce their exposure to them. Net bank financing – the increase in bank debt net of interest payments – of highly unprofitable firms was negative, not positive. That is, the flow of cash was not from the banks to the problem firms, it was from the problem firms to the banks. This shows that Hungarian banks were not soft in 1992–3 – at the same time they were trying to reduce their exposure to their unprofitable borrowers, they were admitting publicly the bad debts problem and were qualifying large portions of their portfolios as bad.

We now turn to the bad debt problem in China. The scale of the bad debt problem can be measured in two ways: classified loans as a per centage of all loans, and the volume of classified loans in relation to the scale of economic activity (e.g. GDP). Table 3.5 presents both indicators for China and selected CEEFSU countries. In the case of the CEEFSU countries, the data are either for the year in which the scale of classified loans reached its peak (Czech Republic, Hungary, Poland) or the most recent data available (Bulgaria, Romania, Russia, Slovakia). The estimate of classified loans in China is only approximate, and in particular these figures may under-state the scale of bad bank debt in China if banks are rolling over loans which firms are not servicing. Cross-country comparisons of the scale of classified loans should also be treated with some caution because of differences in classification schemes as well as differences in the scale of possible understatement of bad debt problems. Nevertheless, it is

Table 3.5   Classified loans, China and CEEFSU countries, 1993–6

Country	As % of total loans	As % of GDP
Bulgaria (1995)	74	31
Czech Republic (1994)	38	27
Hungary (1993)	29	15
Poland (1993)	31	5
Romania (1995)	43	19
Russia (1996)	13–30	1–3
Slovakia (1995)	29	26
China		
1993	13–20	12–19
1995	20	17
1996	22	21

Sources: OECD Economic Surveys, various years (Bulgaria, Czech Republic, Hungary, Poland, Russia, Slovakia), National Bank of Romania *Quarterly Bulletin*; own calculations. For China (1993), estimates of People's Bank of China, for China (1995), PBC estimate of percentage of bad loans in the four largest Chinese commercial banks cited in Woo (1996) and here applied to PBC figures for total credit stock; for China (1996), figure for percentage of bad loans in the four largest Chinese commercial banks cited in *The Economist*, 13 September 1997, and here applied to PBC figures for total credit stock.

clear that the proportion of bank debt in China which the banks have classified as poor or bad, while large at about 20 per cent of total bank debt in 1995, is actually somewhat low compared to that in other transition countries, where figures of 30–40 per cent are more typical. If we measure the scale of classified loans in proportion to GDP, however, the picture is somewhat different – the absolute size of China's bad debt problem, about 20 per cent of GDP in 1995, is comparable in scale to the bad debt problems observed in CEEFSU countries.

The explanation for this can be seen from Tables 3.6 and 3.7. The scale of total credit in China, 88 per cent of GDP in 1995, is large compared to that observed in most CEEFSU countries (Table 3.6). Most of this bank credit consists of lending to firms, and hence we observe that the Chinese firms are heavily indebted compared to their CEEFSU counterparts – Table 3.7 shows that the debt/asset ratio at book value in Chinese enterprises in 1994 was 65 per cent, compared to 30–45 per cent observed in the Czech Republic, Hungary and Poland. It is worth noting that the debt/asset ratios observed in developed Western countries are in the range of 55–75 per cent (Rajan and Zingales, 1995) – i.e. it is the CEEFSU level which is low by international standards and not the Chinese level which is high. It should also be noted that debt/asset ratios in the CEEFSU countries were also low prior to the start of transition, meaning that CEEFSU firms inherited low debt levels from the socialist period.

The explanation for the high debt/asset ratio in Chinese enterprises compared to CEEFSU firms, and for the larger volume of total bank debt in

Table 3.6   Credit to the non-financial sector as a percentage of GDP, in China and CEEFSU countries, 1995

Country	Credit as % of GDP
Bulgaria	41
Czech Republic	64
Hungary	23
Poland	20
Romania	23
Russia	12
Slovakia	59
Slovenia	28
China	88

Source: OECD *Economic Surveys: Russian Federation* (1997), p. 92; IMF, *International Financial Statistics* (December 1997); *Chinese Statistical Bulletin* (1996); own calculations.

China, follows from changes in Chinese government policy towards funding investment. From the start of the reforms in the late 1970s, bank loans have progressively replaced budgetary appropriations as the main source of external funding of investment in fixed capital in SOEs in China. Government expenditure on capital construction amounted to 13 per cent of GDP in 1978, and fell to 7 per cent of GDP by 1975 and only 3 per cent of GDP in 1993. The increased reliance on bank financing of investment is reflected in the higher stock of bank credit and the higher indebtedness of firms. CEEFSU firms, by contrast, at the start of transition in 1989–91 inherited stocks of fixed capital which had been funded largely by government budgets rather than debt, and hence inherited low volumes of debt as well.

The sources of the bad debt problem in China also differ in some respects from those in the CEEFSU economies. Most obviously, China has experienced

Table 3.7   Firm's debt asset ratio (book value), China and CEE countries, 1992–4, per cent

Country	Debt/Asset ratio
Czech Republic (1994)	44
Hungary (1992)	32
Poland (1992)	41
China (1994)	
All industrial enterprises	65
of which:	
state-owned enterprises	68

Sources: CEE countries, Cornelli, Portes and Schaffer (1996); China: *Chinese Statistical Yearbook* (1995), using Tables 12–9, 12–11, 12–12.

continuous economic growth since the start of the reforms. One of the main causes of the bad debt problem in the CEEFSU countries – the deep recessions at the start of transition and the accompanying financial distress of many firms – has no counterpart in China. The causes of the Chinese bad debt problem do, however, resemble some of those operating in the CEEFSU countries, particularly the slower reformers.

While movement towards a market economy has made great progress in China, the financial sector is an exception. The banking sector remains dominated by a few very large state-owned banks. Central planning of goods was progressively abandoned during the reform period, but state direction of bank lending for policy or political purposes continued. In these respects the functioning of China's banking sector resembles those of some of the less rapidly reforming CEEFSU transition countries and, as in these countries, the effect has been to contribute to the growth of bad debts in the banking sector.

The general view in the literature on the Chinese banking system (e.g. World Bank, 1995, Bouin, 1996; Woo, 1996) is roughly as follows. During the reform period, decentralization granted local governments a greater control over state banks' local branches. The greater autonomy of local governments, combined with quantitative credit control, has given rise to political pressure, corruption and collusive behavior between banks, governments and enterprises. Local governments pressure local banks to lend to their controlled SOEs and support local projects to promote local development. The expected economic value of these projects alone presumably would not justify this lending, and hence the recipients of these loans will often not be in a position to service or repay them. Furthermore, when SOEs run into financial difficulties, whether because they are over-indebted or because of other reasons, local governments and enterprises lobby the authorities to direct banks to rescue firms by injecting new loans – a case of the soft budget constraint. To the extent that these loans will not actually be repaid, they can be seen as providing in effect a flow of quasi-fiscal subsidies to enterprises; an additional subsidy element derives from charging low (or negative, in real terms) interest rates.

In this analysis of the Chinese banking sector, the bad debt problem does not resemble that in the faster CEEFSU reformers (e.g. the Czech Republic, Hungary, Poland), which can be characterized as a bad debt stock problem but no major flow problem. In these countries, a large portion of the bad debt stock problem appears to have either been inherited from the pre-transition period in the sense that the recession which accompanied the start of transition meant many firms could not service their debts, or been the result of imprudent lending early in the transition; the flow problem appears small in the sense that cautious lending policies by most state-owned or privatized banks emerged within a couple of years of the start of transition. The Chinese situation is instead more akin to the situation in the slower reformers in the first several years or so of transition (e.g. Bulgaria and many of the countries of the former Soviet Union or FSU), where state direction of credits for political purposes was common: such loans were often made at very negative real interest rates and the principal rapidly deflated, rolled over, or forgiven, and the loans were often directed to distressed and/or politically influential firms.

We now investigate directly this characterization of the Chinese banking sector with the help of a data set of 500-odd Chinese state-owned industrial enterprises for 1991.[8] We apply the method of Bonin and Schaffer (1995) and look at the relationship between net bank financing and firm performance. If net bank financing of poorly performing firms is positive we have evidence of soft budget constraints. That is, if poorly performing firms see an increase in nominal lending greater than the interest they are paying to the banks, the banks are not merely rolling over debts, they are 'throwing good money after bad'.

Net bank financing of firm *i* is defined as:

$$\text{NBF} = \frac{(\text{End-1991 bank debt} - \text{End-1990 bank debt}) - \text{Interest costs (\%)}}{\text{End-1991 total assets}}$$

We measure performance in two ways, using lagged profitability and lagged output growth. Profitability is defined as:

$$\text{Profitability} = \frac{1990 \text{ gross profit} - \text{Profit taxes and other fees (\%)}}{\text{End-1990 total assets}}$$

'Profitability' is defined using the firms' 1990 results for the reason that these should have been known to banks when they were making their 1991 loans. There are problems with profit as a measure of performance, however, since in this case some of the losses experienced by firms may have been owing to price controls, as discussed earlier in this chapter.[9] For this reason, we use an additional performance measure, lagged real output growth. This is defined as:

$$\text{Lagged output growth} = \text{Real increase in output in the two-year} \\ \text{period 1988-90 (\%)}$$

The simplest way to present the data is using a scatterplot, with net bank financing on the vertical axis and either profitability or output growth on the horizontal axis. It is also helpful to be able to distinguish between large and small borrowers, and so we weight each point (firm) in the scatterplot by the size of its end-1991 bank debt – a large point indicates a large debtor. To make the scatterplot more readable, only firms with an end-1991 bank debt in excess of US$ 1 million (at official exchange rates) are plotted.

Figure 3.1 shows the relationship between net bank financing in 1991 and firm profitability in 1990. Most loss-making firms lie above the horizontal axis – i.e. most loss-makers were receiving positive net bank financing. We interpret this as evidence of a 'flow problem' in the Chinese banking sector in 1991 – Chinese banks were not merely rolling over debts of loss-making firms,

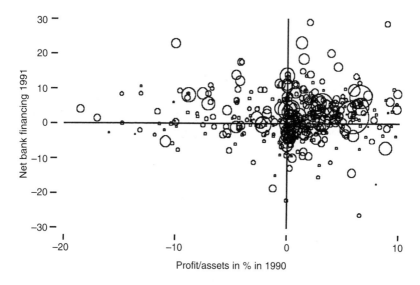

Figure 3.1   NBF v. lagged profit – China 1991

they were 'throwing good money after bad'. These firms, it appears, had soft budget constraints.

Figure 3.2 shows the relationship between net bank financing in 1991 and firm real output growth in 1988–90. About half of firms with real declines in output over the preceding two years received cash injections from their banks. Again, we interpret this as evidence of a flow problem in the banking sector, and of the existence of soft budget constraints.

A comparison with Hungarian firms in 1993 makes an interesting contrast.[10] We use a comprehensive dataset of Hungarian firms as collected by the Central Statistical Office (CSO). As before, in order to make the scatterplot readable, only firms with bank debts in excess of US$ 1 million are plotted. Figure 3.3 shows the relationship between net bank financing in Hungary in 1993 and firm profitability in the preceding year, 1992. In sharp contrast to the Chinese case, almost no loss-making firms in Hungary had positive net bank financing in 1993. The picture is similar if we measure performance by real sales growth in 1992; Figure 3.4 shows that the firms with the largest real declines in output had negative, not positive, net bank financing. In 1993, Hungarian banks were trying to extract themselves from their worst clients. Unlike Chinese banks, they were imposing hard budget constraints on their problem firms.

It is worth noting another important difference between the Chinese and Hungarian cases. In Figures 3.1 and 3.2, we can see that better performing Chinese firms have positive net bank financing. In a sense, the increasing

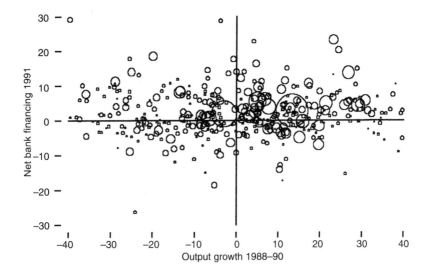

Figure 3.2   NBF v. lagged output growth – China 1991

exposure of Chinese banks to poorly performing firms is counterbalanced by their increased lending to good firms. In Hungary, by contrast, better performing firms have negative net bank financing (Figures 3.3 and 3.4). In our view, this is best interpreted by distinguishing between the supply side (banks) and the demand side (firms) in the market for credit. Real interest rates in 1993 in Hungary were very high, and the Hungarian economy was still contracting. Profitable Hungarian firms probably preferred to reduce their bank lending and instead finance from retained earnings, and in any case in Hungary in 1993 there were relatively few growing firms with a real increase in demand for bank credit. Hungarian banks may have wanted to lend to profitable firms, but such firms didn't want to borrow and there were few such firms anyway. In China in 1991, by contrast, profitable and/or growing firms were willing to borrow, and there were many growing firms to whom banks could lend.

Tax arrears[11]

The problem of tax arrears is quite different from the problem of tax evasion. The answer to tax evasion is improving detection of tax liabilities; the answer to tax arrears is improving collection of tax liabilities that have been accrued, are known both to the tax authority and to the firm, but the firm has not paid.

In the CEEFSU transition countries, virtually all tax arrears are owed by firms rather than individuals. Schaffer (1995, 1996) estimates that the aggregate real

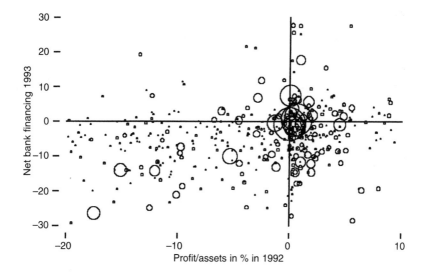

Figure 3.3 NBF v. lagged net profit – Hungary 1993

flow of tax arrears in CEEFSU transition economies is in the order of 1–3 per cent of GDP per annum. This is much higher than we observe in Western countries. The comparable figure in Western economies is the volume of taxes written off as uncollectable, and is a fraction of a percent of GDP

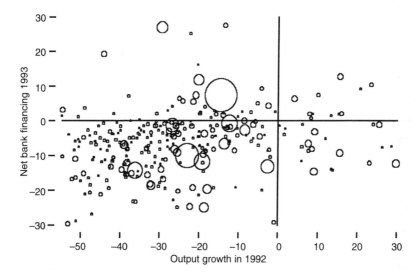

Figure 3.4 NBF v. lagged output growth – Hungary 1993

Table 3.8   Concentration of tax arrears in highly unprofitable firms, Hungary, Poland, and Russia, 1993–4

Country	Highly-unprofitable firms account for:	
	% of firms	*% of tax arrears*
Hungary	10	62
(200 manufacturing firms, 1993)		
Poland	13	74
(200 manufacturing firms, 1993)		
Russia	13	44
(439 industrial firms, 1994)		

Note: 'Highly-unprofitable' firms in Hungary and Poland refer to those whose profit sales ratio is below –10%; in Russia these are firms who described themselves in the survey as 'usually loss-making'.
Source: World Bank Surveys; Schaffer (1996).

per annum. For example, in New Zealand, tax arrears written off as uncollectable in 1994 amounted to 0.3 per cent of GDP.

Tax arrears arise because the state does not pursue firms into liquidation in pursuit of its tax claim and instead tolerates non-payment of taxes, and inflows to the stock of tax arrears continue. The available empirical evidence suggests a large portion of the tax arrears problem is located in financially distressed firms. Because these firms are in serious difficulties, these tax arrears are unlikely ever to be collected. Government toleration of tax arrears means in effect that these firms are being subsidized.

The implication of this is that tax arrears should be highly concentrated in distressed firms, and this is indeed what is found. Table 3.8 presents the results of surveys of firms in Hungary, Poland, and Russia conducted by the World Bank. The most unprofitable 10–15 per cent of firms were separated out and the proportion of tax arrears accounted for by these unprofitable firms were estimated. The results were quite striking – highly unprofitable firms are clearly responsible for much or most of tax arrears: from 44 per cent in Russia to 74 per cent in Poland.[12]

Schaffer (1995) offers the following explanation of why the tax authorities tolerate the accumulation of tax arrears in distressed firms. Because the distressed firm is typically paying its workers and suppliers out of sales revenue, the firm is generating positive value added. If the tax authority allows the firm to continue to operate it may be able to pressure the firm to pay part of its taxes. If the tax authority takes legal action to have the firm liquidated, the liquidation value will be low and little of the overdue tax liabilities will be paid, the value added currently being generated by the firm will be lost, it will take time for the capital and labour freed up to find alternative uses, and in the meantime the resulting unemployment will be politically costly.

The case of tax arrears in China is, to our knowledge, unstudied. The academic, policy and journalistic literature focuses on subsidies, bad debts and trade credit arrears, and tax arrears appear to go unmentioned. This would suggest that, in contrast to the case of the CEEFSU transition countries, tax arrears are not currently a problem in China. The only evidence we have available to us on this come from the survey of Chinese SOEs analyzed above.

We divided the sample of Chinese SOEs in 1991 into 343 profit-makers and 175 loss-makers, and looked at real increases in tax liabilities in the two categories of firms separately. The median real increase in total tax liabilities between end-1990 and end-1991, measured as a percentage of end-year assets,[13] was in fact very small in both categories: the equivalent of 0.1 per cent of assets in the group of loss-makers, and no real increase at all in the group of profit-makers. This is in sharp contrast to the findings reported by Schaffer (1998) using the World Bank survey of 200 Polish enterprises in 1993: in that sample, the median real increase in tax liabilities of very unprofitable firms was the equivalent of a remarkable 12 per cent of end-year assets, compared to less than 1 per cent for other firms. The picture from an examination of the concentration of tax liabilities in loss-making firms is similar. In contrast to the case in the CEEFSU countries, there is no concentration of tax liabilities in the loss-making firms in our sample of Chinese SOEs; loss-makers in 1991 made up 34 per cent of the sample and accounted for 30 per cent of the tax liabilities of the firms in the sample.

This evidence supports the view that tax arrears have indeed not so far presented a financial discipline problem in China. Nevertheless, more research is clearly needed, and the CEEFSU experience suggests that if budget constraints become very hard in China, a tax arrears problem may emerge.

Summary

In parallel with price liberalization, budgetary subsidies have fallen substantially both in China and in CEEFSU transition countries, and are typically associated with remaining price controls. For this reason, it is difficult to demonstrate that remaining subsidies are clear evidence of soft budget constraints.

The scale of trade credit and 'inter-enterprise arrears' in the CEEFSU transition economies, and in China, are roughly comparable to those observed in developed Western economies. More importantly, firms in the CEEFSU countries and in China typically impose financial discipline towards each other. There are, however, some signs that in China trade credit is linked to soft budget constraints, via government policy which has been soft towards firms. In China, as in some of the slower reforming CEEFSU countries, the government has attempted to clear inter-enterprise arrears by injecting credit. As in the CEEFSU cases, the arrears reappeared. This is only natural because trade credit is a normal feature of market economies. We have argued that the best policy in China, as in the CEEFSU countries, is for the government not to attempt to clear such arrears, since this amounts to a bail-out of the enterprise sector and creates moral-hazard problems as firms, anticipating the bail-out, cease paying each other.

We have suggested that, when looking at the bank–enterprise relationship in transition economies, the usual data available on non-performing debt needs to be interpreted carefully, and can usefully be supplemented by using firm-level data to examine the relationship between enterprise performance and net bank financing. We argued that banks in leading CEEFSU transition countries are usually hard and, using Hungary as an example, showed that in 1993 poorly performing Hungarian firms did not receive positive net bank financing. In contrast, banks in China seems to be softer: it is hard for banks to resist political pressure from local governments and enterprises to lend money to financially distressed firms. This was reflected in the enterprise-level data we analyzed: in 1991, poorly performing Chinese firms received positive net bank financing. In other words, although both Hungary and China had bad debt stock problems, only China had a bad debt flow problem. Chinese, but not Hungarian, firms had soft budget constraints.

Tax arrears appear to be an important source of soft budget constraints in CEEFSU countries. The little evidence we have available on China suggests that the situation in China is different and that tax arrears are not, or not yet, a major policy problem in China. More research is called for here.

Notes

*   We would like to thank Juzhong Zhuang for his helpful comments on an earlier version of this chapter and for assisting us with the Chinese enterprise data, and Dic Lo, Duo Qin and Wen-Zhong Ding for their help in obtaining data. An early version of this chapter was presented at the 1996 meeting of the Chinese Economic Association (UK). Portions of it derive from Schaffer (1998). The usual disclaimer applies.

1. 'Soft budget constraint' in this chapter is defined as a form of 'financial indiscipline' in the enterprise sector. Following Kornai (e.g. his 1986 paper in *Kyklos*), the state is paternalistic, hence 'weak' or 'soft', and poorly performing firms will be rescued by the state by some means if they are in trouble and known to be in trouble; poor performance or losses result in subsidies and financing. For a more detailed discussion, see Schaffer (1998).

2. It is worth noting that these sectors are comparable to the range of subsidized sectors observed in developed Western economies.

3. Lo (1997), Table 3.

4. For evidence from Poland, see Belka *et al.* (1995); from Hungary, see Bonin and Schaffer (1995); from Russia, see Alfandari and Schaffer (1996).

5. Well documented examples include Russia in 1992 and Romania on several occasions since 1992.

6. For a model of strategic arrears, see Perotti (1997).

7. Few banks are quick to admit that they have large amounts of bad assets, even when accounting standards are well established and the banks have staff with experience in classifying assets.

8. For a description of the dataset, see Fan, Li and Peng (1989).
9. For example, most of the coal mining firms in the sample were earning negative profits as defined above, but had non-negative retained profits, presumably because of subsidies.
10. The results for 1992 are similar and can be found in Bonin and Schaffer (1995) and Schaffer (1998), to which we refer the reader for a more in-depth analysis.
11. The material in this section draws on Schaffer (1995, 1996, 1998).
12. This is despite the fact that they are accruing fewer taxes than profit-makers, who incur profit liabilities as well as the other taxes.
13. Note that we are looking at total tax liabilities, not just overdue tax liabilities (tax arrears).

Bibliography

Alfandari, G. and M. E. Schaffer (1996) '"Arrears" in the Enterprise Sector', in S. Commander, Q. Fan and M. E. Schaffer (eds), *Enterprise Restructuring and Economic Policy in Russia* (New York: EDI/World Bank).

Belka, M., S. Estrin, M. E. Schaffer and I. J. Singh (1995) 'Enterprise Adjustment in Poland: evidence from a Survey of 200 Private, Privatized, and State-owned Firms', *Centre for Economic Performance Discussion Paper*, 233, April.

Bonin, J. P. and M. E. Schaffer (1995) 'Banks, Firms, Bad Debts and Bankruptcy in Hungary 1991–94', *Centre for Economic Performance Discussion Paper*, 234, April.

Bouin, O. (1996) 'Financial Discipline and State Enterprise Reform in China in the 1990s', in O. Bouin, F. Coricelli and F. Lemoine (eds), *Different Paths to a Market Economy: China and European Economies in Transition* (London and Paris: CEPR/CEPII/OECD).

Broadman, H. G. (1994) 'Meeting the Challenge of Chinese Enterprise Reform', *World Bank Discussion Papers*, 283(Washington, DC: The World Bank).

Coricelli, F., M. D'browski and U. Kosterna (1997) *Fiscal Policy in Transition*, EPI Forum Report 3 (London and New York: CEPR and IEWS).

Cornelli, F., R. Portes and M. E. Schaffer (1996) 'The Capital Structure of Firms in Central and Eastern Europe', in O. Bouin, F. Coricelli and F. Lemoine (eds), *Different Paths to a Market Economy: China and European Economies in Transition* (London and Paris: CEPR/CEPII/OECD).

Fan, Gang (1996) 'Interenterprise Debts and Macroeconomic Performance in China', Institute of Economics, China Academy of Social Sciences.

Fan, Qimiao, Lei Li and Zhaopin Peng (1989) 'The CESRRI Enterprise Panel Survey System: An Introduction', *STICERD China Programme Technical Reports*, 1, December.

Kornai, J. (1986) 'The Soft Budget Constraint', *Kyklos*, 39 (1).

Lo, D. (1997) 'Re-appraising China's State-Owned Industrial Enterprises', *SOAS Department of Working Paper Series* 67, University of London, April.

Perotti, E. (1997) 'Inertial Credit and Opportunistic Arrears in Transition', *European Economic Review*, forthcoming.

Rajan, R. and L. Zingales (1995) 'What Do We Know About Capital Structure? Some Evidence from International Data', *Journal of Finance*, 50 (5), December.

Schaffer, M. E. (1995) 'Government Subsidies to Enterprises in Central and Eastern Europe: Budgetary Subsidies and Tax Arrears', In D. M. G. Newbery (ed.), *Tax and Benefit Reform in Central and Eastern Europe* (London: Centre for Economic Policy Research), pp. 115–144.

Schaffer, M. E. (1996) 'Tax Arrears in Transition Economies', CERT, Heriot-Watt University, mimeo.

Schaffer, M. E. (1998), 'Do Firms in Transition Countries Have Soft Budget Constraints? A Reconsideration of Concepts and Evidence', *Journal of Comparative Economics*, March.

Woo, Wing Thye (1996) 'Financial Intermediation in China', in O. Bouin, F. Coricelli and F. Lemoine (eds.), *Different Paths to a Market Economy: China and European Economies in Transition*, (London and Paris: CEPR/CEPII/OECD).

World Bank (1995) *China: Macroeconomic Stability in a Decentralized Economy.* (Washington, DC: The World Bank).

World Bank (1997) *China's Management of Enterprise Assets: The State as Shareholder* (Washington, DC: The World Bank).

Zou, Liang and Laixiang Sun (1996), 'Interest Rate Policy and Incentives of State-Owned Enterprises in the Transitional China'. *Journal of Comparative Economics,* Vol. 23, No. 3, pp. 292–318.

4
Impact of Reforms on Wage and Employment Determination in Chinese State-owned Enterprises, 1986–91

*Athar Hussain and Juzhong Zhuang**

Introduction

Chinese economic reforms since 1979 have introduced far-reaching changes in the labour market as well as in enterprise governance. In the state sector, which is at the centre of the transition to a market economy, wage determination has gradually been devolved to managers. Incentive pay and bonuses linked to enterprise performance have became widespread and their share in the wage bill has risen steadily. Managerial discretion over recruitment, promotions and also lay-offs has increased. Terminable employment contracts are replacing jobs for life. The labour force, in turn, has acquired greater freedom in choosing and changing jobs. The determination of wages and employment, although of crucial importance for the transition to a market economy, have as yet not been investigated empirically. Studies of transformation of the state sector have largely concentrated on efficiency and productivity (Chen *et al.*, 1988; Dollar, 1990; Jefferson, Rawski and Zheng, 1992; Woo *et al.*, 1993; Groves *et al.*, 1994).

This chapter reports the results of an empirical analysis of wage and employment determination in Chinese state-owned enterprises (SOEs) geared to an assessment of how these have been affected by reforms. Notwithstanding a steady decline in their importance, SOEs remain important: they account for around 50 per cent of industrial output and set norms for wages in the non-state sector. Broadly, the chapter is structured around two questions. First, is there evidence of a link between wages and the financial performance of enterprises, and has this link become stronger over time? This link was absent in the pre-reform period, as enterprise balance sheets had little significance for decision-making. Drawing on the literature on wage determination in market economies (Krueger and Summers, 1988; Abowd and Lemieux, 1993), we regard the emergence of such a link, whether owing to efficiency wages or rent-sharing, to be a significant step towards the transformation of SOEs into organizations akin to firms in a market economy. The second question concerns the relationship at the enterprise level between employment and the wage rate, on the one hand, and employment and output on the other, and how these have changed. In the pre-reform period, these relationships were weak, if not absent, as the wage rate, employment and output in state enterprises were all largely determined by government rather than management. The allocation of labour was based on information supplied by the enterprise management which had no particular incentive to make an efficient use of labour. Employment was weakly related to output and heavily influenced by factors such as preventing urban unemployment. One piece of evidence for this is the large pool of 'surplus' employees inherited by the state sector. As China is still in transit towards being a fully fledged market economy, the chapter lays special emphasis on changes in the determinants of wages and employment over 1986–91, the period covered by the data.

This chapter is based on panel data on 514 SOEs for six years, from 1986 to 1991 (hereafter referred to as the 'enterprise data'). The sampled enterprises are of different sizes, drawn from 33 industries and distributed over cities in 20 out of 30 provinces. Comprising 3084 observations, the data provide information on enterprise location, the labour force, total wage bill, total bonuses, output at constant and current prices, sales revenue, intermediate inputs, profits and the capital stock. The start date of the survey, 1986, comes a year after the generalization of pilot reforms to all SOEs, which was followed by a series of initiatives to transform employment contracts and wage determination in SOEs (Takahara, 1993). The survey period overlaps with the introduction of the Management Responsibility System, whereby enterprise managers are allowed operational independence in return for a contractual obligation to achieve various performance targets. Being a panel, the data lends itself to an investigation of changes in wage and employment determination arising from these reforms.

The chapter is organized as follows. We give an overview of labour reforms in the state sector and present preliminary tabulations and density functions by way of a background to subsequent analysis. We then discuss the estimation equations, outline the estimation strategy and present results. The final section concludes.

Overview of labour reforms and data description

The period covered by the enterprise data (1986–91) was characterized by large macroeconomic fluctuations and alternated between bold reform initiatives and retrenchment. The industrial growth rate ranged between a high 10–15 per cent in 1986–8 and 1991, and a low 5–3 per cent between 1989 and 1990 (SSB, 1993, p. 31). The inflation rate climbed steadily from 1986 to reach an unprecedented 18–19 per cent between 1988 and 1989, which for the first time in a decade led to a fall in the real wage rate. It then fell to a low of 3 per cent in 1990–1, as a result of a stabilization policy. The quick pace of reforms in 1987–8 was followed in 1989–90 by a marked slowdown and a tightening of control on state enterprises, especially after June 1989. The labour system which the reforms were set out to transform was structured around the following three features: first, administrative control on labour migration, second, centralized labour allocation and wage determination; third, lifetime jobs. Whilst some of these have been radically transformed, others still survive in a modified form.

Administrative control on labour migration still survives but is attenuated. Since the mid-1980s rural residents have been able to take up temporary or casual jobs in urban areas, which they have done in rising numbers. But they are not allowed to settle or take up permanent jobs without permission, which is strictly rationed for large cities, though not any longer for small towns. For the present purposes, the migration control has two main effects: first, it insulates the urban labour market from the rural labour market and, second, within urban areas it separates the market for regular employment (reserved for registered urban residents) from the market for casual and temporary employment (also open to rural migrants). In tandem with a high output growth rate, the migration control has kept the unemployment rate among the labour force with urban registration exceptionally low, below 2.6 per cent since 1983 (SSB, 1993, p. 119; for details of how the Chinese unemployment rate is measured see, Fu *et al.*, 1993). It has served to disguise a potentially huge problem of unemployment by confining it to rural areas, though the disguise is wearing thin with the sharp increase in 'temporary' labour migration. Its net effect is to favour workers with urban registration: compared to the rest, they have wider job opportunities and first claim on vacancies in urban areas and enjoy a more secure employment. It has a much stronger impact on SOEs than on non-state enterprises as almost all SOEs are in urban areas. Arguably, the differences in terms of employment and wages are major factors behind the more rapid growth of the non-state than the state industrial sector.

Administrative allocation to jobs in urban areas, which deprived enterprises of control over their labour force and left behind a large pool of surplus employees, has largely disappeared. Labour plans are still drawn but they are no longer prescriptive, and decisions about recruitment and the size of the labourforce have been devolved to the enterprise management. Government agencies continue to play a central role in job placement but both prospective employees and employers have the option of by-passing them, which they increasingly do. Lifetime employment, which left enterprises little scope for adjusting the size and the composition of their labourforce, is on the way out. Since 1986, all new recruitment to blue-collar jobs has been on fixed-term renewable contracts, and the percentage of contract employees in the state sector has since risen to 18.9 in 1992 (SSB, 1993, p. 117). With a percentage as

Table 4.1   Percentage of enterprises reducing labour force by 5 per cent or more, 1987–91

1987 (%)	1988 (%)	1989 (%)	1990 (%)	1991 (%)
3.8	8.5	11.4	9.4	5.9

Source: Own calculations.

high as this the management has considerable flexibility to adjust the labour force through not renewing expiring contracts and fresh recruitment. There are pilot experiment under way to convert all permanent employment into terminable employment, including technical and managerial personnel. Dismissals on the grounds of indiscipline and inability to perform the job have been possible since 1986 (Child, 1994). Management has also been given the option of internally redeploying 'surplus employees' from core to subsidiary activities, predominantly services. Lay-offs (especially in urban areas) require government clearance, but are more widespread than believed (see, for example, Korzec, 1992, p. 42). A survey of 3000 unemployed in Shanghai in 1989 revealed that 43 per cent of them were previously in 'permanent' employment (Fu *et al.*, 1993). The enterprise data provides the figures shown in Table 4.1 of the percentage of enterprises reducing their labourforce by 5 per cent or more, which we assume cannot be due entirely to voluntary quits and retirement.

There is an unemployment insurance scheme for the employees of SOEs, but beneficiaries are very small in number and consist mostly of blue-collar workers laid off following the expiry of their contract (see Fu *et al.*, 1993).

Unlike in the past, employees can now quit jobs easily and there are reports of rising voluntary quits amongst younger employees and those with skills in demand. For example, according to the above-mentioned survey of the unemployed in Shanghai, around 59 per cent of workers previously employed on contract quit voluntarily (Fu *et al.*, 1993). Given the high growth rate of the industrial sector and control on labour migration, the easing of restrictions on voluntary quits has widened market options open to employees and thereby increased their bargaining position, though unevenly across industries and occupations. However, voluntary quit can have a high cost, as housing is predominantly provided by 'work units' (as they are termed in China). This cost is likely to be higher for older than younger workers as the latter may still be on the waiting list for housing. The attachment of housing to jobs is far more important in the state industrial sector than in the non-state sector, a large part of which is in rural areas where housing is predominantly privately owned and not provided by employers.

In sum, economic reforms have provided managers both greater power and incentive to adjust the size and composition of labour force according to the output demand and factor prices, albeit still under certain constraints. They have also given workers a greater, though not complete, freedom to chose and switch jobs. These raise the empirical issue of their impact on the sensitivity of enterprise employment to the wage rate and output, which we examine later.

Turning to wage determination in SOEs, it has gone through a series of reforms since the early 1980s. These have been directed towards two general aims: first, to break away from the highly egalitarian wage structure carried over from the pre-reform era (popularly known as 'breaking the iron rice bowl') and, second, to increase managerial discretion over wages and forge a closer link between wages and individual or enterprise performance. Chinese statistics divide the total wage bill in SOEs under 5 headings (SSB, 1993, p. 105), but for the present purposes these may be collapsed into two according to how they are determined: 'regular wages' and bonuses. Regular wages consist largely of time wages and cost of living subsidies (inflation compensation), which is decided by provincial or municipal authorities as the inflation rate can vary widely across regions. Time wages are set with reference to an official job grade–wage matrix which favours certain industries such as the heavy industry and the coal mining (Korzec, 1992). The matrix is, in principle, no longer prescriptive, simply indicative; and managers have discretion over regular wages through promotion and incentive payments, but that has been limited by administrative control on the wage bill and an 'excess wage tax' (STB, 1993).

The revival of performance-linked bonuses has been the centrepiece of the Chinese wage reforms. Their share in the total wage bill has risen steadily, from a mere 2.3 per cent in 1978 to 24 per cent in 1992 (SSB 1993, p. 105; see also Table 4.2). In principle, they differ from regular wages in two respects: first, they are more closely linked to enterprise performance and, second, they are more variable across enterprises and can go down as well as up. The emphasis has been on the incentive aspect of bonuses; in contrast to Japan, they are not seen as an instrument for reconciling lifetime employment with fluctuations in the financial conditions of enterprises (Freeman and Weitzman, 1987). The indicators of enterprise performance used for the calculation of bonuses have been variable across enterprise and over time. They have included gross output or sales, pre-tax profits, profits tax and qualitative indicators such as technical renovation or product development. Over time, profit (or a closely related variable such as profits tax paid) has gained currency as the main indicator. Bonuses are usually paid in two parts: one part is paid monthly with regular wages, and the other is paid lump sum before the Chinese New Year. They are calibrated in terms of so many months' regular wage. In SOEs, bonuses have been regulated through official guidelines, agreements between enterprises and their supervisory agencies and a tax. The Bonus Tax (introduced in 1985) was levied at progressive rate to bonuses exceeding four months' regular wage (STB, 1993). Both the excess wage and

Table 4.2   Means and CVs[a] of per-head wages, bonuses and profits, simple averages, 1986–91 (current yuan)

	Sample	1986	1987	1988	1989	1990	1991
Sample	All	514	514	514	514	514	514
	P-M[f]	493	492	490	473	416	395
	L-M[g]	21	22	24	41	98	119
TW[b]	All	1451	1643	2060	2358	2651	2885
	P-M	1449	1648	2073	2388	2760	3038
	L-M	1506	1521	1790	2021	2188	2376
RW[c]	All	1148	1251	1536	1745	1978	2131
	P-M	1141	1249	1538	1755	2013	2182
	L-M	1307	1282	1504	1624	1830	1964
BN[d]	All	303	392	524	614	673	754
	P-M	308	399	535	633	747	856
	L-M	199	239	286	397	357	412
PR[e]	All	3486	3641	3696	3071	1963	1792
	P-M	3676	3841	3932	3486	2971	3047
	L-M	−972	−842	−1137	−1721	−231 4	−2372
BN/PR	All	8.7	10.8	14.2	20.0	34.3	42.1

Notes:
a CVs denote coefficients of variation in percentage terms; all CVs are reported in brackets.
b TW denotes total wage per head.
c RW denotes regular wages per head.
d BN denotes bonuses per head.
e PR denotes profit per head.
f P-M denotes profit-makers.
g L-M denotes loss-makers.

the bonus tax are generally regarded to have been ineffective and are to be replaced with a new 'wage regulation tax'.

A stylized picture of wage determination in SOEs, which we use later for the specification of estimation equations, is as follows. Regular wages are predominantly set with reference to the official job grade–wage matrix with low differentials. It is an open question whether regular wages depend on the financial performance of enterprises, an issue which we examine later. In comparison, bonuses, being more closely linked to enterprise performance, are more variable across enterprises and over time. They also lend themselves to bargaining between the management and the labour force. The decentralization of decision-making to the management, as well as furthering economic incentives, also give the two sides power to make effective threats, opening up the possibility of bargaining. The management can threaten to reduce bonus, and the labourforce, in turn, can threaten to withdraw co-operation thus worsening the financial position of enterprise on which managerial performance is judged. Moreover, economic reforms have given both sides some 'market power'. Workers can quit and the management can substitute 'insiders' by 'outsiders' by not renewing expiring contracts and hiring new workers instead. Although not as important as the first, the 'market power' can serve as a tool of bargaining between the management and small groups of workers. The literature on Chinese economic reforms has emphasized the incentive aspect of decentralization, but not the bargaining aspect even though it is equally important (Groves *et al.*, 1994). Bargaining is, however, informal as wages are not formally negotiated in China. A major difference between wage bargaining in a market economy and in the Chinese economy is that a substantial proportion of enterprises are financially non-viable. In such enterprises, bargaining between employees and the management alone cannot determine the bonus, as it depends crucially on the willingness of the government to cover losses. This raises the question of the difference in wage determination between profitable and loss-making enterprises, which we analyze later.

Before proceeding to econometric analysis, we examine summary statistics and density distributions to get a feel for, first, the impact of reforms on regular wages and bonuses and, second, the behaviour of employment and related variables. Table 4.2 presents the means and coefficients of variation of nominal total wage and regular wage rates, and per head bonuses and pre-tax profit for all enterprises and also separately for profit-makers (P-M) and loss-makers (L-M). A notable feature of the sample is a steady rise in the number of loss-makers over the period. Taking the whole sample, the share of bonuses in total wages rose from 21 per cent in 1986 to 27 per cent in 1991 (for figures on all SOEs, see SSB, 1993, p. 105). The 1991 figure is close to the mean ratio of bonuses to total wages in Japan (Freeman and Weitzman, 1987). The rise in the share of bonuses could be interpreted in terms of either an increase in the importance of economic incentives, or a rise in the bargaining position of workers. Both are possible but, as we argue below, the second is an important cause of the change. The low coefficient of variation (CV) for regular wages fits in with the above stylized picture that they do not differ much across enterprises and are not greatly affected by financial performance, if at all. In fact, over the first four years (1986–8) the mean regular wage rate is higher for loss- than for profit-makers. This is due to the preponderance of coal mining enterprises among loss-makers and a comparatively high regular wage rate of miners. In contrast to regular wages, the mean bonus amongst profit-makers is always higher than that amongst loss-makers, which suggests that it bears some link to profit. However, poor financial performance rarely implies zero bonus. Out of 3084 observations over 1986–91, bonuses are zero in only 65 cases. The implication is that enterprises have to pay some bonus regardless of performance. Moreover, as shown by the last row of Table 4.2 (BN/PR) the ratio of bonuses to profit per head for the whole sample rises over time steadily, especially steeply in 1990–1 when bonuses maintain their upward rise despite a sharp drop in profit per head. The implication is that the link between bonuses and profit changed rather than remaining stable; and if performance is measured in terms of profit per head then the rise in the share of bonuses in total wages cannot be explained in terms of incentives. The ability of workers to acquire a greater share of rents would seem to be the main explanation.

Focusing on total wages (regular wage *plus* bonus), how did their distribution change over the period? Its CV does rise over time, suggesting some movement away from egalitarianism, nevertheless a CV of 29 per cent in 1991 is still very low. The legendary iron rice bowl would seem to be only chipped rather than broken.

Figures 4.1a and 4.1b present the density functions of regular wages and bonuses for the whole sample in order to examine how their distribution changed over the period. The density functions are presented only for 1986 and 1991 for clarity. To facilitate cross-comparison the variables are measured relative to their respective annual means, and the density distributions are estimated by kernel smoothing (Silverman, 1986). The most obvious features of Figures 4.1a and 4.1b are, first, the striking difference in the density functions of regular wages and bonuses and, second, an increase in their dispersion. The first establishes the point that bonuses are not simply a mark-up on regular wages and that two are determined differently. Both in 1986 and 1991, regular wages are concentrated in the narrow interval (0.5–1.5) around the mean (equal to 1) and their modes and means coincide. The reforms increase their dispersion, but only within the narrow interval. In contrast, the density function for bonuses is heavily skewed with a short fat left tail. The main affect of the reforms is to further skew the density function to the left, raising the per centage of enterprises with low bonuses.

Turning to the issue of differences in regular wages and bonuses in profit-making and loss-making enterprises, Figures 4.2a and 4.2b present for the whole period (1986–91) the density functions of the ratio of individual regular wages (or bonuses) to the sample mean regular wage (or bonuses) for the year. The striking conclusion from the density functions is that loss-making not only makes a difference to bonuses but also to regular wages. In the case of regular wages, the density function for loss-makers is to the left of that for profit-makers and its mode is located at 0.3 (1 represents the mean wage for the whole sample). The contrast between profit-makers and loss-makers is even more striking in the case of bonuses. Although positive, bonuses in loss-making are considerably lower than those in profit-making enterprises.

To indicate trends in employment and other variables, Table 4.3 presents the growth rates of employment, real output, real wage rate (deflated by the urban price index) and the index of nominal capital stock to labour ratio. No data on hours of work are available. However, the ratio of overtime pay in the total wage bill for SOEs is low and fluctuates very little over time (see SSB, 1993, p. 105). All variables rise steadily over the period, except for an unexpected

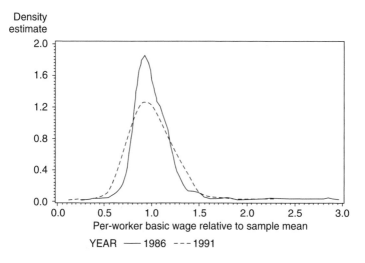

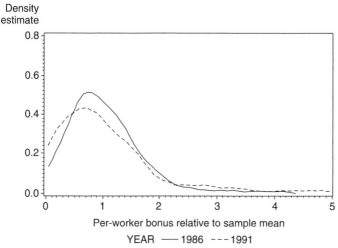

Figure 4.1   Density estimates of regular wages and bonuses, 1986 and 1991
a   Per-worker basic wage (automatic bandwidth)
b   Per-worker bonus (automatic bandwidth)

drop in the mean real regular wage rate in 1989, which is compensated by a large rise in 1990. While the real output growth is high 10 per cent per year, the employment growth is low 2.3 per cent per year. As we shall see later, the estimated elasticity of employment with respect to output is low. Measured in terms of a rise in output per worker, the reforms seem to have been successful in reducing the numbers of surplus employees in the state sector. However,

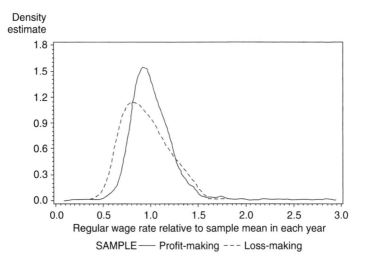

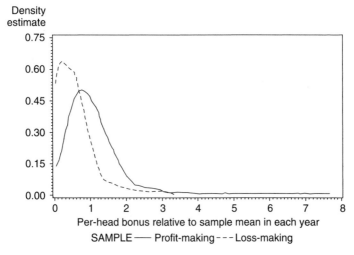

Figure 4.2   Density estimates of regular wages and bonuses for profit- and loss-makers, 1986 and 1991
a   Regular wage rate (automatic bandwidth)
b   Per-head bonus (automatic bandwidth)

since the rise in output per worker is accompanied by a sharp rise in the capital labour ratio (nominal rather than real), at least a part of it would seem to be due to the substitution of capital for labour, which has been encouraged by privileged access of the state sector to loans from the banking system.

Table 4.3 Employment, real output, real wage and capital labour ratio (growth rates), 1986–91[a]

	1986–7	1987–8	1988–9	1989–90	1990–1	Average 1986–91
Employment	4.1	2.7	1.6	0.6	2.5	2.3
	(451)	(353)	(961)	(1144)	(419)	
Real output	14.1	10.4	3.5	1.6	21.6	10.0
	(397)	(413)	(855)	(1228)	(550)	
Real total wage	4.4	5.0	–1.5	11.3	4.1	4.6
	(301)	(381)	(867)	(115)	(324)	
Real regular wage	0.7	3.0	–1.5	13.0	3.1	3.5
	(1739)	(677)	(996)	(116)	(444)	
Real bonus	39.2	34.6	8.1	9.5	28.6	23.3
	(331)	(882)	(883)	(769)	(847)	
Capital per head	130.2	146.2	163.1	179.4	214.3	16.5
1986 = 100	(117)	(128)	(114)	(105)	(112)	

Notes:
a All figures are in percentage terms.
b Figures in parentheses are coefficients of variation.

Specification of estimating equations

The purpose of this section is to outline the analytical framework for specifying and interpreting the estimation equations for the regular wage rate, bonus per head and employment. Since the enterprise data provide no information on the composition of enterprise labourforce, we assume all workers in an enterprise to be alike: they receive the same regular wage and bonus and have the same preference.

Regular wages

Our preliminary hypothesis is that regular wages are largely determined with reference to the official job–wage matrix, and therefore differences in regular wages across enterprises depend mainly on enterprise-specific factors such as the skill composition of the labourforce, industry and the size designation of enterprise (large and medium, or small). A particular issue of interest is whether regular wages also depend on the financial performance of enterprise. The following components-of-variance equation is used to analyze the determinants of the regular wage rate:

$$W_i = \alpha_i + \beta_i + \gamma Z_i \qquad (4.1)$$

W_i denotes the nominal regular wage rate for the ith enterprise, i the mean nominal regular wage rate for the whole state sector (not just the sample) in the province where the enterprise is located. α_i represents enterprise-specific fixed effects and Z_i denotes some measure of financial performance, such as profits and revenue. The mean provincial regular wage rate encapsulates wage determinants common to all SOEs in the province, including inflation compensation. The provincial mean is chosen in preference to the national or the industry mean, for two reasons. First, most SOEs in the sample are under the control of provincial rather than the central government, and the details of the job–wage matrix which structures regular wages are decided by provincial or municipal government in the light of local conditions. Second, in the Chinese context, the industrial classification of an enterprise is generally less important than the government tier controlling the enterprise. We take Z_i to represent quasi-rent per worker (R_i), equal to value added per worker (V_i) *minus* the mean provincial regular wage rate: ($V_i - W_i$). We have chosen quasi-rent rather than profit as the measure of financial performance because the latter excludes the component of regular wages linked to financial performance. As an explanatory variable, quasi-rent suffers from the well known problem of simultaneity bias, which we address by using instrumental variables (indicated below). Given that we are dealing with an economy in flux, we allow coefficient γ on quasi-rent to vary over time, by specifying it as the sum of a common factor γ_0 and a variable component, γ_t (captured by coefficients on a set of slope dummies, γ_{1991} is set equal to 0). The equation for the regular wage rate in levels is:

$$W_{it} = \alpha_i + \beta_{it} + (\gamma_0 + \gamma_t)R_{it} + \varepsilon_{it} \tag{4.2}$$

ε_{it} is used throughout to denote the error term.

Bonuses

We analyze the determination of bonuses per head in terms of a non-co-operative game following the structure set out in Binmore, Rubinstein and Wolinsky (1986). The assumptions are as follows. Bargaining is informal, yearly rather than long-term and individualistic rather than collective and takes place in a deterministic environment. Agreement is reached when it is acceptable to a majority of the labourforce, or the median worker. Workers are concerned only with the total wage rate and their individual risk of lay-off, which is zero for a large majority of state sector employees. The lay-offs which there are in the state sector rather than being random are targeted on a small minority, those lacking appropriate skills and employees at the end of their employment contract. Employment is assumed to be determined by the enterprise management within the constraints imposed by the government. The regular wage rate and employment are already known. The size of bonus per head may have an adverse effect on employment, but we assume this to be sufficiently small to be of concern to most employees, an assumption which we test in the employment equation. Therefore the median employee's utility function has only the total wage rate (*TW*) as argument: U(*TW*), as in Oswald (1993). As standard in wage bargaining models, *U* is assumed to be linear in *TW* and increasing.

In the event of disagreement, the management does not pay any bonus to workers who, in turn, withdraw co-operation. On the grounds of not being credible on a large scale, we disregard market options which the reforms have provided to the two parties, such as quitting the enterprise on workers' part and the replacement of 'insiders' by 'outsiders' on managers' part. What motivates the two sides to reach an agreement is the additional utility, which for workers is bonuses per head ($B = TW - W$). The utility level of the management, scaled in terms of per worker, is a linear function of profit per worker, $\pi = (V - TW)$; V represents value added per worker. In the event of no agreement, profit per worker is π_0, which is assumed to be less than p because of non-co-operation by the labourforce.

The bonus per worker is the solution to the following Nash product:

$$\max_W \gamma \log(TW - W) + (1 - \gamma)\log(V - TW - \pi_0) \qquad (4.3)$$

γ represents the bargaining power of workers and $(1 - \gamma)$ that of the management, $(V - TW)$ and π_0 are profit per worker with and without the agreement. The solution is:

$$B = \gamma(V - W) - \gamma\pi_0 \qquad (4.4)$$

$(V - W)$ is quasi-rent per worker, the pie to be divided, and γ the quasi-rent-splitting parameter. Two sets of issues need to be addressed before estimating an equation based on (4.4). First, the bilateral bargaining model for the determination of bonus makes sense only when quasi-rent per worker is non-negative and not less than bonus per worker. That is, only when the enterprise is profit-making: $\pi = L \{V - (W + B)\}$; 0. In the case of loss-making enterprises, of which there are a substantial number in the sample (Table 4.2), the determination of bonus also involves the government, which has to under-write losses. This issue does not arise when the wage bargaining model is applied to market economies, but it is central in a transitional economy such as the Chinese. We apply the bargaining framework to profit-making enterprise only and examine the pattern of bonuses in loss-making enterprises separately.

The second set of issues concerns estimation and arise due to the form in which wage data is reported. The enterprise data provide only the total wage bill, total bonus and employment. Total regular wages are calculated by subtracting total bonuses from the total wage bill, and both the regular wage and bonus per head are calculated by dividing the respective totals by employment. Given the possibility of measurement errors, we use average provincial regular wage rate as proxy for the individual regular wage rate. Quasi-rent per worker in (4.4) is measured as in (4.2).

We assume that bargaining parameter γ in (4.4) may vary over the sample period and write it as $\gamma_0 + \gamma_t$, the former represents the common factor and latter the time-varying component. Moreover, as π_0, the pay-off for the management in the event of no agreement, is not observed, we subsume it under the enterprise-specific component α_i. The basic estimated bonus equation for profit-making enterprises in levels is:

$$B_{it} = \alpha_i + (\gamma_0 + \gamma_t)R_{it} + \varepsilon_{it} \qquad (4.5)$$

B_{it} and R_{it} are per-head bonuses and quasi-rent for the ith enterprise at the t-th period, respectively. For loss-making enterprises, rather than formulating a model of bonus determination, we simply examine the factors determining the pattern of bonuses, in particular whether they are affected by the size of losses, by means of the following components-of-variance equation:

$$B_{it-} = \alpha + \eta(R_{it-}) + S_i + H_i + P_i \qquad (4.6)$$

B_{it-} and R_{it-} represent per-head mean bonus and quasi-rent in the sub-sample of loss-making enterprises in the t-th year, S_i is the size dummy (large or medium and small); H_i is the industry dummy; P_i is the province dummy.

Employment

We are interested in two questions. First, how does enterprise employment respond to output and to the wage rate, and whether the responses have changed over the period? Second, given the rising importance of bonuses, does employment respond differently to bonuses than it does to regular wages? The employment equation is derived on the supposition that output is produced from three factors – labour, capital and intermediate inputs (raw material and inputs). Rather than deriving the equation from a production function, we proceed in terms of (4.7) which may be regarded as a log-linear approximation to an employment demand equation. Aside from the enterprise-specific constant (α_i), the logarithm of employment in the ith enterprise is related to real output (Q_i), the regular wage (W_i), bonus (B_i), intermediate input price (M_i), all in logs and enterprise-specific. Capital user cost (C) is assumed to be constant across the state sector:

$$L_i = \alpha_i + \sigma Q_i + \phi W_i + \psi B_i + \rho M_i + (\phi - \psi - \rho)C \qquad (4.7)$$

The coefficient on C represents the restriction that the sum of employment elasticities with respect to factor prices sum to zero, which follows from the homogeneity of the cost function. This restriction implies that the equation is invariant to the common deflator used to index wages and other factor prices. σ, which is usually taken to represent returns to scale, is, following the argument in Akerlof (1981), interpreted here as an indicator of the size of pool of surplus employees or of effort on the part of the management to diminish the pool.

Turning to issues which arise in the estimation of (4.7), both the regular wage rate and bonus per head are calculated by dividing respective totals by employment. To correct for the spurious negative correlation this introduces, we use instrumental variables (specified below). Real output, Q, is supplied by the enterprise data, as are total materials and energy cost but not quantities. Intermediate input price is calculated in terms of cost per unit of real output, which means that price change cannot be separated from changes in quantity, which is not an important issue here. Specifying the user cost of capital poses even greater problems in the Chinese than in market economies. As is usual (Card, 1990; Abowd and Lemieux, 1993), we omit it and assume that its effect on employment is picked up by the enterprise-specific constant term and year dummies.

As in the estimating equations for the regular wage rate (4.2) and bonus (4.4), we allow slope coefficients to vary over time, but only those on the regular wage rate and output (σ, ϕ). Since the estimation of time-varying coefficients on four explanatory variables (excluding capital user cost) in (4.7) runs into the problem of non-identification, we assume that the coefficients on bonus and intermediate input price do not vary over time. The basic estimated equation in levels is:

$$L_{it} = \alpha_i + (\sigma_0 + \sigma_t)Q_{it} + (\phi_0 + \phi_t)W_{it} + \psi B_{it} + \rho M_{it} + \varepsilon_{it} \qquad (4.8)$$

Estimating framework and results

For panel-data estimation, the chapter uses the version of 'Generalized Method of Moments' (GMM) due to Arellano and Bond (1991), which is a more efficient extension of the first-difference instrumental variables method for dynamic fixed-effect models suggested earlier by Anderson and Hsiao (1981). The basic idea is to first-difference the equations to eliminate the firm-specific effect, and use all values lagged two period onwards as instruments for the lagged dependent variable and other explanatory variables presumed to be endogenous. The validity of the method depends crucially on the errors in the level equation being serially uncorrelated – i.e. the absence of the second-order serial correlation in the first-difference equation, which is tested by a statistic.

All equations for panel samples are estimated in first differences with or without time dummies. The equations for regular wages (4.2) and for employment (4.4) are estimated for the balanced panel of all enterprises and for the unbalanced panel of profit-making enterprise. The huge variation in the numbers of loss-making enterprises (Table 4.2) rules out panel-data estimation for the sub-sample. The bonus equation is estimated only for profit-making enterprises, and a separate OLS equation is estimated to explain the pattern of bonuses in loss-making enterprises. All but one equation allow time-varying slope coefficients. These are entered as the sum of a fixed and a variable component and the latter is captured through slope dummies. We use instrumental variables whenever there is a risk of simultaneity bias, and these are indicated with the results.

We have data for six years 1986–91; taking first-differences loses one year. We lose an additional year in the case of the employment equation (4.7), owing to the use of the regular wage rate lagged two periods as an instrument for the current regular wage rate. Apart from estimated coefficients and their standard errors which are robust to general heteroscedasticity, we report five test statistics for each equation. Three of these are Wald-tests of joint significance of all explanatory variables excluding year dummies, of year dummies and of slope dummies to capture time variation in coefficients. The fourth is the test statistic for lack of second-order serial correlation in the first-difference residuals, which is asymptotically distributed as $N(0,1)$ under the null of no-second-order serial correlation, and is robust to general hetero-scedasticity. The fifth is the Sargan general misspecification-test in its two-step version, which we use to test the validity of instruments.

Results are presented for regular wages (W), bonuses (B) and employment (L), in order.

Regular wages

The estimated equations are variations on the first difference of (4.2):

$$\Delta W_{it} = \beta \Delta_{it} + \gamma_0 \Delta R_{it} + \gamma_t R_{it} - \gamma_{t-1} R_{it-1} + \Delta \varepsilon_{it}; \gamma_{1991} = 0 \qquad (4.9)$$

All variables are in current prices. γ_0 is the component of the quasi-rent coefficient common to all years (from 1987 to 1991), and γ_t is the change in the coefficient in the t-th year and γ_{1991} is set equal to zero. Three variants of (4.9) are estimated: with and without year dummies and with and without time-varying components γ_t. Each variant is estimated for the whole sample and the sub-sample of profit-making enterprises, but not for loss-makers because of the huge variation in their numbers over the period (Table 4.2). Δ_{it} is the mean regular wage for all of the state sector in the province where the enterprise is located. It is assumed that quasi-rent per head, R, is endogenous. The instruments set includes the current period per-head capital, the ratios of sales to output and of intermediate inputs to output, enterprise-specific output price index (calculated from the enterprise data), industry and time dummies, and current values of all the exogenous variables in the equation. The results are reported in Table 4.4. The instrument set is valid according to the Sargan-test except when both year and slope dummies are left out.

The most striking feature of the results in Table 4.4 is the very high coefficient on the mean provincial regular wage rate (b). The inclusion of year dummies (columns (2), (5)) reduces β, as does the inclusion of a time-varying coefficient on quasi-rent. Moreover, comparing the same specification, β is lower for the sub-sample of profit-making enterprises than for the whole sample. Nevertheless, it is always very high. What the results establish is that year-to-year changes in regular wages in state enterprises in a province move in close tandem. The coefficient on quasi-rent, whether constant or variable over

Table 4.4   Estimated regular wage equation (dependent variable = regular wages per head)

		All			Profit-making		
		(1)	*(2)*	*(3)*	*(4)*	*(5)*	*(6)*
1	Constant	0.0033*	0.0018	0.0048*	0.0048*	0.0023*	0.0073*
		(0.0013)	(0.0013)	(0.0019)	(0.0016)	(0.0014)	(0.0020)
2	Mean provincial	0.9712*	0.8120*	0.8590*	0.9379*	0.7549*	0.7619*
	regular wage rate	(0.0887)[b]	(0.1119)	(0.1161)	(0. 0951)	(0.1193)	(0.1231)
3	Quasi-rent p/h[a]	0.0018	0.0019	0.0008	0.0099	0.01 39	0.0165}
	(Constant component)	(0.0048)	(0.0055)	(0.0090)	(0.006 2)	(0.0077)	(0.0090)
4	Quasi-rent p/h			0.0007			−0.0027
	(1986 component)			(0.0072)			(0.0089)
5	Quasi-rent p/h			−0.0090			−0.0156
	(1987 component)			0.0076			0.0081
6	Quasi-rent p/h			0.0019			−0.0058
	(1988 component)			(0.0066)			(0.0066)
7	Quasi-rent p/h			0.0061			−0.0018
	(1989 component)			(0.0059)			(0.0050)
8	Quasi-rent p/h			0.0136*	0.0063		
	(1990 component)			(0.0052)			(0.0039)
9	Year dummies	No	Yes	No	No	Yes	No
10	Wald-test for joint	120.79*	52.76*	289.19*	98.63*	43.92*	269.48*
	significance	(2)	(2)	(7)	(2)	(2)	(7)
11	Wald significance-test		26.63*			28.44*	
	for year dummies		(5)			(5)	
12	Wald significance-test			24.03*			25.98*
	for slope dummies			(5)			(5)
13	Wald significance-test	0.15	0.12	24.08*	2.48	3.24	26.15
	for quasi-rent p/h	(1)	(1)	(6)	(1)	(1)	(6)
14	Second order serial	0.284	0.227	0.065	0.663	0.530	0.366
	correlation-test N(0,1)	(514)	(514)	(514)	(448)	(448)	(448)
12	Sargan-test for	70.14*	47.66	43.79	70.30*	43.70	43.14
	instrument validity	(39)	(35)	(34)	(39)	(35)	(34)

Notes:

a Quasi-rent per head (p/h) is treated as endogenous. The instruments set includes current period per-head capital, the ratios of sales to output and of intermediate costs to output, enterprise-specific output price index, industry and year dummies and current values of all the exogenous variables in the equation.

b Standard errors, in parantheses, are robust to general heteroscedasticity.

* Significant at 5% or less.

the period, is insignificant in terms of the *t*-test, though the slope dummies are jointly significant in terms of the Wald-test (columns (3), (6)). But they may simply be acting as proxies for the omitted year dummies. The conclusion is that whatever positive impact quasi-rent may have on regular wages is too weak and irregular to reject the null hypothesis that the financial performance of enterprises has no impact on regular wages. This conclusion holds for both the whole sample and the sub-sample of profit-making enterprises. However,

Table 4.5   Estimated bonus equation (dependent variable = bonus per head)

		(1)	(2)	(3)
1	Constant	0.0086*	0.0084*	0.0087*
2	Quasi-rent p/h[a]	0.0409*	0.0793*	0.0768*
3	Quasi-rent p/h		–0.0434*	
4	Quasi-rent p/h		–0.0431*	–0.0405
5	Quasi-rent p/h		–0.0323*	
6	Quasi-rent p/h		–0.0236	
7	Quasi-rent		–0.0055	
8	Year dummies	yes	no	yes
9	Wald-test for joint significance	11.14*	28.08*	20.66*
10	Wald significance-test for year	582.41*		513.46*
11	Wald significance-test for		19.34*	6.54*
12	Second order serial correlation-test	0.448	–0.498	–0.347
13	Sargan-test for instrument validity	49.40	39.45	38.47

Notes:

a Quasi-rent per-head (p/h) is treated as endogenous. Instruments set includes current period per-head capital, ratio of sales to output, ratio of intermediate input costs to output, enterprise-specific output price index, industry and time dummies, and current values of all the exogenous variables in the equation.

b Standard errors, in parentheses, are robust to general heteroscedasticity.

* Significant at 5% or less.

it is interesting to note that, comparing the same specification, γ_0 is always higher for profit-making than for all enterprises.

Bonuses

The estimated bonus equations for profit-making enterprises are based on the first difference of (4.5):

$$\Delta B_{it} = \gamma_0 \Delta R_{it} + \gamma_t R_{it} - \gamma_{t-1} R_{it-1} + \Delta \varepsilon_{it}; \gamma_{1991} = 0 \qquad (4.10)$$

Bonuses in a few cases are zero, which may introduce a truncated sample bias. We have rechecked results using the two-stage procedure, but the estimates are not affected. Results for three specifications are reported in Table 4.5. The instrument set for quasi-rent is the same as in the case of regular wages (4.9). Specification (1) includes year dummies but excludes the time-varying components of the quasi-rent coefficient, γ_t, and vice versa in Specification (2). The coefficient γ_0 is significant in both, but almost twice as high in the second as in the first. In Specification 2 all γ_ts are negative and rise steadily over time; moreover all (except γ_{1990}) are significant. To determine whether they are significantly different from each other (or the time pattern of change), the following iterative procedure is used. Starting with γ_{1990}, the Wald-test is used to test whether it is significantly different from γ_{1991} (which by assumption is zero), and similarly for earlier years. Grouping the years for which γ_ts are insignificantly different, the period 1986–91 divides into two sub-periods: 1986–8 and 1989–91. Specification (3) rests on this two-part division and includes year dummies.

Focusing on Specification (3), the main result is that, in contrast to regular wages, bonuses depend on quasi-rents per worker, and the implementation of the bonus system underwent an important change in 1989 when this dependence became much stronger. The coefficient 0.0768 for the sub-period 1989–91 is more than twice that for 1986–8 (0.0363). The elasticity of bonus with respect to quasi-rent per worker at the means is 0.354 for 1989–91 and 0.33 for 1986–8. These are much higher than elasticity of bonus with respect to profit per worker that Freeman and Weitzman (1987) find for Japan. We also tested Specification (3) with a square term in quasi-rent, but the coefficient on it is insignificant.

To examine the pattern of bonuses in the sub-sample of loss-making enterprises (4.6) was estimated in levels by means of OLS, as the sub-sample is too unbalanced to be treated as a panel:

$$B_{it-} = \alpha + \eta(R_{it-}) + S_i + H_i + \varepsilon_{it} \qquad (4.11)$$

B_{it-} and R_{it-} represent mean bonus and quasi-rent for the sub-sample in each year. The benchmark for the size dummy, S_i, is small and medium enterprises, and the benchmark for the industry dummies H_i is the measuring instruments industry. The results are presented in Table 4.6 and all the test statistics are

Table 4.6 Pattern of bonuses in loss-making enterprises (dependent variable = bonus per head)[a]

1	Constant		0.0159 (0.0207)[b]
2	Quasi-rent p/h		0.0029 (0.0064)
3	Dummy for large-size enterprises;		0.0150 (0.0037)*
	Benchmark: small- and medium-size		
4	No. of industry dummies: 28;	Coal	0.0315 (0.0136)*
	of which significant: 6.	Electricity	0.0551 (0.0203)*
	Benchmark: the instruments	Petroleum	0.0431 (0.0207)*
	industry	Ferrous metals	0.0335 (0.0150)*
		Non-ferrous metals	0.0419 (0.0174)*
		Electrical machinery	0.0300 (0.0152)*
5	No. of province dummies: 19, of which significant: 11		–
6	Adjusted R^2		0.6491
7	Durbin–Watson statistics		1.681
8	First order autocorrelation		0.153
9	F-test statistics		13.231
10	No. of observations		325

Notes:
a OLS estimates.
b Standard errors in parentheses.
* Significant at 5% or less.

satisfactory. The main result is that there is no relation between quasi-rent per worker (negative) and bonuses. Bonuses are higher in large than in medium and small SOEs. Provincial location seem to be more important than the industry to which the enterprise belongs. The industrial classification is important only in the case of coal mining, electricity, petroleum, ferrous and non-ferrous metals and electrical machinery. A particular feature of these industries is that their prices have been more strictly controlled by the government. Presumably, the comparatively high bonuses in these enterprises is a compensation for this.

Employment

Two sets of employment equations are estimated, and these are variations on the first difference of (4.8):

$$\Delta L_{it} = \sigma_0 \Delta Q_{it} + \sigma_t Q_{it} - \sigma_{t-1} Q_{it-1} + \phi_0 \Delta W_{it} + \phi_t W_{it} - \phi_{t-1} W_{it-1} + \psi \Delta B_{it}$$
$$+ \rho \Delta M_{it} + \Delta \varepsilon_{it}; \sigma_{1991}, \phi_{1991} = 0 \tag{4.12}$$

All specifications include year dummies, and (4.12) is estimated with or without lagged employment and for the whole sample and the sub-sample of profit-making enterprises. Output Q is in real terms (supplied by the data) and the factor prices (W, B and M) are deflated by the urban residents' price index. As the equation is in logs, observations with zero bonuses (65 out of 3084) are excluded. It is assumed that output, the regular wage and the bonus all suffer from the simultaneity bias. The instruments set includes output, per-head regular wages and bonuses lagged two period backwards, current period levels and the first differences of mean provincial regular wages and bonuses, per-head capital stock and intermediate inputs price index. For equations including lagged employment, instrument set also includes lagged employment lagged two period onwards. In all cases the instrument set passes the Sargan-test. As the regular wage lagged two is used as an instrument, (4.12) is estimated for the data for five years (1987–91) rather than for six as in the case of regular wages and bonuses.

The results are reported in Table 4.7. All four specifications were first estimated with four time-variable components each for σ_ts and ϕ_ts ($t = 1987, \ldots$ 1990) without year dummies. Using the same iterative procedure as in the case of the equation for bonuses, σ_ts and ϕ_ts were grouped on the basis of whether or not they are significantly different from each other. Having thus reduced their numbers, the specifications were re-estimated with time dummies.

The following three common features of the results stand out. First, while the elasticity of employment with respect to the regular wage is negative and significant, the elasticity of employment with respect to bonus is insignificant. Notwithstanding the 'soft budget constraint' Chinese SOEs respond to regular wages in the same way as firms in a market economy would – though, it seems, less strongly (for a survey of empirical estimates of the wage elasticity, see

Table 4.7   Estimates of employment equations (dependent variable = log employment)[a]

		Full Sample		Sub-sample	
		(1)	(2)	(3)	(4)
1	Constant	–0.162*	–0.0631	–0.1568*	–0.0852*
2	Lagged log employment		0.4232*	0.3870*	
3	Log regular wage	–0.2916*	–0.2098*	–0.3118*	–0. 2337*
4	Log regular wage	0.0884*	0.0435	0.0829*	0.0454
5	Wage elasticity of employment	–	–0.3637	–	–0.3812
6	Log output	0.3367*	0.2399*	0.4059*	0.2729*
7	Log output	–0.0150*	–0.0077	–0.0193*	–0.0102*
8	Output elasticity of employment	–	0.4159	–	0.4452
9	Log bonus	–0.0266	–0.0161	–0.0371	–0.02 88
10	Log intermediate input price	0.0558*	0.0406*	0.0890*	0.055 1*
11	Year dummies	yes	yes	yes	yes
12	Wald-test for joint-significance	40.02 (6)*	148.11 (7)*	31.73*	113.31 (7)*
13	Wald significance-test for year	24.19*	6.63	27.28*	12.96*
14	Wald-test for Regular wage	6.01 (1)*	1.85 (1)	5.40 (1)*	2.55 (1)
	joint significance Output	11.73 (1)*	3.04 (1)	14.92 (1)*	4.43 (1)
15	Second order serial correlation test	–1.018	–1.535	0.369	–1.362
16	Sargan-test for instrument validity	42.85	54.00	36.97	50.17

Notes:

a All equations assume that regular wages, bonuses and output are endogenous. Instruments set includes all lags on the regular wages, bonuses and output from t-2 backwards, the current period levels and the first differences of per-head capital stock, the provincial mean regular wages and mean bonuses and current values of all other exogenous variables.

b Standard errors, in barckets, are robust to general heteroscedasticity.

* Significant 5 per cent or less.

Hamermesh, 1993). But the result for bonuses mean that they are not perceived as a component of the labour cost, rather they are a share of quasi-rent. In this respect, bonuses are akin to the 'profit share' in Weitzman (1986), and different from the firm-specific supplement to the 'outside wage' in Nickell and Wadhwani (1991), which has a negative effect on employment. An important implication of the finding is that the steady rise in bonuses relative to profit per worker over the period (Table 4.2) has not had an adverse impact on employment in the state sector. This finding could be interpreted in terms of an 'efficient contract' but such an interpretation is not appropriate either in the Chinese context or theoretically (Manning, 1987).

Second, the output elasticity of employment is less than 1 and low, below 0.45 in all cases. Like firms in market economies, Chinese SOEs exhibit increasing returns to labour, but more pronounced. Using Akerlof's (1981) analogy of 'jobs as dam sites', the low elasticity may be interpreted in terms of the extent of labour slack or the efforts of the management to reduce the slack.

Third, comparing identical specifications (columns (1) and (3) or (2) and (4)), profit-making enterprises have both a higher regular wage elasticity (in absolute terms) and a higher output elasticity than for the whole sample. They are more responsive to changes in regular wages, and have either less labour slack or are less under pressure to reduce labour slack. Both interpretations are possible, but the former is more likely, given their greater sensitivity to changes in regular wages.

Turning to the differences in the results for specifications with and without lagged employment. Comparing columns (1) and (2) or (3) and (4), the addition of lagged employment raises the elasticities with respect to the regular wage (in absolute terms) and output. But it makes the variable components of the elasticities (σ_ts and ϕ_ts) insignificant. Unlike in the case of bonuses (Table 4.5), variations in coefficient on explanatory variable over time (in this case, σ_ts and ϕ_ts) are less important. However, focusing on specifications without lagged employment (columns (1) and (3)), it is interesting to note that 1989 is the 'watershed', the year when both the wage elasticity of employment (in absolute terms) and coefficient of bonus on quasi-rent rise (Table 4.5, column (3)).

Conclusions

Our main conclusions are as follows:

(1) Regular wages and bonuses (the two principal components of total wages) are determined differently. Regular wages in SOEs in a province follow closely in tandem and do not depend on the financial performance of enterprises, though regular wages in loss-making enterprises tend to be lower than those in profit-making enterprises. The differentials in regular wages seem to be small (Table 4.2). The determination of regular wages does not appear to have changed over the period 1986–91 (Table 4.4).

(2) In contrast to regular wages, bonuses in profit-making enterprises depend on the financial performance of enterprise, and the bargaining power of workers (measured in terms of the share of quasi-rent accruing to them) has risen over time. However, a simple interpretation of the rise in the share of bonuses in total wages in terms of efficiency wage or incentive payment would seem to be doubtful. The reforms have had a tangible impact on the determination of bonuses. Compared to regular wages, they differ more across enterprises (see Figures 4.1 and 4.2).

(3) However, bonuses in loss-making enterprises are predominantly positive and bear no relation to the scale of losses. Bonuses in such enterprises depend on the provincial location of enterprise and also industry. Nevertheless, bonuses in loss-making enterprises tend to be significantly lower than those in profit-making enterprises.

(4) The employment elasticity with respect to regular wages is negative and significant, though on the lower side compared to those found for market economies.

(5) The elasticity of employment with respect to bonuses is insignificant. Bonuses are not perceived as a component of labour cost and their rise over time has had no adverse impact on employment.
(6) The elasticity of employment with respect to output in SOEs is low compared to those found for market economies. This can be interpreted as both a confirmation of labour slack and a sign of a progressive reduction in the pool of surplus employees in SOEs.

Notes

* We would like to thank Richard Freeman and Andrew Oswald for comments and suggestions during the preparation of this chapter, which arises from the ESRC-funded project on 'Public Finance in Transitional Economies – China and Poland'.

Bibliography

Abowd J. A. and T. Lemieux (1993) 'The Effects of Product Market Competition on Collective Bargaining Agreements: The Case of Foreign Competition in Canada', *Quarterly Journal of Economics*, 108, November, pp. 983–1014.
Akerlof G. A. (1981) 'Jobs As Dam Sites', *The Review of Economic Studies*, 48, January, pp. 37–49.
Anderson, T. W. and C. Hsiao (1981) 'Estimation of Dynamic Models with Error Components', *Journal of the American Statistical Association*, 76, pp. 598–606.
Arellano, M. and S. Bond (1991) 'Some Tests of Specification for Panel Data: Monte Carlo Evidence and an Application to Employment Equations', *Review of Economic Studies*, 58, pp. 277–97.
Binmore, K., A. Rubinstein and A. Wolinsky (1986) 'The Nash Bargaining Solution in Economic Modelling', *Rand Journal of Economics*, 17 (2), Summer, pp. 176–88.
Card, D. (1990) 'Unexpected Inflation, Real Wage, and Employment Determination in Union Contracts', *American Economic Review*, 80, pp. 669–88.
Chen, K., H. Wang, Y. Zheng, G. H. Jefferson and Rawski, T. G. (1988) 'Productivity Change in Chinese Industry: 1953–1985', *Journal of Comparative Economics*, 12, pp. 570–91.
Child, J. (1994) *Management in China During the Age of Reform* (Cambrigde: Cambridge University Press).
Dollar, D. (1990) 'Economic Reform and Allocative Efficiency in China's State-Owned Industry', *Economic Development and Cultural Change*, 34, pp. 89–105.
Freeman, R. and M. Weitzman (1987) 'Bonuses and Employment in Japan', *Journal of the Japanese and International Economies*, 1, pp. 168–94.
Fu, G. Z., A. Hussain, S. Pudney and L. Wang (1993) 'Unemployment in Urban China – An Analysis of Survey Data From Shanghai', *Labour*, 7, Spring, pp. 93–123.
Groves, T., Y. Hong, J. McMillan and B. Naughton (1994) 'Autonomy and Incentives in Chinese State Enterprises', *Quarterly Journal of Economics*, 109, February, pp. 183–209.
Hamermesh, D. S. (1993) *Labour Demand* (Princeton: Princeton University Press).
Jefferson, G. H., T. G. Rawski, and Y. Zheng (1992) 'Growth, Efficiency and Convergence in China's State and Collective Industry', *Economic Development and Cultural Change*, 40 (2), pp. 239–66.
Korzec, M. (1992) *Labour and the Failure of Reform in China* (London: Macmillan).
Krueger, A. B. and L. H. Summers (1988) 'Efficiency Wages and the Inter-industry Wage Structure', *Econometrica*, 59, pp. 259–94.

Manning, A. (1987) 'An Integration of Trade Union Models in a Sequential Bargaining Framework', *The Economic Journal*, 97, March, pp. 121–39.

Nickell, S. and S. Wadhwani (1991) 'Employment Determination in British Industry: Investigations Using Micro-Data', *Review of Economic Studies*, 58, pp. 955–69.

Oswald, A. (1993), 'Efficient Contracts are on the Labour Demand Curve', *Labour Economics*, 1, pp. 85–113.

Silverman B. W. (1986) *Density Estimation for Statistics and Data Analysis* (London: Chapman & Hall).

State Statistical Bureau (SSB) (1993) *China Statistical Yearbook 1993* (Beijing: State Statistical Bureau).

State Tax Bureau (STB) (1993) 'The Chinese Tax System' (Beijing: State Tax Bureau), mimeo.

Takahara, A. (1993) *The Politics of Wage Policy in Post-Revolutionary China* (London: Macmillan).

Weitzman, M. (1986) 'Macroeconomic Implications of Profit Sharing', in S. Fischer (ed), *NBER Macroeconomic Annual 1986* (Cambrigde, Man.: MIT Press).

Woo, W. T, W. Hai, Y. Jin and G. Fang (1993) 'How Successful Has Chinese Enterprise Reform Been?', Institute of Governmental Affairs, University of California, Davis.

5
Reform of China's Energy Sector: Slow Progress to an Uncertain Goal

Philip Andrews-Speed

Introduction

The national energy industries are of great importance in China for three reasons. First, they comprise a large part of the industrial sector of the economy.[1] Secondly, the continued growth of China's economy and improvement of people's standard of living will require a sustained increase in energy supply. Thirdly, and in part as a consequence of these first two factors, China's government would appear to accord the energy sector a special status with respect to other industries. Energy is treated more as a strategic issue than as a commodity.

Reform of state-owned enterprises (SOEs) commenced in the mid-1980s and has taken a number of successive forms (Broadman, 1995). Despite the often patchy and slow implementation of these various reform measures, a number of trends can be observed. Managers have obtain greater autonomy and production decisions are taken lower down the chain of command (Rawski, 1995). Market-entry barriers for collectives and private enterprises have been reduced or removed, and price reform has permitted competition in some sectors (Lee and Nellis, 1990; Rawski, 1995).

Though wholesale privatization has seldom occurred, shares have been issued, either free to employees, on local stock exchanges or, more recently, on international exchanges. An increasingly popular, and effective, approach to reform has involved forced mergers between SOES, with consequent job losses. Better-performing companies absorb underperformers – a state sector equivalent of a take-over (*Far Eastern Economic Review*, 1996a). A recent innovation has been the sale of bankrupt state companies through public tender (*China Economic Review*, 1996).

The aims of this chapter are to show how the government's treatment of the energy sector contrasts with the treatment of much of the rest of the economy and to question if this approach is likely to yield the desired results. The 'desired results' or strategic objectives probably include (see, for example, SPC, 1995):

- improving and enlarging the capacity to produce and deliver energy
- improving the productive efficiency and financial performance of the energy sector
- reducing the intensity of energy consumption
- reducing pollution

This chapter looks first at the reforms of the energy industries to date, analyzes their recent performance and, finally, evaluates the reforms against the objectives listed above.

Reform of the energy industries to date

Reform of the energy sector in any transition or developing economy should address three major issues: energy pricing, the structure and ownership of the energy industries and the regulation of investment and competition. This section examines the changes in these components of China's energy industries since the mid-1980s.

Energy prices

Of the three issues mentioned above, pricing is, arguably, the most important and the easiest to address in the short term. From the point of view of the energy industry in a rapidly expanding economy the aim should be to raise prices of domestically produced energy to levels close to long-run marginal cost (LRMC) or border prices so that the necessary investment can be made in new capacity (Gray, 1995). Against this purely economic imperative needs to be set the Chinese government's desire to promote social equity, or rather to reduce the risk of social unrest resulting from massive price rises.

A second dimension of price reform is the degree to which the government releases its control on energy prices and allows the market to take over. Before the mid-1980s, all forms of energy in China, and indeed most goods of any kind, were sold at prices which were set by the government at levels which generally lay well below either international prices or long-run marginal cost. In the last ten years China has made considerable progress in raising energy prices, but rather less in releasing control over energy prices. The prices of the major energy commodities have risen to levels close to LRMC or border prices, but each commodity has been treated in a different manner with respect to how prices are determined.

Coal

In the case of coal the government instituted reform of three types in the mid-1980s: for the first time the price depended on the quality of the coal; the controlled price for coal was increased in local currency terms so that it quadrupled in ten years; and an increasing percentage of coal output could be sold at market prices (Dorian, 1994). By 1994 nearly all coal was being sold through wholesale markets, and prices in coastal provinces were close to international levels (Todd and Zhang, 1994; Thomson, 1996).

Despite this 'liberalization', coal for power stations is still sold at subsidized prices. Consumer prices for coal remain controlled in some cities, but administrations are under pressure to raise prices in order to allow the suppliers to make profits. For example, Beijing planned to double the consumer price for coal briquettes during 1997 (*China Daily*, 1996a).

Oil

From 1983 to 1993 the price of crude oil and of oil products followed a path similar to that of coal. Before 1983 crude oil was sold at a single, state-controlled price, regardless of quality. In 1983 the government introduced a three-tier pricing system. Oil produced within the quota was sold at two fixed prices according to a set proportion. Any oil produced in excess of the quota could be sold at freely negotiated prices. By 1993 the low-price quota level had been removed and two-thirds of the crude was being sold at decontrolled rates close to or exceeding international levels (Troner and Miller, 1995; see Table 5.1).

The price reforms for crude oil were also applied to oil products, and by the early 1990s two-thirds of products were being sold at high or unregulated

Table 5.1   Crude oil pricing, 1983 and 1994

The three-tier pricing system for crude oil introduced in 1983, using official exchange rates at that time

	Y RMB/tonne	US $/tonne	Proportion (%)
Low-price quota crude	100	5.60	66
High-price quota crude	555	31.00	28
Decontrolled	–	–	6

The crude oil-pricing system introduced in 1994, using official exchange rates

	Oilfield	Y RMB/tonne	US $/tonne
In-plan crude	Daqing	745	11.68
	Shengli	684	10.60
Out-of-plan crude	Daqing	1310	20.30
	Shengli	1220	18.90
Mean price		950–1000	14.75–15.50

Note: Shengli crude is heavier than Daqing crude; these two crudes are used as standards for the other crudes in China.
Source: Troner and Miller (1995).

prices (Troner and Miller, 1995). Regional price differences for product were dramatic. In a booming coastal province like Guangdong, 90 per cent of product was being sold at market prices. In poorer, inland regions, all but 35 per cent of product was sold at fixed, subsidized prices (*Far Eastern Economic Review*, 1994).

In 1994 a new system of oil pricing was introduced as part of a package of measures designed to constrain imports and stimulate domestic output. The key element of the new scheme was that all crude oil and products would be sold at prices fixed by the government. The market was abolished, and the average price for crude was close to international levels. Further, the varying quality of the crude was acknowledged by establishing two crude standards, Daqing and Shengli. As international prices for crude oil and products rose dramatically during 1996, the fixed prices in China were raised only modestly.

Thus, having introduced an oil-pricing system which was evolving rapidly towards being an open market, the government has made a rapid retreat. Prices are now tightly controlled and respond only sluggishly to the international markets. This dislocation between domestic and international prices resulted in a severe shortage of gasoil in China in the early part of 1997.

Gas

Natural gas is available in relatively few parts of China and, until recently, was sold close to the location of production. Prices varied greatly between provinces and were set well below LRMC. For example the producer price in Jilin Province was less than US\$ 1.00/mmBTU[2] in 1993.

The years 1994–7 saw substantial increases – for example, to about US\$ 4.00/mmBTU in Jilin Province. An even higher price may soon be charged to Beijing consumers for gas piped from the Ordos Basin, 900 km away.

Electricity

The system for pricing electricity in China has long been and remains extremely complex (World Bank, 1994) and detailed review is beyond the scope of this chapter. However it is clear that the average consumer price has increased from levels around or below RMB Y 0.10/kWh[3] in the 1970s and early 1980s to greater than RMB Y 0.25/kWh (US\$ 3.0c/kWh) in 1994 (World Bank, 1994; Kosmo, 1987; Schramm, 1993). In coastal provinces where coal is the predominant feedstock and new power stations are being constructed with foreign funds, final consumer prices in 1994 lay in the range RMB Y 0.32–0.45/kWh (US\$ 4.0–5.5c/kWh). Average prices in Guangzhou reached RMB Y 0.60–0.70/kWh (US\$ 7.5–8.7 c/kWh) in 1995 (Yang and Yu, 1996). Consumer prices in such regions may now lie close to long-run marginal costs (LRMC), but elsewhere they still fall short (World Bank, 1994; Yang and Yu, 1996). This deficiency is expressed in the continued shortage of capital for the construction of new generating and transmission capacity.

Structure and ownership

As with pricing, the reforms to China's energy industries with respect to structure and ownership have taken diverse routes. Common strands are the continuing high degree of state ownership,[4] the lack of separation of regulator and operator, and the survival of large companies which hope to compete internationally.

Coal mining

The coal industry has seen the most dramatic reform in the energy sector in terms of ownership of production (SPC, 1995) (see Figure 5.1). From less than 10 per cent in 1970, the contribution of collective and private mines has risen to more than 40 per cent of total coal output. This rise has been at the expense of both central ('state') and local government mines, and has occurred over a period when total output of coal increased fourfold. In essence, the state (in the form of the Ministry for Coal Industry) has focused its attention on the largest mines and deposits on which the long-term supply of the country will be based. Small and technically easy deposits have been left to the collective and private enterprises. This has allowed the state to invest heavily in mechanization of existing large mines and the exploitation and development of new ones.

Within the state sector, the Ministry for Coal Industry is both operator and regulator, and has an effective monopoly on the largest deposits. Only in 1996 was the possibility of foreign investment in coal mines formally announced (*Mining Journal*, 1996). Despite its modest contribution to national coal output, the Ministry for Coal Industry has an annual output approaching

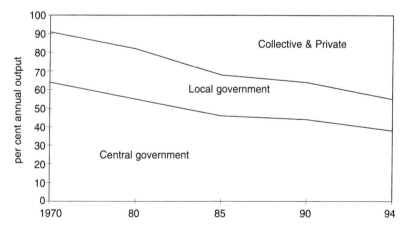

Figure 5.1   Changing ownership of coal production, 1970–94
Source: SPC (1995).

500 million tonnes per year and is the largest producer in global terms. In 1997 it announced an internal reorganization in order to be able to compete internationally (*China Daily*, 1997).

Oil and gas exploration and production

Oil and gas exploration and production remains firmly in the hands of two national oil companies: CNPC[5] for onshore and CNOOC[6] for offshore. Each act as both regulator and operator in their respective territories. Foreign companies may undertake exploration and production under production-sharing agreements with the appropriate company. The Ministry of Geology and Mineral Resources (MGMR) has long been involved in the exploration for hydrocarbons, but this role has only recently been formalized by the creation of a third state oil company, the China National Star Petroleum Corporation.

A limited degree of management autonomy has been granted to individual oilfield administrations within CNPC, though strategic decisions require the support of the centre. Certain oilfields, particularly the smaller, less strategic ones, have become financially independent from the centre, making a profit or loss on their own account. One symptom of this is that the service companies which are part of the individual oilfield companies have been allowed to behave more competitively, and enter bids to provide services in other oilfield regions. The oilfield companies have also sought funding for the development of small fields from local provincial enterprises.

Both CNPC and CNOOC are seeking to become players on the international stage. CNPC has been particularly active, with exploration, production and service projects in Latin America, South-East Asia, the Middle East and the CIS. The principal aim would seem to be to secure crude oil reserves for China's refineries and to make foreign exchange profits from service provision. In this respect CNPC's activities are closely allied to government objectives.

Oil refining and marketing

Oil refining and the marketing of oil products has remained largely in state hands, though the nature of that ownership has changed over the last thirteen years. Sinopec was created in 1983 to take-over and bring order to the refining, petrochemicals and domestic marketing sectors. Only a few refineries and service stations were left in the hands of CNPC or provincial governments.

From the late 1980s this simple structure evolved to one where each player sought to increase its involvement upstream or downstream. Sinopec began to trade internationally, encroaching on the business of the state trader, Sinochem. At the same time Sinochem moved upstream into refining, and CNPC and CNOOC downstream into refining, trading and marketing. Both CNPC and Sinopec lacked trading expertise and so each formed joint ventures with Sinochem (Troner and Miller, 1995).

In addition to this diversification by the main state companies, provincial and local companies were being created to import, market and distribute product. Foreign companies succeeded in entering the sector with oil storage, third-party processing and product imports. In the field of refinery construction at least eight foreign joint-venture (JV) projects were under discussion by 1993 (*Petroleum Economist*, 1995). Sinopec had lost its control over the market and thus its guaranteed level profits.

This trend towards market liberalization was brought to an abrupt halt. The level of oil imports was rising rapidly resulting in stockpiles of product in the north and of crude in the south. In April 1994 the government acted by banning all import rights for both crude and product. Over the following months it instituted a series of reforms designed to increase central control over the importation and marketing of oil products (Troner and Miller, 1995; Tang and Fesharaki, 1995). The dominant positions of Sinopec and Sinochem were re-established in the refining and marketing sector and in the trading sector respectively (*Energy Compass*, 1995; Tang and Fesharaki, 1995). In one step the government reversed ten years of reform. Since that time no new refinery construction deals have been reached with foreign companies.

Electricity production and supply

The state owns some 80 per cent of China's power industry, measured in terms of output. The remaining 20 per cent is owned by collectives and a small number of private investors. Private ownership will remain negligible until new power stations built with foreign funds come onstream during the next few years.

Two phases of reorganization in 1991 and 1993 led to a structure in which the Ministry of Electrical Power owned the power groups and companies throughout China, except in Guangdong, Hainan and Tibet (World Bank, 1994; Yang and Yu, 1996). By this time the number of separate high-voltage grids was down from thirty-two in the early 1980s (Nakajima, 1982) to thirteen. A modest diversification of ownership has been achieved through the emergence of a small number of quasi-independent Chinese power producers such as the Huaneng Group which were only partly owned by the Ministry for Electrical Power. Further diversification has started through the local and international stockmarkets (Yang and Yu, 1996).

As with the oil and coal industries, the Ministry of Electrical Power has acted as both regulator and operator. A new electricity law which came into effect in 1996 implicitly calls for the abolition of this Ministry, and for the creation of a state power company separate from a regulatory agency. The new State Power Corporation was officially inaugurated in January 1997. It remains to be seen whether or not regulatory powers are indeed wrested from the state company.

The government has been appearing to promote foreign investment in power generation. However, procedural delays and inconsistent policy objectives has resulted in a very small number of completed deals. Despite the ever-growing list of suitors and projects, construction has started on less than ten plants and only four have been completed, all in Guangdong with Hong Kong investors (Li and Dorian, 1995).

A distinctive feature of the power industry in China is the high degree of decentralization from the centre to both provincial and county levels within the state administration. This has its roots in the development of the nation's power industry which was fostered at a local level and in the absence of large, regional grids. At present, the approval of central government is required for the construction only of those plants with a capacity greater than 50 MW (Yang and Yu, 1996).

The regulation of investment and competition

Entry barriers

Until the late 1970s competition in any sector of China's economy was effectively non-existent and major investment decisions were made by the central government. The 1980s saw the emergence of competition in certain sectors as the barriers to entry were removed, and private and collective enterprises were allowed to enter market, invest and sell.

China's energy sector has not experienced such liberalization. Entry barriers to parts of the energy industry are clearly higher than for other sectors because of the requirements for capital, technology and skills. However the Chinese government has shown a consistent determination to erect high entry barriers to most segments of the nation's energy sector and to maintain the monopoly powers of the state enterprises. This has applied to those activities with naturally high entry barriers related as capital requirements, as well as to those with low natural entry barriers such as marketing and trading. A study of entry barriers to forty industries in China ranked the four main energy industries in the top nine with respect to magnitude of entry barriers, upstream petroleum being in the highest position (Yang, 1996). The effects of this are clearly seen in the limited number of participants in most segments of China's energy industries, as described above.

Foreign investment

The task of regulating investment and limited competition falls to the Ministry or State Company in the respective industry, which is at once both regulator and operator: the Ministry for Coal Industry, the Ministry of Electrical Power, CNPC, CNOOC and Sinopec. Foreign companies which wish to invest in the energy sector must seek the permission of these authorities who are at the same time a competitor and near-monopolist with interests to protect.

This failure to separate the operator from the regulator has been an important factor in determining the slow pace of foreign investment in China's energy industry. The notable exception has been offshore petroleum exploration and production. In this case CNOOC had no 'turf' to protect as it was created specifically to encourage foreign investment, a task it has carried out creditably well (Andrews-Speed and Gao, 1996).

A further consideration has been the perception of the Chinese government concerning the nature of the requirements of their energy sector. In the power and refining industries, the government believes that their principle requirement is for capital rather than technology or management. With the possible exception of nuclear power stations, the perception seems to be that technology can be purchased directly from suppliers, and that the management skills of major international companies are not required. As a result, foreign funds for the power industry have been raised through loans and stockmarkets (Li and Dorian, 1995; Yang and Yu, 1996). The principal requirement of the upstream petroleum industry onshore would appear to be capital. However, China's offshore industry in the 1980s clearly lacked technical capacity and foreign involvement was assiduously promoted. In contrast foreign investment in the onshore petroleum industry has come late and at a slow pace due to the unattractive nature of the opportunities on offer.

The year 1996 marked a watershed in China's power industry as the first open tender for a BOT (Build–Operate–Transfer) power project was implemented. This resulted in a consortium led by EdF of France being selected to construct the Laibin B power station in Guangxi province. A second round of bidding was held for the construction of a power plant in Changsha, Hunan Province, with a closing date for tenders of 25 September 1997. This period has also been characterized by a substantial increase in the level of interest shown by foreign companies in forming ad hoc joint ventures with Chinese counterparts for the construction of power plants throughout China.

No such breakthrough has occurred in the refining industry. Indeed official announcements during 1997 seemed to confirm that the Chinese government would not permit foreign investment in *new* refineries in the foreseeable future. Investment in upgrades, however, would be allowed.

Regulation of Chinese companies

With respect to large Chinese state companies, the incumbent monopolists have been successful at either excluding or severely limiting competition; this remains the case in upstream petroleum, power and large coal mines. In the one case where competition from sister companies began to emerge, in oil refining and marketing, the 'regulator', Sinopec, lost control and drastic measures had to be taken in 1994 to re-establish its monopoly. Indeed, this action highlights the inability of the current 'regulators/monopolists' to respond to competition as either competitors or regulators.

This regulatory weakness also has expression at the local level. As described above, local enterprises have long been involved in coal mining and power generation. More recently they have invested in refineries, in the development of small oil fields and even in petroleum exploration. The regulation of such activities appears to be left to local governments at provincial or lower levels which lack the skill or the will to regulate closely. Symptoms include a poor quality of output (coal, oil products and power), inefficient exploitation of resources (coal, crude oil), unreported output (crude oil, coal), low thermal efficiency (power) and poor environmental and safety standards (coal, oil refining and power) (Yang and Yu, 1996; Wirtshafter and Shih, 1990; *Mining Journal*, 1994; *China Daily*, 1996b, 1996c; Thomson, 1996).

The recent performance of the energy industries

The previous section has shown that although energy prices have undergone significant reform, the structure of the energy industries has changed little and competition has emerged only to a limited degree. The following section attempts an evaluation of the recent performance of China's energy sector under the following headings: production and delivery of energy; technical and management performance; and financial performance.

The production and delivery of energy

Coal dominates China's energy industry. It accounts for 75 per cent of the country's primary production and about 80 per cent of power generation. Crude oil is the other main source of primary energy, and hydroelectricity contributes most of the remaining 20 per cent of the power generation (DRI World Energy Service, 1996; SPC, 1995). Natural gas provides just 2 per cent of primary energy output. The nuclear power sector is currently very small, but growing fast.

A key component in the ability of each of the major energy industries to deliver energy to the end-user is transport. The crude oil and the coal reserves are concentrated in the north of the country as are oil refineries, while the focus of economic growth lies currently in the south and east (World Bank, 1995). Inefficiencies and capacity shortfalls create major bottlenecks for the transport of most forms of energy, which are largely independent from problems in the production of energy.

The consumption of energy in China has risen rapidly as the economy has grown. Domestic supply has failed to keep pace with demand. As a result, China has become a net importer of energy (DRI World Energy Service, 1996) and a significant proportion of demand for energy remains unsatisfied. To a certain extent this shortfall has been alleviated by falling energy intensity. However, China's energy intensity is relatively high among Asian countries (even in purchasing power parity or ppp terms) and the rate of decline shows signs of easing (DRI World Energy Service, 1996).

The impending shortfall in domestic energy supply has been recognized by the Chinese government. Annual investment in fixed assets in the state energy industries has remained close to or in excess of 20 per cent of the total for SOEs, at a time when this total continues to rise (SSB, 1996a). Despite this generosity, the level of investment in the energy sector fails to deliver the required capacity and output.

The rate of growth of both capacity and output of electrical power is greater than for the other main energy sectors (SPC, 1995). Despite this success, an estimated 10 per cent of demand is unsatisfied and more than 100 million citizens have no access to electricity (Yang and Yu, 1996). Ambitious plans to enlarge the nation's generating and transmission capacity are constantly revised downwards as funds for investment in new or upgraded capacity fail to materialize. To combat the bottlenecks in coal transportation, the industry is emphasizing the construction of power stations near the coal mines in the north of the country (Li and Dorian, 1995).

From having been a major net exporter of oil since the 1970s, China has recently become a net importer of oil and the level of these imports is set to rise (DRI World Energy Service, 1996). The domestic output of crude oil appears to be reaching a plateau close to or just above 3000 mb/d[7] (Troner and Miller, 1995; DRI World Energy Service, 1996). Great effort and expense has been devoted to maintaining production levels in the old fields in the east, and modest incremental production is being achieved from new hydrocarbon provinces offshore and in the far north west. Despite the involvement of foreign companies, exploration success in these regions has not matched expectations, and China is facing considerable difficulty replacing its reserves of crude oil. Forecasts for production levels in the year 2000 are frequently adjusted downwards.

The capacity of the oil refining industry is increasing steadily. Reliable figures are difficult to obtain, and estimates of China's total refining capacity lie in the range 3400–4000 mb/d (*Petroleum Intelligence Weekly*, 1996; *Weekly Petroleum Argos*, 1996; *China Daily*, 1996b). Of greater significance is the apparent major increase of throughput achieved during the last few years,[8] which has to some extent compensated for the poor performance in the early 1990s. This rate of increase of throughput will have to be maintained if the target of 4500 mb/d for the year 2000 is to be achieved.

As the level of net oil imports rises, the key unresolved issue relates to the split of these imports between crude oil and products. Should China decide to, and be able to, create significant additional refining capacity, regardless of the potential excess in East Asia, then imports will be mainly in the form of crude. Should China fail to, or decide not, to devote the funds to building this capacity, the imports will be in the form of product.

China has one of the world's largest reserves of coal and the country is investing heavily in new capacity (British Petroleum, 1996; *Petroleum Economist*, 1995). The coal industry appears to be the most successful in satisfying domestic demand. Output has grown and has, in general terms, kept pace with consumption, allowing the country to raise its modest level of exports (SPC, 1995), but this promising facade hides a number of serious problems. Though the absolute level of coal reserves is high, the reserves *per capita* are less than the world average (Bryne, Shen and Li 1996). Further, the apparent balance of domestic supply and consumption hides a high level of unsatisfied demand (Thomson, 1996). Further challenges in the coal industry relate to transport and pollution.

Technical and management performance

Systematic and reliable data on the technical and management performance of China's state enterprises is not readily available. Some inferences may nonetheless be drawn from published statistics.

The only statistic available which is common to all energy sectors is productivity per man-day. In this respect the power industry has shown the greatest improvement, with production per man-day tripling from 1980 to 1994 (Figure 5.2a). Over the same period the coal industry showed a 100 per cent increase in productivity, and the oil industry (production and refining) a 50 per cent increase.

On the technical front, the performance of the power industry has been less impressive. The average fuel consumption has declined from 398 g/kWh[9] in 1985 to 382 g/kWh in 1994 (Figure 5.2b). The slow rate of decline is caused by the continued predominance of small, inefficient plants (Yang and Yu, 1996). The capacity utilization of thermal plants remains obstinately at a high level of about 60 per cent (SPC, 1995) and transmission and distribution losses are estimated to lie in the range 16–20 per cent (Yang and Yu, 1996).

Investment in new capacity in the coal industry has been accompanied by a rapid increase of mechanization, especially in the state mines (Ministry of Energy, 1992). At the same time, hundreds of thousands of workers have been laid off or transferred to other industries (Wu and Li, 1995).

Estimates of the capacity utilization of oil refineries are handicapped by a lack of reliable data, especially concerning total capacity (see above). Some sources suggest that 1995 saw a massive increase in utilization from 79 per cent to 87 per cent (*Petroleum Intelligence Weekly*, 1996). Regardless of the exact figures, a significant improvement has been achieved through debottlenecking and upgrading.

Assessing the technical performance of an upstream oil industry is difficult, even in an open economy. Figures for exploration success rate, reserves replacement costs or production costs are not readily available in China. Average well production for oil lies at about 60 b/d (Skrebowksi, 1997) and anecdotal evidence suggests that average production rates are not increasing. A key issue is whether China is succeeding in finding new, commercially viable reserves to replace current production. Official figures for discovered reserves are notoriously unreliable and difficult to interpret. The government announced that total discoveries in 1995 amounted to about 5 billion barrels of 'reserves' (*Petroleum Economist*, 1996a, 1996b). Assuming that these 'reserves' equate to resources in place, a recovery factor of 25 per cent would yield reserves equivalent to an annual production of 3400 mb/d. This is marginally larger than present levels of domestic supply and consumption, but significantly lower than consumption forecast for the year 2000 of 4600 mb/d. The key unknowns concern the commercial viability of these 'reserves' and the extent to which the government is prepared to continue subsidizing the exploitation of non-commercial accumulations. One statistic

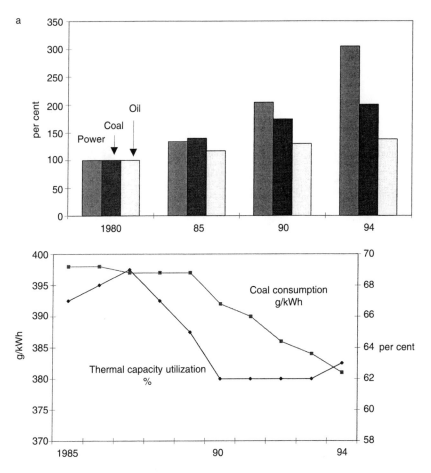

Figure 5.2 Technical and management performance of China's energy industries, 1980–94
a Changes in productivity (physical output per man day), 1980–94 (1980 = 100)
b Technical performance of the power industry, 1985–94
Sources: SSB (1995b); SPC (1995).

which may be indicative of underlying problems is the increase of manpower in the petroleum production industry of about 50 per cent from 1990 to 1994 (SSB, 1995a). During this period crude oil output increased by only 6 per cent.

Financial performance

Assessing the financial performance of Chinese companies is fraught with problems relating to both the accounting conventions and the accuracy and transparency of the reporting. Despite these problems the official, published

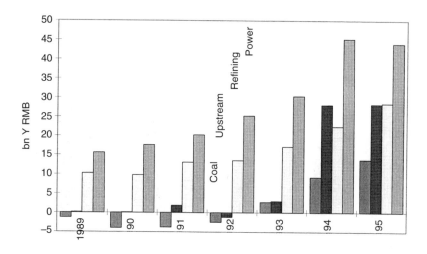

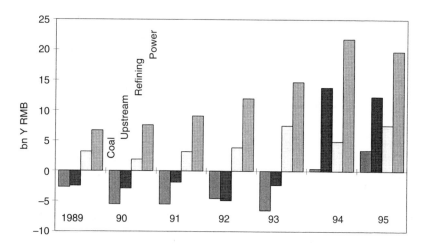

Figure 5.3   Financial performance of individual energy industries
a   Pre-tax profits (billion Yuan RMB)
b   Post-tax profits (billion Yuan RMB)
c   Ratio of pre-tax profits to total assets
d   Ratio of post-tax profits to gross revenue
Sources: SSB (1990, 1991, 1992, 1993, 1995b, 1996b).

figures appear to carry some interesting information concerning the energy industries (Figure 5.3).

The major energy industries all saw improvement in the level of pre-tax and post-tax profits during the period 1989–95. Most notably the coal and

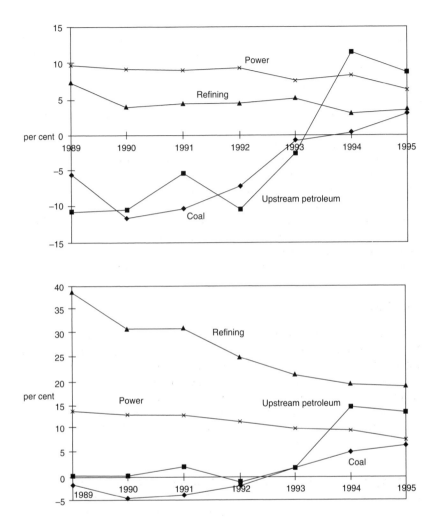

Figure 5.3   (continued)

upstream petroleum industries recorded post-tax profits for the first time in 1994. The coal industry sustained this improvement through 1995, though the profits of the upstream petroleum industry fell back slightly.

The picture concerning profitability is less consistent. The upstream petroleum and coal industries have shown improved profitability when measured against revenue and total assets. In contrast, the refining and power industries have reported a sustained but erratic reduction in profitability over the same period.

Although a detailed interpretation of these figures is not possible, it is noteworthy that the improved profitability of the coal and upstream petroleum industries occurred at a time of rising energy prices. These industries were able to sell their output at significantly higher prices, while input costs may not have risen by the same amount. At the same time, the power and refining industries were squeezed between rapidly rising input costs, on the one hand, and output prices which were not allowed to rise as fast, on the other.

The positive cash flows and relatively respectable profitability of the energy industries is consistent with the picture that the largest state companies are performing better than the small and medium-sized ones (Nolan, 1996). In the light of the comments on technical and managerial performance, it is not evident that the profitability data bears close relation to productive efficiency. Rather, pricing seem to have been the main determinant. However, the ability of the coal industry to sustain its improvements through 1995 may reflect the more radical nature of the technological and management reforms being undertaken in this sector compared to the upstream oil industry.

Conclusions

This chapter has examined the reform of China's energy industries to date and their performance. The energy sector stands in stark contrast to much of the rest of the country's industry. Steps taken to improve productivity and financial performance in other industries have not been applied with the same rigour to the production and distribution of energy. In particular control of much of the energy sector remains centralized, and high entry barriers have resulted in little diversification of ownership and a paucity of competition.

Security of supply

With respect to security of supply, the domestic energy industries are clearly failing to satisfy demand, with the exception of the coal industry. In the case of domestic crude oil supply the main cause is geological, and a miracle is required to reverse the trend of ever-increasing net oil imports. The question is to what extent the government wishes to subsidize domestic exploration and production in order to save foreign exchange.

The domestic output of petroleum products is constrained by the capacity and performance of the refineries. The government faces the choice of whether to improve security of supply by continuing to increase refinery capacity at a time of capacity excess in East Asia or by importing ever-larger quantities of product.

The shortage of electrical power is potentially more damaging than the shortfalls in the other forms of energy, as electricity is not easily substituted or imported. The critical bottleneck appears to be the administrative process for approving projects and, in the case of those funded domestically, the release of funds. The delegation of approval authority to local governments for small projects has at least partially alleviated this problem in the short term.

Productive efficiency and financial performance

Evidence for improved technical performance and productive efficiency in the energy sector is scant, and suggests that improvements have been modest. This situation is likely to be exacerbated where budgetary constraints are soft and where regulatory authority is delegated to local levels. The financial performance of China's energy industries appears to be largely determined by the prices of inputs and outputs, and this makes it difficult to identify the financial impact of any improved productivity.

Reducing energy intensity and pollution

High energy prices and the availability of energy-saving technology are the key to reducing intensities of energy consumption, although the latter issue has not been addressed in this chapter. Considerable progress has been made to raise energy process to levels approaching long-run marginal costs or border prices. However, substantial subsidies still exist because, though prices have risen, they are still controlled and often at a local level. As a result prices across the country fail to keep up with inflation or international prices, and locally prices are well below these levels.

The reduction of pollution from the energy industry depends on reducing the intensity of energy consumption, on effective regulation and on the energy companies having the funds to invest in improved plant. As mentioned above, further progress is required to raise energy prices and drive down energy intensities. Decentralization may stimulate investment, but the quality of environmental and technical regulation in China would appear to decline as authority is delegated to local governments. Finally, considerable improvements in financial performance are required if the energy companies are to have the funds to invest in cleaner plant.

The need for restructuring

An industry should be restructured to achieve specific economic aims, and not just to satisfy political or ideological aspirations. Can China's energy industry rise to the challenges described above in its present structure? The frequent references to the need for reform in the Chinese press suggests that the government realizes that some form of restructuring is required. The recent electricity laws and regulations may herald action at last.

Reform of China's energy sector need not, and probably should not, involve wholesale privatization. The legal framework is now in place for a sustained programme of commercialization and corporatization of the energy indus-tries. A pessimistic prognosis is that failure to act soon is likely to result _ either in the exacerbation of the shortage of energy or in an increased requirement for the government to provide financial support to the energy sector.

Implications for foreign investors in China's energy sector

The outlook for foreign investors, rather than suppliers and banks, does not appear to be bright. With the possible exception of the offshore oil industry and nuclear power, China's energy industries appear to want only money and equipment. At present they are successfully sourcing significant quantities of both with little recourse to foreign direct investment. The government regards the energy sector as being of great strategic importance and therefore significant foreign direct investment is likely to remain unwelcome and tightly controlled until circumstances force dramatic policy and structural changes.

Notes

1. In 1995 the energy industries accounted for 13 per cent of the gross output value, 24 per cent of the pre-tax profits and 15 per cent of the workers in China's whole industrial sector (SSB, 1996a).
2. mmBTU = million British Thermal Units.
3. kWh = kilowatt-hour.
4. State ownership in the energy sector remains higher than for most other industrial sectors in China, with the exception of tobacco, iron and steel, and electronics (Goldstein, 1994).
5. China National Petroleum Corporation.
6. China National Offshore Oil Corporation.
7. mb/d = millions barrels/day.
8. Refinery throughput increased from 2090 mb/d in 1992 to 2950 mb/d in 1995 (SPC, 1995).
9. g/kWh = grams of coal equivalent per kilowatt-hour.

Bibliography

Andrews-Speed, C. P. and Z. Gao (1996) 'China's Legal Regime for Foreign Participation in its Upstream Petroleum Industry: The Foreign Oil Company's View', *Journal of Energy and Natural Resources Law*, 14, pp. 161–78.

British Petroleum (1996) *BP Statistical Review of World Energy 1996* (London: British Petroleum, 1996).

Broadman H. G. (1995) 'Meeting the Challenge of Chinese Enterprise Reform,' *World Bank Discussion Paper*, 283 (Washington DC: World Bank).

Bryne, J. B. Shen and X. Li (1996) 'The Challenge of Sustainability. Balancing China's Energy, Economic and Environmental Goals', *Energy Policy*, 24, pp. 455–62.

China Daily (1996a) 'Prices of Cooking Fuels to Double in Beijing', *China Daily CBnet*, 3 December.

China Daily (1996b) 'SPC Limits Refinery Construction', *China Daily CBnet*, 23 December.

China Daily (1996c) 'Coal Industry Urged to Cut Losses', *China Daily CBnet*, 27 December.

China Daily (1996d) 'Sinopec Expands Reforms', *China Daily CBnet*, 2nd December.

China Daily (1997) 'Reform in Store for Coal Industry', *China Daily CBnet*, 3 January.

China Economic Review (1996) 'Bankrupt Firms for Sale', 6 December, p. 4.

Dorian, J. P. (1994) *Minerals, Energy and Economic Development in China* (Oxford: Clarendon Press).

DRI World Energy Service (1995) *World Energy Forecast Report: Asia/Pacific* (Lexington: DRI/McGraw Hill)

Economist Intelligence Unit (1996) *EIU Country Forecast, China, 2nd quarter 1996* (London: *The Economist*).

Energy Compass (1995) 'China Sideswipes Products Markets as it Hacks Away at Imports', 10 February, p. 9.

Far Eastern Economic Review (1994) 'Energy: Not so Slick. Beijing Faces Tough Choices on Oil Policy', 7 April, pp. 66–8.

Far Eastern Economic Review (1996a) 'Urge to Merge. China Pins Hopes on Mergers to Save State Firms', 23 May, pp. 56–9.

Far Eastern Economic Review (1996b) 'China in Transition', 1 August, p. 23.

Goldstein, C. (1994) 'Mixed (or Mixed Up) Economy', in: F. Ching (ed.), *China in Transition* (Hong Kong: Review Publishing Company), pp. 50–4.

Gray, D. (1995) 'Reforming the Energy Sector in Transition Economies. Selected Experience and lessons', World Bank Discussion Paper, 296 (Washington, DC: World Bank).

Kosmo, M. (1987) *Money to Burn? The High Cost of Energy Subsidies* (Washington, DC: World Resources Institute).

Lee, B. and J. Nellis (1996) 'Enterprise Reform and Privatization in Socialist Economies', *World Bank Discussion paper*, 104 (Washington, DC: World Bank).

Li, B. and J. P. Dorian (1995) 'Change in China's Power Sector', *Energy Policy*, 23, pp. 619–26.

Mining Journal (1994) 'China Cracks Down on Mine Safety', 11 November, p. 339.

Mining Journal (1996) 'Investment in China's Coal', *Mining Journal*, 12 January, p. 25.

Ministry of Energy (1982) *Energy in China 1992* (Beijing: Ministry of Energy).

Nakajima, S. (1982) 'China's Energy Problems: Present and Future', *The Developing Economies*, 20, pp. 472–98.

Nolan, P. (1996) 'Indigenous and International Big Business in China', presentation to Chinese Economic Association, Annual Conference, London, December.

Petroleum Economist (1995) *China: Its Energy Potential* (London: *Petroleum Economist*).

Petroleum Economist (1996a) 'News in Brief', February, p. 42.

Petroleum Economist (1996b) 'News in Brief', April, p. 57.

Petroleum Intelligence Weekly (1996) 'Keen Appetite for Crude Follows Asia Refinery Expansion', 12 February, pp. 1–4.

Rawski, T. G. (1995) 'Implications of China's Reform Experience', *The China Quarterly*, 144, pp. 1150–73.

Schramm, G. (1993) 'Issues and Problems in the Power Sectors of Developing Countries', *Energy Policy*, 21, pp. 735–47.

Skrebowski, C. (1997) 'Coal Dominates but Gas Set to Make Inroads into Energy Sector', *Petroleum Economist*, February, p. 15.

State Planning Commission (SPC) (1995) *'95 Energy Report of China* (Beijing: State Planning Commission).

State Statistical Bureau (SSB) (1990) *China Industrial and Economic Statistical Yearbook 1990* (Beijing: China Statistical Publishing House).

State Statistical Bureau (SSB) (1991) *China Industrial and Economic Statistical Yearbook 1991* (Beijing: China Statistical Publishing House).

State Statistical Bureau (SSB) (1992) *China Industrial and Economic Statistical Yearbook 1992* (Beijing: China Statistical Publishing House).

State Statistical Bureau (SSB) (1993) *China Industrial and Economic Statistical Yearbook 1993* (Beijing: China Statistical Publishing House).

State Statistical Bureau (SSB) (1995a) *China Industrial and Economic Statistical Yearbook 1994* (Beijing: China Statistical Publishing House).

State Statistical Bureau (SSB) (1995b) *China Statistical Yearbook 1995* (Beijing: China Statistical Publishing House).

State Statistical Bureau (SSB) (1996a) *China Statistical Yearbook 1996* (Beijing: China Statistical Publishing House).

State Statistical Bureau (SSB) (1996b) *China Industrial and Economic Statistical Yearbook 1995* (Beijing: China Statistical Publishing House).

Tang, F. C. and F. Fesharaki (1995) 'China – Evolving Oil Trade Patterns and Prospects to 2000', *Natural Resources Forum*, 19, pp. 47–58.

Thomson, E. (1996) 'Reforming China's Coal Industry', *The China Quarterly*, 147, pp. 726–50.

Todd, D. and L. Zhang (1994) 'Ports and Coal Transfer: Hub of China's Energy Supply Policy', *Energy Policy*, 22, pp. 609–21.

Troner, A. and S. J. Miller (1995) *Energy and the New China. Target of Opportunity* (New York: Petroleum Intelligence Weekly).

Weekly Petroleum Argos (1996) 'China: Crude Imports Surge as Refiners Hit Record Runs', 9 September, p. 4.

Wirtshafter, R. M. and E. Shih (1990) 'Decentralisation of China's Electricity Sector: Is small Beautiful?', *World Development*, 18, pp. 505–12.

World Bank (1994) *China – Power Sector Reform: Toward Competition and Improved Performance*, Report 12929-CHA (Washington, DC: World Bank).

World Bank (1995) *'China – Investment Strategies for China's Coal and Electricity Delivery System'*, Report 12687-CHA (Washington, DC: World Bank).

Wu, K. and B. Li (1995) 'Energy Development in China. National Policies and Regional Strategies', *Energy Policy*, 23, pp. 167–78.

Yang, G.(1996) 'Barriers to Entry and Industrial performance in China', presentation to Chinese Economic Association, Annual Conference, London, December.

Yang, M. and X. Yu (1996) 'China's Power Management', *Energy Policy*, 24, pp. 737–57.

Part II

The Rural Sector:
Agriculture and Industry

6

Agriculture's Role in Economic Development: The Case of China*

Shujie Yao

Owing to unrealistic ambitions and poor foresight, many governments of the developing world have tried to industrialize their economies at such a high speed that agricultural growth is suffocated, resulting in low efficiency in industry and poor performance of the entire economy. In many countries, real outcomes contradict the initial policy objectives.

China provides a good example of this strategy. Before economic reforms began in the late 1970s, the government over-emphasized the development of capital-intensive industries at the expense of agriculture, light industry and services. The industrialization strategy resulted in poor agricultural production and low efficiency of the state-industrial sector. With better price and marketing incentives as well as institutional reform, especially the dismantling of the commune system, China has achieved better agricultural growth and industrial efficiency since 1978. One important reason for China's success during economic reforms is that policies have been designed to adjust the unbalanced development structure between agriculture and industry and to encourage farm production. On the one hand, the prices of many agricultural products were raised several times to increase the return to agricultural production. In the late 1980s, some commodities such as vegetables and livestock products were allowed to be marketed freely in the local markets. On the other hand, the rigid administrative controls imposed by the former commune system were scrapped to give farmers more freedom and choice in production and marketing.

China has experienced many economic cycles of booms and busts but it is interesting to note that most boom years were positively related to more favourable agricultural policies whereas all the poor years were negatively related to poor agricultural performance. Although economic growth has not been entirely determined by agricultural production, the Chinese experience indicates that agriculture has been an important driving force of the economy since 1949 even though the share of agricultural output in national income has been declining sharply over time.

In this chapter, the assessment of agriculture's role follows the conventional approach by dividing the contributions of agriculture into four different categories and examines these contributions in the Chinese economy since 1949. The four contributions proposed by Kuznets (1964) and discussed in Ghatak and Ingersent (1984) include (1) product contribution or the forward linkage effect; (2) market contribution or backward linkage effect; (3) factor contribution or inter-sectoral transfers; and (4) foreign exchange contribution. A descriptive analysis of these contributions is presented below.

To understand more precisely how agriculture has been driving the whole national economy, an econometric model is established to unveil the extent of linkages between agriculture and other economic sectors. As conventional econometric models using ordinary least square method (OLS) may yield spurious regression results if the time-series data are not co-integrated, a vector autoregression (VAR) model developed in Johansen and Juselius (1992) is particularly useful for this purpose. Based on a VAR model and time-series data for sectoral GDP indices over 1952–92, three co-integrated vectors are identified among five economic sectors in China, including agriculture, industry, transportation, construction and services.[1]

A weak exogeneity test is then conducted to identify the direction of causality for growth between different sectors. The results suggest that agriculture is weakly exogenous but all the non-agricultural sectors are not. This implies that the growth of agriculture caused the growth of non-agricultural sectors but the growth of the latter did not cause agriculture to grow over the data period. This finding is in agreement with the analyses in other studies (e.g. Won and Lin, 1992). It is a striking result and has important policy implications for China's entire development strategy.

A review of agriculture's role

This section discusses agriculture's contributions to economic development in China since 1949. It follows the conventional approach of examining agriculture's role in the four different aspects of product, market, factor and foreign exchange earning contributions. A more general discussion of these contributions can be found in Kuznets (1964) and Ghatak and Ingersent (1984).

Product contribution

Product contribution is usually measured by the size of agriculture in the national economy. By definition, the importance of agriculture declined steadily over time. In the early 1950s, agriculture accounted for almost 58 per cent of national income but by 1991 it accounted for less than 33 per cent. Over the period 1952–78, agriculture's share in total national income declined by 1.9 per cent per year (Table 6.1).

There are two main reasons for a declining share of agriculture in national income. One is the inevitable trend of economic development which requires a higher growth rate of non-agricultural sectors than agriculture as dictated by

Table 6.1 National income, by sector, 1952–91 (100 million yuan)

Year	National income at 1952 prices[a]	National income indices		As % of national income		
		Index total	Index per capita	Agri. (%)	Industry (%)	Others[b] (%)
1952	589	100.0	100.0	57.7	19.5	22.8
1960	1220	199.1	172.9	27.2	46.3	26.5
1965	1387	197.4	156.4	46.2	36.4	17.4
1970	1926	294.6	204.0	40.4	41.0	18.6
1975	2503	384.7	239.3	37.8	46.0	16.2
1980	3688	516.3	300.7	36.0	48.9	15.1
1985	7020	830.6	456.7	35.5	45.1	19.4
1991	16117	1286.4	646.7	32.7	47.8	19.5
Annual growth rates: Pre-reform period 1978/53		5.68	3.61	−1.89	3.29	−1.38
Annual growth rates: Reform period 1991/78		8.35	6.93	−0.02	−0.25	0.69

Notes:
a National income and indices are at constant 1952 prices.
b 'Others' includes all the other sectors of the national economy.
Source: SSB (CSYB, Chinese edition, 1992), pp. 34–35.

Engel's Law. Engel's law states that as personal disposable income grows as a result of economic development, consumers tend to spend a lower proportion of incremental income on agricultural products. In China, the Engel's law is verified by the very low income elasticities of food demand. For example, the income elasticities of cereals are close to zero or negative although the demands for animal products are more elastic (Table 6.2).

Another reason for slow agricultural growth is government policy which has discriminated against agriculture and the rural population. Before economic reforms, farmers were forced to deliver grains and other agricultural products to the state at very low prices. For example, the procurement prices of grains paid to farmers were less than half of the market prices before 1978 (Lardy, 1983; Yao, 1994). Since 1978, market liberalization, price reform and other policy measures more favourable to agriculture have stimulated agricultural growth. As a result, the declining rate of agriculture's share in national income was reduced to 0.02 per cent per annum in the reform period from 1.9 per cent before 1978 (Table 6.1). This is a powerful example of how government policies can affect agricultural growth.

Although the share of agricultural output in GDP tends to decline because of Engel's Law and government policy biased against agriculture, it is important not to overlook the critical importance of the product contribution of domestic agriculture to the maintenance of an adequate rate of economic growth. More importantly, it needs to be stressed that government policies

Table 6.2   Income elasticities of demand for agricultural products (1988 and 1952–88)

Agricultural products	Urban		Rural	
	Time series	Cross-section	Time series	Cross-section
Cereals	–0.20	–0.33	–0.06	0.15
Pork/beef/mutton	0.34	0.57	0.73	0.26
Poultry	1.66	0.93	1.48	2.16
Eggs	0.52	0.58	1.06	1.66
Fish	0.04	0.59	0.89	4.54

Sources: Data: SSB (CSYB, 1989) household income and expenditure data, estimates: World Bank (1991), p. 12.

deliberately designed to achieve unbalanced development against agriculture can result in poor overall performance of the entire economy. The comparison of economic performance between the pre-reform and reform periods in China potently supports this argument. It is obvious that economic performance was weak in the pre-reform period when agriculture was squeezed hard (through explicit and implicit taxation) to support industrial development. In addition, the institutional framework of the commune system and a set of other political and economic policies (e.g. grain self-sufficiency for every locality and the suppression of commercial activities in rural areas) had helped to suffocate agriculture. The more favourable policies for agriculture in the reform period have achieved better performance not only in agriculture but also in the rest of the economy, even though some bias against agriculture still persists (Yao, 1994; Bhalla, 1990).[2]

The importance of agriculture's product contribution is not only through the provision of food and other agricultural products for a huge population but also through its ability to provide huge amounts of raw materials for industrial production. In addition, although agriculture's share in GNP is relatively small, its share in employment is still large. In 1994, for example, agriculture's share in total employment was 54 per cent although its share in GNP was only 21 per cent (SSB, 1995, pp. 32, 83).

In the early 1950s, over 60 per cent of total industrial production was agriculture-based. Although the dependency of industrial production on agriculture declined over time, by 1992 two-thirds of light industrial output, or 30 per cent of the total industrial production, still relied on agriculture for raw materials (Table 6.3).

Market contribution

'Market contribution' refers to the demand by the agricultural sector for different inputs, such as fertilizers, insecticides, machinery, electricity and transportation, and farmers' consumption effects on the rest of the economy.

Table 6.3 Output values of agriculture-based industries and their shares in total industrial output values, 1952–92 (current prices)

Year	Gross output values of agriculture-based industries (billion yuan)	As % of gross light industrial output values (%)	As % of gross industrial output values (%)
1952	19.5	86.7	55.9
1960	40.5	74.0	24.7
1965	50.5	69.8	36.0
1970	70.7	73.6	34.0
1975	96.3	70.0	30.8
1980	163.9	71.0	33.5
1985	283.2	69.3	32.3
1990	611.9	69.7	32.7
1991	700.0	68.4	31.7
1992	827.9	67.8	29.9

Sources: Ministry of Agriculture (Planning Bureau, 1989), pp. 52–3 & 60–1 for 1952–85, State Statistical Bureau (CSYB, 1991), p. 399 for 1990, (1992), p. 411 for 1991; (1993), p. 417 for 1992.

Agricultural demand for industrial inputs was accelerated by the increasing constraints of arable land and crop area. *Per capita* arable land and crop area declined, respectively, by 2.08 per cent and 1.69 per cent per year between 1953 and 1989 (Yao, 1994, Table 4.6).

Despite the acute shortage of land, China achieved significant growth of *per capita* agricultural output, especially during the reform period. *Per capita* grain output increased by 0.44 per cent per year during 1953–78 and by 1.56 per cent during 1978–89. *Per capita* agricultural output value increased by 0.7 per cent per year during 1953–78 and 4.67 per cent during 1978–89 (Yao, 1994, Tables 2.10 and 2.11).

Sustainable growth has been achieved through steady improvements in land productivity. Increased land productivity, however, has relied on increased use of industrial products, such as fertilizers, insecticides, farm machinery and equipment and electricity. This suggests that an increasing share of agricultural output value is accounted for by the non-farm sectors. For example, grain yield improved almost threefold from 1155 kg/hectare in 1950 to 4004 kg/hectare in 1992. But the use of fertilizers rose by more than 260 times from 0.75 kg/hectare to 196 kg/hectare over the same period. After over 40 years of development, agricultural land became well-irrigated and agricultural production well-mechanized (Table 6.4). Irrigation and mechanization involved large amounts of industrial inputs into agriculture, creating a strong backward linkage effect driving the rapid development of agro-industries.

Table 6.4   Fertilizer use*ᵃ*, irrigation and mechanization indices, 1950–92

Year	Grain yield (kg/ha)	Fertilizer application (kg/ha)	Irrigated area/ Arable land	Tractor plough area/ Arable land
1950	1155	0.75	0.09	0.00
1960	1170	4.50	0.27	0.02
1965	1635	13.50	0.32	0.15
1970	2010	24.75	0.35	0.18
1975	2355	36.00	0.43	0.33
1980	2745	87.00	0.45	0.41
1985	3480	123.60	0.45	0.36
1989	3690	160.86	0.47	0.45
1992	4004	196.63	0.51	0.54

Notes:
a Fertilizer use is calculated as effective contents per hectare of crop area.
Source: 1950–86: Ministry of Agriculture (Planning Bureau, 1989); 1987–9: Ministry of Agriculture (Statistical Materials of Chinese Agriculture, various issues); 1992: SSB (CSYB, 1993), pp. 332, 349, 359, 371.

Farmers' income is largely determined by the rate of agricultural growth. As farmers' incomes grow, they are able to buy more consumer goods produced by the agricultural and non-agricultural sectors. This consumption effect has been widely recognized. Mellor (1976); Mellor and Lele (1973); Hazell and Roell (1983), in particular, have called attention to the potential power of agricultural consumption linkages. Hirschman's (1958) assessment of agriculture as a low-linkage, under-powered engine of growth erred because it neglected these important consumption linkages. As China is still basically agrarian and over three-quarters of the total population live in the countryside (77.58 per cent in 1993, MOA, 1993), the rural community is inevitably the dominant market for many domestically produced consumer goods.

Economic reforms have brought about a sustainable and significant increase in farmers' incomes. As rural incomes grow, farmers are spending a higher proportion of incremental expenditure on manufactured products. For instance, many traditional durable goods – such as TV sets, watches and bicycles – have a limited market in the urban areas, but they have a very strong and expanding market in the countryside (Nolan, 1991).

Factor contribution

Two basic factors – i.e. capital and labour – can be provided by agriculture to the national economy. Capital transfers from agriculture took place mainly in the form of indirect agricultural taxes through forced procurement of agricultural products at below market prices. The Ministry of Agriculture estimated that about 70–80 per cent of total state revenue in the 1950s were from taxing agriculture. Although the share of state revenue from agriculture

Table 6.5   Capital transfers from agriculture, 1957–88 (billion yuan)[a]

	Total transfers[b]	As % of state budget	State subsidy to agriculture[c]	Net transfer
1957	22.1	71		
1965	35.8	76		
1971	38.4	52		
1978	44.2	39		
1984	67.7			
1986	89.4			
1987	104.5			
1988	130.2			
1953–85	680.0			
1978–85	481.5	47.5	224.9	176.8

Notes:

a Values are calculated at current prices.

b Calculated according to the 'scissors difference' and the volumes of trade between agricultural and non-agricultural sectors (for more explanation, see n. 2, p. 148).

c State subsidies to agriculture include state investment in agriculture, input subsidies and all the other possible subsidies to agriculture and the rural areas.

d Most agricultural taxes are in the form of indirect taxation by paying farmers at below-market prices for their products and charging them at above-market prices for inputs and consumer goods. The main beneficiaries are urban industries and consumers.

Source: Ministry of Agriculture (Research Centre of Economic Policy, 1991), pp. 139–41 & 159.

has declined over time, by the mid-1980s, about half of state revenue still came from agriculture (Table 6.5).[3]

Tax revenue from agriculture in Table 6.5 does not include taxes collected from the rural township and village enterprises (RTVEs), a new and dynamic production force since economic reforms. If these were included, they would add 4.2 billion yuan in 1978 and 36.5 billion yuan in 1989, or 4.2 per cent and 13.4 per cent, respectively, of the total state tax revenues (Yao, 1994, Table 3.6). In other words, the total rural/urban capital transfers were much greater than the capital transfers from agriculture to the non-agricultural sectors.

A logical industrialization process should benefit from capital transfers and increased use of cheap agricultural labour. In China, however, industrial development in the pre-reform period did not use much labour from agriculture although rural to urban migration since 1979 has been substantial. Farmers were largely excluded from the industrialization process although they had contributed almost all the accumulated capital assets of the state industries. This was an inevitable outcome of the state industrial policy characterized by high capital intensity and urban bias.

There were two undesirable consequences of this development strategy. First, labour could not be quickly transferred from agriculture to industry, leading to huge under-utilized human resources and depressed labour productivity in agriculture. Secondly, industrial labour was highly expensive as enterprises had to employ only the urban workers who were entitled to various state subsidies. However, high labour costs had to be entirely borne by the enterprises. As a result, domestic industrial goods were not competitive internationally and required heavy protection from the state.

Significant labour transfers from agriculture to industry and other non-farm enterprises were possible during the economic reforms. However, such transfers were confined within the rural economy, characterized by the dramatic development of the RTVEs. Obviously the development of agriculture and non-agricultural enterprises in the rural areas has been mutually beneficial. One great advantage of RTVEs over the state-owned industrial sector is that the former have substantially benefited from using cheap labour released from agriculture. The state sector has 'selfishly' excluded farmers from participation, but it has had to bear the inevitable consequences: low profitability, low growth, and eventually self-destruction as competition from the collective and private sectors, particularly from the RTVEs, intensifies over time.

Foreign exchange contribution

Agricultural exports have been a dominant source of foreign exchange earnings in China. In the 1950s, they accounted for more than 80 per cent of total foreign exchange earnings. Although by the 1980s their dominant position was gradually supplemented by manufactured goods, they still contributed about 40–45 per cent of the total national exports (Table 6.6). As imports of agricultural goods and related products (e.g. chemical fertilizers) are much smaller than agricultural exports, the agricultural sector has been a large net foreign exchange earner.

A co-integration analysis

In this section, a multivariate co-integration analysis is conducted using the vector autoregression model (VAR) developed in Johansen (1988) and Johansen and Juselius (1992). It is based on the estimation of a VAR by maximum likelihood. Detailed discussion of the methodology is referred to Muscatelli and Hurn (1992); Banerjee *et al.* (1993); Harris (1995). Here we present only the general model, the results and their interpretation.

The VAR model

As our objective is to investigate whether agriculture and the rest of the economy are co-integrated, the Chinese economy is divided into five sectors, agriculture, industry, transportation, construction and services. If it is possible to find one or more than one co-integration vector among these sectors, it will be possible to conclude that different sectors of the Chinese economy moved closely together over time. It is also possible to test the hypothesis of weak

Table 6.6 External trade of agricultural products, 1953–92 (billion US$ and %)

Year	Exports[b,c]		Imports[b,c]		Export-imports: (1)–(2)	
	Value (1)	*As % of national total*	*Value* (2)	*As % of national total*	*Value* (3)	*As % of total national imports*
1953[a]	0.83	81.60				
1960	1.36	73.30				
1965	1.54	69.10				
1970	1.68	74.40				
1975	4.41	60.70				
1980	8.82	48.66	6.76	33.75	2.06	10.29
1985	11.99	43.84	8.23	19.48	3.76	8.90
1989	23.88	45.45	15.31	25.89	8.57	14.49
1990	24.50	39.45	13.93	26.12	10.56	19.80
1991	28.12	39.15	15.64	24.52	12.48	19.57
1992	37.02	43.55	22.83	28.32	14.19	17.61

Notes:

a Data for 1953–80 are provided by the import-export departments. Data after 1980 are provided by the customs. These two sources of data may not be consistent.

b Imports and exports under agriculture include two categories: (i) agricultural primary products: foods and processed foods (e.g. live animals, livestock products, fishery products, vegetables, tea and coffee), beverage and tobacco products, industrial raw materials (e.g. leather and cotton), and others (e.g. animal feeds and unclassified live animals); and (ii) agriculture-based light industrial products: cotton yards, clothing and other related textile products for exports; fertilizers, clothing and other related textile products for imports.

c All the import and export values are calculated at current prices in US dollars.

Source: Ministry of Agriculture (Planning Bureau, 1989), p. 517–519 for 1953–80. State Statistical Bureau (CSYB): 1991, p. 618-619; 1992, p. 630-631; 1993, p. 636–637.

exogeneity for any particular sector. In this study, it is particularly interesting to test the null hypothesis that agriculture is weakly exogenous in the system. If the null cannot be rejected, it means that agricultural growth contributes to the growth of other sectors of the economy. The same hypothesis test for exogeneity can be conducted on the non-agricultural sectors to see whether their growth can cause the growth of agriculture.

The time-series data of national income indices in constant prices for the five sectors over 1952–92 (SSB, 1993, p. 34) are used in setting up the model. Although the number of observations (41) is small for a VAR model, the data provides the longest possible time series for the Chinese economy. The variables to be included have been tested for orders of integration and the results (not reported here) suggest that all of the variables are $I(1)$ non-stationary series.[4]

Let x_t denote a (5*1) column vector of the logs of national income indices for agriculture (a), industry (i), transportation (t), construction (c) and services (s), or $x_t = (a, i, t, c, s)$. The VAR model as in Johansen and Juselius (1992) is replicated by (6.1),

$$\Delta x_t = \sum_{i=1}^{p} \pi_i \Delta x_{t-i} + \pi x_{t-1} + \psi z_t + \varepsilon_t \qquad (6.1)$$

where π_is ($i = 1, ..., p$) are (5*5) matrices for the variables Δx_{t-i}; Δx_t are a (5*1) column vector of the first differences of x_t; π is a (5*5) matrix for the variables x_{t-1} which is a (5*1) column vector of the lagged dependent variables; z_t is a (5*s) matrix containing s deterministic variables (such as a time trend, a constant, and any other exogenous variables with $I(0)$ property) for each dependent variable; ε_t is a (5*1) column vector of disturbance terms normally distributed with zero means and constant variances.

The first term in (6.1) will capture the short-run effects on Δx_t. The lagged length (i.e. the value of p) is taken arbitrarily simply to ensure that the residuals are normally and independently distributed (NID) with zero means and constant variances. In our model, it is found that $p = 2$ will be sufficient.

The second term in (6.1) will capture the effect on Δx_t of the disequilibrium from the long-run relationship. As this is our main concern of this study, it is necessary to understand the meaning of the coefficient matrix π which can be factored into $\alpha\beta'$ where both α and β are (5*r) matrices of rank r ($5 \geq r \geq 0$) and β' is the transpose of β. The value of r indicates the number of cointegrating vectors among x_t. The cointegrating vectors can be written as $\beta'x_t$. All these vectors will be integrated of degree zero, or $I(0)$, because the elements in x_t have been tested to be $I(1)$. The loading matrix α gives the weights attached to each cointegrating vector for all the equations.

A time trend is added to both the cointegrating space and the model. It is also necessary to add a dummy variable for the Great Leap Forward movement period of 1958–62 when agricultural production was strongly affected by the unprecedented disastrous harvests and wrong policies for that period. Another dummy variable is added to capture the effect of the post-Mao economic reform. Thus, the deterministic variables in z_t involve a time trend and two dummy variables for 1958–62 and 1979–92.

Estimation and results

The model is run in the CATS sub-routine of RATS developed by Hansen for VAR regression (for detailed technical explanations, see Hansen and Juselius, 1994). Examination of the companion matrix, different residual-tests (mean, standard deviations, autocorrelation and normality), the L-max and Trace-test statistics indicates that there are three co-integration vectors ($r = 3$). With two lagged differences, all the residuals are NID as indicated by the residual analysis in Table 6.7.

The first three rows of β' are selected to be normalized as there are three co-integrating vectors. A close examination of the α matrix indicates that

Table 6.7　Statistics from the residual analysis

Equation	Mean	Std. dev	Normality [a]	R^2
a	0.000	0.045	1.740	0.508
i	0.000	0.091	1.560	0.674
t	0.000	0.082	4.548	0.720
c	0.000	0.053	3.512	0.587
s	0.000	0.052	0.421	0.626

Note:
[a] The Jarque–Bera normality-test statistics has a χ^2 distribution with two degrees of freedom under the null. The critical value at 5% is 5.99. Full detail of the statistics is given in Hendry (1989).

Table 6.8　The α matrix and *t*-values with three co-integration vectors

The α matrix			*t-values for* α		
0.052	–0.139	0.091	0.821	–1.472	0.813
0.632	–0.459	–0.226	4.136	–3.389	–2.877
0.772	–0.212	–0.214	5.720	–1.777	–3.089
0.304	–0.682	–0.498	1.185	–3.006	–3.787
0.266	–0.296	–0.074	2.864	–3.593	–1.561

agriculture may be weakly exogenous as the α values for agriculture are significantly lower than the corresponding α values for other sectors (Table 6.8). The LR-test fails to reject the null that agriculture is weakly exogenous (*p*-value = 0.16 when $\chi^2(3) = 5.14$). Similar tests are carried out on other variables in the system but all yield the same conclusion that none of the other variables are weakly exogenous. Therefore, a final conclusion is drawn that agriculture is the only exogenous variable in the system. By imposing the restriction on α so that agriculture is treated as a weakly exogenous variable, the first three rows of β' are reproduced and normalized. The results are reported in Table 6.9.

As agriculture is found to be weakly exogenous, it is necessary to test whether is also strongly exogenous. If it is, this means that agriculture is not part of the co-integration space, or is totally excluded from the rest of the economy. Hence, only if the null hypothesis of strong exogeneity is rejected can the conclusion drawn from the weak exogeneity test become meaningful. The strong exogeneity test is equivalent to testing whether the three coefficients in the β matrix under agriculture are jointly equal to zero. In the present context, the following version of the estimated β' matrix in Table 6.9 is tested:

$$\hat{\beta}' = \begin{bmatrix} 0 & * & * & * & * \\ 0 & * & * & * & * \\ 0 & * & * & * & * \end{bmatrix}$$

Table 6.9   Co-integration vectors from VAR

Cointegration vectors	Beta transposed, or β'					
	a	*i*	*t*	*c*	*s*	*Trend*
V1	−0.343	−0.541	−1.037	1.000	0.161	0.057
V2	−0.676	1.000	−0.886	0.720	0.397	−0.085
V3	−0.426	−1.186	1.000	0.922	−1.221	0.059

The test is easily carried out in CATS. The LR results reject the null at a 1 per cent significance level (p-value = 0.01 when $\chi^2(2) = 10.42$). The analysis below is therefore based on the weak exogeneity of the agricultural sector. The intuitive explanation is that although agriculture does not benefit from the growth of other sectors, the growth of other sectors benefits from that of agriculture. Agriculture is not totally excluded from the system. It plays an important role in driving the development of the whole economy.

For easy understanding, the three cointegrating vectors in Table 6.9 can be represented by the following equations:

$$c = 0.343a + 0.541i + 1.037t - 0.161s - 0.057\,trend \tag{6.2}$$

$$i = 0.676a + 0.886t - 0.720c - 0.397s + 0.085\,trend \tag{6.3}$$

$$t = 0.426a + 1.186i - 0.922c + 1.221s - 0.059\,trend \tag{6.4}$$

The coefficients on the right-hand side are interpreted as long-run elasticities. In (6.2), for example, the coefficient of *a* is 0.343. It suggests (*ceteris paribus*) that a 10 per cent rise in agricultural national income would raise construction income by 3.43 per cent. In (6.3) and (6.4), the results indicate that a 10 per cent increase in agricultural income would raise the national incomes of industry and transportation by 6.76 and 4.26 per cent, respectively.[5] A positive trend coefficient of 0.085 in (6.3) suggests that the industrial sector grew much faster than the general trend of economic growth. The negative trend coefficients in (6.2) and (6.4) suggest that construction and transportation lagged behind the general trend of economic growth. The existence of bottlenecks in the transportation and construction sectors of the Chinese economy during the data period is clearly reflected in the results.

The existence of three co-integration vectors implies that economic forces were able to bind different sectors together to form a long-run structural equilibrium even though some sectors might have grown much faster than others in the short run. It is interesting to notice that inter-sectoral relationships are not always positive. The signs of the coefficients in (6.2) suggest that construction and services had a negative relationship. This may also be reflected in (6.3), which suggests that both construction and services competed with industries. Transportation is a special sector. Although empirical evidence indicates that there has been under-investment in transportation, the sector's development has a strong and positive impact on industry and services as reflected by the positive coefficients of transportation in (6.2) and (6.3). The development of transportation is also driven by the growth of the industrial and service sectors although it may have been hampered by under-investment in the construction industry (the coefficients in (6.4). Indeed, the government was much in favour of the industrial sector at the expense of other sectors, especially agriculture. Such bias towards industry often created bottlenecks in the economy such as insufficient transportation, lack of raw materials and under-development of services and agriculture. These bottlenecks persisted for decades but periodic efforts were also made to tackle them through large-scale state investments in the relevant areas (e.g. energy and transportation).

The finding that agriculture is exogenous to the system is striking. It suggests that over the data period agriculture contributed to the growth of the non-agricultural sectors but the latter did not contribute to the growth of the former. This result supports the empirical evidence presented earlier. However, further explanations are required to fully understand the reasons for the one-way causality of growth between agriculture and the non-agricultural sectors.

The first argument to support this is by examining available studies conducted by other researchers. There are few similar studies on this issue but the work by Won and Lin (1992) provides some useful information. Although their study is based on a simple regression analysis using OLS techniques and involves only agriculture and industry as two separate sectors, their results suggest that agricultural production has a strong and positive effect on industrial growth but the reverse is not true. As the present analysis is based on a rigorous regression system and involves all the economic sectors, it is more conclusive to say that the development of non-agricultural sectors had little effect on agriculture in the Chinese economy. The following provides some possible explanations for this argument.

First, agriculture has been unfairly treated by government policies. Before economic reforms agriculture was a dominant source of capital accumulation for industrialization and the major net contributor of foreign exchange. Most agricultural surplus was taken away from farmers with little left for investment in agriculture itself. Even after economic reforms, agriculture was still unfairly treated in terms of low investment by the state, high prices of inputs and numerous duties and taxes forced on the rural communities. It is obvious that if terms of trade always work against agriculture, as is the case in China, no matter how fast the other sectors grow they will have little positive effect on agricultural income. On the other hand, had agriculture not been unfairly treated, it would have been possible for it to benefit from the growth of the rest of the economy through equal competition.

Secondly, urban bias and rural–urban segmentation meant that industria-lization in the urban economy had little impact on the rural economy. After 1949, China developed a strict registration system to separate the urban and rural residents. Urban residents were given rights to enter non-agricultural employment whereas rural people were strictly confined to farming. This rural–urban segmentation implied that no matter how quickly the non-agricultural sectors developed, there was no effect on rural employment. An increasing labour force had to work on a declining land area. As farmers could not move to the cities and work in the non-agricultural sectors, agriculture did not benefit from the growth of the rest of the economy. Economic reforms have significantly reduced this urban–rural divide as the township and village enterprises (TVEs) have managed to siphon 20 per cent of farm workers out of agriculture, but the non-agricultural and agricultural linkage effects may require more time to develop at the national level. This is probably why they have not been detected in our present model.

Conclusions

Development experiences in many industrial and developing countries indicate that agriculture's share in GDP declines over time but the share of agricultural labour declines much more slowly, resulting in an increasing income gap between agricultural and non-agricultural workers. A declining role for agriculture is mainly caused by the Engel's Law but government intervention can affect this trend. The experience of China suggests that policies biased against agriculture in an attempt to industrialize the economy quickly have undermined agriculture's contribution to national economic development. However, the Chinese experience is not unique. Many similar developing economies (e.g. Indonesia, the Philippines, Malaysia, Thailand, India and Pakistan) have gone through the same process. The question is whether a deliberate policy against agriculture is good for transforming a developing economy. The answer is 'no' according to the analyses in this chapter.

The importance of agriculture lies not only in its ability to provide food for the population, ample raw materials for domestic industries, tax revenues for the government and exports for foreign exchanges, but also in its ability to sustain a decent income growth rate for the rural population which in turn provides a huge market for the products and services of domestic industries.

A comparison of economic performance before and after the economic reforms in China indicates that speedier capital transfers from agriculture do not necessarily result in higher growth in the rest of the economy. Sustainable economic growth has to depend on a balanced development of agriculture and the industrial sectors. This argument is strongly supported by the regression results, which suggest that agriculture is a dominant driving force for the growth of all the other sectors. Without agriculture providing enough food for the population, materials for industries, large capital transfers to the state revenue and foreign exchange, the entire economy would suffer enormously.

Notes

* The author is grateful to Sarah Cook and Juzhong Zhuang for their valuable comments on earlier versions of this chapter but bears full responsibility for any errors or omissions.

1. According to the State Statistical Bureau (SSB), industrial production at and below the village level was included in agriculture before 1984 but has been included in industry since 1984. For consistency, the data before 1984 are adjusted in line with the new definition since 1984 (SSB, CSYB, Chinese edition, 1993, pp. 402–3).

2. The share of agricultural national income in total national income declined much less sharply after the economic reform than before (Table 6.1) – indirect evidence showing that agriculture was excessively undermined by government policies in the pre-reform era. However, during the economic reform, agriculture has been highly under-invested. The state council agreed in 1979 that the share of agricultural investment as total state investment would be raised to 18 per cent for the period 1980–4, from 14 per cent in 1979, and 12 per cent in the pre-reform period (Lardy, 1983). In implementation, the share was curtailed to about 5 per cent. In the most recent years, this share has been reduced to less than 3 per cent. This reflects the legacy of how agriculture is neglected and how investment decisions are ad hoc and myopic. The heart of the matter lies in a strong tendency for politicians to achieve quick and high economic growth through expanding industries without thoughtful consideration of long-term efficiency and the need to balance the structure of the economy.

3. Government intervention in pricing results in lower prices paid for agricultural goods and higher prices of industrial goods charged to farmers than their respective 'real market values'. The diversion curves of regulated prices away from their real market values look like the two blades of scissors when they are open. The distance of the two blades from the central axis (implicitly referred to as the real market values) measures the degree of diversion of regulated prices from their respective real values. The 'scissors difference', therefore, refers to the sum of the difference between the regulated prices and their real market values of agricultural goods, and that of industrial goods sold to the rural areas. This scissors difference can be illustrated by the Figure 6.1.

4. Standard augmented Dickey–Fuller (ADF)-tests based on the null of non-stationary, as well as non-standard multivariate ADF-tests based on the null of stationarity (obtained from the Johansen modelling procedure), were undertaken. In any event, because of the uncertainty surrounding unit root testing it is useful to proceed with estimating the co-integration model (see Harris, 1995, Chapter 3).

5. There is a great difficulty in identifying the long-run elasticities in a VAR model because the values of the elasticities are affected by the way of normalization. I have tried various ways of normalization on β' and found that the most consistent results are those reported in (6.2)–(6.4). Nevertheless, it is important to note that the signs of these elasticities are more indicative than their absolute values.

Bibliography

Banerjee, A., J. J. Dolado, J. W. Galbraith and D. F. Hendry (1993) *Co-integration, Error-correction, and the Econometric Analysis of Non-Stationary Data* (Oxford: Oxford University Press).

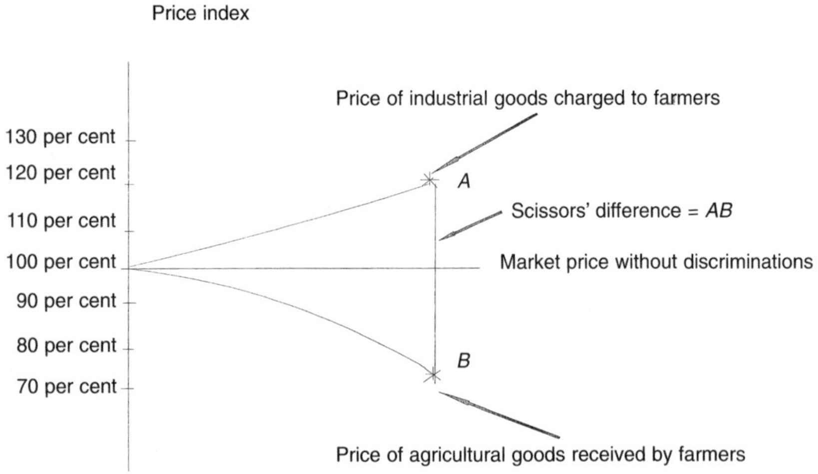

Price index

Figure 6.1   Principle of scissors' difference

Bhalla, A. S. (1990) 'Rural–Urban Disparities in India and China', *World Development,* 18 (8), pp. 1097–1110.

Fei, J. C. and G. Ranis (1964) *Development of the Labour-supply Economy: Theory and Policy* (Homewood, Ill. (Irwin).

Ghatak, S. and K. Ingersent (1984) *Agriculture and Economic Development* (London: Wheatsheaf).

Hansen, H. and K. Juselius (1994) *Manual to Co-integration Analysis of Time Series CATS in RATS,* Institute of Economics, University of Copenhagen.

Harris, R. I. D.(1995) *Using Co-integration Analysis in Econometric Modelling* (London: Harvester)

Hazell, Peter B. R. and A. Roell (1993) 'Rural Growth Linkages: Household Expenditure Patterns in Malaysia and Nigeria', *Research Report,* 41 (Washington, DC: International Food Policy Research Institute).

Hendry, D. F. (1989) *PC-Give: An Interactive Econometric Modelling System, Version 6.0/ 6.01,* Institute of Economics and Statistics, University of Oxford.

Hirschman, A. O. (1958) *The Strategy of Economic Development* (New Haven, Conh: Yale University Press).

Johansen S. (1988) 'Statistical Analysis of Co-integration Vectors', *Journal of Economic Dynamics and Control,* 12, pp. 231–54.

Johansen S. and K. Juselius (1992) 'Testing Structural Hypotheses in a Multivariate Co-integration Analysis of the PP and UIP for UK', *Journal of Econometrics,* 53, pp. 211–44.

Kuznets, S. (1964) 'Economic Growth and the Contribution of Agriculture', in C. K. Eicher and L. W. Witt (eds), *Agriculture in Economic Development* (New York: McGraw-Hill).

Lardy, N. R. (1983) *Agriculture in China's Modern Economic Development* (Cambridge: Cambridge University Press).

Lewis, W. A. (1954) 'Economic Development with Limited Supplies of Labour', *the Manchester Schools,* 22, pp. 139–91.

Mellor, J. W. (1976) *The Economics of Growth: A Strategy for India and the Developing World* (Ithaca, NY: Cornell University Press).

Mellor, J. and U. J. Lele (1973) 'Growth Linkages of the New Food Grain Technologies', *Indian Journal of Agricultural Economics*, 18 (1) January–March, pp. 35–55.

Ministry of Agriculture (MOA) (various issues 1986–93) *Statistical Materials of Chinese Agriculture* (Beijing: Agricultural Publishing House).

Ministry of Agriculture (MOA, Planning Bureau) (1989) *China Rural Statistical Compilation, 1949–86* (Beijing: Agricultural Publishing House).

Ministry of Agriculture (MOA, Research Centre of Economic Policy) (1991) *Rural China: A Review of Policy Research, Volume II* (Beijing: Reform Publishing House).

Muscatelli, V. A. and S. Hurn (1991) 'Co-integration and Dynamic Time Series Models', *Journal of Economic Surveys*, 6, pp. 1–43.

Nolan P. (1991) *Reforms and Social Development in China*, Cambridge University, mimeo.

State Statistical Bureau of China (SSB) (various issues, 1990–5) *China Statistical Yearbook* (Beijing: China Statistical Publishing House).

Won, W. K. and Jinding Lin (1992) 'An Intersectoral Perspective on the Relationship between Agricultural and Industrial Sectors in Chinese Economic Development', in M. Bellamy and B. Greenshields (eds), *Issues in Agricultural Development: Sustainability and Cooperation,* International Association of Agricultural Economics, *Occasional Paper*, 6 (Newcastle upon Tyne: Athenaeum Press).

World Bank (1991) *China: Managing an Agricultural Transformation (Part I – Grain Sector Review), Working Papers, Volume I: Working Papers 1–3* (New York: China Department, Agricultural Operations Division, Asia Regional Office).

Yao, S. (1994) *Economic Reforms and Grain Production in China* (London: Macmillan).

Yao S. and D. Colman (1990) 'Chinese Agricultural Policy and the Grain Problem', *Oxford Agrarian Studies*, 18 (1), pp. 23–34.

7

Property Rights and New Commercial Organizations: A Comparison of Agricultural Reform in China and Russia

Qiren Zhou

Introduction

The transition from a centrally planned to a market economy seems to have been more successful in China than in Russia. While China has been one of the fastest-growing economies in the world since the initiation of market reforms, Russian output has fallen dramatically even after adjusting for problems in under-estimating data. How should we interpret this difference? Does it mean that China's gradualist reform strategy is superior to Russia's strategy of rapid privatization? Does it mean that the Chinese strategy has solved the key problems of transition where Russia has failed? Moreover, does it mean that China can maintain its gradualist strategy to achieve further success? Finally, does it mean that Russia should alter its rapid reform strategy and adopt the Chinese pattern? While scholars who study socialist reform hold different opinions on these issues, based on a comparison of the agricultural reforms which have taken place in China and Russia, I will argue that in the case of agriculture neither Russia nor China have yet solved a fundamental problem. Moreover, Russia's experience of radical privatization of the large, state-owned organizations (SOEs) may hold important lessons for China's reform.

The key element that affects the choice of reform strategy is economic scale – the economic scale of production as well as of transactions. In this chapter I suggest that, owing to the large scale of production in Russia's agricultural sector, Russian agriculture requires reorganization based on a free-enterprise system which will differ from China's agricultural reform through the Household Responsibility System (HRS). For this reason, the Chinese HRS does not provide a model for the successful transformation of Russian agriculture. On the other hand, Chinese rural reforms seem to be slowing down after about ten years of successful development. I argue that one reason for this is the challenge faced by small-scale household producers in entering a large-scale market. China needs to develop market-oriented organizations appropriate to the large scale of the market. The basic problem in both China and Russia is therefore similar: how to organize agriculture, either through small-scale HRS production in China or large farms in Russia, to meet the needs of huge markets. From this standpoint, neither China nor Russia have yet solved the key problem, and China may benefit from the lessons of Russia's radical privatization of large organizations.

Agricultural reform in China

Early reforms in China were initiated locally to de-collectivize the rural economy. The HRS was then extended region by region to the whole country. Collectivized production teams continued to own the land, but the land-use rights were transferred to individual households under a contract specifying the households' obligation to fulfil the state production quota and to pay local public levies to the collective. Under the HRS, individual farmers have become, to some degree, independent land users and family-based cultivators (Zhou, 1988, 1994).

Originally, the HRS was a short-term institutional arrangement with contracts of only one or three years. From 1984, it was permitted to extend HRS contracts for fifteen years in order to provide better incentives for soil conservation and land investment. More recently, in 1994, the central government introduced a new national policy to extend the HRS contract to 30 years. These changes indicate the gradual completion of the transfer of land-use rights from collectives to households in China.

On the other hand, the Chinese government has since 1979 also raised agricultural producer prices and relaxed discriminatory pricing policies and controls over marketing. In contrast to the HRS reform, price and market reforms raised intense conflicts of interest. For rural households, complete price and market reforms implied full product rights: they could make the final decision about how to exercise their land-use rights, what types and amounts of grains or other crops to produce, what proportion of output to sell, what kind of purchasing contract to accept, and so on. While the transfer of these product rights means that farmers face market risks, they also obtain all the benefits from their market activities. For this reason most rural producers asked for and welcomed the market reforms (DI, 1986). Active free markets at the village, township and city levels served to support the HRS reform. Through these small marketing channels, household production could easily obtain the necessary technical and other input support and the services necessary for marketing output.

Small agricultural producers, however, have no access to the so-called 'mass-distribution channels' for agricultural products. That is, they have no access to the trade in major agricultural products such as grain, cotton and sugar; to long-distance or international trade; or to the mass-supply of major agricultural inputs. All these relations with the wholesale system and with the long-distance transport system are controlled by the state-owned 'commercial' sector. During the reform period, this state-owned commercial sector has become more profit-oriented, but it still retains its control over marketing. In other words, it has the dual role of being at the same time both a player and regulator, a situation which has resulted, at least in part, in a 'profitable bureaucracy' or 'bureaucratic commerce'.

On the demand side of the agricultural product market, consumers – especially in urban food markets – are unable to buy food at 'full market prices' unless their salaries are set according to market principles. Without a complete reform of state-owned firms, there is no way to free food markets. Unfortunately, the Chinese urban economy to date remains dominated by the unreformed SOEs. The Chinese government therefore has no alternative but to continue to subsidize food in urban areas. This mixed policy, partially relaxing producer prices on the one hand, but subsidizing food prices on the other, places a heavy financial burden on the central government.

I observe a deeper reform dilemma in China's gradualist strategy. While the government has tried to cut its food subsidy expenditure, the urban population, particularly workers in state-owned firms, 'reasonably' complain that food prices are too high because their salaries are too low. Naturally, the financial burden of subsidies has prevented the government from further freeing agricultural product prices. Instead, the government has been forced to re-control, and then to re-liberalize, major agricultural products prices several times. Since 1993, the state has reinstated monopolies in all regional grain trades, the cotton trade and the market for chemical inputs. The total amount of the grain and cotton quota even increased after 1993.

Under such reform cycles, it is hard to attract investment into 'new channels' of commerce between small household farms and the large urban food markets. The key limitation for investors is that there is no stable expectation of obtaining 'potentially' high profits because of the government's vacillating policies. Under an uncertain policy environment, large always means dangerous, and small is beautiful. Without efficient large commercial companies, however, there is no way of reducing the transaction costs of supplying as large a market as China's.

In contrast, the 'profitable bureaucracy' is very healthy. This sector is never a loser. When the government exercises tight price controls, either because of high inflation or because of the heavy financial burden of subsidies, its only policy tool is the state-owned commercial sector, and therefore the 'control benefits' belong to this sector. When the government loosens its control to boost a 'fast expanding market', this sector again becomes more profitable because it controls all the major commercial channels. In any case, it is impossible to identify clearly what part of the profits earned by this sector is caused by its marketing ability, and what part its monopolistic power. For this sector, it is rational to love the half-reform pattern in China. More regulations mean more opportunities for corruption. This is not 'rent-seeking' but 'rent-making' or, as Professor S. Cheung said of the Indian system, a way to institutionalize corruption (Cheung, 1994).

In summary, after fifteen years' of gradualist reform, there is still a dual-pricing system for agricultural products in China. On the one hand, agricultural producer households can freely dispose of a part of their agricultural production for either market exchange or home consumption. On the other, farmers have to meet quotas and 'sell' quota production to the state-owned commercial sector. In the early reform period, agricultural growth was based on small marketing channels. Subsequently, a delay in the reform of the large state-owned channels has obstructed the further growth of Chinese agriculture. This is at least part of the reason why Chinese agricultural growth slowed down after the mid-1980s. Today, by the best estimate, quota products amount to about 20–30 per cent of total agricultural production, a farmer's home consumption may be about 50–60 per cent, and freely marketed agricultural products amount to only 10–20 per cent (Song, 1995). In other words, the real market relationship accounts for less than half of total marketable agricultural production in China today.

Agricultural reform in Russia

Agricultural reform has been more difficult in Russia. Compared to the Chinese rural reforms, agricultural reform in Russia could be evaluated as 'super' rapid from the viewpoint of the legal process. Private individual farms (i.e. family farms operated by individuals and small groups of farmers) did not emerge in Russia until the late 1980s, ten years after the introduction of the HRS in China. Within four to five years, however, Russia had already established a legal framework to privatize land, addressing issues of land-holding, selling, purchasing, share-holding, mortgages, and so on (Prosterman, Rolfes and Mitchell, 1995). There are two types of privatized farms in Russia: one type is family-based farms, and the other is based on employees becoming share-holders in state or collective farms. In either case, land rights had been distributed to individuals and farm employees in Russia by the early 1990s.

This rapid privatization, however, has not brought about an efficient restructuring of Russian agriculture. Family-based farms have not grown as fast as expected. By 1994, individual farms represented only 6 per cent of agricultural households and 5 per cent of cropland (Prosterman, Rolfes and Mitchell, 1995). Most land and labour resources are organized in large, corporate farms. However, both the size and ownership form of the corporate farms are poorly suited to the real situation. Russian farms still have an average size of about 6000 hectares, and such large farms cannot be managed efficiently either by incentive mechanisms within the farm, or by share trading on secondary markets which are unlikely to develop (World Bank, 1996, p. 59).

Compared to China, where in only three years between 1981 and 1984, almost 99 per cent of collective forms became peasant family-based farms, privatization of farms has been extremely slow in Russia. It is a standard argument in economics that well defined property rights should help in reorganizing economic structures, but why was the restructuring so easy in China in the absence of a well defined land law? And why was it so difficult for Russian agriculture with much more clearly defined land property rights?

I suggest that the key to this question is the economic scale not only of production, but also of transactions. In China, heavy population density has resulted not only in smaller farms on average, but also in highly dispersed small markets. When Chinese farm households adopted the HRS model, it was easy for them to get access to input supplies, technology, trading, financial services and so on, through these small marketing channels. At the start of the HRS reform, these small free markets were adequate to supply the needs of agricultural family-based production with a little surplus.

Russia faces a totally different situation. Given the relatively relaxed labour land ratio, Russia has on average much larger farms. The former distribution mechanism for agricultural inputs, technology and services was very highly concentrated. When this old mechanism broke down, both large and small farms became the 'wrong choice': small family-based producers complained that it was difficult to get inputs from nearby small free markets, while on large farms the old system was restored. This explains, at least in part, why Russian agricultural reforms were so late and faced so many difficulties at the start, in contrast to the Chinese experience.

More recently, however, the pattern of rapid and complete privatization and market liberalization in Russia is showing advantages for improving the support system to agriculture. Based on field work, Wegren (1996) examines the complete food system in Russia, from farm production to the consumer's table. He finds that: (1) food trade policies have been decontrolled, resulting in a more market-based competitive environment; (2) state procurement comprises a much smaller percentage of raw food products than previously; for example, 64 per cent of grain trade occurred through state channels in 1992, but only 3 per cent in 1995 (half-year), and non-state channels gained a larger share; (3) the Russian food system is characterized by less state regulation and intervention and less state protection.

Overall, several reports have pointed out that the dramatic fall in total agricultural output in Russia can be explained by sharply plummeting demand owing to both the cuts in subsidies and the demise of the CMEA market (World Bank, 1996; Zhang, 1996; Sedik, Foster and Liefert, 1996). But Russia has made significant progress in its transformation to a market-oriented system. The production, consumption and trade in agricultural products have become better co-ordinated with the ability of consumers to pay, and production is under considerable pressure to become more efficient. From this perspective therefore, Russian agriculture, rather than undergoing a 'crisis', is performing reasonably well (Sedik, Foster and Liefert, 1996).

Market size, property rights, and new commercial organizations

Both the Chinese and Russian experiences of agricultural reform show that complete reform of the industrial and commercial sectors is necessary for agricultural development. Especially when faced with vast markets, as is the case of both China and Russia, there is no other efficient way of connecting farms to urban markets than through a market-based free enterprise system. As we have argued above, without such a system, the agricultural sector – whether organized for small-scale production as in China or large-scale production as in Russia – cannot efficiently respond to market changes in order to reallocate agricultural resources, is unable to obtain modern inputs and services from other sectors and cannot efficiently contribute to the food system. To use Coase's term, it cannot minimize the huge transaction costs by itself alone.

The success of China's agricultural reform is truly impressive. But the most successful results came during the early period of China's rural reform. These results can be explained by the dramatic increase of agricultural production for home consumption, small-scale family production supported by small markets, and relatively stable demand expansion at the macroeconomic level. Since the mid-1980s, however, Chinese agricultural reform has been at a standstill. This is caused mainly by the delay in reforming the state-owned commercial sector as well as other parts of the state-owned economy. Since 1993, almost all mass-trades of grain, cotton and major inputs have been dominated by de-liberalized policies. Thus there remains a dual system in China today: co-existing with active small family-based and local market-based agriculture is a large, state-owned or state-controlled quota system in which the 'profitable bureaucracy' plays a critical role in increasing, rather than reducing, transaction costs.

In Russia, little positive effect was seen from its early agrarian reform. Given the large scale of production, Russian agriculture needed at once to reform all major distribution systems connecting the agricultural sector to the urban market. Without a complete change here, neither large farms nor peasant farms could operate well. This logic forced Russia to chose a rapid reform strategy, privatizing all aspects of agricultural production, mass-distribution and so on. It is true that Russia suffered a dramatic decline in agricultural output since its reform; but now we are beginning to see the positive effect of the rapid, privatization policy on the Russian food system.

Of course, China differs significantly from Russia in terms of its development level, economic structure, political and social traditions and the international environment. But we can identify one important similarity in both transitions from central planning to a market economy. This concerns how a hierarchical ranking 'distribution' system is replaced by free-enterprise institutions. Free enterprise, I believe, is the only efficient tool for integrating a huge market. Socialist reform will suffer, sooner or later, in one way or another, from a conflict between these two political/economic forces. From this viewpoint, China started earlier, but seems to have been highly indecisive about whether to get into the real campaign; Russia started much later, but she seems to be crossing this river.

Conclusion

Based on the above discussion, my conclusions are very simple: first, a gradualist strategy cannot bring China to a new stage in which both a market system with low levels of exchange continues to flourish, while at the same time a system of so-called 'upstream exchange' – that is, a highly integrated market system – is able to develop. Second, the early model of Chinese agricultural reform – family-based land-user rights plus a small-scale free-market-based support system – did not, could not and should not be expected to settle the problems which Russia has faced. Russia needs a complete change in its large-scale distribution mechanism, and China has no experience in solving this problem. Third, whereas Russia is still in a critical stage of transition, following the Chinese gradualist strategy is not an option. Neither Russia nor China have yet solved the key problem – that is, the organization of agricultural marketing channels. Finally, in order to push the reforms further, China may need to learn from the Russian model of radical privatization of state-owned organizations. While some Chinese people may not like to hear the word 'privatization', they need to find another way, or another word, to solve the real problems that China faces.

As is well known, the pragmatic strategy of 'feeling the stones to cross the river' has been a basic principle of the reform philosophy in China. Since the mid-1980s, China has been grasping one big stone – that of partial reform, involving a new sector which I like to call the 'profitable bureaucracy', and which threatens the economic order, political stability and social justice. The remaining questions which need to be addressed are: Do Chinese policy-makers really want to cross this river? And, if so, how can China do so?

Bibliography

Cheung, S. N. S. (1994) 'Economic Interactions: China vs. Hong Kong', in Wong Gungwu and Wong Siu-lun (eds), *Hong Kong Transition* (Oxford: Oxford University Press), pp. 89–103.

DI (Development Institute), Chinese Academy of Social Sciences (1986), *Reform and Institutional Innovation* (Shanghai: Sanlian Press).

Prosterman, R., L. J. Rolfes, Jr and R. G. Mitchell (1995) 'Russian Agrarian Reform: A Status Report from the Field', *Communist Economies & Economic Transformation*, 7(2), pp. 175–93.

Sedik, D., C. Foster and W. Liefert (1996) 'Economic Reform and Agriculture in the Russian Federation, 1992–95', *Communist Economies & Economic Transformation*, 8 (2), pp. 133–47.

Song, G. (1995) 'Interest Rate, Saving Preference, and Inflation', *Economic Research*, 7.

Wegren, K. S. (1996) 'From Farm to Table: The Food System in Post-Communist Russia,' *Communist Economies & Economic Transformation*, 8(2), pp. 149–83.

World Bank (1996) *From Plan to Market, World Development Report 1996* (Oxford: Oxford University Press).

Zhang, Bing (1996) 'Rural Reform and Agricultural Productivity in Russia', In Hai Wen (ed.), *Russian Economy under Transition* (Beijing: Enterprise Management Press), pp. 86–95.

Zhou Qiren (1988) 'Land System: Valid Property Rights, Long-term Tenancy, and Paid Transfer', *Economic Reference*, 3 (English in FBIS-CHI-88-226, 23 November, pp. 41–6).

Zhou Qiren (1994) 'Rural Reform in China: The Changed Relationship between Property Rights and the State,' *Chinese Social Sciences Quarterly* (Hong Kong), 15 August 1994.

8
Employment, Enterprise and Inequality in Rural China

Sarah Cook

Introduction

Changes in the distribution of income in China since economic reforms were initiated in 1978 have been much researched and debated (see, for example, Adelman and Sunding 1987; Ahmad and Wang, 1991; Griffin and Zhao, 1993). Making use of available aggregate data, early studies highlighted growing regional and rural–urban income disparities, leading to a policy focus on combating poverty and under-development in the poorest and most disadvantaged interior provinces. More recently micro-level data has enabled researchers to examine the growing income disparities at the local (inter-and intra-village and township) levels. These micro-level studies provide opportunities for understanding the mechanisms and processes through which inequalities arise and become entrenched in a period of rapid economic change.

This chapter analyses current patterns of inequality in one rural county in North China with the objective of illuminating the mechanisms underlying the changing distribution of income among rural households. The main focus of inquiry is the effect of different types of employment on the level and distribution of income. As the labour resources and employment opportunities of asset-poor rural households are critical determinants of income and welfare, with different types of employment having distinct distributional implications, understanding who undertakes certain types of activity, and the relationship between employment type and income, will help in identifying the constraints which prevent the poorest households from improving their economic position in the transitional economy.

The data are from a household survey in Zouping County, Shandong Province, collected between 1990 and 1994. Zouping County covers an area of diverse geographical, ecological and economic characteristics and thus represents some of the diversity found within Shandong Province, which is noted for its wealthy coastal regions but also contains a considerable number of farmers living in poverty.[1] In contrast to many studies which focus on regions with a high concentration of poverty, as in the western provinces, or which have experienced rapid development of off-farm employment, as in much of Jiangsu, a study of Zouping County may better capture the features of rural areas at more average levels of income and development.

Following a review of the evidence on inequality in rural China, we examine the relationship between income distribution and employment in Zouping County, using results from other studies to place this in comparative context. Results of a decomposition analysis show the disequalizing effect of non-agricultural employment and, in particular, the large contribution to inequality made by household enterprise income. While these findings are broadly consistent with other studies, this chapter attempts to disaggregate further between types of activities (agricultural and non-agricultural, wage and self-employment).[2] Furthermore, using quantile regressions techniques, this study explores the determinants of household income conditional on being at a particular place in the income distribution. The results suggest that, at the lower end of the income distribution, the contribution to household income of wage and self-employment are similar, findings which suggest different policy conclusions than those drawn from other studies.

Income distribution in rural China – a review of the evidence

Regional trends in income inequality in the post-Mao era have been relatively well documented using the available (primarily provincial-level) data. The overall picture is one of rising rural incomes during the early 1980s with considerably more rapid income growth occuring in the coastal provinces. Income inequality appeared to decline during the period from 1978 to 1983, largely due to the increase in rural incomes which closed the rural–urban gap and thus reduced one major source of inequality.[3] Within rural areas, however, inequality was on the rise. Adelman and Sunding (1987) found that between 1978 and 1983 rural inequality increased owing to decreases in the income share of the poorest 40 per cent and a large increase in the share of the richest one per cent (p. 452). Ahmad and Wang (1991) provide evidence for an increase in income inequality in the mid-1980s, with considerable variation in the incidence of inequality on a regional basis.

With the slowdown of agricultural output growth in the mid-1980s, the distribution of income appears to have widened, with the poorer regions being left further behind in the development process. In a study analyzing sources of inter-provincial inequality, Rozelle (1996) finds rising household and regional inequality, with Gini coefficients increasing from 0.28 to 0.38 between 1983 and 1989. This increase is attributed to the uneven geographic distribution of rural enterprises' income which makes up a rising share of total rural income. Putterman (1993), in his study of Dahe Commune in Henan Province, also shows an upward trend in inequality as measured both by the Gini coefficient and by the ratio of distributed collective income between the 'richest' and 'poorest' teams.

Studies which focus on the spatial dimensions of poverty and inequality have tended to find that a large degree of inequality can be explained by factors which operate at the local level. Rather than viewing inequality as predominantly a regional or 'ecological' phenomenon,[4] increasing evidence points to pockets of poverty existing within wealthy areas, and to rising levels of inter-household variation in incomes. In contrast to Zhu (1991) who found that 'total net household income was evenly distributed among peasant households inside a given rural area' (p. 152),[5] the findings of more recent studies suggest a relatively high level of inter-household inequality within villages and townships. Knight and Song (1993), for example, found that inter-county (within-province) rather than inter-province income variation is a major cause of overall income inequality. Ho (1994), in his study of six villages in Jiangsu Province, estimates village Gini coefficients which range from 0.164 to 0.367. Using data from a 1989 study of rural households in one county in Guangdong Province, Hare (1994) calculates a Gini coefficient of 0.31, a level comparable with other national estimates.

The most comprehensive study of income distribution in China in the 1980s is Griffin and Zhao (1993). Based on a nationwide household survey implemented in 1988,[6] rural–urban differences were found to constitute a major source of inequality, with urban incomes being 2.4 times as high as rural incomes. The national Gini coefficient was 0.38. Within urban areas, inequality was exceptionally low by international standards, with a Gini coefficient of only 0.23. Rural inequality was considerably higher as measured by a Gini coefficient of 0.34. The bottom 20 per cent of the rural population received only 7 per cent of total rural income, as opposed to 41 per cent received by the top two deciles.

The distribution of income in Zouping County is consistent with that found in other household surveys. Average *per capita* income among households in the survey was 1117 yuan in 1990, increasing to 1193 yuan in real terms by 1992.[7] Table 8.1 presents the data by income quartile. Between 1990 and 1992, only the lowest quartile experienced a decrease in average income, although the changes for all groups in real terms were small. The shares going to each quartile were relatively consistent across the three years, with the lowest quartile receiving approximately 11 per cent of income and the top quartile over 40 per cent. The bottom decile received approximately 3 per cent of total income, compared with 24 per cent going to the top decile.

While most studies have been limited to one point in time, when taken together the picture which emerges is of an increase in income inequality since the late 1970s with large income differences along rural–urban and regional lines and growing variation in incomes within villages and townships. Given China's previous egalitarian policies, some increase in inequality was an inevitable outcome of market liberalization. The more important concern here is to identify the determinants of these changing patterns of income distribution which mediate how different households are affected by

Table 8.1   Income level, by quartile, 1990–2

Quartile[a]	1990		1991		1992	
	Average income[b]	*Share of total income*	*Average income*	*Share of total income*	*Average income*	*Share of total income*
1	529 (133)	11.6	553 (158)	11.7	516 (120)	11.2
2	783 (64)	18.5	907 (84)	20.5	888 (102)	18.2
3	1112 (141)	24.6	1195 (117)	26.6	1231 (118)	26.4
4	2053 (547)	45.3	2046 (667)	41.2	2154 (751)	44.2
Total	1117 (646)	100	1172 (651)	100	1193 (718)	100

Notes:
a Quartiles are calculated using *per capita* household income. Each quartile includes approximately 64 households.
b Average *per capita* household income (yuan) in real terms (1990 prices). Standard deviations are given in parentheses.

economic transition. More concretely, can we identify variables which are amenable to policy intervention in order to assist those households which are being left behind in the transition process?

Employment and the distribution of income in Zouping County

One of the key mechanisms through which asset-poor rural households increase their incomes is through enhancing their labour productivity in home production activities, or by gaining access to more remunerative employment opportunities. Recent micro-level studies of income distribution in rural China have highlighted particular patterns in this relationship between employment and distribution, finding a strong relationship between the source of off-farm income and inequality (Hare 1992, 1994; Ho, 1994; Khan *et al.* 1992; Putterman 1993; Zhu 1991). The general trend documented in these studies is that income from off-farm employment is less equitably distributed than that from agriculture, and that the diversification of sources of household income increases income differentials. Not surprisingly, households in the upper ranges of the income distribution tend to receive a larger proportion of their income from non-agricultural activities, while those in the lowest percentiles are heavily dependent on crop agriculture.

These studies, however, reach slightly different conclusions concerning the distributional effect of various forms of non-agricultural income. Hussain, Lanjouw and Stern (1991) and Khan *et al.* (1992) find that off-farm wage income is a major contributor to rural income inequality; in Khan *et al.*'s study, wage income is heavily concentrated in the upper percentiles with 62 per cent going to the top 10 per cent of the population. Ho (1994) and Hare (1994) distinguish between wage work and self-employment and find that the distribution of income from non-agricultural self-employment is particularly

Table 8.2   Percentage share of income source, by quartile, 1990 and 1992

	1990					1992				
	Quartile				Total	Quartile				Total
	1	2	3	4		1	2	3	4	
Agriculture	86.0	79.4	65.8	65.2	74.1	86.4	68.6	64.4	50.1	67.5
Crop	89.8[a]	77.8	59.4	47.3	68.6	91.8	66.0	55.9	32.1	61.6
Non-agriculture	8.2	17.2	29.4	28.9	20.9	11.8	25.0	30.3	43.1	27.5
Wage	5.0	11.3	22.9	14.0	13.3	8.9	18.0	26.2	29.1	20.5
Household sideline	3.2	6.0	6.5	15.0	7.6	2.9	7.0	4.1	14.0	7.0

Notes:
a This reflects 'negative' income from non-crop agriculture owing to investment in fruit trees which have not yet begun to yield returns.

unequal relative to other sources of household income. Using survey data from one county in Guangdong Province, Hare (1992) finds that wage employment has an equalizing effect on incomes, with greater inequality arising from self-employment. Ho (1994) finds an increase in inequality in villages where economic reforms have led to more household-based production.

Patterns of income and employment in the Zouping Household survey appear to support the evidence that household enterprise income is a disequalizing income source. As expected, the poorest households are those for whom agriculture provides the primary – or even sole – source of earned income. For the whole sample, approximately 70 per cent of income comes from agriculture, over 20 per cent from non-agricultural sources, with the remainder being unearned income such as transfers and gifts. Disaggregating by *per capita* income quartile (Table 8.2), households in the bottom quartile receive 85–90 per cent of their income from agriculture, of which virtually all is from staple crop cultivation (primarily wheat, corn and cotton[8]). Only the top quartile has successfully diversified into other agricultural activities: by 1992, it received only 50 per cent of its income from agriculture, of which approximately two-thirds was from crop cultivation. Remaining income sources were more remunerative – specialized agricultural activities, such as animal husbandry (mainly chicken and cattle) and fruit production.

Differences in income patterns among quartiles are clear from Table 8.3. Although households in the lowest quartile received 86 per cent of their income from agriculture in 1990, they received only 14 per cent of total agricultural income. Households in the top quartile, by contrast, received 45 per cent of total agricultural income, but this constituted only 65 per cent of their total income. Income from self-employment as a share of total household income increases for each quartile but rises dramatically in the top quartile, making up approximately 14 per cent of household income for this group – over twice the proportion for the next highest quartile. The top

Table 8.3   Quartile share of income (per cent), by source, 1990 and 1992

Income quartile	1990			1992		
	Agriculture	Wage	Self-employment	Agriculture	Wage	Self-employment
1	14.4	4.3	3.1	15.5	6.4	7.3
2	20.9	15.0	11.8	19.8	15.4	14.5
3	21.8	39.1	17.7	27.1	29.0	10.1
4	42.9	41.6	67.4	37.7	49.0	68.1
Total[a]	100.0	100.0	100.0	100.0	100.0	100.0

Notes:
a Percentage shares may not exactly equal 100 owing to rounding.

quartile in fact received approximately 70 per cent of total income from household enterprises and sidelines, with 46 per cent going to the top decile alone. Wage income is somewhat more equitably distributed, with a slightly larger share accruing to the bottom quartile (9 per cent by 1992) and 25–30 per cent to each of the top two quartiles. These patterns of wage and enterprise income are similar to those found by Hare (1994) but contrast with Khan *et al.*'s (1992) finding that 62 per cent of wage income goes to the top 10 per cent of the population. In the Zouping Household sample, in 1990 only 13 per cent of wage income went to the top 10 per cent while approximately 80 per cent went to the top 50 per cent.

In summary, the poorest households are dependent almost entirely on crop agriculture, wage income is relatively evenly spread among the middle deciles, while households in the upper range of the income distribution have more successfully diversified out of agriculture into private income-generating activities. Successful private enterprises are predominantly non-agricultural, but households in the upper quartile also engage in highly remunerative, specialized agricultural activities. The data support other evidence that enterprise income is indeed a disequalizing source of income, a fact which may be readily explained by the higher capital requirements and risks involved in such undertakings. By contrast, wage jobs may bring lower average returns but require lower initial investment and may provide a more stable source of income, thus offering a safer and more attractive employment option to poor households while offering wealthier households a mechanism for diversifying risk.

The decomposition of inequality by income source

The decomposition of inequality by income source helps to illuminate these relationships between employment and income distribution. An extensive literature exists on the measurement and decomposition of inequality (for example, Atkinson, 1970; Fei, Ranis and Kuo, 1978; Shorrocks, 1980, 1982,

1983). The methodology used here follows that of other studies, notably Khan *et al.* (1992) and Hare (1994), in using a Gini decomposition in order to facilitate comparisons between the studies.

Khan *et al.* (1992) found that income from household production accounts for 62 per cent of inequality[9] and wage income for 18.3 per cent, with the remainder owing to non-wage enterprise income, transfers and other sources (p. 1040). They also look in more detail at two provinces. In Jiangsu Province, income from household production accounts for 46 per cent of income inequality while 36 per cent is explained by wage income. In Hunan Province, household production accounts for 64 per cent of inequality while 15 per cent is due to wage income. Hare's (1994) study in Guangdong finds that, of total income inequality, 42 per cent is explained by the distribution of agricultural income, 25 per cent by self-employment and 27 per cent by wage income.

Results of a decomposition analysis for Zouping County are presented in Tables 8.4 and 8.5. The 'inequality ratio' presented in Table 8.4 is a measure of whether a specific income source is more or less equitably distributed than overall income.[10] Agricultural production accounts for almost 54 per cent of total inequality, but agricultural income in general is more equitably distributed than total income. Disaggregating by source of farm income indicates that crop income is most equitably distributed; more interestingly, specialized agricultural activities, such as fruit cultivation and animal husbandry, are similar to non-farm household enterprises in their disequaliz-ing impact on the distribution of income. The contribution of fruit production to inequality has decreased rapidly, probably owing to the time lag existing between investing in fruit trees (which occurred in Zouping only in the late 1980s and early 1990s) and seeing the financial returns to this investment.[11] These results point to the importance for understanding income distribution of adopting a more nuanced distinction between the types of activities undertaken by rural households. In particular, critical variables may include costs of entry into various activities, capital and technological requirements, degree of specialization and dependence on bureaucratic inputs and services.

The decomposition results (Table 8.4) also show that the ratio of wage income inequality to total income inequality remained relatively stable across the three years. However, the increasing share of income coming from wages since 1990 means that wage income contributes more to overall inequality over time, increasing from 15 to 25 per cent. The contribution of self-employment to income inequality declined in 1992 but varied significantly during this period, reaching 30 per cent in 1991.[12] Given that Khan *et al.* (1992) include both agricultural and non-agicultural production in this category,[13] the results from Zouping appear to be broadly comparable with those for Hunan (Table 8.5), perhaps reflecting similarities in the structure of the two economies.

The above analysis illustrates the critical relationship between employment and inequality. The contribution of a particular income source to inequality

Table 8.4   Decomposition of income, by source, 1990–2

	Income share			'Pseudo-Gini'[a]			Inequality ratio[b]		
	1990	1991	1992	1990	1991	1992	1990	1991	1992
Total income	1.00	1.00	1.00	0.296	0.278	0.299	1.00	1.00	1.00
Agriculture	0.70	0.63	0.63	0.225	0.135	0.213	0.76	0.49	0.71
Crop	0.59	0.55	0.50	0.117	0.049	0.068	0.40	0.18	0.23
Livestock	0.09	0.05	0.08	0.823	0.952	0.999	2.78	3.43	3.34
Fruit	0.01	0.03	0.05	1.00	0.456	0.303	3.38	1.64	1.01
Wage	0.13	0.21	0.21	0.352	0.324	0.354	1.19	1.17	1.18
Self-employment	0.12	0.13	0.10	0.566	0.648	0.477	1.91	2.33	1.59
Other	0.05	0.02	0.06	0.395	0.873	0.347	1.33	3.14	1.16

Notes:

a The 'pseudo-Gini' or concentration index is calculated with the data ordered by *per capita* household income.

b The inequality ratio is the ratio of the 'pseudo-Gini' to the real Gini, which provides a measure of whether income from a particular source is more or less equally distributed than total income.

depends on both the share of total income coming from that source and the variance in the returns to that particular activity. Overall, agriculture still accounts for the largest share of inequality because of its continuing dominant share in total income. However, enterprise income is found in all studies to account for a large and increasing share of inequality even relative to wage income. Further questions concern the mechanisms by which this process

Table 8.5   Percentage contribution to inequality, 1990–2

Percentage of inequality explained by:	Zouping Survey Data			Khan et al. (1992)			Hare 1990
	1990	1991	1992	All Rural	Jiangsu	Hunan	Guang Dong
Agriculture	53.6	30.7	44.7	33.9[a]	46[a]	64[a]	42
Crop	23.6	9.7	11.3				
Livestock	25.8	16.4	26.2				
Fruit	3.1	4.7	4.6				
Wage	15.5	25.1	25.1	39.7	36	15	27
Self-employment	22.2	31.6	16.5				25
Other	6.7	6.1	6.8	(26.4)[b]	(18)[b]	(21)[b]	6

Notes:

a Khan *et al.* (1992) define a category of 'income from production activities' including cash income and home consumption of farm and non-farm goods and services. Thus it includes the 'self-employment' category.

b 'Other' includes categories not included in income in the other surveys, notably rental value of housing. It also includes non-wage income from enterprises, income from property, subsidies, etc. which are included in the Zouping Survey under 'other'.

occurs. In particular, does the variation in income arise from differences in the returns to labour in particular activities determined by an individual's skills, from the nature of the activity itself, or from the institutional environment which might inhibit entry into higher-paying forms of employment? What is the role of location in determining labour demand and access to employment, and how do institutional factors – such as surplus labour or labour market imperfections – affect this relationship between employment and income?

The determinants of rural household income

Standard earnings functions provide a way to examine the effect of exogenous variables on household income, holding other factors constant. When the largest part of household income is derived from labour, as is the case in rural China, this type of analysis goes far towards identifying the key determinants of household income. To explore the distributional implications further, it would be useful to identify whether the results vary for households at different levels of the income distribution. For example, an additional year of education may have a different impact on the income of households in the bottom quartile than those in the top quartile. Estimation of quantile regressions allows us to examine these effects for different income sub-groups. The results of both OLS and quantile regressions are discussed below.

Model specification

The following log-linear incomes function is estimated

$$\ln Y_{it} = \beta_0 + \beta_1 \ln X_{it} + \beta_2 \ln Z_i + \beta_3 \ln V_j + \varepsilon_{it}$$

where Y is *per capita* household income in current yuan (*pcinc*),[14] i denotes the household, t denotes the year (1990–2), X are characteristics which vary by household over time and Z are characteristics which vary by household but are constant over time; V are village dummy variables and ε is the error term. Regressions were run on each year of the data separately, and pooling the three years of data. The variables used in the regressions and their summary statistics are described in Table 8.6.[15]

As the largest share of household income is derived from agriculture, the area and quality of cultivated land are expected to be positively correlated with income. Within villages, land is distributed on a *per capita* basis so that cultivated area is unlikely to be a major source of variation in *per capita* income. Variation occurs when households either rent additional land, reclaim land for cultivation, or (rarely) give up their contract land to others, usually relatives, to farm. Variables used in the model are *per capita* land area allocated to the household (*landpc*),[16] the proportion of flat land (*flat*) which acts as a proxy for land quality, and the number of plots (*plots*) which measures the degree of land fragmentation and is predicted to affect output negatively. Important

Table 8.6   Means and standards deviations of variables used in the analysis, 1990–2[a]

Variable	1990		1991		1992		Pooled	
Per capita income	1061	(610)	1172	(717)	1263	(775)	1166	(708)
Real per capita income	1061	(610)	1128	(690)	1160	(712)	1117	(673)
Allocated land	6.62	(2.8)	6.8	(4)	6.7	(4)	6.7	(3.4)
Per capita land	1.64	(.66)	1.7	(.91)	1.7	(.9)	1.7	(.8)
No. of plots	3.69	(1.2)	3.3	(1.4)	3.3	(1.4)	3.44	(1.3)
Share of flat land	0.97	(.08)	0.99	(.06)	0.98	(.0 9)	0.98	(.07)
Household size	4.1	(1.1)	4	(1)	4	(1)	4	(1)
Av. education (yr)	2.7	(1.5)	2.1	(1)	3.9	(1.7)	2.7	(1.5)
No. of adults	2.1	(1)	2.9	(1)	2.9	(1)	2.9	(1)
Males/workers	0.8	(.25)	0.8	(.26)	0.81	(.26)	0.8	(.26)
If wage employment	0.44		0.46		0.5		0.5	
If enterprise (SE)	0.21		0.14		0.14		0.16	
If Party member	0.22		0.23		0.22		0.22	
If new cadre	0.07		0.09		0.1		0.07	
If old cadre	0.26		0.27		0.26		0.26	
Poor peasant	0.62		0.62		0.62		0.62	
Middle peasant	0.28		0.28		0.28		0.28	
Rich peasant/ landlord	0.09		0.09		0.09		0.09	
Party and cadre	0.11		0.14		0.15		0.14	
Poor and party	0.18		0.19		0.19		0.18	
Poor and cadre	0.13		0.17		0.17		0.16	
Cadre and wage	0.08		0.22		0.14		0.15	
Cadre and SE	0.04		0.012		0.005		0.02	
Party and wage	0.09		0.15		0.1		0.11	
Party and SE	0.06		0.02		0.02		0.03	
Poor and wage	0.27		0.33		0.28		0.29	
Poor and SE	0.13		0.07		0.07		0.09	

Note:
a Data is weighted by village size.

variations in land endowments occur between villages depending on the land population ratio, land quality and irrigation. Such variation can be controlled for using village fixed effects.

Household demographic characteristics affect income in several ways. First, the ratio of adult workers to non-workers determines *per capita* income. The difference between the logs of family size (*pop*) and the number of adults (*adult*) provides a measure of the dependency ratio which is expected to be negatively related to *per capita* income. The differences observed in the type of employment undertaken by men and women suggest that the gender composition of the household may be systematically related to income: the proportion of workers who are male (*malepw*) is expected to be positively correlated with income. The average number of years of education attained by adult household members, *avgeduc*, is included to examine whether, as theory would predict, higher levels of education are rewarded in the labour market.[17]

The dichotomous variables, *wage* and *hhent*, indicate whether or not the household has a member engaged in wage or household enterprise employment, respectively. As the previous sections have shown, there is a strong relationship between the type of employment in which households engage and their income levels. The inclusion of employment variables potentially gives rise to a problem of endogeneity, as individual or household employment choices are assumed to choose employment so as to maximize household income.[18] A justification for including them in the model is that employment choice is not determined entirely within the household. Instead, given the imperfect labour market and excess supply of labour, the assumption is made that off-farm employment is rationed by means of non-market mechanisms so that households are not necessarily able to undertake the employment of their choice. Regressions are presented both with and without the employment variables.

In China's transitional rural economy, it is expected that non-market or bureaucratic mechanisms continue to play an important role in the allocation of economic resources, with political status or connections acting as an important determinant of household income.[19] Indicators of political status are whether the household has a party member (*ccp*), whether a household member is currently a government official (*newcadre*) or was one prior to reform (*oldcadre*), and the family's assigned 'class background' (*poor* and *middle*).[20]

OLS estimation results

Results of the estimation of household income using the pooled data for 1990–2 are presented in Table 8.7 while Table 8.8 summarizes key results, giving the percentage changes and the real (*yuan*) changes in income for a unit change in the independent variables.[21] Land consistently yields significant coefficients of around 0.3. Interestingly, when controlling for household off-farm employment, the effect of *per capita* land on incomes increases by approximately 10 per cent. This result may be due to the effect of moving labour out of agriculture. As labour is able to move off the land, other resources may be more efficiently allocated and the returns to land also increase. Controlling for employment, a one *mu* increase in *per capita* land leads to a 36 per cent increase in *per capita* household income,[22] which translates into an increase in income of 245 yuan at the mean of the income distribution, 112 yuan for the lowest income quartile and 440 for the highest income quartile (Table 8.8).

The variables which measure household composition for the most part operate in the directions predicted by theory. Family size negatively affects incomes: on average, an additional household member reduces *per capita* income by 72 yuan, varying from 33 yuan for the lowest quartile to 133 for the

Table 8.7   Estimates of *per capita* household income (log-linear specification), 1990–2 data[a]

Variable	Model 1		Model 2	
Per capita land	0.268***	(0.104)	0.36***	(0.10)
Plots	−0.011	(0.08)	−0.03	(0.07)
Flat land	−1.1**	(0.57)	−0.78	(0.48)
Family size	−0.166	(0.13)	−0.25**	(0.12)
Adults	0.02	(0.12)	0.06	(0.10)
Male/workers	0.076	(0.088)	0.02	(0.09)
Education	0.193***	(0.06)	0.14**	(0.06)
Poor peasant	−0.18***	(0.06)	−0.186***	(0.05)
Middle peasant	−0.005	(0.069)	−0.033	(0.06)
Party member	0.048	(0.058)	0.067	(0.05)
Old cadre	0.125**	(0.06)	0.095*	(0.05)
New cadre	0.132*	(0.076)	0.12*	(0.06)
Household enterprise			0.31***	(0.05)
Wage employment			0.39***	(0.08)
Adj. R^2	0.41		0.48	
n	756		756	

Notes:

a All regressions are weighted by village size and standard errors corrected accordingly. They are run with village fixed effects and year effects. Standard errors are given in parentheses.

*, **, *** denote respectively significance at 10%, 5% and 1% levels.

highest. Subtracting the coefficients on the number of adults from total family size (log of *adult* and *pop*) gives a measure of the dependency ratio which remains negative as expected, but is not significant at the usual levels. The gender composition of the workforce likewise does not significantly affect household income.

Table 8.8   Conditional change in income, by quartile

Independent variable (x)	Unit change in x	Percentage change in income	Amount (yuan) change in income by quartile				
			Total sample	1	2	3	4
Land	1 mu	36	245	112	181	249	440
Household size	1 person	−0.25	−72	−33	−52	−72	−133
Education	1 year	0.14	83	34	53	65	106
Poor		−17	−197	−90	−146	−200	−354
Party member		6.9	80	37	60	82	144
New cadre		12	144	66	106	146	258
Old cadre		9	116	53	86	117	207
Wage employment		36	416	191	308	423	747
Self-employment		48	556	255	412	565	998

The coefficient on education is positive and significant (except for 1990),[23] and is lower when controlling for employment, indicating higher returns to education in off-farm work. An extra year of education leads to an 83 yuan increase in *per capita* income, varying from 34 yuan for the lowest quartile to 106 yuan for the top quartile.

The remaining variables in the model reported in Table 8.7 are indicators of a household's political status.[24] A significant coefficient of around –0.18 on *poor* means that households with poor class backgrounds receive on average 17 per cent, or 200 *yuan*, less income than households in the omitted category, *rich*. These results are consistent with other studies which have found households with rich peasant or landlord class backgrounds to be particularly successful as private entrepreneurs. The benefit of having a Communist Party member declines by year with a positive and significant effect (17 per cent higher income) only in 1990; it leads to an average increase in income of about 7 per cent or 80 yuan. On the other hand, current cadre status has a significant positive effect only in 1992. The results for cadre status are particularly puzzling as current cadres are by definition wage employees, so that we might expect this variable to pick up the effect of wage employment in the first regression. These results may be explained in part by the correlation between political status variables. For example, a 'good' class background (*poor*) was often a prerequisite for Party membership which in turn was generally necessary to hold government office in the pre-reform era. These interactions are explored further below.

As expected, off-farm employment undertaken by any member of the household is highly correlated with household income. On average, households with wage or private enterprise employment have income levels 36 per cent and 48 per cent higher, respectively, than households without those forms of employment. In 1991 and 1992 the difference in income from having a household enterprise was over 70 per cent. On average, households with wage employment receive 416 yuan more income *per capita*, and those with household enterprises, 556 yuan. This varies from 191 and 255 yuan, respectively, for the lowest quartile, to 747 and 998 yuan for the top quartile. Employment was argued to be, in part, exogenously determined, owing to the nature of the labour market, with political connections providing a key mechanism for access. We should therefore expect political status variables to operate on income at least in part through employment. The results of interactions between these variables are discussed below.

Employment, political status and income

The first regression model presented in Table 8.9 includes interactions among political variables, not controlling for employment. Coefficients on the non-political variables are not notably affected by inclusion of the interaction terms. 'Good' family background (*poor*) has a strong negative effect on income leading

Table 8.9 Estimates of *per capita* household income (log-linear specification), 1990–2 data[a]

Variable	Model 3: political connections		Model 4: employment and political status	
Per capita land	0.27***	(0.1)	0.37***	(0.1)
Plots	–0.03	(0.08)	–0.02	(0.07)
Flat land	–1.1**	(0.5)	–0.68	(0.5)
Family size	–0.18	(0.13)	–0.26**	(0.11)
Adults	0.014	(0.11)	0.05	(0.1)
Male/workers	0.068	(0.09)	0.01	(0.09)
Education	0.2***	(0.06)	0.12**	(0.06)
Poor peasant	–0.17***	(0.06)	–0.27***	(0.06)
Middle peasant	–0.016	(0.07)	–0.004	(0.06)
Party member	0.07	(0.11)	0.02	(0.08)
Cadre	0.27**	(0.12)	0.2**	(0.09)
Party and cadre	–0.04	(0.11)		
Poor and cadre	–0.2*	(0.12)		
Poor and party	0.19	(0.12)		
Enterprise			0.27**	(0.13)
Wage			0.25***	(0.06)
Cadre and wage			–0.04	(0.11)
Cadre and enterprise			–0.43***	(0.11)
Party and wage			0.01	(0.09)
Party and enterprise			0.2*	(0.12)
Poor and wage			0.11	(0.07)
Poor and enterprise			0.26**	(0.14)
Adj. R^2	0.41		0.49	
n	756		756	

Notes:

a Data are weighted by village size. All regressions are run controlling for village effects. Standard errors are given in parentheses.

*, **, *** respectively denote significance at 10%, 5% and 1% levels.

to an average reduction of 16 per cent compared with rich peasant or landlord households. Having a cadre in the household has a significant effect, leading to a 31 per cent increase in income over non-cadre households. Party membership, either alone or interacted with other variables, has no significant effect.[25]

While these results provide some evidence that class background and political position affect household income, the effects over the three years are mixed, and trends towards this influence either increasing or diminishing are unclear. However, the magnitude of the coefficients in certain cases justifies examining them further. One question to address is whether political variables *alone* directly influence household income – that is, are government office or Party membership sufficient to ensure higher earnings, or are these helpful, possibly necessary, but not sufficient characteristics? Interactions between political status and employment variables may reveal one important channel through which political connections operate to affect household incomes.

The results for employment variables in Table 8.9 (model 4) are similar to those presented in Table 8.7. Household enterprise employment increases incomes by as much as 75 per cent, and wage employment by over 40 per cent. Households with a *poor* class background on average have 24 per cent lower incomes than households in the other class categories (*rich* and *middle*). Of households with *poor* class status, those which undertake household sidelines have a 61 per cent income advantage over other households with the same family background, and a 37 per cent advantage over those who are neither from this class background nor undertake self-employment. Households from *poor* class backgrounds who engage in wage employment receive on average 40 per cent more income than other households with the same class status, and 16 per cent more than non-wage households from other class categories. Off-farm employment thus appears to bring substantial improvements in income even for households which might appear disadvantaged by their political status.

Households which have both a cadre and wage employee receive on average 18 per cent more income than non-cadre, wage households, 24 per cent more than non-wage, cadre households and 46 per cent more than households with neither a cadre nor a wage employee. Interestingly, households with current cadres, who are all wage employees, receive higher wages than other households with wage employees despite the common complaints made by cadres of long hours and low remuneration. This result may be owing to the fact that other household members also have wage jobs, the interesting question then being whether having a cadre in the family is an advantage for other household members acquiring such employment. Also noteworthy is the result that households with former cadres (who are not necessarily wage employees) have higher incomes than other non-wage households, suggesting an income advantage to the position not associated with current income.

The interaction between cadre and self-employment is of particular interest as it is contrary to expectations based on other studies. Although cadre–enterprise households receive on average 18 per cent more income than households with neither characteristic, they receive 4 per cent less than non-cadre households and 13 per cent less than other households with enterprises.[26] Perhaps also surprisingly, the interaction of party membership and wage shows very little effect except in 1992 where the interaction leads to a 28 per cent increase over party membership alone, a 9 per cent increase over wage employment alone and a 19 per cent increase over neither. For the interaction between party membership and household enterprise the differences are more striking with an increase of 55 per cent over households with neither characteristic, 53 per cent over Party membership alone and 24 per cent over having a household enterprise.[27]

Possible explanations for the differences which emerge between households with cadres and party members lie in the nature of a cadre's work. Cadres frequently hold time-consuming posts which may leave them ill-placed to manage their own enterprises. They may also be constrained by recent attempts to increase their accountability through elections.[28] However, cadres are also well placed to assist others – for example, in facilitating access to wage employment or valuable resources. The income benefits from such activities, if any, are unlikely to be identified in reported income and we may thus be under-estimating cadre income. Party members who are not cadres may not be subject to the same constraints as cadres but may have similar connections, leaving them better placed to use their political networks to economic advantage within the private sector.

To summarize, the key results of the above analysis confirm that land provides an important basis for household income – the returns to an additional *mu* of land *per capita* are comparable with those from having a household member engaged in wage employment, and slightly lower than those from having a household enterprise. Human capital variables are not highly significant, but the effect of an additional year of education is positive. On the other hand, institutional variables show mixed results. Families formerly classified as poor peasants or hired labour do consistently worse than those which had a 'bad' (rich peasant or landlord) class status, while other measures of status bring positive, though smaller, advantages. Most interestingly, cadres do not appear to be advantaged in undertaking private household enterprise activities.

Quantile regression results

In the above discussion, the relationship between the independent variables and income has been held constant at all points along the income distribution. It is possible, however, that this relationship varies for households with different levels of income. The following analysis relaxes this constraint by using quantile regressions to examine the conditional expectation of income at different points along the distribution.[29] For example, we might expect that the returns to education should be higher for the lower income groups who lack other forms of capital, so that the estimated coefficient will be larger at the lower end of the distribution.

The key results, using the pooled data for 1990–92, are summarized in Table 8.10. Several interesting patterns emerge. First, the conditional distribution of land is U-shaped. At the bottom end of the income distribution, additional land leads to a large increase in income – doubling *per capita* land would lead to a 62 per cent increase in income for the 10th percentile and a 50 per cent increase for the 25th percentile. This effect declines for median income households but then increases to 45 per cent in the top quartile.[30] One explanation for this increase may be the access to complementary inputs among wealthier households which raises the productivity of land.

Household size affects income in an increasingly negative way from the bottom to the top of the income distribution. Interestingly, education has a

Table 8.10   Quantile regression results

Independent variable	Coefficients by income quantile				
	0.10	0.25	0.5	0.75	0.90
Land	0.62	0.50	0.35	0.45	0.44
Household size	–0.10	–0.16	–0.36	–0.40	–0.45
Males per workers	0.17	0.185	–0.03	–0.12	0.01
Education	0.21	0.20	0.22	0.10	0.06
Poor	–0.28	–0.15	–0.09	–0.02	–0.10
Party member	0.03	0.05	0.08	0.02	–0.00
Cadre	0.11	0.10	0.04	0.09	0.17
Wage employment	0.27	0.34	0.31	0.31	0.38
Self-employment	0.29	0.26	0.35	0.47	0.77
Constant	7.40	7.60	8.04	7.74	6.40

larger and more significant effect on the bottom half of the distribution, declining from around 20 per cent for the bottom half of the distribution to results which are not significantly different from zero in the highest decile. A possible explanation is related to employment: education provides a possible entry into off-farm employment for poor households with limited alternative means of access. By contrast, wealthier households, with other advantages such as assets, capital or connections may be able to engage in private enterprise employment where education may play a smaller role.

Of the political variables, good class background provides the most significant result, with a pattern that is consistent with the earlier analysis. It has a large negative (24 per cent) effect at the bottom end of the distribution, becoming insignificantly different from zero for the upper quartile. Thus poor households with a 'bad' class (rich peasant or landlord) background seems to have some advantage but this is outweighed by other factors at the higher end of the distribution. Interestingly, cadre status leads to a positive and significant increase of around 10 per cent in the income of the bottom quartile. This declines for the median group before increasing, although the coefficients for the top groups are not statistically significant.

The trends in the results of the employment variables reinforce the patterns of inequality described above. The returns to off-farm employment, both wage and household enterprise, are similar (just under 30 per cent) at the lowest end of the distribution. The coefficient on wage employment is relatively equal (around 0.3) across all income groups, except in the 90th percentile where it increases to 0.38; by contrast, for enterprise employment it increases in larger increments to 0.47 in the 75th percentile and 0.77 in the 90th percentile. Thus the returns to having a family enterprise are over three times as large for the top as for the bottom decile, a disparity which is considerably larger than that from any other factor.

Conclusion

The results of the preceding analysis broadly support the evidence of studies such as Hare (1994) and Ho (1994) on the contribution to inequality of different income sources, with wage income considerably more equitably distributed than income from self-employment. In terms of methodology, the findings reinforce the argument made by Hare that the broad distinction between farm and non-farm income sources needs to be refined further. In particular, any examination of agricultural income should differentiate between basic crop cultivation and more specialized activities. As with private enterprises, the income from specialized agricultural activities accrues over-whelmingly to the top income quartile, and both these activities share similar features in terms of capital inputs, market access and skills required.

The relationship between income and employment, and intervening variables such as education, depends to a large extent on the institutional context, including the nature of markets. This context affects first, household or individual access to certain types of employment, and second, the returns to labour in a particular activity. As argued earlier, in a labour-surplus economy, non-market rationing mechanisms will generally arise to determine entry into more productive activities. The data allow us to explore these mechanisms more systematically than many previous studies have done. Political variables (Party membership, cadre and class background) continue to affect household incomes, although in varying ways, and do so through different types of employment. In particular, households with a Party member receive higher incomes from household enterprise activities. For households with similar class backgrounds, however, those with off-farm employment are clearly advantaged in income terms suggesting that, even for households which are politically disadvantaged, this is an important route to improve their level of income.

Where markets are the primary allocative mechanism, human capital should become a more important determinant of access and returns to employment. Although the overall returns to education are low, an interesting result of the preceding analysis is the higher return to an additional year of education for the lower income groups who are less likely to have political connections. This may point to the emergence of a labour market which is increasingly responsive to supply-side forces, so that education or skills acquisition again may provide an important channel for assisting low-income households.

Finally, despite broad consensus with the results of other recent studies, the quantile analysis raises questions about the relevant inferences for policy that can be drawn from their findings. Hare (1994) concludes that 'Poor house-holds are unlikely to benefit from policies which simply promote more household-based production' (p. 78) and that increasing the demand for wage labour through the promotion of rural small-scale industry would be a more effective means of raising the incomes of poor households. An alternative interpretation, however, follows from the assumption that an increase in the demand for wage employment will be more effective in targeting the poorest groups only if wage employment yields higher returns than self-employment for this particular income group. The results presented here suggest that the returns to the two types of off-farm employment are similar at the lower end of the income distribution, with the gap widening at higher levels of income. Thus increasing the wage employment opportunities or relaxing some of the constraints on undertaking private activities (for example, by providing access to credit and information about markets) should have a similar impact on the poorest households. Village and township governments may be able to play an important role in promoting such activities among poor households.

Notes

* The author is grateful to Jonathan Morduch, Dwight Perkins, Terry Sicular, Adrian Wood and Shujie Yao for comments on earlier versions of this chapter, but remains solely responsible for any shortcomings.

1. According to Riskin (1994), Shandong has a poverty rate of 6.8 per cent, so that of the province's 82 million inhabitants, 4.5 million are rural poor.

2. Most previous studies have disaggregated only between farm and non-farm employment. An exception is Hare (1994) who demonstrates the importance of distinguishing between wage and self-employment.

3. For example, World Bank (1985) estimates of Gini coefficients for rural China show a decline from 0.26 in 1979 to 0.22 in 1982, and estimates cited in Ahmad and Wang (1991) show a subsequent increase to 0.31 by 1986. Rozelle (1996) provides a summary of rural inequality measures since 1975.

4. Riskin (1994) describes an 'ecological' approach to poverty reduction which 'pictures the poor as confined to poverty regions of great natural adversity' as distinct from a 'socio–economic' model in which the poor live in proximity to other income groups.

5. Zhu's findings are based on a study undertaken in 1985–6 in three counties in Henan Province; income distribution data for the period from 1978 are based on official statistics and local publications (pp. 2–3).

6. The rural survey covered 19 267 households and 83 179 people in the rural areas of all provinces except Tibet and Xinjiang. The urban sample included 10 out of the country's 30 administrative divisions (Griffin and Zhao, 1993 pp. 4–5).

7. In 1990 the exchange rate was 4.8 yuan to one US dollar and in 1993, 5.8 yuan.

8. Cotton is treated as a 'staple' crop here, as it remains subject to government quotas and price controls.

9. However, they do not distinguish between income from agricultural and non-agricultural household production in their decomposition of income.

10. A measure of 1 indicates the same distribution; a measure of 2 would indicate a distribution twice as unequal as the distribution of total income.

11. Fruit production in 1990 was a negative source of income for many households which had invested in trees which had not yet produced fruit.

12. There is likely to be greater error in the reporting or measurement of income from private household activities than most other sources of earned income, which may explain part of the variation across years.

13. Note that additional sources of income included in the data used by Khan *et al.* (1992) mean that the share of each source in the total should be lower.
14. Prices are deflated by an index based on rural consumer prices for Shandong Province taken from SSB (1991, 1992, 1993).
15. Summary statistics of the data are weighted by village size in order to equalize the probability of each household being sampled.
16. Measured in *mu* where 1 *mu* equals 1/15th of a hectare.
17. Other measures, such as the maximum number of years of education or the education level of the household head, were also used and yielded similar results.
18. Ideally, we would like to instrument for employment in the analysis. However, owing to the nature of the relationship between employment and income, it is extremely difficult to identify variables which are correlated with employment but not with income.
19. For a detailed discussion of this debate, see Cook (1998).
20. Class status was assigned to families at the time of the original land reform, based on their income sources for the years 1945–8. In the analysis, *poor* includes the categories of hired labour and poor peasant; *middle* is middle peasant; *rich* includes both rich peasant and landlord, groups which were subjected to persecution during the many political campaigns of the Maoist era. *Rich* is omitted from the regression.
21. The results discussed below are based on the coefficients from model 2, unless otherwise noted; calculations of monetary values use the mean of the weighted data.
22. Average *per capita* land is 1.7 mu and total land per household is around 7. This result means that if a household acquires in total 1 additional mu of land, on average its *per capita* income will increase by 104 yuan.
23. A possible explanation for the increase after 1990 is that, as the wage labour market has expanded, education may have become more important as a determinant of off-farm employment, and thus of income.
24. These variables are all dichotomous variables and the percentage change is calculated as $[\exp(\beta) - 1]$.
25. Perhaps surprisingly, Party membership does not counterbalance the negative effect of 'good' class background (*poor*). By contrast, analysis of agricultural production finds Party membership to have a positive and significant effect on farm output (Cook, 1999).
26. This difference is actually greater in 1991 and 1992 when the coefficient on household sideline employment is larger. For example in 1992, cadre–enterprise households do 56 per cent better than those with neither characteristic, 22 per cent better than other cadre households but 17 per cent worse than other households with enterprises. Note, however, that the number of households with both cadres and private entrepreneurs is very small.
27. These results, however, vary by year: in 1991 the main difference comes from household enterprise *(hhent)* not Party membership *(ccp)* and in 1992 *ccp* actually has a negative effect.
28. In addition to time constraints, there have been recent efforts to regulate the type of activities in which government officials can engage as part of campaigns to reduce corruption.
29. Quantile regressions allow us to estimate the effect of the variables of interest on different income groups, and thus to explore the shape of the conditional distribution. See Deaton (1997); Buchinsky (1994) for further discussion of the method and an empirical application.

30. These results are significant at the 10 per cent level or above. Quantile regression procedures under-estimate the size of the standard errors which are estimated using boot-strapping methods (see STATA, 1993).

Bibliography

Adelman, I. and D. Sunding (1987) 'Economic Policy and Income Distribution in China', *Journal of Comparative Economics* 2 (3), pp. 444–461.

Ahmad, E. and Yan Wang (1991) 'Inequality and Poverty in China: Institutional Change and Public Policy 1978–1988', London School of Economics.

Atkinson, A. (1970) 'Measurement of Inequality', *Journal of Economic Theory*, 2 (3), pp. 244–63.

Buchinsky, M. (1994) 'Changes in the US Wage Structure 1963–1987: Application of Quantile Regression', *Econometrica,* 62 (2) March.

Cook, S. (1998) 'Work Wealth and Power in the Chinese Countryside: Do Political Connections Affect the Returns to Household Labour', in A. Walder (ed.), *Zouping in Transition: The Process of Reform in Rural North China* (Cambridge, Mass: Harvard University Press).

Cook, S. (1999) 'Surplus Labour and Productivity in Chinese Agriculture: Evidence from Household Survey Data', *Journal of Development Studies*, February.

Deaton, A. (1997) *The Analysis of Household Surveys: A Microeconometric Approach to Development Policy* (Baltimore and London: Johns Hopkins University Press).

Fei, J. C. H., G. Ranis and S. W. Y. Kuo (1978) 'Growth and the Family Distribution of Income by Factor Components', *Quarterly Journal of Economics*, 92 (1) pp. 17–53.

Griffin, K. and R. Zhao (1993) (eds) *The Distribution of Income in China* (New York: St Martin's Press).

Hare, D. (1992) 'Rural Nonagricultural Employment, Earnings and Income: Evidence from Farm Households in Southern China', PhD thesis, Stanford University.

Hare, D. (1994) 'Rural Nonagricultural Activities and their Impact on the Distribution of Income: Evidence from Farm Households in Southern China', *China Economic Review*, 4 (1), pp. 59–82.

Ho, Samuel (1994) *Rural China in Transition: Nonagricultural Development in Rural Jiangsu, 1978–1990* (Oxford: Clarendon Press).

Hussain, A., P. Lanjouw and N. Stern (1991) 'Income Inequalities in China: Evidence from Household Survey Data', *London School of Economics Development Economics Research Programme Working Paper*.

Khan, A. R. (1993) 'The Determinants of Household Income in Rural China,' in K. Griffin and R. Zhao (eds), *The Distribution of Income in China* (New York: St Martin's Press).

Khan, A. R., K. Griffin, C. Riskin and R. Zhao (1992) 'Household Income and its Distribution in China', *The China Quarterly*, 132, pp. 1029–61.

Knight, J. and L. Song (1993) 'The Spatial Contribution to Income Inequality in Rural China', *Cambridge Journal of Economics* 17 (2), pp. 195–213.

Putterman, L. (1993) *Continuity and Change in China's Rural Development: Collective and Reform Eras in Perspective* (New York and Oxford: Oxford University Press).

Riskin, C. (1994) 'Chinese Rural Poverty: Marginalized or Dispersed?', *American Economic Review*, 84 (2), pp. 281–4.

Rozelle, S. (1996) 'Stagnation Without Equity: Patterns of Growth and Inequality in China's Rural Economy', *The China Journal*, 35, pp. 63–92.

Shorrocks, A. (1980) 'The Class Of Additively Decomposable Inequality Measures', *Econometrica* 48 (3), pp. 613–625.

Shorrocks, A. (1982). 'Inequality Decomposition by Factor Components', *Econometrica*, 50 (1), pp. 193–211.

Shorrocks, A. (1983) 'The Impact of Income Components on the Distribution of Family Incomes', *The Quarterly Journal of Economics*, May, pp. 311–326.

STATA (1993) *STATA Manuals* (Texas: Stata Press).

State Statistical Bureau (SSB) (1991). *Zhongguo Tongji Nianjian 1990* (*China Statistical Yearbook*) (Beijing: Zhongguo tongji chubanshe).

State Statistical Bureau (SSB) (1992) *Zhongguo Tongji Nianjian 1991* (*China Statistical Yearbook*) (Beijing: Zhongguo tongji chubanshe).

State Statistical Bureau (SSB) (1993) *Zhongguo Tongji Nianjian 1992* (*China Statistical Yearbook*) (Beijing: Zhongguo tongji chubanshe).

World Bank (1985) *China: Long-term Development Issues and Options*, A World Bank Country Economic Report (Baltimore and London: Johns Hopkins University Press for the World Bank).

Zhu, L. (1991) *Rural Reform And Peasant Income in China: The Impact of China's Post-Mao Rural Reforms in Selected Regions* (London: Macmillan).

9
China's Grain Economy and Trade Policy*

Feng Lu

Introduction

China's role in the world market has experienced profound changes over recent decades. In the 1950s, China was a net exporter of grain, especially of rice. This position, however, changed drastically from the early 1960s when China became a net grain importer. In the 1980s, average net imports were more than 9 million tonnes per year, making China a major player in the world food system, and its grain trade policy has inevitably become a topic of considerable academic and political interest.

Recent studies on this topic have primarily concentrated on two aspects. The first is the measurement and analysis of comparative advantage of grain production using various methods such as 'revealed' comparative advantage index, price comparison and the domestic resource cost approach. The second is the estimation of future grain demand and supply upon which China's grain trade prospects are predicted. This chapter approaches the subject from a different perspective. It focuses on the principles and mechanisms upon which China's traditional grain trade policy was based and functioned. It argues that since the mechanism was largely determined by an unique institutional framework with grain self-sufficiency as the most important objective, the changing pattern of grain trade since the 1950s can be largely explained by its special linkage to the domestic grain sector. The analysis provides a useful insight into the current difficulties faced by China's grain trade policy and hence its future evolution.

The chapter is organized as follows. We review the evolution of grain trade policy since the 1950s and raise some puzzling questions about the process. We then discuss the institutional setting and the policy-formation procedure for the grain trade. We then present results of an econometric regression to identify the major determinants of net grain imports, and provide a systematic explanation of the puzzling questions raised earlier on the basis of the analytical results. The final section presents some concluding remarks.

An overview of China's grain trade

Trends and changing pattern of China's grain trade

As indicated in Table 9.1, China's grain trade has experienced substantial shifts in response to a changing economic environment, institutional setting, and policy priorities at different periods of time. The evolution of the grain trade during these different phases is reviewed below.

Phase I: Net export period (the 1950s)

China began large-scale grain exports after the founding of the Republic in 1949. Grain exports were about 1.22 million tonnes in 1950 and jumped to almost 2 million tonnes in 1951. The average exports were well above 2 million tonnes per year in the second half of the decade. Rice and soybean were the most important grains for export. The share of rice and soybean in total grain export was 83 per cent in the period 1953–60 (calculation based on the data from Table 9.1). On the other hand, the magnitude of grain imports was usually small during this period. Net grain exports made a significant contribution to the initial industrialization drive that was in urgent need of an injection of foreign exchange. It is estimated that the ratio of foreign exchange generated by net grain export to total national exports ranged from 12 to 19 per cent during this period (Lu, 1994, p. 118).

Phase II: Famine and recovery period (1960–65)

The large-scale famine from 1959 to 1961 represented a turning point for China's grain trade. China changed from a net exporter in the 1950s into a net importer in the aftermath of the devastating famine that took millions of lives. The famine situation gave the Chinese authorities no choice but to reduce grain exports significantly while increasing imports dramatically from 1960. The annual average grain import was 5.9 million tonnes in this sub-period. Wheat was the most important grain imported by China. The share of wheat in total grain import increased from about two-thirds in 1961 to 93 per cent in 1963 and rose even higher in 1965–6. The pattern of wheat domination in grain imports persists right up to recent years. Huge grain imports had a serious impact on foreign exchange expenditure. It is estimated that the average share of foreign exchange expenditure on net grain imports in total imports was about 13 per cent in this period (Lu, 1994, p. 118).

Phase III: Exchanging rice for wheat (1966–76)

This sub-period coincided with the Cultural Revolution, and was characterized by fierce political struggle and a leftist ideological campaign. Ironically, grain trade policy in this period seemed to be dominated by making practical use of the structural features of the world grain market. As a result, the pattern of exchanging rice for wheat developed. The economic rationale behind exchanging rice for wheat lies in the price differential between rice and wheat

Table 9.1   China's grain trade, 1953–95 (10 000 ton)

Year	Grain imports			Grain exports				
	(1) *Total*	*(2)* *Wheat*	*(3)=(2)/(1)* *(%)*	*(4)* *Total*	*(5)* *Rice*	*(6)* *Soybean*	*(7)* *Maize*	*(8)* *Net import*
1953	1.5	1.4	93.33	182.6	56.1	92.0	n/a	–181.1
1954	3.0	2.7	90.00	171.1	54.0	90.7	n/a	–168.1
1955	18.2	2.2	12.09	223.3	70.0	105.8	n/a	–205.1
1956	14.9	2.3	15.44	265.1	107.7	112.4	n/a	–250.2
1957	16.7	5.0	29.94	209.3	52.9	114.1	n/a	–192.6
1958	22.4	14.8	66.07	288.3	139.7	122.4	n/a	–265.9
1959	0.2	...	n/a	415.8	177.4	172.7	n/a	–415.6
1960	6.6	3.9	59.09	272.0	107.2	111.1	n/a	–265.4
1961	581.0	388.2	66.82	135.5	42.8	40.9	n/a	445.5
1962	492.3	353.6	71.83	103.9	45.8	25.9	n/a	388.4
1963	595.2	558.8	93.88	149.0	68.5	40.9	n/a	446.2
1964	657.0	536.9	81.72	182.1	76.2	59.0	n/a	474.9
1965	640.5	607.3	94.82	241.6	98.5	65.3	n/a	398.9
1966	643.8	621.4	96.52	285.5	148.7	65.1	n/a	358.3
1967	470.2	439.5	93.47	299.4	157.7	67.0	n/a	170.8
1968	459.6	445.1	96.85	260.1	129.9	68.8	n/a	199.5
1969	378.6	374.0	98.78	223.8	117.9	59.5	n/a	154.8
1970	536.0	530.2	98.92	211.9	128.0	47.0	n/a	324.1
1971	317.3	302.2	95.24	264.8	129.2	58.8	n/a	52.5
1972	457.6	433.4	94.71	292.6	142.6	41.2	n/a	165.0
1973	812.8	629.9	77.50	389.3	263.1	40.0	n/a	423.5
1974	812.1	538.3	66.28	364.4	206.1	47.1	n/a	447.7
1975	375.5	349.1	92.97	280.6	163.0	40.5	n/a	94.9
1976	236.7	202.2	85.42	176.5	87.6	20.0	n/a	60.2
1977	734.5	687.6	93.61	165.7	103.3	13.0	n/a	568.8
1978	883.3	766.7	86.80	187.7	143.5	11.3	n/a	695.6
1979	1235.5	871.0	70.50	165.1	105.3	30.6	n/a	1070.4
1980	1342.9	1097.2	81.70	161.8	111.6	11.3	n/a	1181.1
1981	1481.2	1307.1	88.25	126.1	58.3	13.6	n/a	1355.1
1982	1611.7	1353.4	83.97	125.1	45.7	12.7	n/a	1486.6
1983	1343.5	1101.9	82.02	196.3	56.6	33.4	n/a	1147.2
1984	1064.5	1000.0	93.94	344.0	118.9	83.4	91.1	720.5
1985	617.1	563.2	91.27	888.0	101.9	115.1	595.7	–270.9
1986	728.2	575.4	79.02	909.5	95.7	130.1	570.6	–181.3
1987	1627.8	1334.1	81.96	718.7	98.9	171.4	384.7	909.1
1988	1478.8	1391.0	94.06	654.2	70.5	145.9	352.2	824.6
1989	1640.3	1470.3	89.64	622.1	33.9	117.1	349.7	1018.2
1990	1356.4	1233.5	90.94	543.4	30.3	91.0	288.7	813.0
1991	1398.3	1282.5	91.72	1066.0	69.2	106.5	748.7	332.3
1992	1156.9	1034.0	89.38	1445.1	120.4	84.5	1043.5	–288.2
1993	733.0	642.4	87.64	1611.9	170.9	34.5	1178.6	–878.9
1994	901.0			1084.0				–183.0
1995	2027.0			42.0				1985.0

Source: SSB (1994–6), *Phase I: Net Export Period (the 1950s).*

on the world grain market: the price of rice is usually twice as high as that of wheat, although the calorie levels of both grains are similar per physical unit. It is shown in Table 9.1 that China remained a net grain importer during the period, with an average annual import of 2.2 million tonnes. The value of imports, however, was almost the same as that of exports.[1]

Phase IV: Policy adjustment period (1977–84)

The distinct feature of this period was a dramatic surge in grain imports. This was highlighted by the fact that net grain imports reached new records for six years consecutively from 1977 to 1982. In the peak year of 1982, total imports were over 16 million tonnes. It was this huge increase in grain imports that made China one of the most important players in the international grain market.

Phase V: Transitional period (1985–)

There are several striking features of the grain trade during this period. The first was the drastic fluctuation in grain imports and exports which were much wider than in previous periods. The second was China's alternation between net importer and net exporter. Bumper harvests in 1983–4 made China a net grain exporter in 1985 for the first time since the 1950s, but a large reduction in domestic production in the same year forced the country to become a large net importer for subsequent years from 1987 to 1991. China became a net exporter again in 1992–4 with an all-time record high of grain exports in 1994 owing to the unprecedented harvests of the early 1990s. However, grain exports plummeted to almost zero in 1995 and imports reached a new record of over 20 million tonnes. Thirdly, contrary to the usual prediction that China imports large quantities of coarse grains, maize exports have expanded dramatically in recent years, reaching a record of 11.8 million tonnes in 1993 (Table 9.1). These new developments imply that China's grain trade became far more active since the mid-1980s than in any of the previous sub-periods.

Puzzling questions about China's grain trade policy

The above review of the changing pattern of China's grain trade raises many significant questions, four of which are highlighted here:

- First, many people argued that the historical transition into a net importer in the early 1960s was primarily caused by the massive famine from 1959–61. However, grain output dropped dramatically in 1959. Why did China fail to import grain in in 1959 and 1960 to prevent famine?
- Second, grain production recovered to its pre-famine level after 1965. Why did China fail to become a net exporter after 1965?
- Third, why did net grain imports surge to an unprecedented level in the late 1970s and early 1980s although domestic production also increased dramatically at this period following economic reform?

- Fourth, why did the grain trade enter a seemingly unsettled period after the mid-1980s, and what were the implications of this change?

China's grain imports were once described as an enigma (Timmer and Jones, 1986), indicating great difficulty in finding a coherent answer to the above questions. This chapter seeks a systematic explanation to these puzzles based on a coherent analytical framework. The crucial task is to identify the main determinants of China's grain trade. To do this, it is necessary to clarify the special institutional setting and the process by which grain trade policy is formulated.

The institutional setting and policy formulation process

Foreign trade was a monopoly of the government until the economic reforms of the 1980s. As in other centrally planned economies, national import and export plans were drawn up by the state. The Ministry of Foreign Trade (MOFT) exercised control on behalf of the state.[2] Specialized foreign trade corporations supervised by MOFT handled import and export businesses. Of these corporations, the China National Cereals, Oils and Foodstuffs Export and Import Corporation (CNCOFEIC), one of the largest of its type, was in charge of the grain trade. However, what needs to be emphasized here is the particularly high degree of monopoly over the grain trade. This is explained by two facts. First, although foreign trade in most commodities has been largely liberalized since the late 1970s, the grain trade is still monopolized by the state trade corporation or heavily controlled by the state. Secondly, the highest ranking agencies in the central government have been involved in the formulation of grain import plans. In order to clarify this point, we need to look at the policy-making procedure with respect to grain imports.

Accounts of the policy-making process regarding grain imports are scarce. Here I summarize the procedures used in the late 1980s, based mainly on information gathered through interviews with officials and researchers in the Ministry of Commerce (MOC),[3] Ministry of Foreign Economic Relations and Trade (MOFERT), and various research institutes in Beijing. This will be followed by a brief discussion of recent modifications and changes in this context.

The routine procedure involves several stages of policy formulation. First, MOC prepares the draft plan for grain imports. The work is usually undertaken by officials and staff of the Overall Planning Division, Grain Bureau of MOC. The preparation of the draft plan is mainly dependent on the situation of domestic grain demand and supply. MOFERT is usually consulted over the world market situation to facilitate the drawing up of the draft plan.

Secondly, the draft plan is submitted to the State Planning Commission (SPC) which is supposed to examine the feasibility and soundness of the plan from a macroeconomic perspective. Two issues are given particular attention:

(1) The SPC assesses the implications of the grain import plan for foreign exchange allocation, since the pressure of competitive demands for foreign exchange is usually high.
(2) The plan also needs to be examined in the context of the state budget, as grain imports usually involve subsidies from the state.

At the third stage, the preliminary plan is reported to the working meeting of the State Council by SPC, MOC and MOFERT for final examination and approval. Alternatively, the plan may be discussed and a final decision formed at the National Grain Work Conference which is usually held at the end of each year. It should be noted that although the State Council usually makes the final decision, the Political Bureau of the Chinese Communist Party, the most powerful decision-making body in China, can intervene in grain import policy if the situation was regarded as unusual and some special adjustments regarding the domestic grain economy and grain trade are viewed as necessary.

After examination and approval by the State Council, the final decision on grain imports is sent to MOFERT as the annual directive plan which is further assigned to CNCOFEIC for implementation. The implementation of the plan is facilitated by bilateral agreements on the grain trade, if any, and by the processes of investigating and calculating costs, and selecting potential sellers. When all these have been done, the negotiation of transactions begins.

There have been modifications and developments of these procedures in recent years in response to a changing domestic economic environment and external influence. At least three aspects need to be mentioned. First, the institutional framework for grain import policy-making described above was characterized by state monopoly and a rigid annual planning procedure. This system has been challenged by the domestic market-oriented reforms, especially in the grain sector as well as the process of internationalization of the economy. Two reforms were attempted to address these challenges. On the one hand, in order to break the monopoly power of CNCOFEIC in the grain trade, a quota-allocation system has been introduced. Other state-owned companies were assigned the right to engage in grain trade through a licence and quota-allocation system. On the other hand, to achieve better co-ordination between the domestic grain marketing and foreign grain trade, the State Council made the decision to create a new company named Liang Fen, jointly owned by MOFERT and the Ministry of Domestic Trade. However, little is known about the function of the new company, and its role seems quite limited up to now.

Secondly, with a view to playing a more active role in stabilizing the grain market through a grain reserve policy, the central government established the National Grain Reserve Bureau in 1991. The main purposes of the state grain reserves are to stabilize market grain prices and help the victims of natural disasters. The new bureau has been actively involved in grain trade policy-making in recent years. Thirdly, in the past, the delivery system was used to link MOC, which provided domestic grain for exports and received grain from imports on one side, and the state grain trade company on the other. Under the system, MOC delivered domestic grain to CNCOFEIC for export at procurement prices which were usually lower than market prices. On the other hand, the state company delivered imported grain to MOC at fixed prices in line with the price structure for domestic grain transfers. The government would cover any losses if the import price was higher than the delivery price. This policy was abolished in 1994. Under the new system, the state grain trading company acts as a trading agent for MOC and other companies which have export and import quotas and charges fees accordingly.

The above discussion reveals the special features of grain imports in the context of the annual grain plan formulation. Because of the vital importance of grain to people's welfare and to the overall economic plan, grain imports are treated with great care. Government bodies at the highest level are directly involved in formulation of its import plan, and the modifications and developments in recent years have had only a limited impact on changing its basic features.

Determinants and mechanisms of grain trade policy

Many factors which may have influenced grain imports have been discussed in previous studies (Surls, 1978; Wong, 1980; Carter and Zhong, 1991; Chen and Buckwell 1991; World Bank 1991, Garnaut and Ma, 1992; Yao, 1994). These factors may be classified into three groups. The first consists of the conventional structural factors such as relative costs, prices in the world market and foreign exchange availability. They are usually included in trade models for developing economies. The second group of factors is specially related to the context of China's grain imports. It was argued that grain imports in China had been influenced by two special considerations. The first is the argument for variety adjustment and price differentials stated by trade officials. According to this argument, 'the purpose of [grain] importing is to regulate the varieties of food supply' – i.e. importing wheat which is in short supply and exporting rice which is in surplus. Because the rice price has usually been higher than the wheat price on the world market, China's wheat–rice trade has taken advantage of the price differential (*Far Eastern Economic Review*, 44 1964, p. 367). Another consideration is the internal transport bottlenecks and relative transportation costs. It is argued by some western scholars that because of problems and inefficiencies in China's internal transport system, it is cheaper for the eastern coastal cities such as Shanghai and Tianjin to import grains from foreign countries such as Australia, Canada than from the inland grain surplus provinces (Donnithorne, 1970, p. 2). The third group of factors includes grain output, population, income, storage etc. A conventional trade model should also account for these.

Although many factors may potentially have influenced China's grain import policy, their impact is unlikely to be equally important. This chapter focuses only on the institutional factors which in my view are the most important determinants of China's grain imports. In a sense, the primary importance of the domestic grain economy to grain imports in China is self-evident. The fact that wheat usually makes up 80–90 per cent of total grain imports indicates that imported grains have mainly been used for direct human consumption. Considering that the level of grain consumption has been around or only marginally above the level of subsistence requirement for most years of the period, it is arguable that domestic grain demand and supply must be of particular importance to grain imports.

This observation on the relationship between China's domestic grain economy and its grain trade development raises some questions:

- How does domestic grain production influence import policy? With the assumption that the annual grain import plan was formed mainly on the basis of the domestic grain situation, how do planners assess demand and supply?
- What are the indicators of the domestic grain situation?
- Are the indicators reliable, and do they serve their purpose well?

Obviously, the questions need to be addressed in a systematic way so as to establish a coherent linkage between domestic grain production and grain trade.

In a mature market system, there seems to be a natural answer: the relative price of grain may indicate the underlying relationship between supply and demand. The planner may simply take changes in grain price as a signal in this context. However, there was no market mechanism at work in China's domestic grain sector during the sample period. What we had instead was a unique institutional setting which was of vital importance to the function of grain trade policy.

The most important characteristic of the domestic grain economy was that grain distribution had been almost totally controlled by the state since the early 1950s. The system consisted of two basic interrelated aspects:

(1) *Unified purchasing*: the state procured grains from peasants at pre-set quotas and prices. The official prices were substantially lower than market prices that would have prevailed otherwise. After meeting the quota, surplus grain, if there was any, had to be sold to government agencies in most years of the period 1953–78 when free markets were virtually banned; or were allowed to be sold in free markets in other years when free markets existed.

(2) *Unified marketing*: the state supplied grain rations at low prices to the urban non-agricultural population and to a small portion of the rural agricultural

population who were either designated by the government to produce cash crops (such as cotton, peanuts, etc.) or hit by natural calamities (Lu, 1989). Specific levels of grain rations were assigned for different groups of consumers in urban areas and general guidelines were formulated regarding the grain distribution to rural residents who qualified for access to state grain supply.[4] The state also supplied grain by quota to industries which required grain as an input. Although the details of the system were modified or adjusted from time to time, its basic features had not been changed by the mid-1980s.[5]

A direct consequence of the unique institutional setting is that the domestic grain economy was segmented into two parts. One was the state sector which was directly controlled by the state. It covered grain supplies to the non-agricultural population plus a number of rural residents mentioned above. Because by far the greater part of this grain supply was for the non-agricultural population normally residing in urban areas, the state-controlled grain sector may also be referred to as the urban grain sector.[6] The other part of grain supply and demand was for the majority of the agricultural population in rural areas, so it may be called the rural grain sector or the non-state grain sector.[7]

The segmentation of the domestic grain economy had important implications for the grain trade. Considering the questions raised above, owing to the lack of a price mechanism, the relationship between domestic supply and demand had to be assessed by alternative quantitative indicators, such as changes in domestic harvests. Furthermore, under the circumstances of a segmented grain economy, changes in grain imports would be particularly sensitive to demand and supply for grain in the state sector. The main reason is that grain imports have been monopolized by the state and imported grain constituted an important source of grain supply in the state sector. So the situation in the state sector was important in shaping government's decision to import. Investigation of the factors determining the situation in the state grain sector may thus improve our understanding of the quantitative changes in the level of grain imports.

The above observation suggests a special linkage between the quantitative adjustment in the grain trade and the requirements of the state grain sector. We propose a statistical test of the hypothesis regarding this special linkage. In a simple model developed for this purpose, the volume of net grain imports as the dependent variable (*NIM*) is formulated to be related to four variables. The first is the difference between the annual grain purchase and sales by the state (*GX*) that serves as an indicator regarding the demand and supply situation in the state grain sector. The second variable is the growth of domestic grain output over the preceding year (*PRO*) that is expected to reflect the overall situation of domestic production. The third variable is the adjustment in grain trade constrained by trade agreements that sometimes specify purchase commitments for a certain period of time. To investigate the potential partial adjustment in this context, the lagged dependent variable (NIM_{t-1}) is included. Finally, a trend variable (*TRD*) is included aiming to represent the impact of domestic grain shortage as a long-term trend. Obviously this simple model is not expected to provide a formal econometric analysis of the grain trade. It merely serves the purpose of testing the analytical hypothesis regarding the impact of various important factors on the grain trade. On the basis of the hypothesis, *GX* and *PRO* are expected to have a significant impact on grain imports.

As mentioned above, grain imports for a given year were determined primarily by an annual plan. This implies that to formulate a grain import plan for a given year, planners have available information about the domestic grain economy in the preceding years. This suggests that the grain trade is linked to the changes in the domestic grain economy with at least a one-year lag. On the basis of this consideration, the dependent variable of net imports is set to be related to the two main explanatory variables with lags. The length of the lags are essentially determined by data. The data used for analysis are presented in Table 9.2. The equation is estimated in a simple linear form using time series data for the period 1955–94. Results of the OLS estimation are reported below. Figures in parentheses are *t*-statistics.

$$NIM = \begin{array}{cccccc} 0.20 & - & 0.13 \ GX_{t-1} & - & 0.16 \ GX_{t-2} & - & 0.22 \ GX_{t-3} & - & 0.09 \ PRO_{t-2} \\ (0.24) & (2.04) & (2.47) & (3.03) & (2.80) \end{array}$$

$$\begin{array}{ccc} - \ 0.06 \ PRO_{t-3} & + \ 0.15 \ Trend & + \ 0.45 \ NIM_{t-1} \\ (1.94) & (3.60) & (3.84) \end{array}$$

$$R^2(\text{adjusted}) = 0.8148$$

Apart from the highly significant time trend variable and lagged term of the dependent variable, the estimated coefficients for all variables have the negative sign as expected. About 80 per cent of variation in net imports is explained by the fitted equation. The estimated coefficients on the three lagged terms of *GX* (GX_{t-1}, GX_{t-2} and GX_{t-3}) are all significant. The estimated coefficients on *PRO* are significant for two- and three-year lags but not for a one-year lag. The results suggest a rather long lag involved in grain imports. As for the main theme investigated in this chapter, the results seem consistent with the hypothesis regarding the role of institutional factors. On the one hand, given the fact that there was no price signal at work in the domestic grain sector, there was a significant relationship between the change in domestic grain output (*PRO*) and net grain imports. On the other hand, owing to the institutional factors discussed above, grain imports were not only influenced by changes in total grain output, but were also affected by the demand and supply gap (*GX*) in the state trading sector. The magnitude of the absolute values of the coefficients on *GX* are much larger than those on *PRO*, indicating that the state purchases in relation to its sale obligations are more important than the overall situation of grain production in determining grain imports and exports. When the level of state purchases fell short of sale

Table 9.2   Data for the regression analysis, 1952–95 (unit: million tons)

Year	NIMP	GX	PRO	Year	NIMP	GX	PRO
1952	−1.53	7.62	20.23	1974	4.48	0.38	10.33
1953	−1.81	6.45	2.91	1975	0.95	2.89	9.25
1954	−1.68	10.01	2.69	1976	0.60	−3.35	1.79
1955	−2.05	6.75	14.22	1977	5.69	−7.82	−3.58
1956	−2.50	−1.79	9.01	1978	6.96	− 4.05	22.04
1957	−1.93	4.00	2.30	1979	10.70	0.13	27.35
1958	−2.66	3.67	4.95	1980	11.81	−6.81	−11.57
1959	−4.16	11.55	−30.00	1981	13.55	−7.81	4.48
1960	−2.65	−9.25	−26.50	1982	14.87	−5.86	29.48
1961	4.46	−7.79	3.55	1983	11.47	16.40	32.78
1962	3.88	−3.88	12.50	1984	7.21	12.45	20.23
1963	4.46	0.53	10.00	1985	−2.71	−6.90	−28.20
1964	4.75	−0.37	17.50	1986	−1.81	−0.32	12.39
1965	3.99	−2.42	7.03	1987	9.09	7.29	11.48
1966	3.58	0.71	19.47	1988	8.25	−5.86	−8.95
1967	1.71	1.21	3.82	1989	10.18	7.97	13.52
1968	2.00	1.82	−8.76	1990	8.13	30.2 7	38.69
1969	1.55	−3.25	1.91	1991	3.32	13.8 1	10.95
1970	3.24	5.64	28.99	1992	−2.88	−2.16	7.37
1971	0.53	0.32	10.18	1993	−8.79	14.60	13.82
1972	1.65	−7.31	−9.66	1994	−1.83	n.a.	−11.39
1973	4.24	0.60	24.46	1995	19.85	n.a.	21.52

Notes:
NIMP: Grain imports *minus* exports. Data are from SSB, *Yearbook of China's Foreign Economy and Trade*, various issues from 1984. GX: Grain procurement *minus* sale in the state grain sector. Data are from SSB, *Market Statistical Yearbook of China*, (1994).
PRO: The growth of grain output which is defined as the grain output for a given year *minus* the output in the preceding year.
Sources: Data are from SSB, *Statistical Yearbook of China*, various issues from 1983.

obligations, the government had to increase grain imports to maintain a balance between demand and supply. The evidence helps to illustrate the impact of market segmentation on China's grain trade policy.

The political economy of grain trade policy

Several puzzling questions regarding the grain trade were raised. For example,

- Why did China export millions of tonnes of grain in 1959 and 1960 when its population was hit by a famine brought about by a drastic drop in domestic production?
- Why did China fail to become a net exporter after 1965 when its domestic grain production recovered to its pre-famine level?

- Why did imports surge to reach consecutive record levels during 1978–1982 at the same time as its domestic grain output increased dramatically?

The regression results in the previous section provide a simple explanation for these puzzling questions. They are also helpful in understanding the current difficulty faced by policy-makers regarding China's external trade in grain. This section discusses these two issues.

Our estimation results point to the discrepancy between the situation in the state grain sector and the situation of the national food system. For example, although grain production plummeted in 1959, the state purchased 64.12 million tonnes of grain domestically in that year – by far the highest during the period 1950–81. As shown in Table 9.2, the state had a surplus of 11.55 million tonnes – the highest in the entire period 1950–83. The situation in the state sector made it possible for China to increase its net grain export to an unprecedented level of over 4 million tonnes in 1959. However, the grain surplus in the state distribution system disguised a severe food crisis for the vast majority of the rural population, resulting in one of the most devastating famines in human history from 1959 to 1961, when millions of people starved to death. Although panic purchases from the world market were made in 1961, it was too late to prevent a massive famine that prevailed for over two years.

The delayed response of the grain trade to changes in domestic grain production in the late 1950s reveals the importance of political factors behind China's grain procurement policy. It is useful to look at this issue in detail. For most years in the last four decades or so, the grain situation in China was tight. In addition to the grain supply crisis which caused the great famine in 1959–61, grain shortages occurred frequently in other years. Under these circumstances, there were two major objectives set by the government:

(1) To acquire as much grain as possible from the peasants so as to meet the demand in the urban sector. From the government's point of view, this objective is essential to achieving an even more important objective of rapid industrialization.
(2) To maintain an adequate grain supply to meet the basic needs of the agricultural population. However, these two objectives are often in conflict. Transferring a large volume of grain to the state through compulsory procurement at low prices is at odds with the interests of grain producers, and inevitably has an adverse effect on their incentives to produce.[8]

In the 1950s, the state ambitiously acquired all grain surplus from the peasants. To achieve these objectives, the parameters for grain output, self-consumption requirement and surplus had to be calculated accurately for millions of small farmers on an individual basis. This requirement made the policy highly discretionary in nature as it had to be specific with regard to different harvests in different years by individual farmers. Owing to resistance from the huge number of small producers, the implementation of the policy faced enormous difficulties. The need to deal with the difficulties more effectively in part explained why policy-makers pushed forward the agricultural co-operation and then collectivization campaigns much faster than originally planned (Lu, 1989). Several political campaigns brought about the immense pressure that induced the behaviour of over-reporting grain output by grassroots cadres. At the climax of the disastrous Great Leap Forward Campaign in 1958–9, false reports of inflated grain outputs became a nationwide practice. The interplay of political factors created a unique background against which the state achieved the unusual high level of grain procurement in 1959 when the harvest was precariously poor.

The famine of 1959–61 was a catastrophe for the entire population, especially in rural areas. It was also a bitter lesson for policy-makers. The tragedy made one point very clear to the state: although under-fulfilment of the procurement target was bound to cause difficulty, 'successful' procurement of too much grain is far more dangerous. In the light of this lesson, the state had to make an important adjustment in its procurement policy. The previous discretionary policy was adjusted and the new policy specified certain grain procurement targets for different production units that were usually fixed for a period of three–five years. This adjustment aimed to provide a balance check to prevent a tragedy similar to that of 1959–61 from being repeated. It also gave some incentives for production teams to increase grain output since the marginal growth of grain output could be legitimately kept by the teams or sold to the state at higher prices over the fixed period.

Despite its positive effects, the new policy was costly to the state. In recognizing the peasants' partial entitlement to a small proportion of the grain surplus, the state implicitly gave up its previous objective of acquiring all grain surplus from the countryside. Although grain output *per capita* in 1966–76 recovered to the level of the 1950s, the state sector was unable to acquire sufficient grain to make China a net exporter again. Instead the tight situation in the state grain sector necessitated continuous net imports throughout the period. In order to minimize foreign exchange expenditure on grain imports, the deal of exchanging rice for wheat developed into a systematic pattern.

The net import hike in the late 1970s and early 1980s was again mainly driven by the gap between supply and demand in the state grain sector. Nevertheless the underlying cause of the widening gap this time was different from that in 1959–60. The gap was a direct result of the new policy adjustment implemented from the late 1970s that had a far-reaching impact on the Chinese economy. Owing to the policy adjustment in the early 1960s, China successfully avoided any recurrence of a major food crisis. However, food shortages remained a persistent problem throughout the Cultural Revolution period 1966–76. Many political and ideological campaigns aimed at increasing grain output achieved little, if any, desired effect. It became more and more apparent that the slow growth in grain production was primarily caused by the lack of production incentives that in part were due to the state grain procurement policy. At this point, Mao's death and the fall of the 'Gang of Four' represented a historical turning point for agricultural development. After a critical review of the radical economic policy adopted in the Cultural Revolution, policy priorities were adjusted in favour of agricultural and rural development. In order to reduce the peasants' burden and to encourage more production, the state cut the compulsory grain procurement quota by 20 per cent from 37.75 to 30.32 million tonnes during 1979–83 (DDZGLSGZ, 1988, pp. 175–6). This widened the gap between grain demand and supply in the state sector that had to be compensated for through more imports. As a result, the government in 1980 signed grain agreements with major exporters in the world market to secure an annual delivery of more than 10 million tonnes up to 1984 (Lu, 1994, Table 1.5, p. 22).

The above analysis is also useful in understanding China's present grain trade policy. Since the traditional trade regime is so deeply rooted in the old institutional framework, it inevitably faces serious difficulties in a changing economic environment. As revealed above, the primary objective of the grain trade policy was to fill the short-term gap in the domestic grain sector. The trade system was able to serve this objective reasonably well in the pre-reform period. There were two essential conditions for the normal functioning of the system. First, the primary problem in the pre-reform period was on the supply side, reflected in a persistent shortage of grain production. Second, the market mechanism was largely suppressed in the domestic grain sector; almost all marketable surplus was controlled by the state purchasing and selling monopoly. This made it possible for planners to know with reasonable accuracy the basic parameters of the domestic grain sector. On the basis of the information available, planners were able to make quantitative adjustments through an annual plan to balance demand and supply in urban areas.

Recent developments and changes especially from the mid-1980s have had a profound impact on the grain trade:

- First, there is a clear trend of growth in demand because of increasing use for animal feed. At the same time, the fast growth of production costs eroded China's comparative advantage. To meet the growing demand for grains, there is a need to substantially raise producer prices. This, in turn, has an adverse effect on economic stability and external economic relationships.
- Second, the market mechanism has been partially introduced into the grain sector. As a result, the state's control on grain marketing has been substantially reduced.
- Third, grain marketing has faced a glut situation, with so-called 'difficulties in selling grain' several times since the mid-1980s. The previous problem of a persistent grain shortage has been replaced by the new situation where the problems of shortage and glut prevail alternately.[9]

The changing economic environment and institutional setting present fundamental challenges to both the principles and mechanisms of the traditional trade policy. On the one hand, the principle of grain self-sufficiency has been questioned in comparison with the alternative principle of comparative advantage. As the economy is gradually integrated into the international economic system, it seems viable as well as desirable to change the basic objective of the grain trade from mainly bridging short-term gaps between demand and supply to increasing efficiency of resource allocation on the basis of comparative advantage. It is possible to increase economic efficiency and to maintain sustainable growth if China can further integrate its grain economy into the world market. On the other hand, serious problems emerged in the post-reform period because there was inconsistency between the grain trade policy and domestic production. As the controlling power of the state in grain marketing eroded when grain shortage and glut occurred alternately, the planners' task of assessing the grain situation in an annual trade framework became more and more difficult. Since the grain trade is still largely determined in an annual planning framework with a long adjustment lag, it is almost impossible to accommodate effectively short-term fluctuations in the domestic grain market. It is therefore not surprising to observe the discordance between grain import adjustment and domestic grain production in recent years.[10] The grain trade policy needs to be reformed so as to improve its flexibility in responding to changes in the domestic market.

Concluding remarks

Focusing on the relationship between the grain trade and domestic economy, this chapter reveals three central features in China's grain trade policy. First, grain imports have been used to fill the physical gaps between demand and supply in the state sector. The principle of comparative advantage has not been a main motivation behind grain imports and exports. Second, the grain trade policy has developed as an integral part of the traditional central planning system. In fact, it serves as an extension of the state monopoly in grain marketing. Through an annual planning system, the gap between domestic demand and supply is transmitted into import/export demand. Although the foreign trade system as a whole has undergone profound transformation over the last two decades or so, the grain trade is one of the few exceptions and is still heavily regulated in an annual planning framework. Third, there exists a unique mechanism by which traditional grain trade policy is formulated. Because the domestic grain economy is segmented into two relatively independent parts, the state and the rural population, the state marketing authority tends to have a greater influence over import/export decisions.

The above analysis has important policy implications. Since the grain trade system is so deeply rooted in the old institutional framework, it inevitably faces serious challenges in a changing economic environment. On the one hand, the traditional principle of self-sufficiency has been questioned in comparison with an alternative principle of comparative advantage. As the economy is gradually integrating into the international economic system, it seems viable as well as desirable to change the basic objective of the grain trade from mainly bridging short-term gaps between demand and supply into increasing the efficiency of resource allocation. On the other hand, as the domestic grain market increases its significance in adjusting demand and supply, co-ordination between the grain trade and changes in domestic production has become more important for stabilizing the domestic grain market. The annual planning procedure for the grain trade needs to be reformed so as to improve flexibility and to even out the fluctuations in grain supply.

Notes:

[*] The author is grateful for valuable comments and editorial assistance by Shujie Yao, Juzhong Zhuang and Sarah Cook but takes full responsibility for any errors or omissions.

1. The net grain import value for the whole 11 year period is US\$ 126 million, which was only half of that for a single year of 1963 (Lu, 1994, p. 118).

2. MOFT was put in charge of China's foreign trade in 1952. In the institutional streamlining in early 1982, MOFT, the Ministry of Economic Relations with Foreign Countries, the State Import and Export Commissions and Foreign Investment Commission merged into the Ministry of Foreign Economic Relations and Trade (MOFERT).

3. It was later changed into the Ministry of Internal Trade (MIT).

4. In order to fix grain ration levels in the urban areas, the country was divided into two categories of region according to grain production and consumption patterns in the region: those where the staple grain was rice and the other where coarse grain and wheat were the staple food. Urban residents were divided into eight categories depending upon their age and occupation. The categories included 'special heavy physical labourer', 'heavy physical labourer', 'light physical labourer', 'staff members in institutions of administrative bureaucracies and social groups, mental workers', 'students in the universities and middle schools', 'ordinary residents and teenagers over ten years old', etc. Urban consumers were assigned specific grain rations according to the localities in which they lived and the categories of population into which they fell. For example, the monthly ration for the 'special heavy physical labourers' in the rice region was about 25 kg of rice whereas in the second region it was about 27.5 kg of coarse grain and wheat. By the same token, the monthly ration for university and middle school students was 16 kg of rice in the rice region and 17.5 kg of coarse grain and wheat in the second region (DDZGLSGZ, 1988, pp. 90–1). Feed grain was in theory supplied according to actual requirements. However, rations and fodder supply for grain-short households in ordinary grain-producing areas must have been lower than that for grain-surplus households in the same areas. As for peasant households designated by the state to specialize in cash crops, the standards of their ration and fodder supply should not be lower than that of the grain surplus households (DDZGLSGZ, 1988, p. 87).

5. It is worth noting that China's domestic grain market has a long history. However, during the period of the state monopoly of purchasing and marketing, the scale of private grain markets was very small. In certain years, the market was prohibited; in other years when market transactions were permitted, they were subject to severe restrictions. The situation changed substantially when restrictions were gradually removed from the 1980s. The market mechanism has begun to play an active role in the domestic grain economy in recent years.

6. The household registration system in China was directly linked with the grain-ration supply system. Small numbers of people defined as the 'non-agricultural population' might actually live in rural areas and have access to the grain-ration supply from the state; on the other hand, a few urban residents might not have legal urban status and would thus not be eligible for the grain-ration supply.

7. Obviously the two parts of the grain economy were interrelated – e.g. changes in the quantity of grain supply in one part would result in responses in the other, at a given total grain output. However, they were distinct or relatively independent in two aspects. First, the ways in which the two parts functioned were different. The rural grain sector was basically self-sufficient. The state was not directly responsible for allocation of grain in the rural sector, and its control of grain demand and supply in this part of the domestic grain economy was relatively limited and indirect. On the other hand, the grain demand and supply in the urban sector was directly controlled by the state. Secondly, the direction of changes in the two parts of the grain economy might not necessarily coincide. Given certain changes in national average grain output *per capita*, it was perfectly possible for them to move in different directions.

8. For a detailed account of the conflict in dividing the grain surplus in contemporary China, see Oi (1989). However, this problem is not unique to China. 'Mobilizing adequate marketable surplus [grain] for urban consumption' is 'the universal problem' for 'all governments of large developing economies'. 'Fundamentally, the peasants in these countries, where agricultural production is generally precarious, loathe government interference with disposal of their surplus. All are apt to resist the government procurement efforts in any possible way, particularly those involving elements of "squeezing"' (Wong, 1980).

9. Following the first grain selling difficulties in the mid-1980s, the traditional shortage problem struck back from 1986 and dominated the situation for a few years. However the pendulum swung to the glut side in the early 1990s when grain producers again faced widespread problems in selling grain. This changed rather suddenly when grain prices increased dramatically from late 1993 and 1994. A bumper harvest in 1996 created another period of grain glut.

10. For example, net exports peaked in 1993–4 when domestic grain prices rose sharply. The phenomenon of incompatibility between domestic grain market movements and the grain trade attracted wide criticism and concern.

Bibliography

Carter, A. C. and Zhong Funing (1991) 'China's Past and Future Role in the Grain Trade', *Economic Development and Cultural Change*, 39, pp. 791–814.

Chen Liangyu and A. Buckwell (1991) *Chinese Grain Economy and Policy* (London: CAB International).

DDZGLSGZ (1988) *Grain Works in the Contemporary China* (Dangdai zhongguo de liangshi gongzuo) (Beijing: Chinese Social Science Press (Zhongguo shehui kexue chubanshe)).

Donnithorne, A. (1970) *China's Grain: Output, Procurement, Transfers and Trade*, Economic Research Centre, Chinese University of Hong Kong.

Garnaut, R. and Ma Guonan (1992) *Grain in China* (Canberra: Australian Government Publishing Service).

Lu, F.(1989) 'Implementation of the Policy of Grain Unified Purchase and Marketing and Establishment of the Non-market Economy' (Tonggou tongxiao de shixing yu feishichang tizhi de queli), *Teaching and Research* (Jiaoyue yu yanjiu), 3.

Lu, F. (1994) *China's Grain Imports: Policy Evolution and Determinants*, PhD thesis, School of Business and Economic Studies, Leeds University.

Oi, J. C. (1989) *State and Peasant in Contemporary China – The Political Economy of Village Government* (Berkeley: University of California Press).

State Statistical Bureau (SSB) (1993–6) *Statistical Yearbook of China*, various issues.

State Statistical Bureau (SSB) (1994) *Market Statistical Yearbook of China*.

State Statistical Bureau (SSB) (1994–6) *Yearbook of China's Foreign Economy and Trade*, various issues.

Surls, F. W. (1978) 'China Grain Trade', in United States Congress, *Chinese Economy Post-Mao* (Washington, DC: US Government Printing Office).

Timmer, C. P. and J. R. Jones (1986) 'China: An Enigma in the World Grain Trade', in J. R. Jones (ed.), *East–West Agricultural Trade* (Boulder and London: Westview Press).

Wong, J. (1980) 'China's Wheat Import Programme', *Food Policy*, May.

World Bank (1991) *China – Options for Reform in the Grain Sector* (Washington, DC: World Bank).

Yao, S. (1994) *Agricultural Reforms and Grain Production in China* (London: Macmillan).

10
The Economic Behaviour of China's Grain Producers in Transition

John Davis and Liming Wang

Introduction

China's agriculture is in transition both from subsistence to commercial farming and from a centrally planned to a market system. However, the grain sector still has strong characteristics of subsistence agriculture and government control remains strong compared with other crop sectors. Currently, about 73 per cent of arable land is used for grain production, involving millions of agricultural households with very small holdings: about two-thirds of grain output is used for own-consumption in these households. The Chinese government still thinks of grain as the base of the national economy and keeps control of the grain market through the procurement quota, although this has been reduced in significance following economic reforms (see also Chapter 9 in this volume). At present, dual markets for grain co-exist, i.e. the state market and the free market – and grain producers now have to make decisions in the light of two markets and prices: the state quota and price and the free-market price. There has been considerable academic interest in analyzing various aspects of this so-called 'double-track' system in China (e.g. Sicular, 1988; Jin, 1990; Chen, 1990; Cheng *et al.*, 1992; Du, 1995; Ke, 1995). However, there has been relatively little work done in analyzing the microeconomic behaviour of grain producers under *both* traditional subsistence and this new institutional setting. The limited progress in this research area is reflected in the specifications of the major econometric models of China's grain output, few of which have rigorous micro-theoretical foundations.

This chapter explores theoretical models of the microeconomic behaviour of grain producers under the influences of subsistence production, government intervention and the free market. Empirical models of the grain-supply mechanism are then constructed using time-series data; separate analyses are carried out for the pre-reform (1952–78) and post-reform (1978–95) periods.

Theoretical modelling of the Chinese grain producer

This section provides a brief overview of previous theoretical work and then proceeds to develop a graphical analysis of the supply behaviour of a 'typical' grain producer in China. Its purpose is not to provide a precise template for the empirical section which follows. Rather, it is an attempt to highlight in an abstract way some of the special microeconomic features of Chinese grain production which may need to be taken into account in empirical work.

A starting point is the work of Perkins (1966), which examined the transition from a rural market to a planned economy in the mid-1950s and the subsequent interaction of market and plan. Wang (1980) used a graphical analysis of supply in an attempt to explain government price policy but neglected the probable differences in the supply curves of the market and planned economies. Sicular (1983) was the first to provide a Chinese agricultural household model in the planned economy, incorporating a utility-maximization assumption subject to a budget, a production function and a quota constraint. Her subsequent work (Sicular, 1988) in a double-track pricing context highlighted the importance of the market rather than the state quota price in determining farmers' production behaviour. Her work was a major contribution to understanding Chinese agricultural household behaviour and emphasized the need for empirical studies to take account of both the state-procurement and market prices.

However, producer decisions to sell to the state or free market are complicated if quota evasion is common and the market price alone may fail to call the tune. Chen (1990) extended Sicular's model from a three-good to a multiple-good case. He explicitly recognized differences in behaviour among agricultural households in the state and free markets but, like Sicular, did not incorporate quota-evasion formally into his model. Using a diagrammatic approach, Jin (1990) suggested that changes in both the state-quota and free-market prices may give rise to two possible adjustment effects, a marginal and a quantum adjustment. Based on Jin's work, Cheng *et al.* (1992) developed a more formal theoretical model in which agricultural households were regarded as profit-maximizers with a special profit function. They also pointed to the possibility of disequilibrium in the form of quantum changes in supply as 'thresholds of weighted average decisions are reached'. However, both studies failed to take account of the possible effects of production for subsistence needs on farm-household behaviour. It is clear that significant challenges remain in modelling the microeconomic behaviour of grain producers in China; in the remainder of this section we adopt a graphical analysis to explore the supply behaviour of a 'typical' grain producer, taking account of subsistence needs and the possible effects of government interventions. Comparisons are made with the situation which might exist for a commercial producer operating in a free market-context.

The supply schedule of a semi-commercial grain producer in China

It is assumed that the producer has two primary goals. The first is production for subsistence needs: in China today, two-thirds of grain output is used for producers' household consumption. The second is that beyond subsistence needs the producer pursues profit-maximization: this is consistent with Perkins (1966)

> within the scope of his limited knowledge and given the high risks involved in almost any agricultural undertaking in China ... [the producer] has attempted to maximise his expected return.

A marginal cost and supply curve can thus be constructed as shown in Figure 10.1.

In Figure 10.1(i), *MC* is the producer's marginal cost curve. $Q = Q_c$ is the quantity of subsistence grain demanded and supplied by the producer's household: it must be produced regardless of changes in price. Beyond Q_c, the producer will behave according to a profit-maximizing goal. This gives rise to the supply schedule *DCS* shown in Figure 10.1(ii). Thus, we can say that: (a) at prices above P_c the supply and marginal cost schedules coincide; (b) the price at which market supply ceases (P_c) is higher than that (P_o) in a commercial market economy; and (c) for any price below P_c output (Q_c) will be higher than that of a commercial producer, although none of this is sold on the market.

The supply schedule under the influence of government grain policy

Two important elements of policy impinge directly namely, mandatory delivery quotas[1] and the 'double-track' pricing system in which the state fixed price and the free market price co-exist. In principle, under this system once

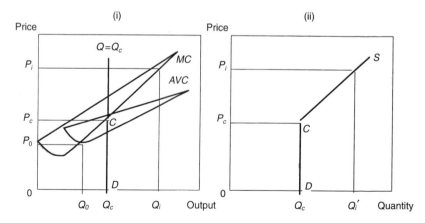

Figure 10.1 Supply schedule of a Chinese grain producer under subsistence production

mandatory grain delivery quotas are filled at the state price, the producer may sell surplus grain on the free market, or to the state, usually at the higher price. However, in practice the situation is more complicated owing to the prevalence of quota evasion in the increasingly liberal environment after economic reform. In what follows, two possible cases are examined through the lens of neoclassical economic theory. In the first case, it is assumed that the grain producer has no choices but fully meets the quota at any cost – i.e. there is no significant quota evasion. In the second, it is assumed that the grain producer chooses to under-supply the quota at negligible cost – i.e. there is quota evasion.

No quota evasion

This case may be further divided into two sub-cases, illustrated in Figure 10.2, according to whether the state price P_s is lower than or equal to P_c or higher than P_c. Where $P_s \leq P_c$, suppose that the quota and the state procurement price are set at $Q_s - Q_c$ and Ps, respectively. P_f and $Q_f - Q_s$ represent the price and the amount traded in the free market. The producer has to fulfil the quota at price P_s and suffers a loss equivalent to the area of triangle ABC. Beyond the quota, the producer pursues a profit maximization goal by increasing supply along her MC curve in the free market. Two possible cases are shown in Figure 10.2(a). In panel (i) the actual MC schedule beyond B is shown to lie below that of a producer in a market economy with no state control, and converges with the latter at the point of maximum output. This configuration, arguably, may be justified as a result of state subsidization of fertilizers, insecticides etc. Another factor is the relative abundance of rural labour in China: Stevens and Jabara (1988) have pointed out that labour in most developed nations represents at least half of the value of non-land resources used in agricultural production. Also, Xu and Peel (1991) have argued that the cost of labour is rarely taken into account by rural households in their productive activities. However, this point may be less valid in recent years following the rapid development of the Township and Village Enterprises (TVEs). Thus, the actual supply schedule in this case is given by $DCBS$. An alternative model is shown in panel (ii). In this case it is suggested that the supply schedule is not continuous but actually has a discontinuity depicted by the vertical distance AB. After meeting the quota the producer will not supply to the market until the price rises to P^*. If such a discontinuity exists the effects on output of changes in prices and costs are difficult to predict. This idea of a discontinuity is consistent with the views of Shi (1991), who proposed that the marginal cost schedule was disjointed.

In Figure 10.2(b) where $P_s > P_c$ the outcomes are similar. However, in this case, as a free-market producers' output would be Q_b, the loss ABE suffered by the producer under quota is now smaller than the loss ABC in Figure 10.2(a): there is also now a surplus generated on output $Q_b - Q_c$, represented by the area BCF. Finally, the supply schedule discontinuity, AE, is now smaller.

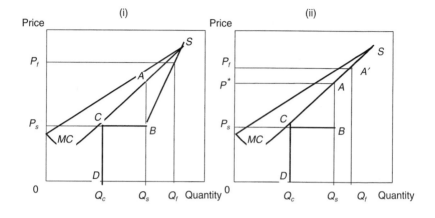

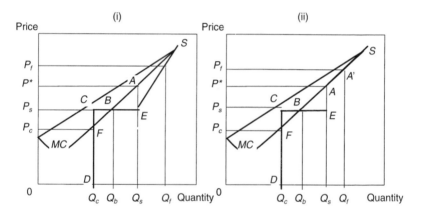

Figure 10.2   Supply schedule of a Chinese grain producer under quota (no quota evasion)
a $P_s \leq P_c$
b $P_s > P_c$

Three additional implications of this analysis should be mentioned.

(1) As a result of the priority given to subsistence needs and state quota, supply may tend to be less responsive to price changes compared with commercial production in a market economy: over certain price ranges there may be very little, if any, supply response.
(2) The market equilibrium price will tend to be lower and quantity higher than in a market economy. Owing to the effects of both subsistence production and quota, grain sown area and output in China will tend to be

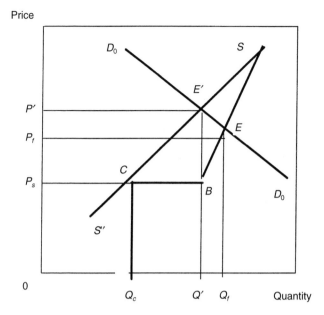

Figure 10.3   Free-market and Chinese-market equilibria

higher for a given price level than would be the case if a market economy prevailed. Figure 10.3 reproduces the supply schedules of Figure 10.2(a) panel (i), and superimposes a market demand schedule D_0D_0. The equilibrium for the market economy case is given by $P'Q'$. However, in the Chinese market case under subsistence production, state quota and artificially low input prices, the equilibrium price (P_f) is lower and output (Q_f) is higher.

(3) The extent of influence of the free market price may be relatively limited in the Chinese case. For example, in Figure 10.2(a) panel (ii), it is evident there will be no supply response to market prices in the range $P_s - P^*$.

With quota evasion

Here we explore the possible impact of quota-evasion on supply behaviour: it is assumed that the producer can evade quota at negligible cost. It is difficult to be precise about the current level of quota evasion but there is evidence that it has been significant in the past especially during the first half of the 1980s.[2] In Figure 10.4 the quota is $Q_s - Q_c$ and the state and free market prices are P_s and P_f, respectively. If the producer's output is Q_s a loss equivalent to ABC is incurred. At the free-market price P_f and output Q_f a producer's surplus equivalent to the area ADE is earned: in this example, it is assumed that ADE

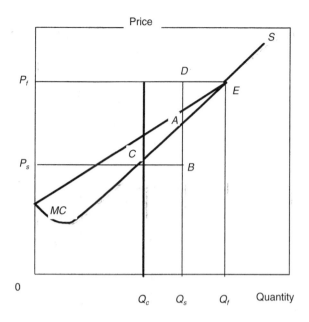

Figure 10.4   Supply schedule of a Chinese grain producer under quota (with quota evasion) $P_s \leq P_c$

equals *ABC*. It thus can be seen that where the free market-price is below P_f the producer may decide to avoid quota so as not to incur the loss ABC. If the price rises above P_f the producer will find it possible to supply quota and begin to earn a surplus in the market. It is possible then to identify three phases of supply: (a) a phase of constant output Q_c where the market price is below P_f; (b) a 'quantum jump' from Q_c to Q_f at price P_f; and (c) a phase of marginal adjustment where the market price rises above P_f. It can be seen that a change in the state and free-market price relativity may be instrumental in setting off a quantum change (rise or fall) in output. This type of phenomenon is unlikely to occur in a free market. It should be stressed that although it is possible to predict quantum changes at the micro level these may not be apparent at the macro level. One reason is that producers have different underlying cost functions and therefore the critical market price for example for a 'quantum jump' to occur will not be the same for all producers.

Empirical modelling of grain supply

Given the economic and political importance of grain in China it is essential to try to understand the complex web of factors underlying supply from both theoretical and empirical standpoints. This section explores empirical models of grain supply which attempt to take account of the special characteristics of supply identified in previous sections and the changes which occurred during the period 1952–95.

Agricultural supply response involves estimating the quantitative response in supply of farm commodities to changes in product prices, input prices and other relevant measurable aspects of the changing environment of agricultural production (Colman, 1983). The conventional specification of a supply-response function is based on a neoclassical economics framework that assumes profit maximization behaviour by producers in a market environment. As discussed in the previous section, however, producer behaviour under the Chinese centrally planned system and the post-1978 'socialist market system' has been much more constrained than in a market economy. In this section, therefore, empirical models will be developed which seek in a pragmatic way to capture the nature of grain production and policy interactions in China's pre and post-reform periods.

The nature of grain production and policy interactions

Grain-sown acreage and yield

Figure 10.5 shows the very different trends in grain sown acreage and yield between 1952 and 1995. Despite the fall in acreage, total output increased by 184 per cent from 164 to 466 million tonnes. The growth in output was due almost entirely to improvements in yield.

As Chen and Buckwell (1991) have pointed out, the high population-land ratio has meant that increasing output by bringing more land under cultivation has not been an available option. Following Nerlove (1958), the supply response of annual crops has often been analyzed using acreage sown

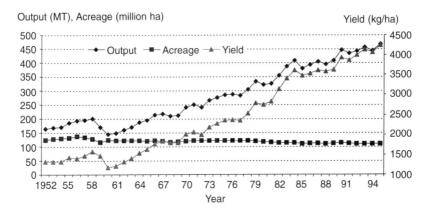

Figure 10.5   Trends of grain output, sown acreage and yield, 1952–95
Source: Chinese Statistical Yearbook (various issues)

as the proxy for output. The argument is that producers have more control over area and that yield is determined by factors such as technology and weather which are beyond producers' control (Gunawardana and Oczkowski, 1992). In this study, however, for the purpose of comparison between the pre- and post-reform periods, acreage and yield responses are treated as distinctly separate aspects of grain supply. The authors take the view that a fuller understanding of supply behaviour in a changing environment can be achieved by analyzing acreage and yield responses separately.

Subsistence-grain farming

In any analysis of the production of basic food crops in developing economies, a fundamental question about the link between total production and the marketed portion must be resolved (Askari, 1976). In discussing the impact of subsistence farming in China, Buck (1937) in his book, *Land Utilization in China*, claimed that even if we can put a price on a crop, there are doubts as to how far it really represents its value to a subsistence agricultural community. Most of the crop may be grown for subsistence consumption, and only a small and unrepresentative part of it traded for money (Clark and Haswell, 1964). Buck's description is still to a large extent applicable in China's grain sector today. At least 200 million rural households out of 215 million in total are currently engaged in grain production. For these small-scale households some minimum own-grain consumption (not cash needs) is the starting point, since survival is the most essential goal of production activities. As a result, on average only about 350 kg of grain is traded on the market by each household in a year (Ke, 1995). Figure 10.6 shows that about 37 per cent of grain produced in 1995 was sold on the market, the rest of it was for subsistence purposes. Although there has been significant specialization and 'commercialization' of grain production in the reform period, subsistence remains a fundamental

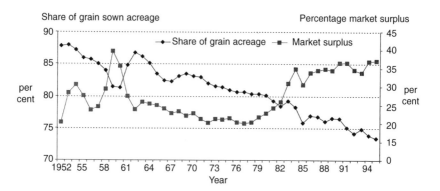

Figure 10.6   Share of grain-sown acreage and proportion of market surplus, 1952–95
Source: Chinese Statistical Yearbook (various issues).

influencing factor in Chinese grain producers' supply behaviour, especially the allocation of sown acreage.

Prices and government policy

From the historical point of view, the changes in Chinese government policies and prices have passed through two distinctive periods, dichotomized by the economic reforms started in 1978. In the pre-reform period, government non-price policies had been very active in trying to influence grain supply. Apart from direct control of the pricing system, four related non-price measures were used: (a) a compulsory planned sown area; (b) a delivery quota system; (c) subsidies on agricultural inputs; and (d) an incentive policy called 'three links', whereby producers would be guaranteed a fixed amount of high-grade chemical fertilizer, diesel oil and cash-advance awards for grain deliveries to the state. These non-price policies tended to predominate and prices appeared to play a relatively minor role in guiding grain supply before the reforms. The long-depressed state procurement prices, in combination with the prevalence of planning in grain production, resulted in a depression of farmers' grain production incentives and inefficiency in resource allocation.

At the beginning of the reforms, the decision to increase state procurement prices, reduce grain procurement quotas and allow producers to sell grain surplus in free markets after fulfilling the state quota reflected an intention to increase the roles of prices and markets (Wang and Davis, 1992). After several bumper harvests in the early 1980s more market-oriented reforms were launched in 1985. The state no longer set mandatory plans for grain production and the state obligatory procurement quotas for grain were replaced by purchasing contracts between the state and farmers. All these reforms reduced the role of government intervention and increased the role of prices and markets in guiding grain production. Although such policy changes are difficult to quantify, it is important nevertheless to attempt to capture their effects. In short, it may be expected that prices have become more important determinants of supply in the post-reform period.

Rural institutional changes

The transition from the Collective to the Household Responsibility System (HRS) between 1978 and 1984 was accompanied by strong growth in yield. Lin (1987) attributed rapid growth in agricultural production to the HRS; he found that 20 per cent of productivity growth and 60 per cent of production growth was attributable to institutional change. McMillan, Whalley and Zhu (1989), using an accounting approach, concluded that 22 per cent of the increase in productivity of Chinese agriculture between 1978 and 1984 was due to higher prices and 78 per cent to institutional change. Fan (1991), using a frontier production function, concluded that 27 per cent of production growth was contributed by institutional change. Although these findings on the relative importance of the HRS diverge, they all attribute importance to this development.

However, following the institutional changes in the early 1980s, the expansion of irrigation systems which accounted for most of the yield growth in the past has stagnated. After peaking in 1984, the growth rates of grain yields declined for the first time since the early 1960s (Huang and Rozelle, 1995). This decelerating yield trend in the late 1980s has caused some researchers to raise questions about the effects of the institutional change on the development of irrigation systems in rural China. Under the HRS, a much smaller core of individuals with more fragmented land is responsible for farming, and it has become more difficult to organize routine maintenance and to initiate new irrigation projects (Liu, 1994). Stone (1988) argued that one cause of the failure is the inadequate specification of ownership rights under HRS, leading to over-use and neglect of maintenance of irrigation systems. Thus, it is well accepted by most researchers that Chinese development efforts during the reform period have been less successful in expanding the irrigated area than during the pre-reform period.

Model specification and estimation

The literature by Chinese researchers on modelling Chinese agriculture has only really developed since the 1980s. Early models were mainly used for output projection and selection of farming structure, rather than for supply and policy analysis. Previous modelling work on China's grain supply had similarly concentrated on output forecasting and either ignored the basic features of grain production in China as discussed in the last section, or treated them superficially. Exceptions include Carter and Zhong's (1988) work on China's grain production, consumption and trade, which tried to measure the impact of government policy on China's grain production. The virtue of their approach was the explicit recognition of the impact of policy on grain production by taking policy instruments as major variables in the model. They suggested that, ideally, one could not exclude policy influences on grain-sown area and yield. However, there is only one economic policy instrument (purchasing price of grain) employed in their model as an explanatory variable. Some very important instruments, especially non-price policies, were omitted. Another problem was that only one exogenous variable (population) was used in the sown-area equation, and this probably explains a rather small proportion of the changes in grain-sown area. It is true that population growth would shift farmland into non-farm usage. However, the long-term declining proportion of grain sown area to total sown area (see Figure 10.6) and shorter-term fluctuations since the early 1950s cannot be explained simply by population growth.

A second notable exception is the research of Chen and Buckwell (1991), who examine the main factors which determine peasants' grain-supply response. They identify systematic policy patterns within the apparently bewildering series of changes in policy which influenced the historical development of Chinese grain production. However, in their model supply response was not disaggregated into sown-area and yield components.

Although prices were employed as major variables in their model, non-price policies were not given enough attention. Dummy variables were used to indicate two policy pattern changes. However, there are limitations in using dummy variables in Chinese grain-sector modelling. One is the difficulty in defining the stages of a policy's impact – i.e. the exact timing of when the policy is announced, when it is having full effect and how it is fine-tuned. Another is the fixity of agricultural assets and the inelastic nature of supply and demand; these contrast with the abrupt changes introduced when dummy variables are used (Halbrendt and Gempesaw, 1990). For these reasons, as Chen and Buckwell themselves pointed out, two policy patterns are not adequately represented as a strict dichotomy – 'policy on' versus 'policy off'. This may explain the poor statistical performance of their equations when dummy variables were employed. The challenge which remains is how to simplify and quantify the complexity of policy impacts, especially non-price policies, on producers' responses whilst taking account of their subsistence objectives.

Although the empirical analysis below takes account of basic elements of the theoretical framework outlined above, it cannot reflect it precisely. This is caused partly by data and statistical limitations. For example, state and free-market price data tend to be highly collinear; the estimation problem is consequently compounded by the presence of multicollinearity. To provide a practical basis for the empirical work the models are therefore specified to reflect key features of grain production and policy interaction. The grain-sown acreage and yield functions are specified separately as follows.

Sown acreage $\quad \ln SA_t = \alpha_0 + \alpha_1 \ln PV_t + \alpha_2 \ln MS_t + \alpha_3 \ln P_{g(t-1)}$
$$+ \alpha_4 \ln P_{k(t-1)} + \mu_t$$

Yield $\quad \ln Y = \beta_0 + \beta_1 \ln IR + \beta_2 \ln WD + \beta_3 Dic + \beta_4 T + v$

where SA is the share of grain sown acreage to total crops

$\quad$ Y is the yield of grain crops (kg/*mu*, 1 *mu* = 1/15 hectare)

$\quad$ PV is a policy variable, represented by average output *per capita* in the previous two years

$\quad$ MS is the level of self-subsistence represented by the average proportion of market surplus in total production in the previous two years

$\quad$ P_g is the weighted average of state and free-market purchasing price index for grain (1951 = 100)

$\quad$ P_k is the purchasing price index for oil crops (1951 = 100) (Both P_g and P_k were deflated by the total retail price index for the rural area)

$\quad$ IR is the proportion of area irrigated

$\quad$ WD is the weather condition represented by the area affected by natural disaster

$\quad$ Dic is the dummy variable for institutional changes

$\quad$ T is the time trend.

The variables

SA: The reason for using share of sown acreage in total crop acreage is that grain-sown acreage itself has often been under-stated in the Chinese official statistics. There are two underlying reasons for this. One is that farmers have for years systematically under-reported the quantity of land as a way of reducing their taxes (Crook, 1994). The other concerns local governments' desire to declare higher yield figures. Figures for arable land obtained by other sources (e.g. remote sensing from a US satellite; Crook, 1992; State Land Administration, 1994; Wu and Kirke, 1994) have been much greater than the official figures. A Chinese report based on the results of a 'National Survey of the Present Situation of Land Uses' has indicated that the total farmland is 133.3 million hectares, almost 40 per cent higher than the Chinese official statistics of 95 million hectares in 1995 (*People's Daily*, 1996).

PV (the *policy variable*):   There are clearly measurement problems here. The national agricultural plan in China is based mainly on the balance of grain production and consumption annually. Therefore, policy-makers in the central government keep a watchful eye on the changes in grain output *per capita*. Where this figure has declined for two or three years continually, the central government will adjust policy to encourage producers to grow more grain. However, the policy adjustment has been mainly through non-price measures such as the 'three links policy'. Former Vice Prime Minister, Yao Yilin, has stated, 'the changes in China's grain policies are mainly dependent on the output, i.e. the average output *per capita*' (Yao, 1988). Thus it was necessary to find a proxy variable which would adequately reflect the extent of non-price policies in a particular year. Bearing in mind the approach adopted by government it was decided to use the average grain output *per capita* in the previous two years. This combined relative simplicity with realism.

MS (the *subsistence variable*):   This is measured as the average amount of grain sold on the market as a proportion of total output in the previous two years. It is an indirect indicator of the level of subsistence. In compliance with the long-standing policy of national and local self-sufficiency for grain in China, agricultural producers nationwide had to allocate certain land for grain production irrespective of the suitability of the soil and agro–climatic conditions of the area. However, during the reform process there has been greater specialization and diversification of production, resulting in more grain-marketed surplus being available from a smaller sown acreage. Thus as more surplus is produced there may be a tendency for land to be switched out of grain production.

P_g *and* P_k *(the price variables)*:   There have been many prices which could be called the 'farm-gate price', including the quota price, above-quota price, negotiated price, contract price and market price. In this study, data on the grain-purchasing price indices (P_g) refer to the weighted average of all prices offered by the state marketing system and the free market for grains. The purchasing price for cash crops (P_k) is another factor influencing producers' behaviour. The main competitive crops are cotton and oil; both of them were tried in the initial specification and it appeared that the purchasing price of oil crops was more relevant. For both P_g and P_k, a simple assumption was made namely that the price in year $t - 1$ was the expected price in year t.

IR (irrigated area): The aggregate irrigation area has been regarded as an important assistance to grain yield growth during the pre-reform era. The organization of China's rural areas into collectives contributed to expansion of the irrigated area from 18 per cent in 1952 to over 45 per cent in 1978, an increase of nearly 20 million hectares (Huang and Rozelle, 1955). During the reform period, however, growth in the effective irrigated area stagnated. By 1995, the proportion of cultivated area under irrigation reached 52 per cent, an increase of only 4.3 million hectares (SSB, 1996).

WD (weather condition): The variable chosen as the indicator of weather condition was the proportion of total cropped area affected by natural disasters. Weather can be an over-riding factor in explaining grain output variations in China (Kueh, 1986). A negative relationship between the weather indicator and grain yield is expected.

Dic (dummy variables for institutional changes):   These changes in rural China have progressed through four major stages. The first was the period of collectivization from 1952 to 1958. Following this, in 1959, the government decided to push for an even higher ideological structure – i.e. the people's communes. This mass movement, with its colossal mismanagement of agricultural production, resulted in a three years' disaster between 1959 and 1961. In 1962, the communal system of production was therefore modified, with production decision-making reverting to the production team level which lasted until 1978 when economic reform started. The final period of institutional change was the transition from collective farming to the HRS after 1978. An attempt has been made to measure the effects of these major changes through the use of dummy variables. This was done by specifying a dummy variable, $D = 0$ for each year 1962–77; $D = -1$ for each year 1959–61. For the periods 1952–8 and 1978–95 the dummy variables in each year were given a value equivalent to the proportion of independent farm households in total production units, in order to reflect the extent of institutional change.

T (technological progress): This has worked as one of the main engines of growth in grain yield in China. Increased use of modern inputs, such as chemical fertilizers, irrigation, weed and pest control and high-yielding crop varieties, etc, have been the main areas of focus for improvement and for capital investment in the last four decades. Unfortunately, there has been little progress made in characterizing and modelling technical progress by means of empirical analysis. Often it is handled using a time trend as an indicator; this is the approach used in this study to represent a set of technology shifters, apart from irrigation.

Research on Chinese agricultural development has always been hampered by data problems, especially for research conducted outside the country. Most data used in this study were obtained from various issues of the *Chinese Statistical Yearbook*. Some were provided by the Ministry of Internal Trade and other published sources. Seemingly Unrelated Regressions (SUR) were estimated using EViews. Sown acreage and yield functions are estimated separately for the periods of 1952–95 and the pre-reform (1952–78) and post-reform (1978–95) periods. Furthermore, in testing for structural stability of regression models, Chow's Forecast-Test was used to examine whether there existed a structural change between the pre- and post-reform periods.

Results

The coefficients of the grain acreage and yield equations are shown in Table 10.1. Both sets of equations have high explanatory power, with adjusted R^2 values not lower than 0.90 for sown acreage and 0.93 for yield. Of greater interest are the values of the individual coefficients and comparisons between the pre- and post-reform periods. The signs of the coefficients are in line with *a priori* expectations. In the acreage equations the proxy for non-price policies – i.e. grain output *per capita* in the previous two years (PV) – had a negative influence on sown acreage. In the pre-reform period these policies were highly significant determinants but in the post-reform period they became insignificant. This is consistent with the change in government approach after 1978 when fewer administrative controls (especially the substantial reduction of government procurement quota) on sown acreage were used. Thus the PV variable appears to have worked well as an indicator of non-price policies. The influence of grain price (P_g) was positive in both periods but only in the post-reform period did it play a highly significant role in influencing acreage allocation. The results for both PV and P_g are consistent with the more market-led policies adopted following the reforms, with grain prices playing a much more important role in acreage response. The co-efficient for the price of oil crops (P_k) tends to confirm the high level of competition between grain and oil crops in both periods. The negative coefficients for the subsistence variable (MS) in both periods confirm that as marketable surplus increased there was a greater propensity to shift land out of grain production. As the proportion of marketable surplus increased in the post-reform period this relationship became more important – i.e. in terms of the magnitude of the coefficients. These results confirm that the level of self-subsistence has always been a significant factor influencing the grain sown acreage.

In the yield equations, the dummy variables representing institutional changes were highly significant in both periods. This suggests that the

Table 10.1 Comparison of pre- and post-reform periods for grain-supply response, 1952–95[a]

	Sown-acreage share				Yield		
Variable	1952–95	1952–78	1978–95	Variable	1952–95	1952–78	1978–95
Intercept	1.003***	1.005***	-0.417	Intercept	4.869***	4.873***	4.912***
	(11.94)	(7.16)	(-0.83)		(19.30)	(14.14)	(11.17)
PV	-0.179***	-0.165***	-0.050	IR	0.459***	0.488**	0.488
	(-10.32)	(-7.53)	(-0.61)		(2.95)	(2.25)	(1.41)
MS	-0.062***	-0.046***	-0.179***	WD	-0.061***	-0.084***	-0.102***
	(-6.01)	(-3.23)	(-5.01)		(-3.04)	(-2.97)	(-3.46)
$P_{g(t-1)}$	0.030*	0.034*	0.131***	Dic	0.216***	0.185***	0.183***
	(1.90)	(1.88)	(3.72)		(5.85)	(3.43)	(5.53)
$P_{k(t-1)}$	-0.081***	-0.097***	-0.090***	T	0.017***	0.014**	0.016***
	(-5.92)	(-8.23)	(-3.10)		(4.10)	(2.32)	(3.04)
R^2	0.94	0.91	0.90	R^2	0.98	0.93	0.98
DW	0.92	1.90	1.47	DW	1.36	1.71	1.36
Chow-test[b]							
F-statistic[c]	3.26***				0.61		
(p-value)	(0.006)				(0.846)		
LR[d]	58.90***				19.94		
(p-value)	(0.000003)				(0.336)		

Notes:

a The coefficients are the estimated elasticity values.

b In the forecast version of the Chow-test, the data set was split into pre- and post-reform periods.

c The F-statistics and LR-statistics from the Chow-test indicate that the acreage response function has undergone a structural change following the economic reform; however, there is no such structural break in yield response. The insignificant test results for the yield function could be partly explained by the fact that the dummy variable Dic had already taken account of the effects of institutional change on yield in the reform period.

d LR denotes Log-Likelihood Ratio.

e Values in parentheses are the t-ratios.

Significance:*** = 1%;** = 5%;* = 10% level.

institutional changes towards the commune system in the 1950s depressed the growth of grain yield. By contrast, the institutional reform towards greater decentralization of responsibility and control of production by households has had a very positive influence on grain yields. The estimated results for the irrigation variable (*IR*) demonstrate that grain-yield growth was assisted by very rapid expansion of the irrigation system in the pre-reform era; the same effect was not evident in the reform period. The positive effect of institutional change on yield during the reform period was therefore partly offset by a failure to maintain and expand the irrigation system in rural China. This may have been a key factor causing the decelerating yield trend in the late 1980s. The magnitude of the effect of weather condition (*WD*) on grain yield is somewhat greater in the reform compared with that in the pre-reform era. It seems reasonable from the agronomic point of view that the weakened irrigation system following the reforms has made grain production more vulnerable to adverse weather conditions. The results for technological progress (*T*) reinforce the message that improvement in technology (plus other factors picked up by the time-trend variable) has worked as an engine of grain yield growth in China in both eras.

Summary and conclusions

In this chapter the economic behaviour of Chinese grain producers in the transition period has been investigated through theoretical and empirical analyses. The need for a detailed understanding of the constraints imposed on producers both as a result of their own subsistence needs and as a consequence of government intervention and the institutional framework has been highlighted. The typical shape of supply curves in the Chinese mixed economy was explored in the graphical analysis. The findings of the empirical modelling exercise indicated that economic reforms in rural China have brought about more market-like behaviour, particularly in relation to sown-acreage decisions. The main features of the supply-response behaviour of Chinese grain producers and their policy implications can be summarized as follows:

- First, government non-price policy (e.g. the grain-delivery quota) played an important role in affecting producers' supply behaviour, especially in the allocation of sown acreage. The graphical analysis suggests that the government procurement quota impeded producers from pursuing a goal of profit-maximization and forced them to bear a loss on quota production. The empirical results indicate that non-price policy became a less influential factor in sown acreage response following the rural reforms in China.
- Secondly, the results from both the theoretical and empirical analyses suggest that subsistence grain farming is an important factor influencing

producers' supply behaviour. The transition from subsistence to commercial farming and rising marketable surplus will tend to shift land out of grain production. China, with limited land endowment, will therefore be more dependent on future improvements in production conditions and uptake of new technologies if it wishes to continue to meet the nation's food demand largely from its own resources.

- Thirdly, apart from the subsistence and survival goal, profitability is another key factor of concern to producers in the process of grain-supply response. This is indicated by the fact that grain-producers respond to changes in both grain and oil crop prices in their decisions on acreage allocation. The empirical results also indicate that grain purchase prices became a more significant factor in acreage response following the economic reforms.
- Fourthly, the empirical findings indicate that the process of institutional change from collectives to HRS has been an important source of yield growth in the reform period, but has had a negative influence on the maintenance and expansion of the irrigation system. These results reinforce the conclusion that improvements in technologies and production conditions are crucial for China's efforts to bring about further increases in grain yield. An important issue that confronts China now is how to improve production conditions in order to ensure sustainable growth in grain production. This is especially true for the irrigation system given the current institutional constraints posed by the HRS.
- Finally, the complex reality of grain production in China certainly has not been fully captured by the models presented in this chapter. It may be somewhat contrived to bend the nation's arcane grain system into this abstract neoclassical setting. The models and their results should be kept in perspective. However, they do underscore the need for a sound understanding of the effects of policy changes on producers' economic behaviour in China's grain sector. Further grain reforms should be underpinned by such knowledge.

Notes

1. The name for these quotas was changed from the 'planned procurement' to the so-called 'contract procurement' in 1985. However, the implementation of 'voluntary contracts' since then, in practice, has been little different from the old obligatory quotas. See Wang and Davis (1992) for a detailed discussion.
2. In the early stage of economic reform, for example, the total deliveries of grain to the market grew at more than 10 per cent a year, but quota fulfilment declined from 94.6 per cent to 80 per cent from 1979 to 1981.

Bibliography

Askari, H. (1976) *Agricultural Supply Response: A Survey of the Econometric Evidence* (New York: Praeger), pp. 383–9.

Buck, J. L. (1937) *Land Utilization in China* (University of Nanking; reprinted 1964 Paragon Books).

Carter, C. A. and F. N. Zhong (1988) *China's Grain Production and Trade: An Economic Analysis* (Boulder: Westview).

Chen, D. (1990) *Plan and Market(s): A Theoretical Model of the Chinese Grain Economy*, PhD dissertation, Iowa State University.

Chen, L. and A. Buckwell (1991) *Chinese Grain Economy and Policy* (London: CAB International).

Cheng, Y., Chan, M. and Tsang, S. (1992) 'Price Responsiveness of Chinese Agricultural Production under the Double-track System', paper for the Conference on Prospects for China's Agricultural Development in the 1990s, Beijing, 20–25 August.

Clark, C. and M. Haswell (1964) *'The Economics of Subsistence Agriculture* (London: Macmillan), p. 50.

Colman, D. (1983) 'A Review of the Arts of Supply Response Analysis', *Review of Marketing and Agricultural Economics*, 51 (3), pp. 201–30.

Crook, F. W. (1994) 'Underreporting of China's Cultivated Land', *Asia and Pacific Rim Agriculture and Trade Notes*, ERS, USDA, Washington, DC

Crook, F. W. (1994) 'Could China Starve the World? Comments on Lester Brown's Article', *Asia and Pacific Rim Agriculture and Trade Notes* ERS, USDA, Washington, DC, 1 September.

Du, W. C. (1995) *Agricultural Marketed Surplus Response in China* (Avebury).

Fan, Shenggen (1991) 'Effects of Technological Change and Institutional Reform on Production Growth in Chinese Agriculture', *American Journal of Agricultural Economics*, 73 (2), pp. 266–75.

Gunawardana, P. J. and E. A. Oczkowski (1992) 'Government Policies and Agricultural Supply response: Paddy in Sri Lanka', *Journal of Agricultural Economics*, 43 (2), pp. 231–42.

Halbrendt, C. and C. Gempesaw (1990) 'A Policy Analysis of China's Wheat Economy, *American Journal of Agricultural Economics*, 72 (2), pp. 269–78.

Huang, Jikun and S. Rozelle (1995) 'Environmental Stress and Grain Yields in China', *American Journal of Agricultural Economics*, 77 (4), pp. 853–64.

Jin, Hehui (1990) 'Plan, Market and the Supply Behaviour of Grain Producers in China', *Economic Research* (Jingji Yanjiu), September, pp. 62–68.

Ke, B. S. (1995) *China's Grain Market and Policy* (Beijing: China's Agricultural Press).

Kueh, Y. Y. (1986) Weather Cycles and Agricultural Instability in China', *Journal of Agricultural Economics*, 37 (1), pp. 101–4.

Lin, Justin Yifu (1987) 'Household Farm, Co-operative Farm, and Efficiency: Evidence from Rural Decollectivization in China', *Economic Growth Centre Work Paper*, 533, Yale University.

Liu, Minquan (1994) 'Commune, Responsibility System and China's Agriculture', in Fan and P. Nolan (eds), *China's Economic Reforms: The Costs and Benefits of Incrementalism* (London: Macmillan) pp. 104–36.

McMillan, J., J. Whalley and L. J. Zhu (1989) 'The Impact of China's Economic Reforms on Agricultural Productivity Growth', *Journal of Political Economy*, 97 (4), pp. 781–807.

Nerlove, M. (1958) *The Dynamics of Supply: Estimation of Farmers' Response to Price* (Baltimore: Johns Hopkins University Press).

People's Daily (1996) (Overseas edition), 25 June, p. 1 (in Chinese).

Perkins, D. H. (1966) *Market Control and Planning in Communist China* (Cambridge: Cambridge University Press).

Shi, X. (1991) 'Micro-analysis of China's Macro-control Policies in Agriculture', *Finance and Trade Economics* (Caimao Jingji), 12 December, pp. 11–16.

Sicular, T. (1983) *Market Restrictions in Chinese Agriculture: A Microeconomic Analysis*, PhD dissertation, Yale University.

Sicular, T. (1988) 'Plan and Market in China's Agriculture Commerce', *Journal of Political Economy*, 96 (2), pp. 283–307.

State Land Administration of the PR, China (1994) *China, Land Resources, Use and Productivity Assessments Project*, Main Report (Beijing).

State Statistical Bureau (SSB) (various issues), *Chinese Statistical Yearbook*.

Stevens, R. D. and C. L. Jabara (1988) *Agricultural Development Principles* (Baltimore: The Johns Hopkins University Press).

Stone, B. (1988) 'Developments in Agricultural Technology', *The China Quarterly*, 116 (4), pp. 767–822.

Wang, L. and J. Davis (1992) 'The Development of Reform of the Rural Marketing System in China', in E. B. Vermeer (ed.), *From Peasant to Entrepreneur: Growth and Change in Rural China* (Amsterdam: Pudoc Wageningen) pp. 69–82.

Wang, T. E. (1980) *Economic Policies and Price Stability in China*, Centre for Chinese Studies, Institute of East Asian Studies, University of California, Berkeley.

Wu, Z. and A. Kirke (1994) 'An Assessment of Some Key Chinese Agricultural Statistics', *China Information*, 9 (1).

Xu, G. and L. J. Peel (1991) *The Agriculture of China* (Oxford: Oxford University Press).

Yao, Y. (1988) 'Emphasis Must be Laid on the Grain Issue', in F. Zhao, *et al.* (eds), *China Today: Food Grain* (Beijing: Social Science Publishing House of China).

11
Labour Productivity of Rural Industry: A Cross-Sectional Analysis*

Fiona Carmichael, Hui Tan and Meibing Fu

Introduction

The Chinese economy has been growing rapidly since 1979. Real GDP rose by more than 10 per cent per year from 1979 to 1993 (State Statistical Bureau, 1994). Rural reforms[1] and trade liberalization are two of the most important factors responsible for China's economic 'miracle'.[2] These are reflected in rapid growth of rural industrial output and exports: between 1993 and 1994 the contribution of rural industry output to China's total GNP (US$ 526bn) rose from one-quarter to one-third. In the same period the value of all Chinese exports grew by nearly 32 per cent, to US$ 121bn. The effects of economic reforms and trade liberalization are inter-related as economic reforms have enabled rural industry to take full advantage of trade liberalization. Rural industry exports grew by 40 per cent between 1990 and 1994. By 1994 the value of rural industry exports was 339.8bn RMB (US$ 41bn), or more than one-third of the country's total exports (*People's Daily*, 1995).

Rural industry exports have established an important link between the domestic and international markets. This chapter focuses on the structure and prospects for development of rural industry exports. 'Rural industries' are defined by the Ministry of Agriculture, Livestock and Fishery (1994) as 'enterprises owned collectively by village and township governments, or enterprises owned privately by individuals, or enterprises owned jointly by the parties mentioned above and foreign investors'. 'Rural industry exports' are 'goods produced for export by rural industry enterprises and may be exported directly by themselves or export agencies'.[3]

In China, foreign trade is seen as a major source of economic development, and a fast-growing export base is similarly seen as the key to long-term rural development (Lardy, 1992; Hsu, 1989). Chen (1994) argues that long-term investment (mainly from outside China) has been a major source of this growth. The growth of foreign direct investment (FDI) can certainly explain some of the unevenness of rural industry development, as FDI is heavily concentrated in the eastern provinces, particularly in Guangdong, Shanghai and Fujian (World Bank, 1988). Since the penetration of FDI into the central and western regions has so far been limited this concentration of FDI can partly account for the much faster development of the eastern provinces. Other studies have stressed more strongly the role of China's economic reform, implying that sustained or higher growth necessitates the implementation of further reforms in rural areas (e.g. Zweig, 1991). The roles of long-term investment and economic reform in rural industry export growth have clearly been important, but here we look to productivity differentials as the key to understanding the prospects for sustained growth in the future.

We are interested in the efficiency of rural industrial output because we are concerned not only with the determinants of the rapid growth that has already been experienced in this sector but also with what the future holds. Because economic reform generates, essentially, one-off gains sustained growth will depend largely on efficiency gains and/or technological innovation.[4] With regard to the former, Bowles and Dong (1994) argue that the doubling of output per person between 1977 and 1987 was in part the result of significant increases in factor productivity in both the state and non-state sectors. Technological innovation may have been less important during this period, but will certainly have a role to play in the future. Here, our analysis is limited to a cross-section study of industry output as opposed to R&D developments, and we concentrate on productivity.[5] We examine inter-industry and inter-province productivity differentials in rural industry exports in order to throw some light on the pattern of output growth across the different Chinese sectors and regions. More efficient regions and industries will be more competitive and likely to grow more quickly, but are there any lessons that can be learned from the more efficient sectors by the less efficient?

Our analysis of inter-industry and inter-province productivity differentials addresses this question by indicating the relative strengths and weaknesses of particular paths of development on a regional and industry basis. The results should provide some indication to policy-makers as to where the opportunities for future development, particularly in the central and western provinces, best lie. This is an issue of some importance, in that failure to deal with regional income inequalities[6] associated with uneven development will encourage further labour migration from the poorer to the richer, coastal provinces. Migration of this kind has already lead to certain socially undesirable developments. For example, in Guangdong immigrant labour is employed on less favourable terms than local labour (Bowles and Dong, 1994, p. 75). Further migration to urban areas will inevitably generate more social problems for the immigrants and their families as well as the local population. The development of rural industry in the less developed regions is therefore crucial for the lives and welfare of both the rural and urban population (for further discussion see Yao, 1997).

Our chapter is organized as follows. We describe our data and include a descriptive analysis at the industry, provincial and regional levels. We then conduct some econometric analysis to examine the overall relationships between productivity, firm size and labour utilization. A number of characteristic variables are incorporated in the model to reflect the different ways in which exports are administered. We then conclude with some policy recommendations.

Data analysis

All the data quoted in this study come from *The Rural Industry Year Book–1994* (Ministry of Agriculture, Livestock and Fishery) which was the latest edition at the time of writing. The data relate to the ten most export-oriented rural industries in 28 provinces.

For each industry and province data were collected relating to the number of firms, the number of workers, the total value of exports and the value of stocks and work in progress.[7] From these data we are able to construct a measure of labour productivity by computing the average value of exports per worker. We can also measure firm size by the average value of exports per firm and labour utilization is indicated by the average number of workers per firm.[8] Total exports were further broken down into three constituent parts relating to their administration: direct and indirect exports and export related labour revenue. In *The Rural Industry Year Book*, 'direct exports' are exports administered through state-owned (but not necessarily directly under state control) import and export agencies or by the producers themselves. Direct exports are therefore further sub-divided into (a) exports administered by state-owned agencies[9] and (b) exports administered directly by the producer. 'Indirect exports' are exports produced for export by Chinese enterprises but the export process is handled by overseas agencies (mainly in Hong Kong and Macao). Export-related labour revenue is derived by Chinese enterprises from the provision of a workplace and labour force while raw materials, intermediate goods, production equipment, production technology and sales of products are wholly provided and administered by overseas agencies.

Industrial development in China is strongly influenced by national and regional policy.[10] Policy is designed with the aim of stimulating fast and/or stable growth and the success or failure of policies is measured in these terms. Since 1979 government industry policy has generally been supportive of rural industry exports, and success is reflected in the figures quoted above. However, aggregated records hide 'winners' and 'losers' and our analysis is about identifying relative success and/or failure at the industry and provincial level. At each level of analysis we therefore compare relative output performance in terms of total and *per capita* output. Unfortunately data limitations at this level of aggregation prevent us from taking the descriptive analysis much further. However, we are able to draw some tentative hypotheses which are tested in the multiple regression analysis.

Table 11.1   Exports, by industry: total and per capita exports and administrative shares, 1994

Industry	Total exports (¥m)	% by a government agency	% by producer	% by an overseas agency	% by labour-related	Value of stocks and work in progress (¥m)	Exports per worker (¥)
Light	44 619	35.43	22.45	10.14	31.99	4 382	25 800
Clothing	36 341	45.72	18.78	13.91	21.59	3 029	31 400
Other	26 620	41.71	18.96	19.47	19.86	10 563	23 600
Textiles	28 847	59.29	11.95	17.71	11.05	4 154	30 400
Arts/Crafts	21 528	50.63	10.31	27.93	11.14	3 007	14 500
Mechanical	14 556	58.92	10.06	25.44	5.58	3 647	28 900
Food	12 872	52.71	21.9	22.72	2.67	2 424	43 600
Chemicals	10 958	59.12	9.47	24.63	6.78	2 368	43 300
Silk	8 311	61.71	5.61	31.78	0.91	911	29 100
Minerals	68 671	59.72	11.41	28.34	0.38	1 249	31 000
All industry average	21 152	52.50	14.09	22.21	11.20	3 572	30 016

Source: Ministry of Agriculture, Livestock and Fishery (1994).

Analysis by industry

Table 11.1 shows the value of exports by industry and *per capita* output. In addition Table 11.1 shows the percentage of exports administered by direct and indirect methods and the value of stocks and work in progress. In 1993, the average value of exports per industry was ¥21 152 million. The value of light industry exports was the highest, accounting for 21.1 per cent of all rural industry exports. The clothing and textile industries had the second and third highest outputs. The value of output of the mineral industry was the lowest and the value of output from the silk industry was also relatively low at ¥8311 million. Together these two industries contributed only 7.1 per cent to the total.

For all industries the largest share of exports is administered directly through a state owned import–export agency. However, in light industries nearly 32 per cent of the value of exports is earned through labour-related services and 22.45 per cent of exports are administered directly by producers. But on average the share of exports managed directly by producers is relatively small. This indicates the degree to which the state has retained its stake in rural industry. The value of stocks and work in progress is also low, on average only amounting to 14.5 per cent of total output (exports *plus* stocks and work in progress).

The average value of exports per worker by industry in 1993 was ¥30 016. Table 11.1 shows that food and chemical industries recorded the highest levels of output per head. Output per head was lowest in 'other industries' and the arts and crafts industry. While light industry had the highest output value, it recorded only the third lowest level of labour productivity. On the other hand the mineral industry had the lowest value of output and ranked fourth in terms of labour productivity. One interpretation is that workers in industries such as food and chemicals are more efficient than workers in light industries even though they contribute less to total output. Industry-specific character- istics will explain some of these differences but firm size and labour utilization practices are also likely to be important. For example, large firms can benefit from economies of scale and in chemicals, the most productive industry, average firm size, measured by exports per firm, is also high (¥4.94 million compared with an average of ¥3.16 million).

Analysis by province

Table 11.2 shows total and *per capita* exports and the value of stocks and work in progress by province.[11] The average value of exports is ¥7554 million and the value of exports is highest in Jiangsu, Guangdong and Zhejiang. These three provinces account for more than half of rural industry exports. Only Shangdong and Fujian produce anywhere near the same value of exports and these five provinces are the only provinces where the value of exports is above the average, indicating that the distribution is highly skewed. The value of output in Hainan province is the lowest of all, less than 0.1 per cent of the value of rural industry exports in Jiangsu. Stocks and work in progress make up only a small proportion of total output except in Neimenggu, Yunnan, Shaanxi, Sichuan and Hebei, where the share of stock holdings in total output is over twice the province average of 14.45 per cent. In Hebei stock holdings account for over 50 per cent of total output.

Average output per worker is ¥22 000 and the standard deviation is ¥9100. The value of output per worker is the highest in Jiangsu and the lowest in Neimenggu. Although the total output value of exports is so high in Guangdong, in terms of labour productivity Guangdong ranks only 17th, behind Heilongjiang. This suggests that there are diseconomies associated with the concentration of production in Guangdong but not in Jiangsu. Firm size and differences in labour utilization[12] may explain some of these differences. For example, firms are larger in Jiangsu and Heilongjiang than in Guangdong (average exports per firm are ¥8.14 million, ¥2.51 million and ¥1.75 million, respectively compared with an industry average of ¥1.86 million).

In some western provinces such as Guizhou, Ningxia, Qinghai and Xinjiang total output is low, but labour productivity is relatively high. For example, output value per worker in Guizhou is ¥22 300, which is above average. These provinces are comparatively under-developed owing to their distance from the developed eastern provinces (and by implication the international markets), outdated communication methods and, perhaps more importantly, a poorly skilled workforce. Their relative success in productivity terms is therefore very encouraging for overall Chinese development and the development of rural exports in particular.

Table 11.2   Exports, by province: total and *per capita* exports and value of stocks and work in progress, 1994.

Province	Total exports (¥m)	Stocks and work in progress (¥m)	Exports per worker (¥)
Jiangsu	62 009	4 805	41 500
Guangdong	45 561	1 775	17 900
Zhejiang	28 109	3 304	34 400
Shangdong	19 914	6 523	22 800
Fujian	17 754	2 272	36 500
Liaoning	7 392	1 854	36 600
Tianjin	6 124	1 106	33 200
Hebei	4 448	8 364	16 900
Beijing	4 322	1 231	36 300
Henan	2 850	1 083	10 400
Hubei	2 366	472	24 200
Hunan	2 066	222	18 100
Anhui	1 928	398	16 300
Sichuan	1 281	718	10 500
Jiangxi	1 081	374	16 000
Shanxi	1 059	100	15 400
Guangxi	942	144	15 000
Jilin	600	223	24 300
Shaanxi	406	322	15 400
Heilongjiang	337	90	18 900
Yunnan	216	158	14 100
Guizhou	148	28	22 300
Gansu	148	18	12 500
Neimenggu	142	67	10 200
Qinghai	138	48	19 900
Ningxia	86	20	19 900
Xinjiang	66	8	18 400
Hainan	32	4	16 700
Province average	7 554	1 279	22 000

Source: Ministry of Agriculture, Livestock and Fishery (1994).

Industrial structure by region

Table 11.3 shows the industrial structure of the eastern, central and western regions of China. Average productivity is much higher in the east than in the central or western provinces. Table 11.3 gives some indication as to how much of this difference is explained by industrial structure,[13] showing that the specialization of the eastern provinces in clothing, light industry and textiles is reflected by China as a whole underlining the contribution of the output of these provinces to total output. Clothing is also the third most productive

Table 11.3 Industrial structure, by region, percentage share of total exports, 1994.

Industry	All provinces	Eastern provinces[a]	Central provinces[b]	Western provinces[c]
Arts and crafts	10.18	9.53	21.42	5.42
Chemicals	6.37	6.29	7.1	9.27
Clothing	16.84	17.2	13.78	3.59
Food	8.21	8.17	8.4	10.15
Light	18.16	18.68	11.7	9.83
Mechanical	6.99	7.03	6.28	7.31
Minerals	3.12	2.52	10.25	14.92
Silk	4.13	4.29	0.91	7.52
Textiles	14.93	15.24	9.6	17.08
Other	11.08	11.07	10.57	14.91

Notes:

a The eastern provinces are: Beijing, Tianjin, Fujian, Guangxi, Hebei, Hainan, Liaoning, Jiangsu, Zhejiang, Shangdong, Guangdong.

b The central provinces are: Shanxi, Heilongjiang, Anhui, Jiangxi, Jilin, Henan, Hubei, Hunan, Neimenggu.

c The western provinces are Guizhou, Yunnan, Shaanxi, Gansu, Qinghai, Ningxia, Sichuan and Xinjiang.

Source: Ministry of Agriculture, Livestock and Fishery (1994).

industry. The provinces of central China have tended to specialize in arts and crafts production which is the least productive sector but clothing is also important. In the west, while textiles and minerals are the most important sectors, a significant share of output is concentrated in the relatively inefficient 'other industries'. The share of chemical production (the most productive industry) is also higher in the west than in – the central or eastern provinces. Such considerations suggest that the higher than average productivity in the eastern provinces is only partly explained by the industrial mix in the three regions.

If industrial structure cannot fully explain the productivity advantages of the eastern provinces, then provincial specific factors may be important. Not least of these will have been the coastal location of most eastern provinces, which has made them more accessible to FDI and international markets. However, not all the eastern provinces are amongst the most productive. The productivity ranking of Guangdong is relatively low and the pattern of industry in that province throws some light on the matter. Guangdong's output is dominated by light industry which is the third least productive industry. The reason why light industry is so important to rural industry in Guangdong is that more than two-thirds of Hong Kong investment in China is located in this province employing around 3 million workers in Chinese–Hong Kong joint ventures, most of which are in light industry (Cheng, 1978).

In the central and western provinces the highest shares of output are in arts and crafts and textiles, respectively. Both industries are traditional and rely quite heavily on raw materials. The indication is that the pattern of industry in the central and western provinces is in part the result of a less advanced state of industrial development compared with that in the eastern provinces. Lack of technology, skilled labour and investment in the western region, in particular, means that provinces disadvantaged in these ways have been constrained to export mainly raw materials and primary processed products.[14] In addition management and organizational skills are likely to be less developed.

The differences in industrial structure between the eastern, central and western provinces go some way towards explaining the inter-provincial productivity differentials highlighted in Table 11.2. The three regions are clearly at different stages of industrial development associated with different competitive advantages. In the eastern provinces, rural industry developed earlier and consequently is more technologically advanced, the labour force is more skilled, there is greater investment, greater availability of marketing information and easier access to export channels. The central and western provinces are disadvantaged in all these respects. On the other hand, these two regions have a cheaper labour force and rich stocks of natural resources. However, the central and local governments have to take measures, both financial and technical, to encourage the development of rural industry in these areas in order to make the most of these advantages. As we have seen the structure of industry is linked to the pattern of inter-provincial productivity differentials. Thus policies need to be adopted to encourage the relocation of productive industries – such as chemicals, textiles and clothing – to the central and western regions. Investment in human resource development should also be undertaken. Firms in eastern provinces will lose out only if they fail to upgrade to a more capital- and technology-intensive industrial structure.

Regression analysis

Regression analysis is employed in order to test two main hypotheses. First, productivity differentials are determined by firm size, labour utilization and the way in which exports are administered. Second, productivity differentials are also determined by industrial-, provincial- and region-specific characteristics.[15]

Methodology

In order to test the first hypothesis we regress our productivity measure on independent variables constructed to reflect firm size, labour utilization and the coverage of different administration methods. In order to test for the existence of industry-, province- and regional-specific effects we employ two different variants of the least squares dummy variable model. In each, it is assumed that differences across industries, provinces or regions can be captured by estimating individual specific constant terms. The first variant of the model includes an overall constant term in the standard way as well as dummy variables for nine of ten industries and 27 of the provinces (or two of three regions). In this model the intercept takes up the influence of an omitted category which acts as a base or benchmark to which the included categories are compared. The dummy variable coefficients for the remaining categories measure the extent to which they differ from this base. The usual *t*-ratio for each included category implies a test of the hypothesis that the relevant coefficient equals zero. In the second variant of the model there is no overall constant and a dummy variable is included for each of either the ten industries or 28 provinces (or the three regions). One of either the industry or province (or regional) dummy variables must still be dropped in order to avoid perfect collinearity, as in the standard case.[16] The two methods are computationally equivalent but the interpretation of the dummy variable coefficients is quite different. With no intercept, the dummy variable coefficients reflect expected productivity for each category and we can test the hypothesis that the constant terms are all equal using an F-test (Greene, 1990, Chapter 16, Kennedy, 1992, Chapter 14).

Dependent and independent variables

Our dependent variable in the regressions is our productivity measure, exports per worker (*EXPERHD*). Dichotomous variables for the ten industries (I_i for $I = 1–10$), 28 provinces (P_j for $j = 1–28$) and three regions (R_k for $k = 1–3$) were constructed by allowing the relevant variable to equal 1 when the observation relates to the particular industry, province or region and zero otherwise.

Firm size is measured by average exports per firm (*EXPF*) and labour utilization is proxied by the average number of workers per firm (*WPF*). *WPF* can also be regarded as a measure of firm size and including *WPF* and *EXPF* in the same regressions is likely to lead to problems associated with multi-collinearity. However, any significant relationship between *WPF* and *EXPERHD* after allowing separately for firm size through *EXPF* can be taken to reflect employment effects over and above those associated with firm size. We expect firm size to have a positive effect on productivity owing to economies of scale. After allowing for firm size (by including *EXPF*) we expect *WPF* to be related negatively to productivity as, for a given firm size, hiring more workers will ultimately lead to diminishing average product.

Four main methods of export administration were identified. These were (1) exports administered by state owned import–export agencies; (2) exports administered directly by the producer, (3) indirect exports where the export process is handled by overseas agencies (mainly in Hong Kong and Macao); and (4) exports administered as labour-related revenue. Variables were constructed measuring the percentage of total exports administered by each of methods 1–3, *EXIM*, *PRODUCER* and *INDIRECT,* respectively. As values for the last category were either zero or missing for several provinces, exports administered as labour-related revenue was taken as the excluded category.

Table 11.4   Summary statistics of major variables

Variable[a]	Mean	Std. dev.	Minimum	Maximum
EXPERHD*	2.3761	1.4176	0.2906	7.691
EXPF	321.62	290.96	2.739	1923
WPF	137.68	109.84	2.457	901.5
EXIM	40.468	22.962	0	100
PRODUCER	14.573	18.819	0	100
INDIRECT	29.236	22.196	0	100
STOCKS	19.284	17.175	−18.27[c]	91.62

Notes:
a *EXPERHD* = value of exports per worker; *EXPF* = value of exports per firm; *WPF* = number of workers per firm; *EXIM* = percentage of exports administered by import–export agencies; *PRODUCER* = percentage of exports administered by producers; *INDIRECT* = percentage of exports administered by overseas agencies; *STOCKS* = percentage of total output held as stocks or work in progress.
* In units of ¥10 000.
c The negative sign is an accounting anomaly indicating that stocks or work in progress recorded as output in one accounting period are exported in another.
Source: Ministry of Agriculture, Livestock and Fishery (1994).

The incentive arguments in support of the market system suggest that the ability of firms to administer exports directly should encourage efficiency. Inasmuch as these arguments carry weight, we should expect a more positive relationship between *PRODUCER* and *EXPERHD* than between the latter and either *EXIM* or *INDIRECT*. However, precisely because the value of the excluded category was mostly either very small or zero some problems with multicollinearity were foreseen with the inclusion of these three administration variables in the same equation. We also measure the percentage of total output that is held as stocks or work in progress, *STOCKS*. We expect *STOCKS* to be negatively related to our efficiency measure as large stock holdings indicate over-production and badly co-ordinated marketing strategies which are both a symptom of inefficient management.[17] Table 11.4 presents summary statistics for all the continuous variables used in our regressions.

Our generalized estimating equation can now be presented as:

$$EXPERHD = \alpha_1 + \alpha_2 EXPF + \alpha_3 WPF + \alpha_4 EXIM + \alpha_5 PROD + \alpha_6 INDIRECT$$
$$+ \alpha_7 STOCKS + \Sigma\theta_i I_i + \Sigma\pi_j P_j \ (\text{or } \Sigma\rho_k R_k)$$

We expect $\alpha_2 > 0$, α_3, $\alpha_7 < 0$, $\alpha_5 > \alpha_4$, α_6 and have no *a priori* expectation with respect to the signs of θ_i, π_j or ρ_k. However, without allowing for firm size or labour utilization we expect the signs on the dummy variables representing the most (least) productive industries, provinces and regions to be positive (negative).

Results

Tables 11.5 and 11.6 present the results of our regressions including an overall constant term, the I–1 industry dummy variables and either the j–1 province variables or the k–1 regional variables. In Table 11.5 the regional variables are included as independent variables while in Table 11.6 the 27 province dummy variables are included. The equations in Table 11.5 are less cumbersome and have more degrees of freedom but some of the information conveyed, including the province variables, is lost when the regional variables are included instead. The results of estimating (6) in Table 11.5 using the second variant of the dummy variable model (excluding an overall constant term) are presented in Tables 11.7 and 11.8 along with relevant test statistics.

In (1) of Table 11.5 the independent variables are nine of the ten industry dummy variables and the eastern and western regional dummies, R_1 and R_3. The excluded categories taken up in the constant term (which is significant and positive) are silk (the 6th most productive industry) and the regional dummy for the central region. The signs and coefficients on all the industry variables except arts and crafts are positive. All except arts and crafts and textiles are significant. This suggests that when regional differences are allowed for all the industries except arts and crafts and textiles have a productivity advantage over silk. The largest coefficient, and therefore the largest productivity advantage, is associated with chemicals, while the smallest significant productivity advantage is associated with the mechanical industry. The sign on R_3 is negative and that on R_1 is positive as expected, while the influence of the latter is significant at the 1 per cent level.

In (2) we add *WPF* which takes a positive sign but is not significant.[18] In (3) we include *EXPF* which takes a positive sign as expected and is highly significant. *WPF* also gains significance at the 1 per cent level and takes a negative sign. This indicates that the number of workers per firm has a negative influence on productivity when firm size is allowed for separately, in line with our expectations. However, R_1 is less significant, the sign on R_3 is positive and the coefficients on the industry variables are much smaller in (3) than in (2). This, taken together with the sign change on *WPF* and the high level of significance of both *WPF* and *EXPF*, suggests that (3) suffers from problems with multicollinearity owing to the inclusion of two highly correlated variables.[19] In (4) *WPF* is dropped, the influence of *EXPF* is almost halved while that of the industry variables is in line with (1)–(2) and R_1 regains significance at the 1 per cent level. *EXPF* is still significant at the 1 per cent level but it is clear that it is the inclusion of *WPF* with *EXPF* that leads to problems with multicollinearity and not simply the inclusion of *EXPF*. Although multicollinearity does not lead to any bias it does make it difficult to entangle the different influences in (3) and as *WPF* is not significant in (2) it is excluded from (5) where we test for the significance of the administration variables and *STOCKS*. However, the sign change on *WPF* once firm size is

Table 11.5   Dependent variable: *EXPERHD*, with regional dummy variables

Variable	eqn (1)	eqn (2)	eqn (3)	eqn (4)	eqn (5)	eqn (6)
Constant	1.14	1.02	1.228	0.195	0.13	0.769
	$(3.96^{***})^a$	(3.01^{***})	(5.7^{***})	(0.83)	(0.25)	(2.65^{***})
Arts and crafts	−0.19	−0.111	0.062	0.63	0.67	0.129
	(-0.53)	(-0.3)	(0.26)	(2.21^{**})	(2.03^{**})	(0.44)
Chemicals	1.523	1.588	0.86	1.63	1.864	1.169
	(4.21^{***})	(4.24^{***})	(3.57^{***})	(5.84^{***})	(5.78^{***})	(3.95^{***})
Clothing	1.331	1.372	0.421	1.074	1.007	0.389
	(3.62^{***})	(3.68^{***})	(1.74^{*})	(3.78^{***})	$(3.1^{**}{}^{*})$	(1.33)
Food	1.449	1.534	1.026	1.88	1.891	1. 148
	(4.04^{***})	(4.03^{***})	(4.22^{***})	(6.75^{***})	$(6.0 7^{***})$	(3.97^{***})
Light	0.943	1.001	0.594	1.203	1.184	0.603
	(2.63^{***})	(2.71^{***})	(2.52^{**})	(4.33^{***})	(3.69^{***})	(2.11^{**})
Mechanical	0.921	0.973	0.545	1.108	1.053	0.657
	(2.48^{**})	(2.56^{**})	(2.25^{**})	(3.86^{***})	(3.15^{***})	(2.23^{**})
Minerals	1.046	1.112	0.497	1.234	1.173	0.596
	(2.92^{***})	(2.99^{***})	(2.09^{**})	(4.45^{***})	(3.56^{***})	(2.01^{**})
Textiles	0.388	0.407	0.21	0.427	0.377	0.134
	(1.07)	(1.11)	(0.9)	(1.52)	(1.17)	(0.48)
Other	1.166	1.246	0.816	1.602	1.494	0.862
	(3.25^{***})	(3.3^{***})	(3.38^{***})	(5.75^{***})	(4.55^{***})	(2.9^{***})
Eastern provinces	0.99	0.9982	0.262	0.449	0.375	0.295
	(5.64^{***})	(5.58^{***})	(2.22^{**})	(3.16^{***})	(2.39^{**})	(2.35^{**})
Western provinces	−0.217	−0.239	0.036	−0.234	−0.377	−0.075
	(-1.07)	(-1.16)	(0.28)	(-1.49)	(-1.86^{*})	(-0.42)
EXPF			0.005	0.003	0.0027	0.0038
			(18.9^{***})	(12.8^{***})	(10.6^{***})	(14.4^{***})
EXIM					0.009	0.0086
					(1.73^{*})	(2.783^{***})
PRODUCER					0.001	0.0097
					(0.19)	(2.781^{***})
INDIRECT					−0.001	
					(-0.27)	
STOCKS					−0.009	−0.0024
					(-1.61)	(-0.6)
WPF			0.0005	−0.007		−0.0053
			(0.68)	(-10.7^{***})		(-7.5^{***})
R^2 adj	0.268	0.266	0.704	0.564	0.639	0.726
F	9.37^{***}	8.61^{***}	47.14^{***}	28.11^{***}	$20.5 9^{***}$	32.11^{***}
Log-likelihood	−401.74	−401.5	−286.02	−3 35.73	−209.73	−198.97

Notes:
a t-statistics in parenthesis.
*** indicates significance at the 1% level, ** indicates significance at the 5% level and * indicates significance at the 10% level.
Explanations of variables are given in Table 11.4.

Table 11.6   Dependent variable: *EXPERHD*, with province dummy variables

Variable	eqn (1)	eqn (2)	Variable	eqn (1)	eqn (2)
Constant	0.826	0.361	Jiangsu	2.851	0.727
	(1.66)*[a]	(0.92)		(5.17***)	(1.83*)
Arts and crafts	–0.09	0.128	Zhejiang	1.781	1.038
	(–0.27)	(0.57)		(3.23***)	(2.81***)
Chemicals	1.65	1.136	Anhui	0.088	0.56
	(4.92***)	(5.0***)		(0.16)	(1.53)
Clothing	1.427	0.608	Fujian	1.737	1.599
	(4.19***)	(2.69***)		(3.15***)	(4.36***)
Food	1.588	1.278	Jiangxi	0.123	0.716
	(4.78***)	(5.6***)		(0.22)	(1.89*)
Light	1.082	0.7	Shangdong	1.191	0.946
	(3.26***)	(3.13***)		(2.16**)	(2.54**)
Mechanical	0.999	0.761	Henan	–0.2	0.457
	(2.92***)	(3.34***)		(–0.36)	(1.22)
Minerals	1.186	0.693	Hubei	0.338	0.498
	(3.57***)	(3.05***)		(0.61)	(1.36)
Textiles	0.488	0.316	Hunan	0.602	0.827
	(1.45)	(1.46)		1.092)	(2.28*)
Other	1.271	1.048	Guangdong	0.442	0.885
	(3.82***)	(4.61***)		(0.8)	(2.35**)
EXPF		0.004	Guangxi	–0.087	0.526
		(14.2***)		(–0.15)	(1.42)
EXIM		0.006	Hainan	0.016	0.799
		(2.26**)		(0.03)	(1.61)
STOCKS		–0.0083	Sichuan	–0.182	0.912
		(–2.44**)		(–0.33)	(2.41*)
WPF		–0.0059	Guizhou	0.125	0.465
		(–9.3***)		(0.21)	(1.14)
Beijing	1.173	0.765	Yunnan	–0.125	1.2
	(2.13**)	(2.05***)		(–0.22)	(3.05***)
Tianjin	1.693	0.713	Shaanxi	0.224	0.874
	(3.07***)	(1.91*)		(0.41)	(2.32**)
Hebei	0.273	0.865	Gangsu	–0.261	0.255
	(0.49)	(2.28**)		(–0.46)	(0.67)
Shanxi	0.641	0.921	Qinghai	0.934	1.286
	(1.16)	(2.52**)		(1.03)	(2.2**)
Neimenggu	–0.138	0.17	Ningxia	–0.108	0.292
	(–0.25)	(0.43)		(–0.19)	(0.75)
Liaoning	1.522	1.4			
	(2.76***)	(3.79***)	R² adj	0.381	0.75
Jilin	0.495	0.969	F	5.31***	19.16***
	(0.9)	(2.6***)			
Heilongjiang	–0.119	0.594	Log-	– 366.58	–233.04
	(–0.21)	(1.49)	likelihood		

Notes:
t-statistics in parenthesis.
*** indicates significance at the 1% level, ** indicates significance at the 5% level and * indicates significance at the 10% level.
Explanations of variables are given in Table 11.4.

allowed for in (3) and the higher R^2 (R^2 is unaffected by multicollinearity) suggests that firms can employ too many workers. Whereas the positive influence of *EXPF* confirms that there are economies of scale to be earned in Chinese rural industry the evidence of (3) is that these are not attainable simply by employing more and more workers.[20]

In (5) we add the export administration variables and *STOCKS*. Only the influence of *EXIM* is significant[21] and *INDIRECT* takes a negative sign. The coefficient on *EXIM* is also the largest and suggests that state owned import–export agencies are managing rural industry exports relatively efficiently. However, the lack of significance of *PRODUCER* in (5) was found to be the result of also including *INDIRECT*. We took this to indicate problems with multicollinearity owing to the inclusion of these three administration variables in the same equation. Since the influence of *INDIRECT* remained insignificant with the exclusion of *PRODUCER* the former was dropped in (6). The influence of *STOCKS* in (5) is negative as expected but is not significant. R_3 is significant at the 10 per cent level, suggesting that after allowing for different administration practices productivity in western provinces is significantly lower than in both eastern or central provinces

In (6) as well as excluding *INDIRECT* we include *WPF* which, as in (2) is highly significant. R_3 is no longer significant, suggesting that lower productivity in the west is at least in part due to the employment of surplus labour. The influence of *PRODUCER* in (6) is significant at the 1 per cent level and the related coefficient is larger than that of *EXIM*. This indicates that exports administered directly by the producer are produced as, if not more, efficiently than exports administered through an import–export agency. This is consistent with the incentive arguments in support of the market system. However, the more positive influence of *PRODUCER* may have as much to do with Chinese institutional arrangements as at present only the largest producers are entitled to arrange their own trade agreements. On the other hand, there will clearly be private incentives to bypass the agency middle-men (as well as disadvantages associated with inexperience) and greater economic freedom is likely to lead to more direct producer control of exports.[22] As a result of including *WPF*, *STOCKS* is even less significant than in (5). This suggests that the negative influence of *WPF* is a much better indicator of inefficiency across regions. The R^2 indicates that (6) is predicting nearly 73 per cent of the variation in *EXPERHD*.

In (1) of Table 11.6, the independent variables are nine of the ten industry dummy variables and 27 of the 28 provincial dummies. The excluded categories taken up in the constant term are silk and Xinjiang, the 15th most productive province. The signs of the provincial dummies were much as expected. There are positive signs on the most efficient provinces, Jiangsu, Liaoning, Beijing, Fujian and Zhejiang in the east and the central province of Shanxi and the largest coefficient is associated with Jiangsu, the most efficient province. There are also negative coefficients on the least productive provinces, Neimenggu, Gansu, Sichuan and Yunnan in the west and the central province of Henan. However, the largest (absolutely) negative coefficient is associated with Gansu, the fourth least efficient province, and not Neimenggu, but neither are significant. Only the positive influences of Beijing, Tianjin, Liaoning, Jiangsu, Zhejiang, Fujian and Shangdong are significant and all of these are eastern provinces. The indication is that while the least productive provinces are not significantly less efficient than Xinjiang the productivity of the most productive provinces is significantly greater than that of the median province.

(2) in Table 11.6 is equivalent to (6) in Table 11.5. In addition, because the value of *PRODUCER* was either zero valued or missing for most industries in some provinces it had to be excluded from (2) (in order to avoid to perfect multicollinearity). In (2) *STOCKS* is negative and significant at the 5 per cent level. This suggests that some of the least competitive producers are over-estimating the size of their market and that there is a need for greater access to market information. That *STOCKS* is significant in Table 11.6 but not in Table 11.5 indicates that the consequences of poor stock-holding management on productivity are different across provinces. None of the province variables take negative signs suggesting that most of the competitive disadvantage of provinces less productive than Xinjiang can be explained in terms of the other variables in (2) (this is also suggested by the low level of significance of R_3 in Table 11.5). However the same cannot be said for the competitive advantage of eastern provinces such as Liaoning or indeed Fujian which has the largest positive effect on productivity of any province. More province effects are significant in (2) than in (1) in Table 11.6, but still only 14 province effects are significant at the 5 per cent level or above. More than half of these effects are associated with eastern provinces and only three with western provinces. R^2 is higher in (2) than in (6) of Table 11.5 but for presentational convenience we take the latter as the basis for testing model 2 in Tables 11.7 and 11.8.[23]

The results of estimating (6) excluding the overall constant term and employing *I*–1 industry dummy variables but all three dummy variables indicating the *k*th region are presented in Table 11.7 along with relevant test statistics. The results of estimating (6) in Table 11.5 excluding the overall constant term and employing only *k*–1 regional dummy variables but all ten dummy variables indicating the *i*th industry are presented in Table 11.8, along with relevant test statistics. The fixed effects in Tables 11.7 and 11.8 measure the individual influences of (respectively) R_j and I_i. For example, the coefficient of 1.938 for the chemical industry in Table 11.8 indicates that average productivity in the chemical industry for given values of the other independent variables is ¥19 380, whereas the coefficient of 1.169 for the chemical industry in (6) indicates that the difference between average productivity in the silk and chemical industries is ¥11 690. The evidence of Tables 11.7 and 11.8 supports the claim that there are significant regional and industry fixed effects that act on productivity; the chi-squared and F-statistics

Table 11.7 Dependent variable: *EXPERHD*, testing for regional fixed effects

Variable	Arts and crafts	Chemicals	Clothing	Food	Light	Mechanical	Minerals	Textiles	Other	EXPF	EXIM	PRODUCER	STOCKS	WPF
Coefficient	0.133	1.178	0.398	1.154	0.607	0.661	0.601	0.136	0.867	0.0038	0.0085	0.0095	-0.0026	-0.0053
t-statistic	0.449	3.968***	1.359	3.98***	2.127**	2.24**	2.025**	0.486	2.91***	14.37***	2.81***	2.77***	-0.641	-7.43***

Estimated fixed effects

Group	Coefficient	Standard error
Eastern provinces	1.066	0.298
Central provinces	0.775	0.29
Western provinces	0.683	0.335

Test		χ^2	F
1	Model (2) vs (1)	37.572***	20.453***
2	Model (3) vs (1)	253.581***	35.117***
3	Model (4) vs (1)	261.523***	32.139***
4	Model (4) vs (2)	223.951***	27.894***
5	Model (4) vs (3)	7.942**	3.691**

Test statistics

Model	Log-likelihood	R^2
(1) Constant term only	-329.67	0
(2) Group effects only	-310.884	0.18
(3) x variables only	-202.879	0.739
(4) X and group effects	-198.908	0.749

Notes: ***, ** and * indicate significance at the 1%, 5% and 10% levels, respectively.

Table 11.8   Dependent variable: *EXPERHD*, testing for industry fixed effects

Variable	Eastern provinces	Western provinces	EXPF	EXIM	PRODUCER	STOCKS	WPF
Coefficient	0.295	−0.075	0.0038	0.0086	0.0096	−0.0024	−0.005
t-statistic	2.35**	−0.422	14.43***	2.783***	2.781***	−0.603	−7.5***

Estimated fixed effects

Industry	Coefficient	Standard error
Arts and crafts	0.898	0.253
Chemicals	1.938	0.245
Clothing	1.158	0.250
Food	1.917	0.230
Light	1.372	0.251
Mechanical	1.426	0.261
Minerals	1.365	0.266
Silk	0.769	0.291
Textiles	0.903	0.263
Other	1.631	0.247

Test	χ^2		F
1	Model (2) vs (1)	26.75***	3.024***
2	Model (3) vs (1)	218.47***	56.29***
3	Model (4) vs (1)	261.4***	32.112***
4	Model (4) vs (2)	234.646***	60.466***
5	Model (4) vs (3)	46.93***	4.874***

Test statistics

Model	Log-likelihood	R^2
(1) Constant term only	−329.67	0
(2) Group effects only	−316.293	0.132
(3) *x* variables only	−220.435	0.685
(4) *x* and group effects	−198.97	0.749

Notes:
***, ** and * indicate significance at the 1%, 5% and 10% levels, respectively.

are highly significant for both sets of group effects in tests 1 and 5 of Tables 11.7 and 11.8. This confirms that the inter-industry and inter-province productivity differentials in our data are not fully explained by firm size, employment, the way in which exports are administered and value of stock holdings, which is not altogether surprising. Together, these factors explain approximately 44 per cent of the variation in productivity. Industry-specific characteristics explain approximately 13 per cent of the variation while industry- and region-specific characteristics together explain around 31 per cent of the variation in productivity.

To summarize, our results suggest that firm size, administration methods and employment and stock holding practices are important determinants of inter-industry, province and regional productivity differentials. The influence of firm size is particularly significant implying that economies of scale are important for Chinese rural industry exports. There are some small efficiency gains associated with allowing exports to be administrated directly by the producer but the administration of exports through state-owned import–export agencies does not appear to be associated with serious incentive problems. There is also some evidence that stock holdings are negatively associated with efficiency but that this effect is less important when province fixed effects are not taken into account. The negative relationship between employment per firm and productivity strongly suggests that it is possible to employ too much labour, and that some firms are doing just that. However, the evidence for this conclusion is weakened by the presence of multi-collinearity in our estimation process and it would be wrong to recommend wholesale labour rationalization on the basis of it – especially given the negative social consequences of such a policy.[24] Our results also imply that there are important industry region- and province-specific effects that remain unexplained. The identification of the origins of such effects is the basis of ongoing research.

Conclusion

China is the largest agricultural country in the world today, with a rural population of 800 million. Rural industrialization is seen as the key to improving the living standards of these 800 million people and the development of rural industry has played an important part in rapid expansion of the Chinese economy (OECD, 1985). However, development has been uneven with the relatively successful eastern provinces reaping most of the benefits in terms of both domestic and international markets. In this chapter we have considered the uneven nature of rural industry development in terms of inter-industry and inter-province productivity differentials. Our contention is that rural industry development in the central and western regions of China depends on establishing a competitive industrial base. Long-term competitiveness requires maintaining efficiency (as well as cost) advantages in line with those achieved in the east. A first step towards improving efficiency can be taken by identifying the most productive eastern provinces and the conditions most conducive to their relative advantage. The second step would be to try to emulate those conditions in the central and western provinces. It is the first step of identification that we have embarked on in this chapter.

Our results based on 280 observations over 28 provinces and ten rural industries in 1993 indicate that exports of food and chemicals are produced the most efficiently. This implies that rural producers could secure a longer-term competitive advantage on the international markets by specializing in these industries rather than in arts and crafts, for instance. However, industrial structure did not explain all the variance in productivity. We found that after allowing for industrial structure the eastern province of Jiangsu, which had the highest output, was significantly more productive than any other while Neimenggu, Yunnan, Sichuan and Gansu in the west and Henan in the central region are the least productive. The eastern provinces as a group were also found to perform significantly better than those in the central region and the exports of the latter were produced more efficiently than those in the western provinces. The regional differences remained when we controlled for firm size and employment, different administrative methods and stock holding practices. We found that firm size had a strong positive influence on productivity indicating the importance of economies of scale. State-owned import–export agencies were shown not to have such adverse effects on productivity as might have been predicted. Higher stock holdings were taken as evidence of poor planning and were negatively associated with productivity, indicating a need for improved information services. More controversially, our evidence also suggests that more labour-intensive methods can lead to efficiency losses.

Our data revealed nothing about capital intensity or technology and it is likely that the much of the competitive advantage of the eastern provinces could be explained in these terms. In addition different patterns of ownership[25] and management methods are likely to be important. As the international structure of industry becomes more capital- and technology-intensive China's rural industries will also need to move in this direction. The western provinces will need to move the fastest, as they already have a long way to go in order to catch up with industrial change in the east. Worldwide trade protectionism is another issue that also needs to be addressed by Chinese policy-makers.

Our analysis of rural industry exports leads us to the conclusion that rural development in the central and western regions of China requires improvements in efficiency in provinces such as Henan and Neimenggu. Sensible investment strategies need to be undertaken with a view to establishing a competitive advantage in the less developed provinces. Industrial structure, firm organization, labour utilization, administrative methods and access to market information have all been identified as important determinants of productivity differentials. Future research needs to examine the roles of these factors in more detail in order that more precise policy recommendations can be made. Research employing case studies should prove particularly enlightening.

Notes

* This chapter reports on the work of a collaborative research project between the Department of International Economics, Renmin University of China and the Department of Economics, University of Salford. The project's overall remit is 'economic reform and rural industry in China' and the link between the two universities is funded by the British Council. We would like to acknowledge the help and advice given by Shujie Yao in the final preparation of this chapter. We are also very grateful to R. Ward for invaluable research and technical assistance.

1. See Faure (1989) for a discussion of pre-liberalization conditions in rural areas and the early development of rural industry.

2. The World Bank (1991) stresses the importance of a market friendly approach to economic development and claims that 'the most striking [of China's economic reforms] were the rural reforms that introduced price and ownership incentives for farmer's. Liu and Garnaut (1992) assess the gains from trade liberalization in a similarly positive light. However, Bowles and Dong (1994) argue that market reforms and the 'open-door' policy provide at best an incomplete explanation of China's economic success and stress instead the role of the local state and the continued existence of social ownership in the form of rural collective industries. Liu Binyan (1992) places the credit for China's economic performance less with the government than with ordinary Chinese people and makes this claim with particular reference to the rapid development of village and township industries.

3. The largest proportion of rural industry is collectively owned under the administrative control or direct ownership of local-level governments at the township and village level. In 1992, 26.6 per cent of rural industry workers were employed in enterprises owned by township governments and 34.7 per cent were employed in enterprises owned by village governments. In the same year, 31.1 per cent of rural industry workers were employed in privately owned enterprises and 7.6 per cent in co-operatives (Bowles and Dong, 1994, Table 3). Although market forces in the western tradition are gaining ground rapidly in China the ownership structure of Chinese industry is clearly very different from that in the west: the latter is based almost entirely on individual property rights while the former, as Luo (1990, p. 140) argues, is heavily tinged with Chinese tradition.

4. There may also be crises in the impacts of reforms leading to policy reversals.

5. For a review of productivity since 1979 see Kam-tim Lau and Brada (1990).

6. Kueh and Ash (1993) argue that the shift of higher incomes to peasants in the first half of the 1980s was only temporary largely because of the CCP's determination to protect the centralized urban core of industry.

7. Unfortunately, there was no comparable data relating to the skill level of the workforce, capital utilization or the value of capital. Such data are available only in relation to *domestic* or *total* (domestic *plus* exports) rural industry output, and is anyway disaggregated to a lower level than the data on exports and therefore not strictly comparable. Because of the way the data is collected aggregation up would also have been difficult and to a large extent ad hoc.

8. The average number of workers per firm may also be regarded as a measure of firm size. However, if firm size by output is taken into account, firm size by employment can be taken as a proxy for labour intensity (in the absence of data on capital utilization, see n. 7)

9. See Page (1987) for details of the role of export–import agencies in China.

10. Regional policies have played a very important role in economic development. For instance, regional policy-makers in the eastern provinces has been quicker to grant

producers the right to export directly, opening up further opportunities for trade in the more developed regions. Coincidentally it is noted that the highest proportion of total exports administered directly by producers is in the light industry and the largest share of light industry output is produced in the eastern region, notably in Guandong. While regional development policy in this case was consistent with national policy there are also conflicts of interests between levels of government hierarchy (Watson, 1992), for example the instances of provincial protectionism that emerged in the 1980s.

11. Data for Shanghai and Tibet were not available.

12. The average number of workers per firm over all provinces is only 104.4 which is quite low as the median firm in the state-owned sector employs between 300 and 1000 workers. One explanation is that rural industry is still in a primary stage of development associated with low technology and poor working conditions.

13. The average value of exports per worker over the ten industries in the eastern provinces is ¥30 040 while in the central and western provinces it is much lower, ¥20 008 and ¥18 275, respectively.

14. This may be seen in the importance of 'other industries' in the western provinces where 'other industry' output is likely to vary considerably according to local conditions in terms of both the availability of resources and demand.

15. Our data is effectively structured as a panel with ten industry cross-sections observed over 28 different provinces (or three regions). We can test for either one- or two-way fixed effects by industry and/or province (or region) (Greene, 1991, Chapter 29). Evidence of province fixed effects over industries, for instance, can be taken to imply that factors we have been unable to account for such as technology which interact positively with productivity are concentrated in those provinces with the largest fixed effects.

16. A third model (Greene, 1991, Chapter 29) estimates the two full sets of fixed effects simultaneously and includes an overall constant term. To avoid multicollinearity the restriction that $\theta_i = \pi_j = 0$ is imposed. This model was estimated and the results are available on request but they are not directly comparable with those reported because of the imposed restriction.

17. This claim is supported by the case of Hebei which ranks low in productivity terms and firms' stock holdings are high (Table 11.2).

18. Although the unadjusted R^2 is higher for (2) than for (1) (0.3 instead of 0.299) the insignificance of *WPF* leads to a lower *adjusted R^2*.

19. The correlation coefficient between *EXPF* and *WPF* is 0.58, which is significant at the 1 per cent level.

20. The coefficient of 0.0038 on *EXPF* in (6), although significant, is quite small and implies that ¥10 000 increase in output per firm would increase output per worker by only ¥38 and a ¥1million increase in *EXPF* would increase productivity by ¥3800.

21. In other words, significantly different from exports administered in terms of labour-related revenue.

22. Whether this will be in the long-term interest of the Chinese economy as a whole remains to be seen. Our evidence suggests that the gains from private incentives may be very small and as Howell (1993) points out economic reforms can create tension between micro-level dynamism and self-interest and the macro-level requirement for stability. In Howell's view such tension has been one of the causes of policy upswings and downswings in economic reform.

23. The results of estimating the variant of the dummy variable model employing province instead of regional variables are available on request from the authors.

Our results indicate that the province effects are significantly different and the associated R^2 for model 4 (X and province group effects) is 0.792 (see Tables 11.7 and 11.8).

24. Particularly as social security provision for unemployed people in rural areas is sparse and highly variable (Hussain, 1994).

25. In 1993, 66.7 per cent of the gross value of all industrial output in the western provinces was produced in the state-owned sector and 24.5 per cent was produced in the collective sector. In the eastern provinces (excluding Guangdong and Fujian) the corresponding figures were 41.7 per cent and 45.6 per cent, respectively and in Fujian and Guangdong 34.5 per cent and 34.1 per cent (State Statistical Bureau, 1993, pp. 415–16).

Bibliography

Bowles, P. and X. Dong (1994) 'Current Successes and the Future Challenges in China's Economic Reforms', *New Left Review*, 208, pp. 49–76.

Chen, Y. (1994) 'Rural Industry and the Development of the Export Orientated Economy', *International Trade Review*, 6, pp. 22–57.

Cheng, Y.K. (1978, first published in 1956) *Foreign Trade and Industrial Development of China: An Historical Integration* (Washington, DC: University of Washington Press).

Faure, D. (1989) *The Rural Economy of Pre-Liberalization China: Trade Expansion and Peasant Lives* (Hong Kong: Oxford University Press).

Greene, W. H. (1990) *Econometric Analysis* (New York: St Martin's Press).

Greene, W. H. (1991) *Limdep Users Manual* (New York: Econometric Software).

Howell, J. (1993) *China Opens its Doors: The Politics of Economic Transition* (Hemel Hempstead: Harvester Wheatsheaf).

Hsu, J. C. (1989) *China's Foreign Trade Reforms: Impact on Growth and Stability*, (Cambridge: Cambridge University Press).

Hussain, A. (1994) 'Social Security in Present-day China and Its Reform', *Chinese Programme Discussion Paper*, 29, London School of Economics.

Kennedy, P. (1992) *A Guide to Econometrics* (Oxford: Blackwell).

Kueh, Y. Y. and R. F. Ash (eds) (1993) *Economic Trends in Chinese Agriculture: The Impact of post-Mao Reforms* (Oxford: Clarenden Press).

Lardy, N. R. (1992) *Foreign Trade and Economic Reform in China, 1978–1990* (Cambridge: Cambridge University Press).

Lau, K. and J. Brada (1990) 'Technological Progress and Technical Efficiency in Chinese Industrial Growth: A Frontier Production Function Approach', *China Economic Review*, 1 (2) pp. 113–24.

Liu, Binyan (1992) 'The Future of China', *New Left Review*, 194, pp. 5–16.

Liu, G. and R. Garnaut (1992) *Economic Reform and Internationalism: China and the Pacific Region* (Canberra: The Pacific Trade and Development Conference Secretariat, Australian National University).

Luo, X. (1990) 'Ownership and Status Stratification', in W. Byrd and L. Qingsong (eds) *China's Rural Industry: Structure, Development and Reform* (Oxford: Oxford university Press).

Ministry of Agriculture, Livestock and Fishery (1994) *The Rural Industry Year Book–1994* (Beijing: Agricultural Press).

Organization of Economic Cooperation and Development (OECD) (1985) *Agriculture in China: Prospects for Production and Trade* (Paris: OECD).

Page, K. (1987) *Trade Contacts in China: a Directory of Import and Export Corporations* (London: China Prospect Publishing House).

People's Daily (1995) (Overseas Edition), 26 March.

State Statistical Bureau (1993–4) *Statistical Year Books of China* (Beijing: Statistical Publishing House).

Watson, A. (ed.) (1992) *Economic Reform and Social Change in China* (London: Routledge).

World Bank (1988) 'China: External Trade and Capital', *World Bank Country Study* (Washington, DC: World Bank).

World Bank (1991) *World Development Report* (Washington. DC; World Bank), p. 38.

Yao, Shujie (1997) 'Industrialization and Spatial Income Inequality in Rural China, 1986–92' *Economics of Transition*, 5(1), pp. 97–112.

Zweig, D. (1991) 'Internationalizing China's Countryside: The Political Economy of Exports from Rural Industry', *China Quarterly*, 128, December, pp. 716–74.

Part III

Modelling Transition and Structural Change

12

On Macro-modelling of Transitional Economies, with Special Reference to the Case of China

Duo Qin[*]

Introduction

Macroeconomic studies of transitional economies have become an exciting and challenging field of research since the dramatic collapse of the East European Socialist Bloc and the disintegration of the Soviet Union around 1990. Rapid changes of these economies took many economists by surprise and they found themselves in need of theories which could offer sound guidance to the reform programmes of these economies. Publications on transitional economies have been piling up rapidly over the last few years, but it is an interesting question whether economic research has kept pace with the rapid transition.

The literature has been expanding and diversifying so rapidly that it makes the task of carrying out an unbiased and up-to-date survey virtually impossible. To make the present survey manageable, I shall make no attempt to itemize who has done what. Instead, I shall focus on methodological issues in the hope that this will assist future research. The survey will put more emphasis on research in applied modelling, and thus restrict discussions of theoretical models largely within the range of positive economics.

The structure of the chapter is straightforward. We first outline the background, then discuss current main research issues and results. We then examine attempts at modelling the Chinese macroeconomy, since this book is dedicated to studies of economic reforms in China. The final section concludes the survey with a few critical observations concerning the current research methodologies.

Background studies: Modelling centrally planned economies

Modelling the centrally planned economies (CPEs) was considered only a minor, sideline subject during the seventies and eighties. Much of the work can be categorized into two schools: the economics of disequilibrium and the economics of shortage. A detailed and extensive discussion of the two schools has been provided by Davis and Charemza (1989); and the main methodological features of the two schools are now sketched.

The economics of disequilibrium is built upon the basis of orthodox general equilibrium theory of a perfect free-market economy. It regards chronic excess demand as the principal feature of the CPEs and explains it as distortion of the general equilibrium state. The distortion is formalized in a 'min condition' – i.e. the minimum quantity in the simultaneous supply and demand of a particular market. The market itself is described by a Walrasian general equilibrium model. Once appended with the min condition, the model is extended to include another relationship characterising the disequilibrium generating mechanism underlying the min condition. The extension is normally done in an ad hoc way (cf. Quandt, 1988).

The shortage approach originated in Kornai's famous book *Economics of Shortage* (1980). Instead of taking the orthodox general equilibrium viewpoint, Kornai tried to describe and to theorize about the CPEs in their own right. Essentially, he attributed the prevalent shortages to the ways in which firms responded to various types of 'soft budget constraints' which they faced within a CPE environment (Kornai, 1986). Kornai maintained that, despite the presence and the persistence of shortages, the CPEs should be regarded as being in a state of macroeconomic equilibrium, albeit a non-Walrasian equilibrium which is inefficient by market clearance criteria, in the sense that they followed certain dynamically stable reproduction norms. Kornai referred to these norms as 'shortages', and in a macro model, he proposed to represent them by a type of variable called 'the shortage indices' (Kornai, 1982).

There are two important differences between the two schools which deserve particular attention. The first lies in the connotation of the term 'equilibrium'. The excess demand described in the economics of disequilibrium is essentially a static concept. The concept centres on the market general equilibrium with little concern for the adjustment costs of the disequilibrium correction.[1] On the other hand, the equilibrium state in the economics of shortages is essentially a dynamic process. This aspect is highlighted subsequently in the studies carried out by Ickes (1986, 1990), who constructs a theoretical framework for macro-modelling of dynamic disequilibrium. Unfortunately, Ickes' work has received little attention in the literature. The second difference concerns the level of representative agents whose behaviour is regarded as the cause of the disequilibrium or shortage. In the economics of disequilibrium, the level is generally assigned to the planners at the macro-level, characterized by the ad hoc additional relationship brought in by the min condition, whereas the behaviour of micro-agents follows the standard market principles. In contrast, the economics of shortage attributes chronic shortages to the behaviour of micro agents, i.e. to their rational reactions to the central plans. This line of research has consequently assumed a microeconomic-oriented direction – that is to say, it became concentrated on modelling how state-owned firms react to soft budget constraints. Applied macro-studies of the CPEs were therefore dominated by the static and orthodox theories of the disequilibrium school.

Another factor affecting the applied macro-studies relates to technical problems associated with the measurement of both the min condition and the shortage index. Econometrically, these variables can all be treated as latent variables. However, the issue of how to compose aggregate indicators uniquely and suitably as proxies for shortage indices has been regarded as more of a statistical than an econometric problem, whereas the min condition in a disequilibrium model has provided econometricians with an engaging estimation exercise. As a result, various tools for estimating disequilibrium models have been invented, for example Bowden (1978), Maddala (1983) and Quandt (1988).

In spite of the advances in estimation techniques, evidence from applied models is far from conclusive in providing a unanimous verdict for or against the main propositions of either school cf. Portes (1989). This has led some modellers to fit macro-models based directly on standard economic theories (Chow, 1985, 1987, for example).

Modelling economic reforms

The literature on the post-socialist transition has exploded since the turn of 1990. Many issues have been discussed, and the approaches to reforms have been varied. But so far the literature has been dominated by country studies reporting and documenting the reforms (Blanchard, Froot and Sachs, 1994; Kornai, 1995). Textbooks on the subject have also appeared (such as Gros and Steinherr, 1995; Lavigne, 1995). Neither country studies nor textbooks are covered by the present discussion. Instead, it will be focused narrowly upon the nascent and relatively meagre literature which tackles the subject via the formal modelling approach.

Theoretical modelling

The disappearance of the Berlin Wall abruptly made models of the CPEs obsolete. Pondering over the current theoretical debates concerning the optimal reform paths of the post-socialist transition, one fails, however, to identify drastic 'structural breaks' in the philosophies between the current debates and those of the two schools sketched above. To a large extent, the so-called 'big-bang' approach can be seen as originating from the economics of disequilibrium, since the shock therapy is based broadly upon the belief that disequilibrium in CPEs is generated by elements of the centrally planned mechanism, such as the price control mechanism (Lipton and Sachs, 1990). On the other hand, arguments in favour of the gradualist approach are largely in accord with the economics of shortage (Kornai, 1990; Murrell, 1992, for example). Moreover, the focal points of current debates actually relate very closely to the two issues highlighted above, namely, the dynamic–static state and the macro–micro position.

An outstanding problem of the 'big-bang' approach is the likelihood of serious macroeconomic instability caused by severe regime shocks. This has impelled economists to face the dynamics of the transitional phase of a regime shock. An immediate approach to the issue is to investigate the economic optimality of the transitional phase subject to the adjustment costs induced by the shock. Studies along these lines utilize aggregate dynamic models. The model analysis has led to discussions of the credibility of 'big-bang' programmes – i.e. what magnitude of shocks can an economy absorb without losing its macro-stability (Coricelli and Milesi-Ferretti, 1993, for example). This problem can be rephrased as one of searching for the limit/boundary of shock endurance. Answers to the problem depend on the micro-structure of the economy and the nature as well as the magnitude of the shocks. A key structural characteristic of transitional economies is a rapidly growing private sector along with a steadily declining state-owned sector. Hence two-sector dynamic models have overtaken aggregate-static models – e.g. the pioneer model developed by Aghion (1993). As far as the impact of various types and sizes of shocks is concerned, another issue has surfaced – namely, the issue of policy sequencing with respect to the optimal speed as well as macroeconomic stability of reforms, since many policy shocks are interdependent, and often complementary with each other, but with different time effects. Pioneer work on this issue has been carried out by Dewatripont and Roland (1992, 1996); their work links the issue of how to design reforms with welfare economics.

On the other hand, the rise of the multisector modelling approach has attracted mainstream economists into investigating the positive aspects of transitional economies from a more micro-perspective than was implied in the economics of disequilibrium approach. Macro-modellers who adhere to the conventional apparatus of comparative-static analysis have tended to ascribe the special features of a transitional economy to a non-market optimization sector of state-owned enterprises (SOEs), rather than to the government macro-policies alone, and towards explaining the SOEs' behaviour by the soft budget rationale. For example, Lin (1993) analyzed the effects of wage and price liberalization via a monetary model built upon Kornai's notion of shortage; Bennett and Dixon (1995) studied the relationship between the SOE sector and the private sector by a macro-model built within a general equilibrium framework; Brandt and Zhu (1995) explored the framework further by relating the soft budget behaviour of the SOEs to the misallocation of resources between the SOE sector and the private sector, and attributed the intensified inflation cycles which are frequently observed during transition to the misallocation. These positive models often contain interesting and testable implications for empirical studies. These models have, however, highlighted two serious drawbacks of the general equilibrium approach. First, the approach provides little economic rationale to explain the behaviour of

SOEs as rigorously as those for the behaviour of firms of the private sector. Secondly, it lacks effective means of delineating the adjustment processes of agents facing drastic regime changes.

One remedy is to regard the SOEs as a monopolistic sector by replacing the assumption of perfect competition implied in the general equilibrium setting with that of imperfect competition (for example, Yin, 1997). But the remedy is only partial, especially in view of the important aspect of transitional dynamics. An alternative remedy is to conceptualize the economic rationale of the behaviour of the SOEs directly in a dynamic setting with imperfect (both intertemporal and intersectoral) information. An important pioneer work along these lines is Dewatripont and Maskin (1995), who postulate a theory which explains excess credit demand of firms under soft budget constraints in terms of the institutional arrangement of financing organizations – i.e. centralized versus decentralized credit markets. The theory suggests that SOEs are rational optimizers, only their optimization is conditioned upon the given institutional arrangement. In fact, this line of thought has been pursued earlier by Murrell and Wang (1993), who tried to set up a formal institutional explanation of the gradualness of the transition via a growth model of the private sector. Such research contributes to as well as embodies the recent revival of institutional economics, most notably by using evolutionary models adapted from biology to characterize the evolutionary dynamics of economies undergoing technical and social innovations (Chiaromonte and Dosi, 1993; Coriat and Dosi, 1995; and also the survey by Nelson, 1995, for example).

Problems of modelling transitional economies have also prompted main-stream economists to re-examine the fundamental weakness of the conventional equilibrium approach. A substantial contribution has been made by Sargent, who attributes the key weakness of dynamic general equilibrium models to the rational expectations conceptualization of the dynamics and proposes to renovate it by 'bounded rationality' (1993). In contrast to the full information and homogeneity assumptions of rational expectation models, bounded rationality allows for heterogeneous micro-agents and for the possibility that each agent possesses only limited information. Moreover, it brings macro-theories much closer to empirical measurement and thus to testability by identifying the agents' learning processes with recursive estimation methods in econometric modelling (cf. also Sargent, 1996; Hansen and Sargent, 1996). Furthermore, the identification establishes the analogy between modelling economically bounded rational agents and the simulation of artificial intelligence in the neural network research (Sargent, 1993; Cho and Sargent, 1995, for example).

Empirical modelling[3]

Similar to theoretical modelling, empirical modelling of transitional econo-mies has been both varied and active. But distinct from theoretical economists, empirical modellers tend to turn to statistical and computational means for solutions when models based upon conventional economic theories fail to produce empirically satisfactory results.

Most macroeconometric models of transitional economies are based on simple, stereotyped theories within the general equilibrium framework. When empirical results of such models turn out to be unsatisfactory, often because of the non-constancy of the estimated parameter and/or non-white noise residuals, it is natural for modellers to attribute these results to the drastic reforms and present them as evidence of 'structural breaks' or 'regime shifts'. The focal point of empirical modelling of transitional economies therefore has become centred upon the issue of how to model structural breaks.

An extreme stance is to abandon macroeconometric modelling altogether. The argument for the abandonment is that the market equilibrium foundation of macroeconometric models is totally inappropriate for describing the behavioural norms of agents adapting as well as contributing to the changing post-socialist transitional economies. It is argued therefore that these models are bound to produce poor econometric results in fitting highly erratic data. To circumvent the problem, modellers should try first to understand the micro-agents' behavioural norms during transitions. A handy tool for that lies with the artificial intelligence system technique. For example, Moss and Kuznetsova (1996) experiment with a simulated Russian model in search of a workable account of the learning processes of several production sectors under different macro-policy shocks, by adjusting the model iteratively via comparison of the model-generated macro-aggregates with actual macro-statistics.

Within the econometric arena, there has been a strong tendency to treat model failures and parameter breaks purely by statistical means. This is evident from many works both of econometric tool-makers – i.e. theoretical econometrics – and of tool users – i.e. applied econometrics (Broemeling and Tsurumi, 1987; Hackl and Westlund, 1992, for example). Prior to the collapse of the Berlin Wall, econometrics had experienced a period of substantial renovation in time-series analyses. The renovation stemmed mainly from a growing awareness of non-stationary properties commonly observable from macroeconomic time-series data (Hendry, 1995). To those econometricians fully alert to such time-series complications, data observations from the post-socialist transitional economies are viewed as fresh evidence of non-stationarity. There has therefore been a significant upsurge in developing statistical tests for parameter non-constancy for non-stationary time-series data in the literature (the special issues of *Journal of Business and Economic Statistics* 1992; *Journal of Econometrics* 1996; and Chu, Stinchcombe and White, 1996).

While parameter breaks are more or less uniformly treated as 'structural breaks' in statistical tests, applied modellers disagree with each other in how to handle and explain them. Methodologically, their explanations and prescriptions can be broadly categorized into two groups. One group opts to maintain the invariance of the *a priori* chosen structural models, and attributes the breaks to shifts of the relevant parameter values, such as certain basic propensities. In other words, parameter breaks are handled by means of time-varying parameter (TVP) estimation methods (Hens, 1992; Blangiewicz and Charemza, 1993; Hall and Koparanova, 1995; and Song, Liu and Romilly 1996, for example). The other group also tries to maintain the validity of the *a priori* chosen structural models. But it chooses to regard parameter breaks as model mis-specifications, and seeks to resolve the problem by *ad hoc* augmentations of the basic structural models (Qin, 1994; Girardin, 1996; Qin and Vanags, 1996, for example). The two groups are hereinafter referred to as the estimation approach and the specification approach respectively.

An implicit but crucial assumption underpinning the estimation approach is that the estimated model corresponds to the actual data-generating process. More precisely, the assumption entails three suppositions: (a) the correctness of the theoretical formulation, (b) the time-dependency of theoretical parameters and (c) the relative independence in sampling such that the usual *ceteris paribus* conditions of the theory are largely satisfied. None seems to hold with high probability for the application of empirical models based upon standard and simple theories to data from relatively short and volatile transitional periods.

As mentioned above, the specification approach also attempts to maintain standard theories. But instead of relaxing the assumption that structural parameters are constant, it tries to achieve this by decomposing data into two parts – one corresponding to the long-run equilibrium described by standard theories and the other to be assigned to short-run and transitional factors reflecting country-specific or institutional features. In other words, it attributes parameter breaks of simple models to a mismatch between the *ceteris paribus* assumption required of these models and the data information from given samples, and it identifies certain institutional variables to account approximately for the mismatch. A major advantage of this approach is the detachment of fundamental theoretical relationships from sample-period specific factors, whereas its major weakness lies in its ad hoc data-mining procedure in specifying the institutional variables, leaving it an open issue as how to justify uniquely these variables.

The case of China

Nearly twenty years of a gradual reform process have made China a theoretically interesting as well as data-rich object of study. The relevant literature is scattered in books, and is more concentrated in academic journals such as *Journal of Asian Economics, Journal of Comparative Economics, Economics of Transition, Economics of Planning*, as well as journals devoted to China studies, such as *China Economic Review*, and also numerous journals in Chinese, such as *Economic Research Journal* (Monthly) and *Quantitative and Technical Economic Research*.

Table 12.1   Key features of theoretical models

Approach	Equilibrium/ disequilibrium	Soft budget/ institutional
Key features of transition	SOEs non-optimization/ monopolistic	SOEs optimize with respect to soft budget institution
Micro–macro interaction	Micro-aggregate to macro	Micro-aggregate to and interact with macro
Dynamics	Comparative-static	Comparative-static/ business cycles
Testability	Parameter ranges	Parameter ranges/ macro-fluctuations
Examples	Bennett and Dixon (1996); Yin (1997)	Wang (1991); Brandt and Zhu (1995)

The literature falls largely within the framework already described. Tables 12.1 and 12.2 outline some main features based on a small selection of the recent theoretical and empirical results. From a critical perspective, we observe the following:

(a) *The link between theoretical and empirical works remains weak.* Theoretical and applied modellers have apparently been working separately in spite of the fact that a number of theoretical models have followed closely the general or partial equilibrium tradition, (Yu, 1994; Bennett and Dixon, 1996; Yin, 1997, for example) and carry testable implications. However, an encouraging sign can be seen in Fry (1996), in which the calibrated parameter values for model simulation have been taken from a number of empirical results.

Table 12.2   Key features of empirical models

Approach	Structural model/ cointegration	TVP structural model	Calibrated structural model
Theory base	Partial equilibrium	Partial equilibrium	Computable general equilibrium
Key features of transition	Additional institutional variables	Changing values of structural parameters	Disequilibrium solutions
Micro–macro interaction	Implicit in the ratio form of institutional variables	No	Explicitly linked by sectors
Dynamics	Partial adjustment/ ADL or VAR[a]	ADL	Comparative static
Examples	Yi (1993); Qin (1994); Girardin (1996)	Song, Liu and Romilly (1996)	Zhuang (1996)

Note:

[a] ADL denotes autoregressive distributed-lag model and VAR denotes vector autoregressive model.

(b) There is a strong move to explore *micro-macro interaction in theoretical modelling*. This is not only seen from models following the conventional equilibrium approach, as those cited above, but also from models incorporating the soft budget behaviour of the SOEs into the macro-movement of China's economic transition (Wang, 1991; Brandt and Zhu, 1995, for example).

(c) There is little sign of micro–macro interaction in empirical modelling but the advance in the use of *statistical methods* is apparent. Empirical studies at the micro-level are more numerous than those at the macro-level, but dialogues between the two sides seem absent. However, the paper by Zhuang (1996) made a courageous attempt to change the situation. In macro-empirical modelling, progress is the most noticeable in the use of statistical methods; a good example of this can be traced in the money-demand studies from the early work of Chow (1987), to Burton and Ha (1990), Yi (1993), Qin (1994), and the work of Girardin (1996).

(d) A gap between the studies carried out by economists *in China* and those done *outside China*. In general, works published in China have been rich in characterizing the transitional process but relatively poor in presenting it via formal models. Although econometric methods have become widely accepted, the majority of empirical studies remains simple, informal and data descriptive.

(e) A lag between the implications of *empirical model results* and what are considered to be the most interesting and imperative issues by *theorists or policy-makers*. This is most manifest in the concentrated efforts at measuring long-run equilibrium relations empirically, although the transitional dynamics during the reforms has been the principal concern.

What should we learn from modelling reforms?

A major deficiency in modelling transitional economies lies in the inadequate communication between theorists and applied modellers. This is discernible from the lack of references to the relevant works on both sides, such as the lack of awareness of the institutional models developed by Murrell (1992) and Murrell and Wang (1993) in the applied specification search for institutional variables by Qin (1994) and Qin and Vanags (1996), and also in the lack of reference to Sargent's work on bounded rationality (1993) and neural networks (Cho and Sargent, 1995) in the simulation model by Moss and Kuznetsova (1996).

From an applied economist's viewpoint, the deficiency stems from a severely partial attention to advances in econometrics and inadequate attention to those in economics. As pointed out above, the wide awareness of nonstationarity in economic time series has led applied modellers to try and use the latest statistical apparatus for the problem. On the other hand, most of the theoretical models used in applied studies depend upon simple, stereotyped theories. There is also a tendency to try to circumvent modelling problems by purely statistical means even when the theories are already inconsistent with the sample data. As a result, the inconsistency is frequently camouflaged by complicated technical devices. The most remarkable instance of this kind is the confusion concerning the concept of 'structure' (Hackl and Westlund, 1992, Introduction). To most economists, the concept of 'structure' denotes certain behavioural patterns/regularities delineated by a theoretical relationship. To some econometricians, however, the behavioural content becomes dispensable. Indeed, it is not difficult to find empirical illustrations of 'structural breaks' based upon single-variable time-series models such as autoregressive models. A model of this kind is devoid of economic structure from the viewpoint of economists, but nevertheless represents the statistical structure of the variable concerned, provided that the assumption of model autonomy holds approximately for the sample periods. Here, model autonomy means the independence of the joint distribution – e.g. $P(XY)$, underpinning the model, e.g. $Y_t = \beta X + \epsilon_t$, with respect to the marginal distribution of other possibly omitted variables , i.e.:

$$P(YXZ) = {}^{\text{i.d.}}P(YX)P(X)$$

where 'i.d.' denotes independent distribution and $P(YXZ)$ underlies the model $Y_t = \beta X + \lambda Z + \epsilon_i$. The independence seldom holds with the marginal distributions of most economic time series – i.e. the case when X represents solely the lagged information of Y, let alone for the particular circumstance of the post-socialist transition. Hence, attempts to demonstrate parameter nonconstancy in simple models such as $Y_t = \beta X + \epsilon_t$ and to interpret the estimated β_t. as evidence of structural breaks can easily be nonsensical and misleading (Qin, 1997).

The theoretical disputes were summarized above into two issues – namely, dynamics versus steady state, and macro-structure versus micro-structure. The problems of empirical modelling of the transition can also be viewed from these two perspectives. Too much emphasis has been put on the testing and estimating of co-integrated relations embedded in macroeconometric models, leaving insufficient attention to the implicit assumptions of the models concerning the economic interpretations of the long-run co-integrations. In particular, these relations are determined largely by the choice of variables. The choice depends on the modeller's knowledge of and preference from the menu of all relevant theoretical models. When the theoretical models come from the general equilibrium setting, their relevance to modelling transitional economies can be rather thin. More importantly, since the estimated long-run relations are closely dependent on both the types of reform shocks experienced and the samples used, it may well be wrong to infer from the resulting nonconstant or implausible estimates that either the long-run theory is incorrect or its parameters are time-varying. In short, the focus on long-run relations corresponds poorly to the theorization of the transitional dynamics, and estimates using data from transitional periods may mismatch the theoretical long-run equilibrium. Actually, such a mismatch simply confirms to the view, already acknowledged by economists, that the transitional process is beyond the general equilibrium setting of most standard theories. In other words, data from the transitional periods is likely to carry important information which is omitted by the *ceteris paribus* assumptions of standard general equilibrium relations. Moreover, such information tends to affect the estimates of the long-run parameters owing to its correlation with the variables included in the long-run relations.

A constructive message suggests that applied modellers should try to separate and decompose the long-run relations from the data so as to concentrate on the transitional features. In a way, the decomposition amounts to assuming the long-run relations 'co-breaking' (Hendry, 1997). Whether the assumption holds will then depend upon how the transitional features are to be represented and modelled. Since institutional variables normally take the form of ratios between different sectors, for example the output ratio between the SOEs and the whole economy, or the productivity ratio between the SOEs and the private sector, applied modelling in search of the appropriate institutional representation leads to the second issue – namely, the appropriate choice of macro–micro level of analysis. Given the subject matter of investigation, the problem is often revealed by heterogeneity in agents' behaviour as one of excessive aggregation and one can identify this by the need for additional institutional variables. On the other hand, we should also be able to view successful use of institutional variables in certain empirical studies as suggesting that homogeneity holds approximately at the sectoral level from which these variables are constructed. For example, if the institutional variable made of the productivity ratio between the SOEs and the private sector is found useful in modelling inflation, this may imply homogeneity within the sector of the SOEs and the private sector, respectively, as far as the inflation-generating process is concerned. However, more research is required before we can establish the exact link between heterogeneous micro-adjustment processes and their aggregate contribution to the complexity of macro-dynamics. Obviously, establishing the link forms a prerequisite for the validity of aggregate macroeconometric models.

To conclude, research in modelling transitional economies cannot be fruitful unless the model structures correspond to the structures of the economies under investigation. To achieve such correspondences, an improved channel of exchange is required not only between theoretical and applied modellers, or between macro- and micro-economists, but also between academic modellers and country specialists as well as policy makers.

Notes

* I would like to thank Sarah Cook, Steve Pollock, Alf Vanags, Juzhong Zhuang and my colleagues at QMW for their valuable comments.

1. Qin and Lu (1996) demonstrate the dynamic implication of a simple and standard disequilibrium model to bring to light the limitation in dynamic specification of the model.
2. The transition in Eastern Europe appears to form the main stimulus for Sargent to embark on the issue. This is best seen from the initial section entitled 'Equilibria and transition' of Chapter 1 of Sargent (1993).
3. Here, we leave aside the issue of measurement problems in data collection induced by drastic reforms. (See Blangiewicz, Bolt and Charemza, 1994; Fischer, Sahay and Végh, 1996 for discussions on the issue). Notice, however, that measurement problems have often been used too easily as the justification for poorly chosen or misspecified models.

Bibliography

Aghion, P. (1993) 'Economic Reform in Eastern Europe', *European Economic Review*, 37, pp. 525–32.

Bennett, J. and H. D. Dixon (1995) 'Macroeconomic Equilibrium and Reform in a Transitional Economy', *European Economic Review*, 39, pp. 1465–85.

Bennett, J. and H. D. Dixon (1996) 'A Macro-theoretic Model of the Chinese Economy', *Journal of Comparative Economics*, 22 277–94.

Blanchard, O. J., K. A. Froot and J. D. Sachs (eds), *The Transition in Eastern Europe*, (Chicago and London: University of Chicago Press).

Blangiewicz, M. and W. W. Charemza (1993) 'Evolutionary Economic Reform and Policy Issues: A Structural VAR Approach', *Centre for Economic Forecasting Discussion Paper*, 23–93, London Business School.

Blangiewicz, M., T. W. Bolt and W. W. Charemza(1994) 'Alternative Data for the Dynamic Modelling of the East European Transformation', *Journal of Economic and Social Measurement*, 20 pp. 1–23.

Bowden, R. J. (1978) *The Econometrics of Disequilibrium* (Amsterdam: North-Holland).

Brandt, L. and X. Zhu (1998) 'Soft Budget Constraints and Inflation Cycles: A Positive Model of the Post-Reform Chinese Economy', University of Toronto, Mimeo.

Broemeling, D. and H. Tsurumi (1987) *Econometrics and Structural Change* (New York: Marcel Dekker).

Burton D. and J. Ha (1990) 'Economic Reform and the Demand for Money in China', *IMF Working Paper*, 90/42.

Chiaromonte, F. and G. Dosi (1993) 'Heterogeneity, Competition, and Macroeconomic Dynamics', *Structural Change and Economic Dynamics*, 4, pp. 39–63.

Cho, I-K. and T. J. Sargent (1995) 'Neural Networks for Encoding and Adapting in Dynamic Economics', Department of Economics, University of Chicago, mimeo

Chow, G. C. (1985) 'A Model of Chinese National Income Determination', *Journal of Political Economics*, 93, pp. 782–92.

Chow, G. C. (1987) 'Money and Price Level Determination in China', *Journal of Comparative Economics*, 11, pp. 319–33.

Chu, C.-S. J., M. Stinchcombe and H. White (1996) 'Monitoring Structural Change', *Econometrica*, 64, pp. 1045–65.

Coriat, B. and G. Dosi (1995) 'The Institutional Embeddedness of Economic Change: An Appraisal of the 'Evolutionary' and 'Regulationist' Research Programmes', *IIASA Working Papers*, 95–117.

Coricelli, F. and G. M. Milesi-Ferretti (1993) 'On the Credibility of "Big Bang" Programs', *European Economic Review*, 37, pp. 387–95.

Davis, C. and W. Charemza (eds) (1989) *Models of Disequilibrium and Shortage in Centrally Planned Economies* (London: Chapman & Hall).

Dewatripont, M. and E. Maskin (1995) 'Credit and Efficiency in Centralised and Decentralised Economies', *Review of Economic Studies*, 62 pp. 541–55.

Dewatripont, M. and G. Roland (1992) 'The Virtues of Gradualism and Legitimacy in the Transition to a Market Economy', *Economic Journal*, 102, pp. 291–300.

Dewatripont, M. and G. Roland (1996) 'Transition as a Process of Large-scale Institutional Change', *Economics of Transition*, 4, pp. 1–30.

Fischer, S., R. Sahay and C. A. Végh (1996) 'Stabilisation and Growth in Transition Economics: The Early Experience', *Journal of Economic Perspectives*, 10, pp. 45–66.

Fry, M. J. (1996) 'Can Seigniorage Revenue Keep China's Financial System Afloat?', *International Finance Group Working Papers*, 96–09, University of Birmingham.

Girardin, E. (1996) 'Is There a Long Run Demand for Currency in China?', *Economics of Planning*, 6, pp. 169–84.

Gros, D. and A. Steinherr (1995) *Winds of Change: Economic Transition in Central and Eastern Europe*, London and New York: Longman.

Hackl, P. and A. H. Westlund (eds) (1992) *Economic Structural Change* (Berlin: Springer-Verlag).

Hall, S. G. and M. S. Koparanova (1995) 'Modelling and Forecasting Structural Change in Transition: the Case of Bulgaria', *Centre for Economic Forecasting Discussion Papers*. 6–95, London Business School.

Hansen, L. P. and T. J. Sargent (1996) *Recursive Linear Models of Dynamic Economies*, University of Chicago, mimeo.

Hendry, D. F. (1995) *Dynamic Econometrics* (Oxford: Oxford University Press).

Hendry, D. F. (1997) 'The Econometrics of Macroeconomic Forecasting', *The Economic Journal*, 107, pp. 1330–57.

Hens, L. M. A. (1992) 'On Modelling Capital Flows when the International Financial System is in Transition', in J. W. Owsinski *et al.* (eds), *Transition to Advanced Market Economies* (Warsaw: The Association of Polish Operational Research Societies).

Ickes, B. W. (1986) 'On the Economics of Taut Plans', *Journal of Comparative Economics*, 10, pp. 388–99.

Ickes, B. W. (1990) 'A Macroeconomic Model for Centrally Planned Economies', *Journal of Macroeconomics*, 12, pp. 23–45.

Kornai, J. (1980) *Economics of Shortage* (Amsterdam: North-Holland).

Kornai, J. (1982) *Growth, Shortage and Efficiency: A Macrodynamic Model of the Socialist Economy* (Oxford: Basil Blackwell).

Kornai, J. (1986) *Contradictions and Dilemmas: Studies on the Socialist Economy and Society* (Cambridge, Man.: MIT Press).

Kornai, J. (1990) *The Road to a Free Economy* (New York: Norton).

Kornai, J. (1995) *Highway and Byways: Studies on Reform and Post Communist Transition* (Cambridge, Man,: MIT Press).

Lavigne, M. (1995) *The Economics of Transition: From Socialist Economy to Market Economy* (London: Macmillan).

Lin, S.-K. (1993) 'A Monetary Model of a Shortage Economy', *IMF Staff Papers*, 40, pp. 369–94.

Lipton D. and J. Sachs (1990) 'Creating a Market Economy in Eastern Europe: The Case of Poland', *Brookings Papers on Economic Activity*, 1, pp. 75–147.

Maddala, G. S. (1983) *Limited-dependent and Qualitative Variables* (Cambridge: Cambridge University Press).

Moss, S. and O. Kuznetsova (1996) 'Modelling the Process of Market Emergence', in J. W. Owsinski and J. Nahorski (eds), *Modelling and Analysing Economies in Transition* (Warsaw:).

Murrell, P. (1992) 'Evolution in Economics and in the Economic Reform of the Centrally Planned Economies', in C. C. Clague and G. Rausser (eds), *Emerging Market Economies in Eastern Europe* (Oxford: Basil Blackwell).

Murrell, P. and Y. Wang (1993) 'When Privatization Should be Delayed: The Effect of Communist Legacies on Organizational and Institutional Reforms', *Journal of Comparative Economics*, 17, pp. 385–406.

Nelson, R. R. (1995) 'Recent Evolutionary Theorising about Economic Change', *Journal of Economic Literature*, 33, pp. 48–90.

Portes, R. (1989) 'The Theory and Measurement of Macrocosmic Disequilibrium in Centrally Planned Economies', in C. Davis and W. Charemza (eds), *Models of Disequilibrium and Shortage in Centrally Planned Economies* (London: Chapmall & Hall).

Qin, D. (1994) 'Money Demand in China: The Effect of Economic Reform', *Journal of Asian Economics*, 5, pp. 253–71.

Qin, D. (1997) 'A Critique on Macroeconometric Modelling of Structural Changes', *Department of Economics Discussion Paper*, 368, Queen Mary and Westfield College.

Qin, D. and M. Lu (1996) 'Dynamic Structure of Disequilibrium Models', *Department of Economics Discussion Paper*, 9631, University of Southampton.

Qin, D. and A. Vanags (1996) 'Modelling the Inflation Process in Transitional Economies: Empirical Comparison of Poland, Hungary and Czech Republic', *Economics of Planning*, 6 , pp. 3–24.

Quandt, R. E. (1988) *The Econometrics of Disequilibrium* (Oxford: Basil Blackwell).

Sargent, T. J. (1993) *Bounded Rationality in Macroeconomics* (Oxford: Clarendon Press).

Sargent, T. J. (1996) *Recursive Macroeconomic Theory*, University of Chicago mimeo.

Song, H., X. Liu and P. Romilly (1996) 'A Time-varying Parameter Approach to the Chinese Aggregate Consumption Function', *Economics of Planning*, 6, pp. 185–203.

Wang, Y. (1991) 'Government Reform, Fixed Capital Investment Expansion and Inflation: A Behaviour Model Based on the Chinese Experience', *China Economic Review*, 2, pp. 3–27.

Yi, G. (1993) 'Towards Estimating the Demand for Money in China', *Economics of Planning*, 26, pp. 243–70.

Yin, X. (1997) 'A Micro-Macroeconomic Analysis of the Chinese Economy with Imperfect Competition', *China Economic Review*, 8, pp. 31–51.

Yu, Y. (1994) *Macroeconomic Analysis and the Design of Stabilisation Policy in China*, DPhil. thesis, Oxford University.

Zhuang, J. (1996) 'Estimating Distortions in the Chinese Economy: A General Equilibrium Approach', *Economica*, 63, pp. 543–68.

13
Structural Changes in Employment and Investment in China: 1985–94*

Aying Liu

Introduction

One of the most striking features of China's economic reform is the increasing polarization between the prosperous eastern coastal provinces and the still relatively backward north and western parts of the country. Regional income inequality has been widening considerably under economic reforms (Yao, 1997). This has been accompanied by dramatic changes in the employment and investment structures at both national and regional level. First, there is an increasing surplus of labour released from agriculture owing to increased labour productivity and shortage of land. Second, an increasing number of workers and staff employed by state-owned industries have become unemployed or under-employed. Third, and most impressively, the country's investment emphasis has been shifting or diversifying away from agriculture and manufacturing to the service sector, and from heavy and defence-based industries to light industries (Zhao, 1996). Indeed, economic reform has led to significant changes in employment and investments across regions. Such changes have contributed to substantial regional disparities in economic growth and incomes as different regions now have different industrial structures and development policies.

Several studies on spatial disparity in China are found in the existing literature. Yao (1997) uses a Gini decomposition procedure to examine regional income inequality in rural China; Zhao (1996) uses time-series data to compare regional disparities between the development policies under Mao and Deng. There are also other studies (Knight and Song, 1993; Griffin and Zhao, 1993; Hussain, Lanjouw and Stern, 1994), but it appears that all of them examine disparity in terms of income distribution, and their analysis is usually carried out at the aggregate regional level (i.e. east, central and west of China).

While sharing the concerns of others about the widening regional income gap, this chapter argues that it is more interesting and useful to conduct an analysis based on employment and investment disparities which may, to a large extent, explain the income gap. It is also argued that while a highly aggregated regional analysis is useful for providing an overall picture for political and social analysis, it may be less analytically useful in trying to understand factors determining the real differences between provinces within a region. The analysis of provincial-level disparities may reveal some real problems reflecting specific economic policies, since the province is China's basic and constant administrative unit, at which level most economic policies are formulated and economic activities are organized and managed.

Using the shift-share method, this chapter investigates the driving force behind the changes of employment and investment structures over a ten-year period (1985–94). Our interests here are focused on whether the disparities of employment and investment in different provinces were caused by the industrial mix or by some other factors.

The rest of this chapter is organized as follows. We give a brief introduction to the shift-share method and the data used in the study, and then present the results of a shift-share analysis based on employment and investment changes for all provinces by aggregate industrial sectors. We provide the results from analyzing three selected provinces at detailed sectoral level to reveal the underlying nature of the problems faced by those regions – i.e. their industrial structures. This leads to a discussion of policy and its effects on regions. The final section draws some conclusions.

Shift-share analysis

Shift-share is a standardized and useful analytical tool for spatial analysis. Since its introduction in 1960, it has been widely used for analyses of regional employment, structural change affecting different industries, industrial location, migration and economic growth. The method (together with its merits and limitations) is extensively discussed in Stillwell (1970), Fothergill and Gudgin (1979), Stevens and Moore (1980), Casler (1989), Armstrong and Taylor (1993, section 7.1) and Hoppes (1994). Some examples of its use in examining employment change, growth and productivity are found in Moore and Rhodes (1973); Randall (1973); Healey and Clark (1984); and Ishikawa (1992), among others.

Over the years, the basic technique has been extended and refined. A number of alternative models have appeared in the literature, such in Esteban-Marquilas (1972) and Arcelus (1984). Some of those models have enriched or improved the original method by linking shift-share with other techniques such as statistics (Berzeg, 1978, 1984; Kurre and Weller, 1989), information theory (Theil and Gosh, 1980), and stochastic regression functions (Arcelus, 1984; Knudson and Barff; 1991). The classic formulation, however, remains the most dominant model in empirical work.

This study adopts the most basic version of the model discussed in Dunn (1960) and Armstrong and Taylor (1993). Let ΔE_{ij} denote the change of employment for the ith industry in region j from the base period to the end period. By definition, it is the product of total employment of the ith sector in region j in the base period, denoted by E_{ij0}, multiplied by the growth rate of employment of the ith sector in region j over the whole period, denoted by R_{ij}. The relationship is expressed in equation (13.1).

$$\Delta E_{ij} = E_{ij0} R_{ij} \qquad (13.1)$$

Further, let R_k and R_{ik} denote the employment growth rates for the country and for the ith sector of the country, respectively; (13.1) can then be decomposed into three components as expressed in (13.2).

$$\Delta E_{ij} = E_{ij0} R_k + E_{ij0}(R_{ik} - R_k) + E_{ij0}(R_{ij} - R_{ik}) \qquad (13.2)$$

The first term on the right-hand side of (13.2) is usually called the *national component* of growth. It shows, *ceteris paribus*, the effect on the sector of the local economy, if sector i in location j exactly matched the national trend (R_k). The second term in (13.2) is the *structural component*. It calculates the change in the ith sector that can be attributed to the region's industry mix. If the region has a 'favourable' mix, comprising more fast growing industries, it will, *ceteris paribus*, experience faster employment growth than the rest of the country.

However, having a favourable industrial structure in the base period is neither a necessary nor a sufficient condition for faster growth. Hence the third term in (13.2) is the *differential* (or *residual*) *component*. It is that part of regional change not 'explained' by the national and structural components. It is a catch-all for measuring the extent to which an industry in the region grew faster (shown by a positive value) or slower (shown by a negative value) than would have occurred had the local industry experienced the national growth rate. The sign and size of the structural and differential components therefore have very important economic implications in terms of structural adjustment and improvement in local competitiveness.

Following Randall (1973), (13.2) can be rearranged as (13.3):

$$\Delta E_{ij} - E_{ij0} R_k = E_{ij0}(R_{ik} - R_k) + E_{ij0}(R_{ij} - R_{ik}) \qquad (13.3)$$

The left-hand side is called the *net relative change* (NRC), meaning the difference between the actual change and the national component. It shows whether growth of the ith sector in region j is faster or slower than the national average growth, irrespective of industrial structure. NRC can therefore be regarded as an index of relative performance, which the right-hand side seeks to explain.

The data used in this study are drawn from *China Statistical Yearbook* (SSB, 1985–95). Three sets of regional and sectoral data are employed in both absolute and growth rate terms: (1) national income (NI), (2) employment and (3) investment in capital construction. While NI is used as an indicator of

Table 13.1   Changes in employment and investment in capital construction, by sectors, 1985–94, per cent

	Total	Agriculture		Industry		Services	
	Actual	Actual	NRC	Actual	NRC	Actual	NRC
Employment	23	7	–16	33	9	73	50
Investment	447	62	–385	427	–20	489	42

economic development, employment and investment data are used for analyzing some of the reasons behind the disparities in NI.

Results of spatial disparity analysis

An overall view of the changes

Over the period 1985–94, China's economy experienced strong growth, for example, national investment in capital construction increased in real terms by 447 per cent, and employment by 23 per cent. Such growth was by no means even across sectors and regions (see Table 13.1).

Table 13.1 clearly shows a dramatic shift between three highly aggregated sectors over the period. While the agricultural sector declined by −16 per cent in employment and −385 per cent in investment in terms of NRC, the industrial sector experienced relative growth of 9 per cent in employment and −20 per cent in investment, and the service sector attracted both more labour and investment with relative growth rates of 50 per cent and 42 per cent, respectively. Given the national and structural influence on overall economic growth, however, the actual changes varied from one region to another. The difference between the actual and relative changes can be apportioned to the regional industry-mix component and the differential component, and it is to this that we now turn at a more spatially disaggregated level.

Changes in employment

Table 13.2 illustrates a detailed picture of change at the provincial level, showing what was happening to employment and investment over the period in terms of NRC broken down into structural and residual components (see (13.3)).

For a succinct picture, provinces are grouped and ranked by sectors, according to the components' share of NRC (Table 13.3).

Tables 13.2 and 13.3 together show some important points of employment changes over the period:

- First, agriculture experienced a relative decline (negative NRC) in most provinces, except Jilin, Guizhou and Yunnan. Some provinces even

	Agriculture				Industry				Services			
	Change (000)		Share of NRC[a] (%)		Change (000)		Share of NRC (%)		Change (000)		Share of NRC[a] (%)	
	Actual	NRC	Structural	Differential	Actual	NRC	Structural	Differential	Actual	NRC	Structural	Differential
Beijing	-230	-456	34	66	215	-377	-64	164	1084	565	197	-97
Tianjin	-135	-365	44	56	59	-480	-45	145	392	94	675	-575
Hebei	1209	-2650	101	-1	2648	1328	40	60	2923	1997	99	1
Shanxi	666	-661	140	-40	945	142	229	-129	1048	430	307	-207
I. Mongolia	362	-794	101	-1	454	41	405	-305	892	505	164	-64
Liaoning	-60	-1534	67	33	378	-1086	-62	162	1915	946	219	-119
Jilin	1518	532	-129	229	565	-102	-265	365	1211	722	145	-45
Heilongjiang	293	-947	91	9	841	-210	-203	303	1254	555	270	-170
Shanghai	-599	-898	23	77	-187	-1173	-34	134	767	273	388	-288
Jiangsu	-1231	-5287	53	47	1811	-675	-149	249	3048	1699	170	-70
Zhejiang	-801	-3768	55	45	1817	306	199	-99	2899	2022	93	7
Anhui	1741	-2324	122	-22	1798	946	36	64	3305	2560	62	38
Fujian	870	-781	147	-47	1461	938	23	77	1664	1159	93	7
Jiangxi	938	-1465	114	-14	845	193	137	-37	2659	2077	60	40
Shandong	1611	-3928	98	2	3898	2250	30	70	2556	2280	120	-20
Henan	2937	-3052	137	-37	3464	2259	22	78	4158	3090	74	26
Hubei	501	-2716	83	17	851	-287	-160	260	2483	1515	137	-37
Hunan	1269	-3457	95	5	1747	875	40	60	3942	3159	53	47
Guangdong	-1716	-5995	50	50	4368	2960	19	81	5901	4497	67	33
Guangxi	1164	-2260	106	-6	1052	673	23	77	2751	2277	45	55
Sichuan	2152	-6741	92	8	2845	1207	55	45	6408	5043	58	42
Guizhou	3066	605	-283	383	442	123	105	-5	1391	1066	65	35
Yunnan	3224	155	-1379	1479	356	-53	-312	412	951	489	202	-102
Tibet	24	-175	79	21	-3	-15	-32	132	14	14	529	-429
Shaanxi	1620	-457	316	-216	461	-207	-131	231	1463	971	109	-9
Gansu	974	-380	248	-148	643	320	41	59	628	150	680	-580
Qinghai	216	-45	405	-305	0	-93	-40	140	163	86	190	-90
Ningxia	254	-15	1229	-1129	120	43	73	27	206	140	102	-2
Xinjiang	156	-670	86	14	268	46	193	-93	508	261	203	-103

Note:
[a] A minus sign indicates that this component was operating in the opposite direction from the direction of NRC. The indication is applied to all relevant tables in this chapter hereafter.

Table 13.3 Rankings of employment changes of provinces, 1985–94

Province	Agriculture	Industry	Services
Top 7	Jilin, Guizhou, Yunnan, Ningxia, Qinghai, Shaanxi, Gansu	Guangdong, Henan, Fujian, Guangxi, Shandong, Anhui, Hebei	Sichuan, Guangdong, Hunan, Henan, Anhui, Guangxi, Jiangxi
Middle 7	Shandong, Inner Mongolia , Hebei, Guangxi, Hunan, Jiangxi, Sichuan	Guizhou, Jiangxi, Xinjiang, Sichuan, Zhejiang, Shanxi, Inner Mongolia	Hebei, Ningxia, Fujian, Shaanxi, Shandong, Hubei, Jilin
Bottom 7	Shanghai, Beijing, Tianjin, Guangdong, Jiangsu, Zhejiang, Liaoning	Tibet, Qinghai, Tianjin Shanghai, Liaoning, Beijing, Shaanxi	Gansu, Tianjin, Tibet, Shanghai, Shanxi, Heilongjiang, Liaoning

experienced an absolute decline (negative actual changes). The decline was mainly influenced by the structural component; this is particularly true in the metropolitan cities (Beijing, Tianjin and Shanghai), the southern coastal provinces (e.g. Jiangsu, Zhejiang and Guangdong) and the provinces with large share of industry already (e.g. Liaoning).

- Second, the general trend of employment in the industrial sector was a large increase in the fast-growing (e.g. Guangdong, Jiangsu, Zhejiang and Shandong) or catch-up provinces (e.g. Henan, Hebei and Anhui), and a slow increase in either the most industrialized cities (e.g. Tianjin) and provinces (e.g. Liaoning), or the least developed provinces (e.g. Qinghai, Ningxia and Yunnan). The structural component played a positive role in the sector's increase in employment in all provinces, but the differential component played a positive role only in the fast-growing or catch-up provinces, and a negative role in the rest.
- Third, the increase of employment in the service sector was predominantly due to the structural component; 'other factors' made positive contributions to growth in some provinces (e.g. Guangxi, Hunan, Guangdong) and negative in others (e.g. Gansu, Tianjin).
- Fourth, the shift of employment from the agricultural sector to the industrial and service sectors largely reflects the process of industrialization. The main feature of employment change in the municipalities and industrial provinces was not expansionary but rather shifts between sectors, and their shares of employment in the national total, were declining as a result of low growth in employment. For some new developing provinces, high employment growth occurred owing to both structural changes and the expansion of their economic scale.

It is very interesting to notice from Table 13.3 that there are four different patterns of employment change.

(1) The *Guangdong model* was characterized by shifting employment from agriculture to industry and services, while overall employment increased rapidly. The causality of the increase was shared by both of its industrial mix and its location.
(2) The *Shandong model* enlarged its employment share in the industrial sector considerably, with a moderate reduction in agriculture and a proportional growth in services.
(3) The *Liaoning* model revealed some critical problems facing those economies largely dependent upon state-owned heavy and military-based industries. Net relative change in employment in those provinces performed poorly in all sectors. There was a serious unemployment or under-employment problem in the local economy under economic reforms and rapid structural transformation.
(4) The *Gansu model* was representative of the northernwestern provinces where natural conditions are poor and agriculture plays a dominant role in the economies. The model was characterized by a continuous increase in agricultural employment, an average growth in industry and below-national average growth in services.

These growth models in employment, as will be seen later, are borne out once again by the patterns of change in investment.

Change in investment

To gain further insights into the scale of regional disparity, it may be interesting to undertake a separate analysis of the changes in investment.

During the Maoist period, China's development strategy was geographically-oriented towards the interior central and the western regions, and sectorally-oriented towards military production in the so-called 'Third-Front' industries. As Zhao (1996) points out, more than 50 per cent of national investment went to a few interior provinces with Liaoning alone gaining 11.6 per cent of national investment over the period 1953–62, and Sichuan 13.6 per cent during the period 1966–70. These investments generally received the lowest economic return. Since the reform, China has radically changed its national development priorities from the interior provinces to the coastal (eastern) provinces. A package of economic policies was designed and implemented on investment, foreign trade, taxation and land-rental, in favour of the so-called 'special economic zones' (SEZs). Investment was then heavily concentrated in the southern and eastern coastal provinces in general and Guangdong in particular. Massive investment into the coastal provinces has greatly improved their economic position. For instance, between 1985 and

1992, Guangdong jumped from eighth to fourth in *per capita* national income (NI) rankings (only below the three municipalities, Beijing, Tianjin and Shanghai) and from seventh to first in the growth rate rankings.

Like the change in employment, the change in investment occurred also in terms of share and shift. It is related not only to national growth trends and structural changes, but also to local performance. Table 13.4 provides the results of shift-share analysis for all provinces of China.

With the overall national investment increasing at 447 per cent over the period 1985–94, a shift of investment between sectors occurred: net relative investment shrank by 385 per cent in agriculture and 20 per cent in industry, and increased by 42 per cent in services. Given this national trend, investment changes in different provinces show some clear patterns. In agriculture, all provinces (except Tibet) had negative NRCs, and suffered from the unfavourable national trend towards agriculture. Some provinces, however, performed better than others. For example, the differential component of agriculture in Hebei was −54 per cent against its NRC (−136 per cent), which means better local performance reduced 54 per cent of the effect of its unfavourable industrial mix. The provinces that performed better in agriculture include Jilin, Heilongjiang, Shanghai, Zhejiang, Fujian, Jiangxi, Guangdong, Guangxi, Yunnan and Xinjiang. On the other hand, with the nationwide increase in services, some provinces performed poorly. Liaoning, for instance, had an NRC of −4898 million yuan, of which its differential component contributed 129 per cent, cancelling 29 per cent of the sectoral effect. Other provinces which performed poorly include Shanxi, Jilin, Heilongjiang, Anhui, Hubei, Guizhou, Shaanxi, Gansu, Qinghai, Xinjiang, Beijing, Tianjin, Jiangsu, Sichuan and Tibet. The results in Table 13.4 reveal the following points:

- First, the investment shortage in agriculture spread over the whole country, and about ten provinces experienced an absolute decline. This decline was closely associated with the structural component and can be explained by the instability in agricultural production over the period.
- Secondly, the variation of investment in the industrial sector was mainly related to the differential rather than the structural component. While Guangdong increased its investment in both industries and services, the rest of the coastal provinces were shifting investments from industry towards services, and the less developed provinces were struggling to increase their investments in industries. The service sector in general received increasing investments. The largest increase occurred in the eastern coastal provinces, especially in Shanghai and Guangdong. This was attributed to a favourable industry mix and remarkable local performance. An exceptional case was found in Jiangsu and Sichuan, where poor local performance concealed the structural advantage of 14 per cent and 61 per cent, respectively.

Table 13.4 Structural and differential components of NRC in investment (million yuan)

Province	Agriculture				Industry				Services			
	Change (million)		Share of NRC (%)		Change (million)		Share of NRC (%)		Change (million)		Share of NRC (%)	
	Actual	NRC	Structural	Differential	Actual	NRC	Structural	Differential	Actual	NRC	Structural	Differential
Beijing	30	-305	95	5	7920	2186	-12	112	15152	-3021	-56	156
Tianjin	-12	-182	80	20	6338	452	-59	159	2715	-2661	-19	119
Hebei	106	-136	154	-54	9090	198	-203	303	9280	871	90	10
Shanxi	-24	-395	81	19	4979	-10945	7	93	3402	-3030	-20	120
I. Mongolia	-9	-286	83	17	7432	2208	-11	111	3262	-1041	-38	138
Liaoning	22	-533	90	10	15808	1839	-34	134	10457	-4898	-29	129
Jilin	52	-279	102	-2	7159	1255	-21	121	4131	-33	-1165	1265
Heilongjiang	308	-560	134	-34	4950	-10504	7	93	6080	-3148	-27	127
Shanghai	72	-232	113	-13	8588	-8566	9	91	34514	20049	7	93
Jiangsu	29	-311	94	6	8131	-5462	11	89	12647	955	114	-14
Zhejiang	90	-344	109	-9	6587	1184	-21	121	12280	4032	19	81
Anhui	-72	-868	79	21	4734	-4037	10	90	4075	-1136	-43	143
Fujian	72	-308	106	-6	5502	-1167	26	74	8850	2914	19	81
Jiangxi	81	-241	115	-15	2841	-1820	12	88	3945	962	29	71
Shandong	64	-629	95	5	10119	-5796	12	88	15196	4023	26	74
Henan	-27	-886	84	16	9729	-451	102	-2	10449	4920	10	90
Hubei	-20	-1116	85	15	14793	6312	-6	106	7213	-1357	-59	159
Hunan	-19	-431	82	18	5220	49	-473	573	8114	2626	19	81
Guangdong	357	-1821	103	-3	43329	22458	-4	104	41826	16165	15	85
Guangxi	105	-409	108	-8	5239	1790	-9	109	6824	2248	19	81
Sichuan	48	-610	93	7	12183	-350	161	-61	12008	656	161	-61
Guizhou	3	-158	88	12	2706	-170	76	24	1763	-1073	-25	125
Yunnan	118	-343	116	-16	4197	212	-85	185	6008	1692	24	76
Tibet	58	31	-74	174	487	-184	16	84	864	-272	-39	139
Shaanxi	-1	-278	86	14	4328	-1755	16	84	3308	-2981	-20	120
Gansu	-148	-984	73	27	2491	-1964	10	90	1679	-1067	-24	124
Qinghai	6	-155	89	11	1047	-2674	6	94	380	-1977	-11	111
Ningxia	-12	-254	82	18	1273	-1438	9	91	324	-852	-13	113
Xinjiang	204	-615	115	-15	10698	5474	-4	104	3555	-1294	-35	135
Total	1481	-50528	96	4	227898	-11666	93	7	250301	32269	63	37

It is clear that over the period, the national economic environment was favourable to the service sector, and detrimental to agriculture. The eastern coastal provinces were in the process of diversification, while the western inland provinces in the process of industrialization. Table 13.5 provides the rankings of provinces by investment growth.

A close examination of the results reveals four investment growth models similar to the four employment growth models:

(1) The *Guangdong model* focused its investment strategy heavily upon industry and services. Consequently, the local economy attracted large investments, mostly accounted for by the differential component.
(2) The *Shandong model* invested proportionally among different sectors with a slight bias towards services. The differential component contributed about 74 per cent to its positive NRC.
(3) The *Liaoning model* had to invest substantially in industry to maintain its traditional economic structure (we call this 'passive investment'). Given a certain amount of investment, therefore, investment in other sectors had to be low. Despite the remarkable inadequacy (negative NRC figures) of investment in services and agriculture and the unfavourable structural component of the industrial sector, Liaoning still invested considerably in its industries. The differential component of industrial investment was 134 per cent. This made up for its structural loss of 34 per cent, but was at the expense of slow diversification out of old industries.
(4) The *Gansu model,* with its low level of competitiveness, had negative NRC for investment in all sectors. Low investment could be explained by the sectoral trend in agriculture, but for other sectors it could be explained only by its poor competitiveness.

Table 13.5   Rankings of investment changes of provinces, 1985–94

Province	Agriculture	Industry	Services
Top 7	Hebei, Heilongjiang, Yunnan, Jiangxi, Xinjiang, Guangxi, Yunnan,	Guangdong, Xinjiang, Hubei, Guangxi, I. Mongolia Beijing, Zhejiang	Shanghai, Guangdong, Fujian, Zhejiang, Henan, Jiangsu, Shandong
Middle 7	Guangdong, Shandong, Beijing, Jilin, Guangxi, Jiangsu, Sichuan	Hunan, Hebei, Sichuan, Henan, Liaoning, Fujian, Shandong	Hebei, Beijing, Jiangxi, Sichuan, Hubei, Jilin, Tibet
Bottom 7	Gansu, Anhui, Ningxia, Shanxi, Hunan, Henan, Liaoning	Qinghai, Shanxi, Heilongjiang, Ningxia, Anhui, Shanghai, Gansu	Qinghai, Ningxia, Shaanxi, Gansu, Shanxi, Liaoning, Guizhou,

Results of sectoral disaggregate analysis for three selected provinces

As argued earlier, spatial analysis for all provinces with highly aggregated sectors is useful in providing a broad picture of the national economy. It may, however, conceal the difference in industrial structure and performance at provincial levels. From the regional policy-making viewpoint, it would be more useful to conduct the analysis at a refined sectoral level. Data available at disaggregated level (SSB, 1985–95) make it possible for us to carry out a provincial comparison analysis at the 16-sector classification, but we will report only detailed results of the nine sectors which are of paramount importance.

Three provinces – namely, Liaoning, Guangdong and Gansu – are selected in this section. The selection is based upon the following considerations:

(1) The size of employment changes between 1985 and 1994;
(2) The representativeness of different types of regional economies in terms of industrial structures and economic growth.
(3) Their representitiveness of geographical location.

Major economic features of the three provinces are highlighted in Table 13.6.

Traditionally, Liaoning is one of the most industrialized provinces in China, its economy depending largely on heavy industry, especially the steel, machinery and chemical industries. For a 15-year period (1953–67), the province alone received about 11 per cent of total national investment among the 30 provinces. Employment share in 1985 was 35.9 per cent in agriculture, much below the national average, and 40.2 per cent in industry, nearly double the national average. Guangdong is a coastal province; in 1985, its employment structure was about the same as the national average, and its *per capita* NI ranked number eight. Gansu is one of the poorest regions in the country in terms of its infrastructure, development stage, and natural condition – a large

Table 13.6   Changes in GDP and employment structure, selected provinces, 1985–94

| | GDP | | Employment structure (%) | | | | | |
| | (Yuan/per head) | | 1985 | | | 1994 | | |
	1985	1994	Agriculture	Industry	Services	Agriculture	Industry	Services
China	856	3679	63.7	20.9	15.3	54.3	22.7	23.0
Liaoning	1469	5015	35.9	40.2	23.9	31.2	38.5	30.3
Guangdong	1005	4938	60.4	19.7	19.9	42.7	26.7	30.6
Gansu	669	1600	62.8	14.6	22.6	59.0	17.7	23.3

Table 13.7   Structural changes, 1985–94, per cent

	Employment				Investment				National income			
	Total	A	I	S	Total	A	I	S	Total	A	I	S
All China	23.3	5.0	34.0	84.2	447.3	61.9	427.1	488.9	296.3	163.6	393.6	201.3
Liaoning	13.8	–1.0	9.0	44.0	393.5	17.7	484.3	324.5	218.3	225.4	225.3	267.1
Guangdong	28.0	–9.3	73.4	96.3	785.2	73.3	851.1	792.1	451.1	192.1	740.9	326.0
Gansu	24.2	16.7	50.3	28.3	223.8	–79.1	242.2	286.3	221.8	179.7	226.3	330.9

Notes: A = agriculture; I = industry, S = Services.

proportion of its land is located either in the Loess Plateau or in the Gobi desert. During the so-called 'Third-Front' development period (1966–70), the province had a number of military-based projects, and established many large-scale SOEs in the machinery, chemical, iron and steel industries. A large proportion of the labourforce was and still is engaged in extensively managed agriculture.

After 15 years of reform, especially now that current reform has reached the most sensitive sector of the economy – the state-owned industries – fundamental changes have occurred in all aspects of economic structure at the provincial level. Liaoning, as one of the most important industrial bases in China, faces the typical problems of the Soviet-type planned economy, such as an unbalanced industrial mix with enormous inefficiency, significant unemployment and under-employment in the SOEs, and heavy dependence on a few traditional industries governed by central planning. Guangdong has followed the newly industrialized countries' (NICs) path, and has been one of the most rapidly growing regional economies. It has achieved the highest growth in employment, investment and *per capita* income. It attracted 10.65 per cent of total national investment in the early 1990s, and accounted for 58 per cent of the total foreign investments in 1979–88 and 37.7 per cent in 1989–92. Gansu has some typical problems confronted by most Third World countries, such as low productivity, lack of investment, and poor economic infrastructure. Beside its low economic growth, Gansu's economic position seems to be more vulnerable than before:

(1) High employment growth and low investments imply a decline in the capital/labour ratio.
(2) An absolute increase in employment and an absolute decrease in investment in agriculture means that the province is being left further behind in the country's industrialization process.

Table 13.7 outlines the structural changes in the three selected provinces, with the national average provided as a benchmark for comparison.

Changes in employment structure

Table 13.8 presents the results of a shift-share analysis in employment change by sector over the period 1985–94. Had these three provinces followed the national trend, they should have respectively created 4.107 million, 7.091 million and 2.24 million more jobs. Instead, Liaoning had a negative NRC (−1.675 million), as did Gansu (−0.364 million); only Guangdong had a positive NRC of 1.469 million. The results in Table 13.8 show some interesting and clear patterns of employment change:

- First, let us look at the decomposition of NRCs for these three provinces. NRC was −1.675 million in Liaoning, of which 81 per cent of the positive effect from its favourable industrial mix was cancelled out by the 181 per cent negative effect from the poor local performance. In Guangdong, NRC was 1.469 million, 86.4 per cent of which was contributed by the structural component and 13.6 per cent by the differential component. The problem of NRC in Gansu (−0.364 million) was not as serious as in Liaoning in quantity terms, but decomposition of the change suggests that Gansu's local performance was extremely poor, attributing 441.8 per cent of the negative growth and cancelling 1.244 million jobs from its structural component. This implies some serious policy problems at the provincial level.

- Secondly, analyses by the major sectors of three provinces reveal some further insights. Liaoning benefited from its industrial mix in all sectors except agriculture, and suffered from its local performance in all sectors except banking and insurance and education and arts. The problem was particularly serious in manufacturing and energy, construction and others. In the case of Guangdong, both the structural and differential components contributed positively to fast growth of local employment in all sectors (except agriculture and education), remarkably in others, construction, wholesale and retail and estate and social services. This implies a great strength and competitiveness of the provincial economy in terms of its economic structure and other local factors. Overall employment growth in Gansu was mainly driven by a national trend and its industrial mix, the local factors contributing positively only to agriculture, manufacturing and energy, and education. Had the national and structural components been netted out, the situation would have been much worse than it actually was, especially in 'others', transportation and telecommunication and estate and social services.

- Thirdly, it is interesting to note that three largest gaining sectors (i.e. others, manufacture and energy, and wholesale and retail) of Guangdong were directly or indirectly linked to foreign trade, especially the 'others' sector. This is mainly explained by Deng's SEZ policy and its coastal location. The same can be said to explain the second largest losing sector ('others') in

Table 13.8   Major changing sectors in employment, 1985–94

Sector	Actual change (000)	National component (000)	NRC (000)	Structural component		Difference component	
				Quantity (000)	As % of NRC	Quantity (000)	As % of NRC
Liaoning							
Total change	*2432*	*4107*	*–1675*	*1357*	*–81.0*	*–3032*	*181.0*
Agriculture	–61	1474	–1535	–1027	66.9	–508	33.1
Manufacturing and energy	349	1403	–1054	350	–33.2	– 1404	133.2
Construction	287	248	39	328	834.1	– 289	–734.7
Transport and telecom	338	152	186	191	102.4	–4	–2.4
Wholesale and retail	818	322	496	591	119.3	–96	–19.3
Banking and insurance	76	16	60	47	77.4	14	22.6
Estate and social services	153	87	66	139	211.3	–73	–111.3
Education and arts	69	126	–57	–56	99.4	–1	0.6
Others[a]	324	101	223	832	373.0	–609	–273.0
Guangdong							
Total change	*8560*	*7091*	*1469*	*1269*	*86.4*	*200*	*13.6*
Agriculture	–1713	4279	–5992	–2982	49.8	–3010	50.2
Manufacturing and energy	3180	1039	2141	259	12.1	1881	87.9
Construction	1231	359	872	476	54.6	3 96	45.4
Transport and telecom	516	210	306	264	86.2	42	13.8
Wholesale and retail	1541	454	1087	833	76.7	253	23.3
Banking and insurance	145	23	122	68	56.2	53	43.8
Estate and social service	464	63	401	100	25.0	301	75.0
Education and arts	217	154	63	–69	–110.4	132	210.4
Others[a]	2808	287	2521	2370	94.0	151	6.0
Gansu							
Total change	*1876*	*2240*	*–364*	*1244*	*–341*	*– 1608*	*441.8*
Agriculture	894	1372	–478	–956	200.0	478	–100.0
Manufacturing and energy	358	271	87	68	77.9	19	22. 1
Construction	135	87	48	115	238.2	–67	–138.2
Transport and telecom	69	60	9	75	814.3	–66	– 714.3
Wholesale and retail	205	83	122	153	125.5	–31	–25.5
Banking and insurance	22	7	15	19	123.8	–4	–23.8
Estate and social services	23	18	5	28	529.0	–23	–429.0
Education and arts	42	55	–13	–25	194.3	12	–94.3
Others[a]	78	216	–138	1777	–1292.0	–1915	1392.0

Note:

a 'Others' refers to those not included in the statistics of staff and workers but actually participating in production or services and receiving incomes (e.g., re-employed retirees, non-government paid teachers, foreigners).

Gansu but in the opposite direction. Because its remote and hinterland location and its backward economic infrastructure, Gansu's share of foreign trade and foreign investments were extremely small compared with those of other regions. There are hardly any sizeable joint ventures or foreign companies in Gansu to create employment. It is also interesting to note that the booming economy of Guangdong creates massive demand for construction and hence a huge employment opportunity to the sector. In economies such as Liaoning or Gansu, on the contrary, the growing trend in construction was weakened by their local components, precisely by the slow growth of other sectors. This phenomenon can be explained by the neoclassical theory of multiplier–accelerator interaction.

The results in Table 13.8 point to four conclusions:

- First, a large proportion of job destruction took place in agriculture throughout the country. This may be inevitable and necessary in a transitional economy like China. Absolute employment growth in agriculture happened only in remote and backward regions where employment opportunity from other sectors was critically limited.
- Second, manufacturing and energy and construction were generally in an up-trend, but this was not always true in those regions, such as Liaoning, where state-owned heavy and military industries dominated the regional economy. Thus, industrial structural adjustment becomes an urgent and critical task.
- Third, the diversification of a traditional economy, dominated by agriculture or heavy industry, into a modern economy with a large proportion of service-related sectors becomes increasingly important in employment growth. Nevertheless, service-related sectors cannot be developed alone, they are closely related to growth in agriculture and manufacturing.
- Fourth, employment growth was strongly correlated with the growth of the trade-related sectors. Guangdong's is an excellent case in this regard.

Changes in investment structure

As seen from Table 13.9, investments in capital construction increased in all (aggregated) sectors in the selected three provinces except agriculture in Gansu. Over the period, investment growth in Guangdong was remarkably above the national average: 75.6 per cent overall, 17.7 per cent in agriculture, 84 per cent in industry and 73.6 per cent in services.

In contrast, the growth in Gansu was extremely low: absolutely negative growth rate (−79 per cent) in agriculture, 54 per cent below the national average in industry and 13 per cent below the national average in services. In Liaoning, relatively high growth took place only in the industrial sector. For

Table 13.9   Major changing sectors in capital construction investment, 1985–94 (million yuan)

Sector	Actual change	National component	NRC	Structural component Quantity	As % of	Difference component Quantity	As % of
Liaoning							
Total change	*26288*	*29875*	*–3587*	*1044*	*–29.1*	*–4630*	*129.1*
Agriculture	22	555	–553	–478	89.7	–55	10.3
Manufacturing and energy	15149	13208	1941	–822	–42.3	2762	142.3
Construction	659	760	–101	339	–334.2	–440	434.2
Transport and telecom	2473	4383	–1910	2078	–108.8	–3988	208.8
Wholesale and retail	965	1337	–372	180	–48.5	–553	148.5
Banking and insurance	722	286	436	399	91.7	36	8.3
Estate and social services	2765	3328	–563	891	–158.3	–1454	258.3
Education and arts	652	2254	–1602	–1320	82.4	–282	17.6
Others	413	367	46	–259	–560.3	305	660.3
Guangdong							
Total change	*85512*	*48710*	*36811*	*594*	*1.6*	*36217*	*98.4*
Agriculture	357	2178	–1821	–1877	103.0	55	–3.0
Manufacturing and energy	39012	20235	18777	–1259	–6.7	20036	106.7
Construction	4317	635	3682	283	7.7	3 399	92.3
Transport and telecom	20349	5645	14704	2676	18.2	1 2028	81.8
Wholesale and retail	1036	2903	–1867	392	–21.0	–2259	121.0
Banking and insurance	432	738	–306	1030	–336.5	–1336	436.5
Estate and social services	11580	7371	4209	1974	46.9	2234	53.1
Education and arts	2360	3534	–1174	–2069	176.3	8 95	–76.3
Others	808	1315	–507	–928	183.1	42 1	–83.1
Gansu							
Total change	*4020*	*8047*	*–4027*	*–1219*	*30.3*	*–2808*	*69.7*
Agriculture	–148	836	–984	–721	73.2	–264	26.8
Manuf. and energy	2399	4339	–1940	–270	13.9	–1670	86.1
Construction	92	116	–24	52	–213.3	–76	313.3
Transport and telecom	253	394	–141	187	–132.7	–327	232.7
Wholesale and retail	237	188	49	25	51.6	24	48.4
Banking and insurance	115	45	70	62	88.8	8	11.2
Estate and social services	127	349	–222	93	–42.1	–315	142.1
Education and arts	160	729	–569	–427	75.0	–142	25.0
Others	–11	157	–168	–111	66.0	–5 7	34.0

the analysis of regional investment policies, it is necessary to decompose the influential factors by components. Table 13.9 presents the shift-share results.

For Liaoning, six out of nine sectors presented here were influenced negatively by the differential component, four out of nine were affected negatively by the structural component, only the banking and insurance sector was affected positively by both. Furthermore, it is interesting to note that the highest differential component can be found in the 'others' sector which includes foreign companies and joint ventures. This reflects the fact that Liaoning received an increasing amount of foreign investment, which shared 7.6 per cent of the national total in 1994. All this indicates that an adjustment of investment structure was urgently required. The increase in investments should be emphasized in its construction, transport and telecommunication and estate and social services to give full play to its favourable industrial mix.

In Guangdong, the NRC of 36 811 million yuan was decomposed into a positive structural component (1.6 per cent) and a positive differential component (98.4 per cent). Despite the negative effects of the structural factor in banking and insurance, wholesale and retail and manufacturing and energy, it achieved an outstanding performance in all those sectors.

Gansu had an NRC of –4027 million yuan, 30.3 per cent of which was attributed to its industry mix, and 69.7 per cent to poor local performance. Indeed, apart from wholesale and retail, and banking and insurance, the differential component played a negative role in all the other sectors. This implies that the problem of investment in Gansu was serious not only in its scale, but also in its structure.

Conclusions

This chapter has assessed the structural changes in employment and investment in China over the period 1985–94 from three aspects: the national trend, industrial mix and local performance. The analysis and discussion lead to the following conclusions:

- The disparity of economic growth between the east-coastal provinces (e.g. Guangdong) and the interior hinterland provinces (e.g. Gansu) was closely related to different competitiveness in attracting production factors. It is explained mainly by local industrial mix in the base year and individual performance during the data period. Of course, some external factors, such as biased government policies, geographical location and external shocks, also played a role in the process.
- The country's economic structure was undergoing a dramatic change in both employment and investment in capital construction. First, the shift of employment from agriculture to other sectors may be necessary in an industrialization process and inevitable as the result of the increase in agricultural productivity. However, the dramatic decline of investments in agriculture mostly affected the poor in the northwestern parts of the country, including 60 million rural population who are in poverty. If the current trend cannot be changed, it will create more serious social, economic and even political problems in the future. Lack of agricultural investments has undermined sustainable development in the sector which is responsible for feeding the huge and ever-increasing population.

Secondly, the relative decline of industry that occurred in both the most and the least industrialized provinces have different implications: for the former it means a forward adjustment towards a diversified modern economy with an increasing share of services; for the latter, it means a backward adjustment towards a more agriculture-dominated economy. Thirdly, the relatively high increase in investments with a relatively low increase in employment in most south-coastal provinces resulted in a much higher capital/labour ratio than that in the northwestern provinces. This will generate larger profit shares, higher savings rates and higher competitiveness to attract more factor inputs, and thus higher growth rates the former provinces. Given the country's limited labour and capital resources, this will eventually widen the current spatial disparities even further.

- Analysing three selected regional development patterns reveals various problems being faced by different provinces in terms of industrial structures and regional policies. Liaoning suffered from its industrial mix inherited from the planned system. It has been highly vulnerable to external shocks, such as substantial cuts in defence spending, and industrial reorganization (at the national level) away from heavy industries which are of significant importance to the local economy. When an economy faces such external shocks, quick reactions to diversify and reorganize its industrial structure become fundamentally necessary and important, especially for increasing employment opportunities. For the regional economies like Gansu, problems are rather persistent and pervasive. Poor infrastructure and remote location impose a number of constraints on economic development. Biased reform policies in favour of the more advanced regions have helped widen the disparities between the rich and poor regions. From an equality viewpoint, the central government should reverse its current policy so as to be more favourable towards the northwestern provinces.

Note

*   I am indebted to Shujie Yao and Sarah Cook for their comments, but remain solely responsible for any shortcomings.

Bibliography

Arcelus, F. J. (1984) 'An Extension of Shift-share Analysis', *Growth and Change*, 15, pp. 3–8.

Armstrong H. and J. Taylor (1993) *Regional Economics and Policy*, 2nd edn, (London: Harvester Wheatheaf).

Berzeg , K. (1978) 'The Empirical Content of Shift-share Analysis', *Journal of Regional Science*, 18, pp. 463–9.

Casler, S. D. (1989) 'A Theoretical Context for Shift and Share Analysis', *Regional Studies*, 23, pp. 43–8.

Dunn Jr, E. S. (1960) 'A Statistical and Analytical Technique for Regional Analysis', *Papers of the Regional Science Association*, 6, pp. 97–112.

Esteban-Marquilas, J. M. (1972) 'A Reinterpretation of Shift-share Analysis', *Regional and Urban Economics*, 2 (3), pp. 246–55.

Fothergill, S. and G. Gudgin (1979) 'In Defence of Shift-share Analysis', *Regional and Urban Economics*, 12, pp. 249–255.

Griffin, K. and R. Zhao (1993) *The Distribution of Income in China* (New York: St. Martin's Press).

Healey, M. and D. Clark (1984) 'Industrial Decline and Government Response in the West Midlands: The Case of Coventry', *Regional Studies*, 18, pp. 303–18.

Hoppes, R. B. (1994) 'Rejoinder: Industry-level Shift-share Analysis', *Economic Development Quarterly*, 8, 214–17.

Hussain, A., P. Lanjouw and N. Stern (1994) 'Income Inequalities in China: Evidence from Household Survey Data', *World Development*, 22 (12), pp. 77–96.

Ishikawa, Y. (1992) 'The 1970s' Migration Turnaround in Japan Revisited: A Shift-share Approach', *Papers in Regional Science: The Journal of RSAI*, 71(2), pp. 153–73.

Knight, J. and L. Song (1993) 'The Spatial Contribution to Income Inequality in Rural China', *Cambridge Journal of Economics*, 103, pp. 1221–27.

Kurre, J. A. and B. R. Weller (1989) 'Forecasting the Local Economy, Using Time-series and Shift-share Techniques', *Environment and Planning A*, 21, pp. 753–70.

Knudson, D. and R. Barff (1991) 'Shift-share Analysis as a Linear Model', *Environment and Planning*, 23, pp. 421–31.

Liu, A. and D. Clark (1995) 'Industrial Reorganization of a Defence Based Regional Economy after the Cold War: The case of Portsmouth in Britain', *Discussion Paper*, 62, Department of Economics, University of Portsmouth.

Moore, B. C. and J. Rhodes (1973) 'Evaluating the Effects of British Regional Economic Policy', *Economic Journal*, 83, pp. 87–110.

Randall, J. N. (1973) 'Shift-share Analysis as a Guide to the Employment Performance of West Central Scotland', *Scottish Journal of Political Economy*, 20, pp. 1–26.

Selting, A. C. and S. Loveridge (1994) 'Testing Dynamic Shift-share', *Regional Science Perspectives*, 24, pp. 23–41.

State Statistical Bureau (SSB) of PRC (1985–95) *China Statistical Yearbook* (Beijing: Statistical Publishing House).

Stevens, B. H. and C. L. Moore (1980) 'A Critical Review of the Literature on Shift-share as a Forecasting technique', *Journal of Regional Science*, 20, 4, pp. 419–37.

Stillwell, F. J. B. (1970) 'Further Thoughts on the Shift and Share Approach', *Urban Studies*, 4, pp. 451–8.

Theil, H. and R. Gosh (1980) 'A Comparison of Shift-share and the RAS Adjustment', *Regional Science and Urban Economics*, 10, pp. 175–80.

Yao, S. (1997) 'Industrialization and Spatial Income Inequality in Rural China: 1986–92, *Economics of Transition*, 5(1), pp. 97–112.

Zhao, X. (1996) 'Spatial Disparities and Economic Development in China, 1953–92: A Comparative Study,' *Development and Change*, 27, pp. 131–63.

14
Economic Reforms and the Stability of Long-run Demand for Money in China: Some Results from Co-integration Tests*

Chaodong Huang

Introduction

The demand for money function is a macroeconomic relationship of crucial importance. It forms the key linkage between the monetary sector and the real sector in basic macroeconomic models, and has direct policy relevance as the channels and effects of monetary policy are captured by the functional form and parameter values of this relationship. Indeed, the formulation and effectiveness of monetary policy largely depend on the existence and stability of the relationship between monetary aggregates and economic activities, price, and interest. This chapter aims to investigate the implication of economic reforms on money demand in China, focusing on the long-run stability of broad and narrow monetary aggregates. The issue of stability of the demand for money arises naturally both from China's economic transformation and its inadequate treatment in most previous studies.

There exists a vast literature on the theoretical and empirical studies of the demand for money, most of which are related to industrial countries.[1] In comparison, research in the context of the Chinese economy is less plentiful. Previous work includes Chow (1987); Portes and Santorum (1987); Burton and Ha (1990); Peebles (1991); Yi (1993); Hafer and Kutan (1993, 1994); Huang (1994); Qin (1994); Tseng *et al.* (1994); Girardin (1996), among others. Various issues related to the specification and estimation of the demand for money function in China have been addressed in these studies. For example, Chow's early work (1987), using data for 1952–83, suggests that a model based on the quantity theory provides a reasonable first approximation for money demand in China. Portes and Santorum (1987) studies the money and goods markets in the disequilibrium framework. Later studies typically estimated the money demand by error-correction models. While these research results have undoubtedly enhanced our understanding of the subject significantly, there still remain some basic problems which have not been adequately dealt with.

One such issue is the stability of the money demand function. This is particularly relevant to the Chinese economy. Since the late 1970s the economy has been undergoing a fundamental reform which has introduced profound changes to its institution and the behaviour of economic agents. As a result, it is most likely that previously held behavioural relations may break down. Such breakdowns have been detected for other economies which have experienced institutional reforms or drastic changes in economic conditions,[2] and should be similarly examined for the Chinese economy as well. It appears that previous studies on money demand in China did not address the issue adequately. Some simply ignored it, others worked only on sub-sample of the post-reform economy, based on the prior belief that structural breaks must have occurred. Such treatment of this important issue cannot be regarded as satisfactory. The effect of economic reforms on the behaviour of the economy has to be investigated and understood, rigorous testing of model stability is also needed for an adequate model of money demand function and for the design and conduct of monetary policy.

It is therefore the purpose of this chapter to address this problem. The questions raised are whether the reforms have resulted in structural breaks in the empirical equation of money demand in China, and how such breaks, if detected, may be interpreted in terms of institutional and behavioural changes introduced in the transition of a planning-dominated economy to a market-oriented economy. In particular, the focus of investigation will be on the existence and stability of a long-run money-demand function, since this has to be established before one can move on to formulate an error-correction-type model to characterize the short-run dynamic adjustment.

The plan of the chapter is as follows. We briefly review the Chinese economic reform experience and its relationship to the behaviour of money demand; we then introduce the model. Methodological issues of stability tests for the money-demand function are considered before the empirical results are presented. The final section summarizes and concludes.

China's reform: the emergence of a monetary economy

The Chinese economic reform since 1978 has not only brought about a period of unprecedented rapid and sustained growth but also fundamental changes to the way the economy operates. Such changes are characterized by a transition from a planning-based command economy to a market-based monetary economy. The aggregate behaviour of money demand is likely to show the effects of these changes.

Prior to the reform, the Chinese economic system remained largely a Soviet-type socialist economy, despite frequent political upheavals and various attempts by the leadership to introduce modifications to the system, including the disastrous Great Leap Forward in 1958. Ownership structure of the economy was dominated by the state sectors. The central co-ordinating mechanism of all economic activities was the comprehensive plan at all levels from the central authorities down to the basic production units, covering detailed economic decisions from production to distribution, from consumption to accumulation, from flows of goods to flows of funds, as well as the allocation of both physical and human resources. The plans were implemented through administrative directives, and market activities were kept to a minimum. In such a planned and command economy, prices were highly distorted and rigid. Though the central attributes of money, as a medium of exchange, a unit of account and a store of value remained valid, the role of money was very limited, for it became subordinate to planning. The banking system was completely state-owned and tightly controlled; there was no separation of central banking from other commercial banking activities. Finally, individuals' decisions on consumption and saving were also subject to strong interventions. Most consumers' goods were not freely traded, and there was no financial market to provide diversified financial instruments for investors.

All this has been changed by the gradual but far-reaching reform which was introduced into nearly all areas including agricultural production, enterprise management, product pricing, investment fund allocation, macroeconomic control, employment system, trade and exchange rate management and financial sectors. Comprehensive central planning has been abolished; in its place are various markets for commodities and factors with participants of varying degrees of autonomy. State dominance in ownership structure has diminished, while township and village enterprises (TVEs) and foreign funded joint ventures (JVs) outperform those in the state sectors. Central to the reform is the establishment of a market system within which competition is promoted and the role of government transformed from a direct organizer of economic activities to an indirect regulator.

To see how far market forces have replaced the planning apparatus in economic co-ordination, Table 14.1 shows the proportion of output and sales subject to administrative and market pricing. At the beginning of the reform period, market pricing had little role to play. Through the reform years its role grew steadily and by the early 1990s covered nearly 70 per cent of agricultural output, 65 per cent of industrial output and 80 per cent of retail sales. The rest was subject to fixed prices or the more flexible guided prices.

The reforms have also given much greater freedom for individuals in making their consumption and saving decisions, by liberalizing the goods markets and by cultivating a financial market. Private savings have grown rapidly since the reform started and responded readily to market signals, in sharp contrast to their behaviour in the pre-reform period. In the pre-reform years private incomes were kept very low and savings were almost negligible. The saving ratio averaged 4.6 per cent and had changed little over the period 1952–78. The same ratio over the period 1979–93 registered 31 per cent, and by 1993

Table 14.1   Relative importance of market and administrative pricing, 1978–92, per cent

	1978	1987	1990	1992
Agricultural output				
Fixed prices	92.6	29.4	25.0	17.0
Guided prices	1.8	16.8	23.4	15.0
Market prices	5.6	53.8	51.6	68.0
Industrial output				
Fixed prices	97.0	Na	44.6	20.0
Guided prices	0.0	Na	19.0	15.0
Market prices	3.0	Na	36.4	65.0
Retail sales				
Fixed prices	97.0	33.7	29.7	10.0
Guided prices	0.0	28.0	17.2	10.0
Market prices	3.0	38.3	53.1	80.0

Sources: Bell *et al.* (1993).

private individuals had savings equal to about 60 per cent of the national income, as shown by Figure 14.1 below.

In the reforms of the financial sector, the People's Bank has been established as the central bank and all its commercial banking functions transferred to the specialized banks. New financial institutions have been created to provide a variety of instruments and services to customers. Securities markets emerged with the first issues of treasury bonds in 1981. A secondary market for government securities, enterprises bonds and shares gradually formed, and in 1990–1, two securities exchanges in Shanghai and Shenzhen were officially opened.

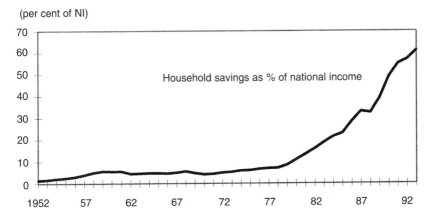

(per cent of NI)

Figure 14.1   Household savings in China, 1952–93
Source: China's Statistics Yearbook (various issues).

(per cent of NI)

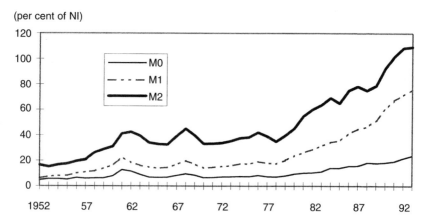

Figure 14.2   Money/GDP ratios in China, 1952–93
Source: China's Statistics Yearbook (various issues).

The change from a physically-based planned economy to a system relying on the market mechanism for the exchange of goods gives money a much more powerful role. Demand for money can be expected to increase substantially. On the other hand, the developments in the financial sector have greatly facilitated the provision of financial services. These factors have contributed to a significant magnetization process, which is a key feature of the post-reform Chinese economy. Figure 14.2 plots the ratios of various monetary aggregates over the national income, clearly showing such a process.

Undoubtedly all the changes discussed above will have an impact on the behaviour of aggregate money demand in the Chinese economy. It could be expected that a structural relationship might break down due to such institutional changes. Whether and how structural changes take place in the demand for money function are examined in the remaining sections.

Model specification

The standard specification of a money-demand function is as follows (Goldfeld and Sichel, 1990; Laidler, 1993):

$$\frac{M_D}{P} = AR^\beta X^\gamma E \tag{14.1}$$

where M_D is demand for nominal money, P is the price level, R is a representative nominal rate of interest, X is the scale variable representing income or wealth, and E is a multiplicative error term. This is a fairly general functional form, to which a wide varieties of models with different theoretical approaches or emphasis can ultimately converge. Most previous studies of the demand for money in China also adopt a model represented by (14.1).[3]

The above relationship is formulated as demand for real money, with a unitary price elasticity imposed. This is supported by economic theories and most empirical results, and is the basic functional form to be used in the following empirical study. However, price homogeneity is a testable hypothesis. There is some evidence which suggests that long-run price elasticities are significantly less than unity in some major industrial countries (Boughton, 1991a). Furthermore, some previous studies on money demand in China are actually formulated in nominal balances. For these reasons, we will also test the more general formulation of demand for nominal money, allowing the price elasticity to depart from unity.

Nominal interest R is to capture the opportunity cost of holding money. Some investigators prefer to use some measures of inflation, or use inflation as an additional variable. However, the impact of inflation expectations on money demand has never been resolved theoretically (Steindl, 1973; Artis and Lewis, 1991), and in most empirical studies such impact is taken to be reflected in the nominal interest rates. Moreover, there is a problem in distinguishing non-zero long-run inflation elasticities from non-zero short-run price elasticities. That is, a standard error-correction model based on a long-run demand for real money allowing for inflation effect will be indistinguishable from that based on a long run function expressed in terms of demand for nominal balances. Because of these theoretical and practical problems, and since our study will allow a test of demand for nominal money, we will not explicitly include an inflation term in the model.

(14.1) can be transformed into a log-linear form in (14.1a), with lower-case letters representing logarithms of the corresponding variables:

$$m - p = \alpha + \beta r + \gamma x + e \qquad (14.1a)$$

From the theoretical point of view, (14.1) or (14.1a) represents a rather general specification of the money-demand function. For empirical studies, however, the model is inadequate in that it assumes instantaneous adjustment in money holding toward its desired levels once those determinants change. This assumption of instantaneous market-clearing is unlikely to hold in reality: adjustment requires time, both because it involves costs and because expectations are not always fulfilled. To capture the sluggish adjustment of money demand toward its desired levels, dynamic models have to be formulated which often employ the hypothesis of partial adjustment, particularly in earlier studies (Chow, 1966; Goldfeld, 1973). More recent econometric practice tends to adopt error-correction models (Hendry and Mizon, 1978; Boughton, 1991b), which may be regarded as a more general, intertemporal version of partial adjustment. The dynamic error-correction model of the demand for money based on (14.1a) is as follows:

$$\Delta(m - p)_t = \lambda_0(L)\Delta(m - p)_{t-1} + \lambda_1(L)\Delta r_t + \lambda_2(L)\Delta x_t$$
$$- \lambda_3[(m - p) - (m - p)^*]_{t-1} + \varepsilon_t \tag{14.2}$$

where Δ is the first difference, $\lambda_i(L)$ is a finite polynomial in lag operator L, and $(m - p)^*$ represented the fitted values from (14.1a).

In the above setting, (14.1a) is interpreted as the long-run demand for money, whereas (14.2) characterizes the short-run dynamic process in which money holdings adjust toward their desired levels.

The analytical framework for testing money demand stability

The estimation of an error-correction model of money demand is carried out in two steps. The first involves establishing a co-integrated relationship between money demand and its long-run determinants, as suggested by (14.1a). In the second, a general distributed lag model is estimated which contains the first differences of both the dependent and independent variables plus the error-correction term from the residuals of the co-integrated relation obtained in the first step, as specified by (14.2). Statistical tests are conducted to ensure that the variables included are all stationary series, thus avoiding the problem of spurious regression (Granger and Newbold, 1974). The general model is gradually reduced to its most parsimonious form, following testing procedures in the general to specific modelling methodology.

Stability testing can be conveniently discussed and conducted within the above framework. The Chinese economic reforms have introduced into the economy changes in the institutional arrangements and agents' behaviour, and may have caused instability in either the long-run or short-run demand for money function, or even in both of these relationships. For example, reforms might cause a one-time level shift in money demand, which will be reflected in the instability of the intercept α in (14.1a). Long-run elasticities might also be changed, so that the coefficients in (14.1a) will exhibit instability. If the short-run behaviour is also affected, there will be instability in the coefficients of λs in (14.2) as well. The effects of the reform can also be detected by observing the significance level of variables, as the importance of such variables may be altered by the reforms.

The testing of the long-run stability is related to the co-integration test.[4] In a relatively stable institutional environment, economic theory predicts that money demand is a stable function of a small number of explanatory variables, typically income and interest rates (Lucas, 1988). A long-run equilibrium relationship is therefore expected to exist between money, income and interest rates in such environments, and can be revealed by testing for the presence of co-integration among these variables. On the other hand, a rejection of co-integration indicates that these variables are not related in a stable and predictable manner over the sample period, possibly owing to changing institutions. In particular, if co-integration between these variables is found to exist for certain sample period characterized by a stable environment but cease to exist for an extended sample which includes periods of economic reforms, this may suggest that the previously stable long-run relationship has become unstable because of the changing environment introduced by the economic reforms.

If co-integration can be established, it is then legitimate to estimate an error-correction model with the co-integrating relationship included. Stability of the short-run money-demand process can then be tested by applying a class of conventional techniques to the dynamic model. These techniques include the Chow-test, predictive failure-test and the CUSUM- and CUSUMSQ- tests (Pesaran *et al.*, 1985).

Empirical results and discussions

This section presents and discusses the empirical results concerning the stability of the long-run demand for money in China. The effects of the economic reforms on money demand are assessed and interpreted in light of these results. Detailed variable definitions and data sources available on request. The econometric package used is Microfit 3.0 (Pesaran and Pesaran, 1991). The co-integration tests follow Johansen's maximum-likelihood procedures (Johansen, 1988; Johansen and Juselius, 1990), but Engle and Granger's (1987) residual-based procedure is also used to provide additional check when necessary.

Testing the order of integration

Prior to the co-integration test, the order of integration of the relevant variables has to be determined, because the presence of co-integration between a number of variables requires that these variables are integrated of the same order. The unit-root-tests of the variables concerned are presented in Table 14.2. Three monetary aggregates are considered: currency in circulation (termed *m0* here), currency *plus* savings deposits from rural and urban households (called *m1*), and currency *plus* all deposits which include saving deposits from both households and institutions (*m2*). The scale variable is the national income y. Both money stocks m and income y are real variables, transformed from nominal series by the national income deflator. r is nominal interest rate. All variables are in logarithms.

Clearly, none of the variables are stationary in level forms. Differenced once, these variables appear to be stationary. With one exception, all statistics for the first differences reject unambiguously non-stationarity at the 5 per cent significant level. The exception is the $ADF_t(3)$ statistic for $\Delta m2$. However, its value is very close to the critical value, and will probably reject the null at the 10 per cent level. Based on this observation, together with evidence from its graph and other statistics for this variable (DF_c, DF_t and $ADF_c(3)$), the

Table 14.2   Unit-root tests of main variables[a]

	DF_c	DF_t	$ADF_c(3)$	$ADF_t(3)$
		Levels		
Critical value	−2.9339	−3.5217	−2.9400	−3.5313
m0	1.1709	−0.4230	1.1463	−0.4516
m1	1.0338	−0.2007	0.6846	−1.0349
m2	0.9954	−0.5206	0.6578	−1.0222
y	0.5993	−1.5839	1.0421	−1.3537
r	−2.9298	−2.4643	−1.7479	−2.0833
		First differences		
Critical value	−2.9358	−3.5247	−2.9422	−3.5348
$\Delta m0$	−5.5833	−5.9652	−3.0638	−4.0261
$\Delta m1$	−3.8049	−4.0349	−3.5081	−4.2482
$\Delta m2$	−4.2684	−4.2695	−2.9963	−3.1927
Δy	−4.3928	−4.4677	−3.7165	−4.1453
Δr	−5.4125	−6.2670	−3.1939	−4.2074

Notes: Data sample, 1952–93. Critical values are given at 5 per cent significance levels.
DF_c Dickey–Fuller-test with a constant.
DF_t Dickey–Fuller-test with a constant and a trend.
$ADF_c(3)$ Augmented Dickey–Fuller-test with a constant, 3 lags.
$ADF_t(3)$ Augmented Dickey–Fuller-test with a constant and a trend, 3 lags.

stationarity of $\Delta m2$ seems to be assured. It is therefore concluded that the order of integration of all the variables under consideration is one – i.e. they all follow an $I(1)$ process.

Co-integration tests

Having determined the order of integration of the basic variables, we can now employ the techniques of co-integration tests to investigate the behaviour of the long-run demand for money in China. The basic long-run model is given by (14.1a). Because there are different definitions for money, and both narrow and broad money are used in previous studies, we use three monetary aggregates here – currency in circulation $m0$, currency *plus* savings deposits from rural and urban households $m1$ and currency *plus* all deposits which include saving deposits from both households and institutions $m2$. The tests report two statistics from the Johansen procedure, *statistic-1* is the likelihood-ratio-test based on maximal eigenvalue of the stochastic matrix, *statistic-2* is the likelihood-ratio-test based on trace of the stochastic matrix. The whole sample covers the period from 1952 to 1993. The co-integration tests are applied to two sub-periods, 1952 to 1978 and 1973 to 1993, respectively, as well as the entire sample period. A constant term is included in the co-integrating equations.

Applying the co-integration test to the basic model, the following results are obtained.

Narrow money m0

Co-integration-test results for narrow money *m0* are presented in Table 14.3 for three different periods. The first sample of 1952–78 covered the pre-reform period, whereas the second sample of 1973–93 was dominated by the post-reform period. Both periods represented relatively continuous, homogeneous economic regimes. The selection of the second period is also based on practical considerations for the degree of freedom – that is, to increase the sample size without changing the nature of the economic regime under consideration. By 1973, the Cultural Revolution had essentially come to its end and the pragmatic leaders represented by Zhou Enlai and Deng Xiaoping started making serious efforts to redirect the country towards economic development. Those several years before the launch of economic reform in 1978 might well

Table 14.3   Cointegration-test result on *m0*: Johansen procedure

Sample period	q – number of Co-integrating vectors: H_0	Test statistic Statistic-1	Statistic-2	Possible co-integrating vectors (PCIV) (normalized on real money balance)
1954–78	$q = 0$	34.1788**	50.6359**	1 PCIV:
	$q \leq 1$	9.8805	16.4570	$m0 = -4.0226 + 0.66491\, y - 0.40999\, r$
	$q \leq 2$	6.5765	6.5765	
1973–93	$q = 0$	28.1305**	46.9612**	*1 PCIV:
	$q \leq 1$	12.1391	18.8307*	$m0 = -24.01 + 3.5320\, y - 2.7334\, r$
	$q \leq 2$	6.6916	6.6916	
1954–93	$q = 0$	29.0782**	52.0374**	3 PCIVs:
	$q \leq 1$	12.2427	22.9593**	$m0 = -12.4098 + 1.6806\, y + 0.45468\, r$
	$q \leq 2$	10.7166	10.7166**	$m0 = -9.4604 + 1.2079\, y + 0.48056\, r$
				$m0 = -12.2958 + 1.7113\, y - 0.10225\, r$

Notes: *significant at 90% critical values; **significant at 95% critical values.
Statistic-1: LR-test based on maximal eigenvalue of the stochastic matrix, relevant critical values are:

Null	Alternative	95% Critical value	90% Critical value
$q = 0$	$q = 1$	22.0020	19.7660
$q <= 1$	$q = 2$	15.6720	13.7520
$q <= 2$	$q = 3$	9.2430	7.5250

Statistic-2: LR-test based on trace of the stochastic matrix, relevant critical values are:

Null	Alternative	95% Critical value	90% Critical value
$q = 0$	$q >= 1$	34.9100	32.0030
$q <= 1$	$q >= 2$	19.9640	17.8520
$q <= 2$	$q = 3$	9.2430	7.5250

be regarded as a preparatory period. The third sample in Table 14.3 includes both pre-reform and post-reform periods.

The tests reveal that in both the first and the second data samples, a unique co-integrating vector exists between real money balance $m0$, real income y and nominal interest rate r. Inspection of the residuals also supports this conclusion. Such co-integrating relationships may be interpreted as the long-run money-demand function for the economy with the institutional environments established in the period concerned. As will be expected for a long-run demand function, the normalized co-integration equations show a positive effect from income and a negative effect from interest rates on the demand for money.

Though the presence of a long-run money-demand function is established for each of the relatively homogenous periods, it is also discovered that parameters in these two relationships are substantially different from each other. Most obviously, the magnitude of all the co-efficients increased significantly in the later period, reflecting the monetization process caused primarily by the transformation from a planned economy towards a monetary economy. Indeed, the parameter values of the two models can be interpreted only in the context of the institutional characteristics of the Chinese economy in these different periods. In the first sample period, income elasticity was found to be below unity. This did not necessarily indicate the existence of the economy of scale in money holding.[5] Rather, it was more likely to reflect the fact that in a planned economy a large proportion of the transactions were conducted without money as a means of exchange. The pursuit of a 'purer' model of socialism under Mao's regime increased the dominance of the planning sector and diminished other sectors. As a result, the increase of aggregate income led only to a less-than-proportional increase in the demand for money. In the second sample period, it was the reverse that was taking place. The role of central planning diminished in the process of marketization. In addition, there were other factors which also contributed to the monetization of the Chinese economy: the economy becoming more open, the structure of the economy undergoing secular changes with fast growth of the services sector, the mushrooming of township industries reducing the farming population. These developments implied that the share of monetary assets in income grew significantly during the second sample period. As a result money growth exceeded income growth, with an estimated income elasticity lying far above unity. The interest rate elasticity is also found to increase greatly in the second period. This may reflect a greater awareness of financial prudence of the general public in a more changeable and market-oriented environment.

The parameter changes in the two long-run equations are evidence of the instability of the money demand in the Chinese economy. Further insight can be gained from the results of co-integration test applied to the basic model over the whole sample, also shown in Table 14.3. For the third sample period

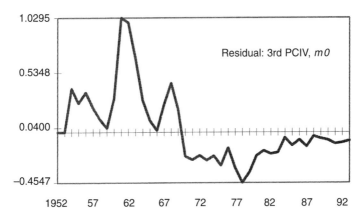

Figure 14.3   Residuals of the 3rd PCIV for *m0* (1954–93) in Table 14.3

of 1952–93, the maximal eigenvalue-test supports the presence of one co-integrating vector, whereas the trace-test indicates that there may exist three such vectors. These three possible relationships are estimated and also shown in Table 14.3. The first two have the wrong sign for the interest elasticity. Only the third one has the right sign of co-efficients expected for a demand function. However, if we examine the residuals of these possible co-integrating vectors, they appear to be non-stationary. The residuals of the third vector is given in Figure 14.3. From the graph, evidence of structural break can also be found. Two different regimes seem to exist over this long period with the early 1970s as the switching point.

When there are multiple co-integrations in the system, these co-integrating vectors span a space in which any linear combination of them may also be a co-integrating vector.[6] In this case, the single-equation estimation of the Engle-Granger (1987) procedure yields coefficients which are weighted average of the Johansen maximum-likelihood estimators (Arestis and Biefang-Frisancho Mariscal, 1993). In order to further check the co-integration property of the variables over the whole sample, we apply the Engle–Granger procedure and get the equation in Table 14.4.

The unit-root-tests reject co-integration at 95 per cent critical values. This result lends additional support for the conclusion drawn from the above tests based on the Johansen procedure that no stable long-run function of money demand exists for the entire sample period.

To summarize, co-integration is present for separate samples representing the pre-reform and post-reform economies, but not for the whole period. Substantial difference in the long-run demand for narrow money is observed for the two regimes. Economic reform has indeed resulted in instability in the long-run demand for money in the Chinese economy.

Table 14.4   Co-integration test for *m0*: unit-root-tests

$m0 = -10.7287 + 1.4508\ y + 0.16407\ r$, $R^2 = 0.96449$ D.W. $= 0.58032$
    (0.37561) (0.044579) (0.075586)

Sample 1952–93, $T = 42$, OLS estimation, standard error in brackets.

Unit-root-tests for residuals:

Statistic	Sample	Observations	Value
DF	1953 1993	41	−2.8358(−3.9546)
ADF(1)	1954–1993	40	−3.6239(−3.9601)
ADF(2)	1955–1993	39	−2.9555(−3.9659)
ADF(3)	1956–1993	38	−2.4452(−3.9720)
ADF(4)	1957–1993	37	−1.7015(−3.9784)

95% critical values in brackets when available.

Before we leave this sub-section, a brief qualification for the above interpretation may be useful. The theories of co-integration have established that co-integrating vectors can be interpreted as long-run equilibrium relationships (Engle and Granger 1991). Therefore, in the above discussion, we interpreted the estimated co-integrating vectors as the long-run money-demand functions. However, it should be recognized that the precise concept of 'long run' itself has not been clearly defined in economics, as argued in Granger (1993). For the money-demand equation discussed here, the presence of a non-unitary income elasticity presents some problems when viewed from a long run perspective. For in the very long-run, it cannot be sustainable for the share of monetary assets in income in an economy to increase without limits. The time horizon in which such a relationship is valid may be more appropriately referred to as 'medium' rather than 'long' run. The existence of a unique co-integrating vector here reflects a stable relationship between money and the other variables over a period when the economic institution is unchanged, but owing to the monetization process in a developing economy the growth in money exceeds that in income. The stability of such a relationship is nevertheless useful for policy formulation, which requires a reasonable length of time but not necessarily the vaguely defined long run.

Broad money m1 and m2

Similar tests are also carried out for the broad definitions of money *m1* and *m2*, with results presented in Table 14.5, Parts I and II.

For *m1*, the narrower definition of broad money which include currency *plus* household deposits, the evidence seems to point to the non-existence of co-integration. The maximal eigenvalue-test rules out any such co-integration between the variables in the basic long-run model for all sample periods, whereas the trace-test has presented a somewhat different picture. As can be

Table 14.5 Co-integration-test result on broad money: Johansen procedure

Sample period	q – number of Co-integrating vectors: H_0	Test statistic Statistic-1	Statistic-2	Possible co-integrating vectors (PCIV) (normalized on real money balance)
			Part I m1	
1954–78	$q = 0$	15.1703	25.0578	
	$q \leq 1$	6.6519	9.8876	Co-integration not found
	$q \leq 2$	3.2358	3.2358	
1973–93	$q = 0$	19.0737	36.5955**	1 PCIV:
	$q \leq 1$	12.5066	17.2218	$m1 = -15.5697 + 2.2398\,y - 0.35243\,r$
	$q \leq 2$	4.7152	4.7152	
1954–93	$q = 0$	18.4151	34.6159*	1 PCIV:
	$q \leq 1$	10.3323	16.2008	$m1 = -13.7399 + 1.9324\,y + 0.71494\,r$
	$q \leq 2$	5.8685	5.8685	
			Part II m2	
1954–78	$q = 0$	27.8818**	40.1649**	1 PCIV:
	$q \leq 1$	8.0840	12.2831	$m2 = -0.87092 + 0.51181\,y - 0.77679\,r$
	$q \leq 2$	4.1992	4.1992	
1973–93	$q = 0$	19.8051*	38.8988**	1 PCIV:
	$q \leq 1$	12.6386	19.0937*	$m2 = -12.0695 + 1.8655\,y - 0.3248\,r$
	$q \leq 2$	6.4551	6.4551	
1954–93	$q = 0$	22.7640**	42.4086**	1 PCIV:
	$q \leq 1$	12.1370	19.6456*	$m2 = -10.296 + 1.6185\,y + 0.29551\,r$
	$q \leq 2$	7.5086	7.5086	

Note: See Table 14.3.

seen from Table 14.5, in 1954–78, both tests unambiguously reject co-integration. For the sample of 1973–93, only the trace-test gives support for the existence of one co-integrating vector at the 95 per cent critical value. The normalized equation may be interpreted as a long-run demand for money function for the period concerned. The obviously large value of income elasticity (larger than unity) is again a reflection of the monetization process in the economic reform period. Because of the absence of the corresponding relationship for the first sample period, here we cannot make comparison for money-demand behaviour under different regimes, as we did for *m0* above. As for the whole sample period, there is only one very weak indication that there might be one co-integrating vector. This is given by the trace statistic at the 10 per cent significant level. We then check the stationarity of the residuals from such possible co-integrating vector, which rejects the existence of co-integration. Figure 14.4 gives the plot of the residuals.

Turning now to the broader measure of monetary aggregate *m2*. The tests identify one unique co-integrating vector for the pre-reform regime. This co-integration represents the long-run relationship of demand for broad money *m2* for that period. The small income elasticity reflected the institutional features of the China economy under central planning system of the time, as

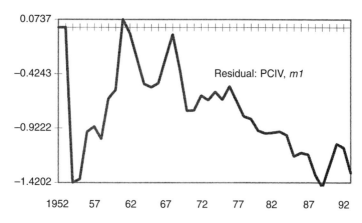

Figure 14.4   Residuals of the PCIV for *m1* (1954–93) in Table 14.5, Part I

we argued earlier in the model of *m0*. For the second sample period, co-integration is also established, giving a long-run demand function of the post-reform period. Compared with its counterpart in the first sample, once again we observe a larger-than-unity elasticity with respect to income. This is expected, given the development in the economy and the economic institution, as has been explained before. However, the elasticity with respect to interest rates decreases in its magnitude compared with that in the pre-reform model. This contrasts the observations we have on the models for narrow money, *m0*. One possible explanation may be given as follows. For the non-interest-bearing narrow money, *r* may be regarded as a good measure for opportunity costs and therefore would be expected to have a negative effect on money holding. On the other hand, for saving-deposit accounts, which form a large part of broad money, *m2*, *r* may be regarded as a proxy for the so-called 'own rates'. It would therefore be expected to have a positive effect on demand for this interest-bearing component of the monetary aggregates. In the pre-reform economy, savings were very low and did not play a significant role in the portfolio-decision-process of agents. The reforms promoted fast economic growth and resulted in a steady increase in saving deposits. The positive effect identified above tended to exert greater and greater importance; as a result, the overall interest elasticity decreases as compared with the pre-reform model. Of course, it would be more desirable to distinguish the two different effects, but data availability prevents us from doing so. Data on interest rates in China is rare and incomplete; the interest rate series used is the only continuous series available, and is used in all previous studies.

When the co-integration test is applied to the sample of 1954–93, the statistics suggest one possible co-integrating vector. But this vector, when interpreted as money-demand function, has a positive interest coefficient,

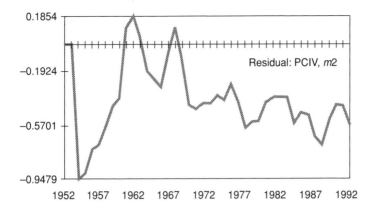

Figure 14.5   Residuals of the PCIV for *m2* (1954–93) in Table 14.5, Part II

which is opposite to those in the two separate models. More seriously, when we further check the residuals of the relationship, given in Figure 14.5, the plot exhibits non-stationarity.

To provide additional information regarding the possibility of co-integration, we use the Engle–Granger procedure to obtain the following static regression result, in Table 14.6.

The unit-root-test of the residuals rejects the co-integration hypothesis at the 5 per cent significance level. From all the evidence reviewed, it can reasonably be concluded that a long-run stable relationship of the demand for *m2* does not exist for 1954–93. The separate models for the first two samples have shown instability in the parameters of the long-run broad money-

Table 14.6   Co-integration-test for *m2*: Unit-root-tests

$m2 = -9.8065 + 1.5787\ y - 0.055323\ r$, $R^2 = 0.97134\ DW = 0.41197$
      (0.36715) (0.043575) (0.073884)

Sample 1952–93, $T = 42$, OLS estimation, standard error in brackets.

Unit-root-tests for residuals

Statistic	Sample	Observations	Value
DF	1953–1993	41	–2.1687(–3.9546)
ADF(1)	1954–1993	40	–3.3986(–3.9601)
ADF(2)	1955–1993	39	–2.4022(–3.9659)
ADF(3)	1956–1993	38	–2.4191(–3.9720)
ADF(4)	1957–1993	37	–2.1185(–3.9784)

95% critical values in brackets when available.

demand for the Chinese economy, and the co-integration-test applying to the sample of 1954–93 also leads to the same conclusion.

In light of all the evidence for testing both the narrow and broad measures of the monetary aggregates in the Chinese economy over the period 1952–93, some observations regarding the stability of the long-run demand for money in China may be drawn. As we can see, the general conclusion emerging from these test results is the following. In a relatively stable regime, co-integration between real money balances and real income and nominal interests does exist. In both the pre-reform and the post-reform period, there are co-integrating vectors which can be interpreted as long-run money-demand-function for the particular regimes. However, these relationships differ substantially in coefficient values and hence in their economic implications for money-demand in the economy under different regimes as well. When we examine this co-integration in the whole sample encompassing both regimes, the separately-held long-run relationships break down. A stable long-run money-demand function did not exist over this whole period. This breakdown of long-run money demand reflects the effect of the economic reform.

Further tests[7]

This section briefly reports two more test results. They provide further evidence on the structural instability of the long-run money-demand function under consideration, and therefore increase the robustness of the conclusions drawn from co-integration tests in the last section. One of the tests employs recursive estimation techniques and the other involves relaxing the assumption of price homogeneity.

Recursive least square (RLS) estimation

Though perhaps less formal and rigorous, the use of the RLS method proves very informative and widely used in detecting structural stability of empirical models. The method is therefore used here as a supplementary tool to shed some light on the issue of stability in money-demand.

Using the RLS method to estimate the long-run money-demand function (14.1a) for the three aggregates of $m0$, $m1$ and $m2$, we obtain the time paths of the relevant parameters. The results are not shown to save space. It is clear from these results that all parameters change significantly in the sample period covering 1952–93. The three different money aggregates share similar paths of their parameter changes. Particularly, the changes appear to conform to the pattern of the economic reform. The examination of these parameters indicates that structural changes in the long-run demand function seem to have occurred when the reform was introduced, hence the whole period can be reasonably split into two separate regimes, both being relatively stable.

Testing for the nominal balances

In the literature on the study of money-demand functions, the assumption of price homogeneity is usually imposed for theoretical reasons, so that the demand for money is formulated in terms of real rather than nominal balances. Available empirical evidence tends to support such theoretical prediction (see Laidler, 1993). In the above exercises, we also followed this practice and constructed the models for real money-demand. However, such an assumption is empirically testable, and there is some evidence, though small in number, which shows a non-unitary price elasticity (e.g. Boughton, 1991a). More importantly, some previous studies on money-demand in China did use nominal balances (Hafer and Kutan, 1994; Huang, 1994). It is therefore necessary to examine the Chinese money-demand function formulated in nominal terms as well. After all, a model allowing for the possibility of price non-homogeneity is more general, encompassing the special case when real money-demand is the dependent variable.

The test results, based on similar techniques but on the demand for nominal money, support the conclusion of a structural break in the money-demand function. The results also contrast those of Hafer and Kutan (1994), who found co-integration between nominal money *M1* and the national income deflator, real income and nominal interest rates using a shorter sample from 1952 to 1988.

Concluding remarks

This chapter investigates the implication of economic reforms on money-demand in China, focusing on the long-run stability and predictability of broad and narrow monetary aggregates. It suggests that previous work on money-demand in China has not adequately addressed the problem, and the present study employs techniques of co-integration and recursive estimation to shed some light on this important issue.

Results based on both co-integration tests and the RLS estimation reveal that the long-run demand for money in China, both narrowly and broadly defined, has exhibited considerable instability in the period 1952–93. The conclusion holds whether the demand for money is formulated in terms of real or nominal balances. The instability is closely related to the economic reforms introduced in the late 1970s. Changes in the institutional environments and agents' behaviour owing to the market-oriented reforms are the major sources of the observed structural breakdown in the long-run money-demand function. For relatively homogeneous economic regimes corresponding broadly to the pre-reform and post-reform periods, stable relationships can be identified which can be reasonably interpreted as long-run money-demand functions for the economy concerned. Both income elasticity and interest elasticity are found to reflect characteristically the working of the economic system and the behaviour of agents under the particular regimes. Specifically, the income elasticity in the pre-reform economy was far below unity, owing to the low degree of monetary economy and the building up of a central planning system in that period. On the other hand, the post-reform period witnessed large-scale marketization and significant changes in the economic structure; as a result a substantial monetization process took place, leading to the observation of an income elasticity far exceeding unity. The changes in interest elasticity also suggest a greater awareness of financial prudence and sizeable increase in savings owing to the economic reforms.

Notes

*   I am grateful to Wojciech Charemza, Zuzhong Zhuang and participants in the 7th Annual Conference of the Chinese Economic Association (UK) for helpful comments. The contents are the sole responsibility of the author.
1.   Among them a selection of examples are Boughton (1991a, 1991b), Goldfeld (1973, 1976); Hall, Hendry and Wilcox (1989); Hendry and Ericsson (1991a, 1991b); Miller (1991): Comprehensive surveys are found in Artis and Lewis (1991); Boughton (1992); Cuthbertson (1991); Goldfeld and Sichel (1990); Laidler (1993).
2.   Goldfeld (1973, 1976); Leventakis and Brissimis (1991); Tseng and Corker (1991).
3.   See the references cited in the Introduction.
4.   The arguments follow closely those of Tseng and Corker (1991).
5.   The classic Baumol–Tobin model demonstrates the presence of the economies of scale in the holding of money. See, Baumol (1952); Tobin (1956).
6.   See the discussion in Clements and Mizon (1991) and examples of such transformation in Adam (1991), Arestis and Biefang-Frisancho Mariscal (1993).
7.   Detailed results for tests in this section are not shown to save space. They are available from the author on request.

Bibliography

Adam, C. S. (1991) 'Financial Innovation and the Demand for M3 in the UK 1975–86', *Oxford Bulletin of Economics and Statistics*, 53(4), pp. 401–24.

Arestis, P. and I. Biefang-Frisancho Mariscal (1993) 'Wage Determination in the UK: Further Empirical Results Using Cointegration', *Applied Economics*, 26.

Artis, M. J. and M. K. Lewis (1991) *Money in Britain: Monetary Policy, Innovation and Europe* (Oxford: Philip Allan).

Baumol, W. J. (1952) 'The Transactions Demand for Cash: An Inventory Theoretic Approach', *Quarterly Journal of Economics*, 66, November, pp. 545–56.

Bell, M. W. *et al.* (1993) 'China at the Threshold of a Market Economy', *Occasional Paper*, 107 (Washington, DC: IMF).

Boughton, J. M. (1991a) 'Long-run Money-Demand in Large Industrial Countries', *IMF Staff Papers*, 38, March.

Boughton, J. M. (1991b) 'Money Demand in Five Major Countries: Estimating and Interpreting Error Correction Models', in M. P. Taylor (ed.), *Money and Financial Markets* (Oxford: Basil Blackwell).

Boughton, J. M. (1992) 'International Comparisons of Money-Demand: A Review Essay', *IMF Working Paper*, WP/92/7, Research Department.

Burton, D. and J. Ha (1990) 'Economic Reform and the Demand for Money in China', *IMF Working Paper*, WP/90/42, Asian Department.

Chow, G. C. (1960) 'Tests of Equality between Sets of Coefficients in Two Linear Regressions', *Econometrica*, 28(3), July, pp. 591–605.

Chow, G. C. (1966) 'On The Long-run and Short-run Demand for Money', *Journal of Political Economy*, 74, April, pp. 111–31.

Chow, G. C. (1987) 'Money and Price Level Determination in China', *Journal of Comparative Economics*, 11, September, pp. 319–33.

Clements, M. P. and G. E. Mizon (1991) 'Empirical Analysis of Macroeconomic Time Series', *European Economic Review*, 35, pp. 887–932.

Cuthbertson, K. (1991) 'Modelling the Demand for Money', Chapter 1 in C. J. Green and D. T. Llewellyn (eds), *Surveys in Monetary Economics*, vol. I, (Oxford: Basil Blackwell).

Engle, R. F. and C. W. J. Granger (1987) 'Co-integration and Error Correction: Representation, Estimation, and Testing', *Econometrica*, 55, pp. 251–76.

Engle, R. F. and C. W. J. Granger (eds) (1991) *Long-run Economic Relationships*. (Oxford: Oxford University Press).

Girardin, E. (1996) 'In Search of a Stable Demand for Money Function for China', *Economic of Planning*, 29 (3), pp. 169–84.

Goldfeld, S. M. (1973) 'The Demand for Money Revisited', *Brookings Papers on Economic Activity*, 3, pp. 577–638.

Goldfeld, S. M. (1976) 'The Case of Missing Money', *Brookings Papers on Economic Activity*, 3, pp. 683–730.

Goldfeld, S. M. and D. E. Sichel (1990) 'The Demand for Money', Chapter 8 in B. M. Friedman and F. H. Hahn (eds), *Handbook of Monetary Economics*, vol. I., (New York: Elsevier Science).

Granger, C. W. J. (1993) 'What we are Learning about the Long Run?', *Economic Journal*, 103(417), March, pp. 307–17.

Granger, C. W. J. and P. Newbold (1973) 'Spurious Regressions in Econometrics', *Journal of Econometrics*, 2 (July), pp. 111–20.

Hafer, R. W. and A. M. Kutan (1993) 'Further Evidence on Money, Output and Prices in China', *Journal of Comparative Economics*, September, pp. 701–9.

Hafer, R. W. and A. M. Kutan (1994) 'Economic Reform and Long-run Money Demand in China: Implications for Monetary Policy', *Southern Economic Journal*, 60(4), pp. 936–45.

Hall, S. G., S. G. B. Henry and J. B. Wilcox (1989) 'The Long-run Determination of the UK Monetary Aggregates', *Bank of England Discussion Papers*, 41.

Hendry, D. F. (1983) 'Econometric Modelling: The 'Consumption Function' in Retrospect', *Scottish Journal of Political Economy*, 30(3), July, pp. 193–220.

Hendry, D. and N. R. Ericsson (1991a) 'An Econometric Analysis of UK Monetary Demand in *Monetary Trends in the United States and the United Kingdom* by Milton Friedman and Anna J. Schwartz', *American Economic Review*, 81, March, pp. 8–38.

Hendry, D. and N. R. Ericsson (1991b) 'Modelling the Demand for Narrow Money in the United Kingdom and the United States', *European Economic Review*, 35, May, pp. 833–81.

Hendry, D. and G. E. Mizon (1978) 'Serial Correlation as a Convenient Simplification, Not a Nuisance: a Comment on a Study of Demand for Money by the Bank of England', *Economic Journal*, 88, September), pp. 549–63.

Huang, G. (1994) 'Money Demand in China in the Reform Period: An Error Correction Model', *Applied Economics*, 26, pp. 713–9.

Johansen, S. (1988) 'Statistical Analysis of Cointegration Vectors', *Journal of Economic Dynamics and Control*, 12, pp. 231–54.

Johansen, S. and K. Juselius (1990) 'Maximum Likelihood Estimation and Inference on Cointegration – With Application to the Demand for Money', *Oxford Bulletin of Economics and Statistics*, 52(2), pp. 169–210.

Laidler, D. E. W. (1993) *The Demand for Money: Theories, Evidence and Problems*, 4th ed (New York: HarperCollins).

Leventakis, J. A. and S. N. Brissimis (1991) 'Instability of the US Money Demand Function', *Journal of Economic Survey*, 5(2).

Lucas Jr, R. E, (1988) 'Money Demand in the United States: A Quantitative Review', in K. Brunner and B. T. McCallum (eds), *Money, Cycles and Exchange Rates: Essays in Honour of Allan H. Meltzer*, Carnegie–Rochester Conference Series on Public Policy, vol. 29 (Amsterdam: North-Holland).

Miller, S. M. (1991) 'Money Dynamics: An Application of Cointegration and Error-correction Modelling', *Journal of Money, Credit, and Banking*, 23(2), pp. 139–54.

Pesaran, M. H. and B. Pesaran (1991) 'Microfit: An Econometric Software Package', *User Manual* (Oxford: Oxford University Press).

Pesaran, H., M. R. P. Smith and J. B. Yeo (1975) 'Testing for Structural Stability and Predictive Failure: A Review', *Manchester School of Ecobomic and Social Studies*, 53(3): 1280–95.

Peebles, G. (1991) *Money in the People's Republic of China: A Comparative Perspective*, (Sydney: Allen & Unwin).

Portes, R. and A. Santorum (1987) 'Money and Consumption Goods Markets in China', *Journal of Comparative Economics*, 11, September, pp. 354–71.

Qin, D. (1994) 'Money Demand in China: The Effect of Economic Reform', *Journal of Asian Economics*, 5(2), Summer, pp. 253–71.

State Statistical Bureau (SSB) (various years) *China's Statistical Yearbook* (Beijing: China's Statistics Press) (in Chinese).

Steindl, F. G. (1973) 'Price Expectations and Interest Rates', *Journal of Money, Credit, and Banking*, November.

Tobin, J. (1956) 'The Interest Elasticity of the Transactions Demand for Cash', *Review of Economics and Statistics*, 38, pp. 241–7.

Tseng, W. and R. Corker (1991) 'Financial Liberalization, Money Demand, and Monetary policy in Asian Countries', *IMF Occasional Paper*, 84, IMF, July.

Tseng, W., H. E. Khor, K. Kochhar, D. Mihaljek and D. Burton (1994) 'Economic Reform in China: A New Phase'. *IMF Occasional Paper*, 114, November.

Yi, G. (1993), 'Towards Estimating the Demand for Money in China', *Economics of Planning*, 26 (3).

15
Is There Any Stable Long-run Equilibrium Relationship between Aggregate Consumption and Income in China?

Haiyan Song, Xiaming Liu and Peter Romilly

Introduction

Following Chow's (1985) seminal quantitative investigation of the relationship between aggregate consumption and income in China, a number of studies have been carried out in this area. These include Portes and Santorum (1987), Qian (1988) and Qin (1991). While these studies are all based on the lifecycle/permanent income-type hypotheses, their empirical results are far from reaching a consensus. Applying switching regression models with 1979 as the break point, Qian (1988) finds that there is a marked difference in consumer behaviour before and after the economic reform. Song, Liu and Romilly (1996) use the Kalman filter approach to estimate the Chinese aggregate consumption function and find that both the average propensity to consume (APC) and marginal propensity to consume (MPC) have changed over time. The instability of the APC and MPC are found to be associated with the political and economic regime shifts. However, in her dynamic error-correction consumption model, Qin (1991) detects no significant changes in the propensity to consume – i.e. there is a constant long-run equilibrium relationship between consumption expenditure and income.

The issue of whether there is any stable long-run equilibrium relationship between consumption and income in China has two important implications. Theoretically, do economic and political policies/shocks affect consumer behaviour within a fixed parameter framework, or is consumer behaviour conformable to the Lucas (1976) critique? Empirically, what quantitative techniques should be employed in the study of the Chinese aggregate consumption function?

Founded on the Soviet model in the 1950s, China was traditionally a centrally planned economy (CPE) and there have been frequent changes in economic, political and social conditions since then. These include the economic strategy, where priority was given to heavy industry in the first Five-Year Plan, the economic programme of the Great Leap Forward in 1958, the 1960–2 economic adjustment period, the Cultural Revolution between 1966 and 1976, and various economic and social reforms since 1979 which have been transforming China's CPE into a socialist market economy with an increasing degree of openness to the outside world.

Political, economic and social changes have happened throughout the history of the People's Republic of China (PRC), and some of them have had sustained rather than once-and-for-all effects on Chinese consumer behaviour. Thus, it is of interest to investigate whether there is any stable long-run relationship between consumption and income in China, and whether it is sufficient to regard the year 1979 as the only switching point in China's consumption patterns.

In this study, both the traditional co-integration testing approach developed by Engle and Granger (1987) and the time-varying parameter (TVP) co-integration technique proposed by Granger (1991) and Granger and Lee (1991) are applied to investigate the nature of the long-run relationship between consumption and income in China. The parameters of interest are the long-run APC and MPC.

The rest of the chapter is organized as follows. We briefly introduce the concepts and tests of TVP co-integration, and then compare the empirical results of traditional and TVP co-integration tests of the Chinese aggregate consumption function. The TVP average propensity to consume and TVP marginal propensity to consume are examined and the final section concludes.

An introduction to TVP co-integration

The standard co-integration technique uses constant parameters to postulate a stable long-run equilibrium relationship among economic variables. If a pair of economic variables, x_t and y_t are both characterized as $I(1)$ and their linear combination is $I(0)$, series x_t and y_t are said to be co-integrated. The Engle and Granger (1987) two-stage test for co-integration between x_t and y_t can first be used to estimate the following co-integration regression (the constant term is omitted for convenience):

$$y_t = \alpha x_t + u_t \tag{15.1}$$

where u_t is the residual and is the co-integration parameter (or vector in the case of more than one independent variable). The second step is to test whether the estimated residual, $\hat{u}_t$ is $I(0)$ using the Dickey–Fuller test procedure. The implication of the co-integration relationship is that the variables in levels form will have a constant equilibrium relationship in the long run, though they may temporarily diverge from equilibrium in the short run. There is always a mechanism that prevents the variables drifting too far away from each other. This mechanism is termed the 'error-correction mechanism' (ECM). The ECM may be obtained from (15.1) as:

$$\Delta y_t = \beta \Delta x_t - \gamma(y - \alpha x)_{t-1} + e_t \tag{15.2}$$

where the parameter γ implies that the economic agent removes units from the disequilibrium $(y - \alpha x)_{t-1}$ occurring in the last period in order to achieve equilibrium in the current period.

In reality, one expects that a long-run equilibrium relationship, if it exists, may not remain constant (i.e. there are structural breaks) owing to changes in taste, expectations and economic polices. If structural changes can be identified at specific times, zero-one dummy variables may be employed in (15.1) to capture their effects. In practice, the breaks may not be easily identified – the co-integration parameter(s) may change in a smooth rather than sharp manner. Thus, dummy variables may be of little help. Recognizing the possibility of structural changes in the long-run equilibrium relationship, Granger and Lee (1991) and Granger (1991) have proposed simulating the possible change in the long-run equilibrium relationship using a time-varying co-integration method. Instead of assuming a constant relationship, the co-integration parameter is allowed to be time-varying:

$$y_t = \alpha_t x_t + u_t \tag{15.3}$$

If there exists a time–varying parameter, α_t, that causes $u_t = y_t - \alpha_t x_t$ to be $I(0)$, we say that x_t and y_t are co-integrated with time-varying parameters.

The change in the co-integration parameter(s) may be modelled by a time-series representation, such as an ARMA(p, q) process. A simple form of time-series representation is the AR(1) process:

$$\alpha_t = \phi_0 + \phi_1 \alpha_{t-1} + \varepsilon_t \tag{15.4}$$

where ε_t in (15.4) is i.i.d with $E(\varepsilon_t) = 0$.

It has been shown by many researchers (see, for example, Engle and Watson, 1987; Granger and Lee, 1991) that time-varying parameters in long-run level models usually have unit roots. In particular, most of the time-varying parameters can be simulated by a random-walk process, that is $\phi_0 = 0$ and $\phi_1 = 1$ in (15.4). Under these circumstances, TVP co-integration should be considered.

An obvious procedure to test for TVP co-integration is to estimate (15.3) and (15.4) via the Kalman filter algorithm and test the integration properties of the estimated residual, $\hat{u}_t$ using the standard augmented Dickey–Fuller-test. If the estimated $\hat{u}_t$ is $I(0)$, this might suggest a TVP co-integration relationship between x_t and y_t. However, there is a probability that the detected TVP co-integration might be a spurious one when the estimated time-varying parameter is expressed by

$$\hat{\alpha}_t = (y_t/x_t) + \xi_t \tag{15.5}$$

where ξ_t is $I(0)$ with zero mean.

This can be seen by substituting (15.5) into the estimated (15.3):

$$\hat{u}_t = y_t - \hat{\alpha}_t x_t = -\xi_t x_t \tag{15.6}$$

It is clear that $\hat{u}_t$ is always stationary since $(-\xi_t x_t)$ is $I(0)$. However, this happens because $\hat{\alpha}_t = (y_t/x_t) + \xi_t$, and not because x_t and y_t are co-integrated. Given the possibility of obtaining a spurious TVP co-integration relationship, Granger and Lee (1991) propose an alternative procedure of testing for TVP co-integration which is outlined as follows:

(a) Test that the variables involved are $I(1)$ or TVP–$I(1)$. In this study we use the Dickey–Fuller-type-tests to examine the integration properties of the data since no tests have been developed for testing TVP–$I(1)$.
(b) Estimate the TVP co-integration regression of (15.3) and generate the one-period-ahead *ex post* forecasts over a certain period.
(c) Estimate a number of alternative models with constant parameters including constant parameter error-correction and VAR models and obtain one-period-ahead forecasts of these models over the same period.
(d) Select the best forecasting models from the alternative constant parameter specifications.
(e) Calculate the correlation coefficient between the forecasting errors from the TVP model and those from the constant-parameter model using

$$r = \frac{\Sigma(\hat{e}_j^c + \hat{e}_i^t)(\hat{e}_i^c - \hat{e}_i^t)}{\sqrt{\Sigma(\hat{e}_i^c + \hat{e}_i^t)\Sigma(\hat{e}_t^c - \hat{e}_t^t)}} \tag{15.7}$$

where $\hat{e}_t^c$ and $\hat{e}_t^t$ are one-step-ahead forecast errors from the constant-parameter model and the TVP-co-integration model, respectively. We would expect that the correlation between the forecasts from the TVP model and those from the constant-parameter model is zero, since by assumption the forecast errors from the two models should be unbiased and uncorrelated.

(f) Calculate a t-statistic based on r:

$$t = \frac{r}{\sqrt{(1 - r^2)/(n - 2)}} \tag{15.8}$$

to test for equality of the forecast errors from the TVP and constant-parameter models. If the calculated $t > -0.72$[1], it would imply that the TVP-co-integration model performs better than the constant-parameter model and therefore the TVP-co-integration relationship should be accepted.

Empirical results

Our empirical test is based on a generalized consumption function of the form:

$$C_t = KY^\eta \varepsilon_t \qquad (15.9)$$

where C_t and Y_t are aggregate consumer expenditure on non-durable goods and national income available, respectively, K and η are constant parameters, and ε_t is the error term which is i.i.d $(1, \delta)$.

The time series used in the estimation of the consumption function are from the Macroeconomic Analysis System (MEAS) database published by the State Information Centre of China (1995). The consumption variable is real personal consumption (RPC) and the income used is real national income available (RNIA) to urban and rural residents. Both series are annual and observations range from 1952 to 1993.

To test whether the consumption and income variables are co-integrated, (15.9) may be written as:

$$c_t = \alpha_1 + \alpha_2 y_t + u_t \qquad (15.10)$$

where the lower-case letters represent the equivalent upper-case variables in logarithms, $\alpha_1 = \ln(K), \alpha_2 = \eta$ and $u_t = \ln(\varepsilon_t)$. (15.10) is the constant-parameter co-integration regression and (α_1, α_2) is the co-integration vector.

If the underlying data-generating process of (15.10) is changing over time, (15.10) can be easily extended to a TVP co-integration regression:

$$c_t = \alpha_{1t} + \alpha_{2t} y_t + u_t \qquad (15.11)$$

and the time-varying parameters α_{1t} and α_{2t} are assumed to follow a random process:

$$\alpha_{it} = \alpha_{it-1} + w_{it} \qquad i = 1, 2 \qquad (15.12)$$

A random-walk specification is used to model the time-varying parameters following the recommendation of Engle and Watson (1987, p. 249), who suggest that this specification is a convenient way of capturing the changes in consumer behaviour caused by the effects of structural changes and policy shocks.

Before testing for a co-integration relationship between consumption and income, the integration orders of the two series are examined using the standard ADF-test procedure. The results are shown in Table 15.1.

The ADF-test results suggest that both consumption and income are $I(1)$ variables.

The Engle and Granger two-stage co-integration test is performed on the error term from the co-integration regression (15.10) using the constant-parameter approach. The reported ADF(2) statistic of -3.426 suggests that consumption and income are co-integrated at the 5 per cent significance level.

Table 15.1   Integration-test results

Variable	ADF	Variable	ADF
c_t	−1.576(5)	Δc_t	−3.887 (4)**
y_t	−1.372(5)	Δy_t	−3.766(4)**

Notes:
a The figures in parentheses are the numbers of lagged dependent variables in the ADF-test.
** Indicates that the unit-root hypothesis is rejected at the 5% significance level.

However, using 1979 as the breakpoint, the Chow (Chow, 1960) breakpoint-test statistic of $F(2, 36) = 3.19$ suggests that the variances of the residuals of (15.10) are significantly different for the periods 1952–78 and 1978–93 at the 5 per cent significance level. Furthermore, if we use 1963 (the end of the Great Leap Forward movement), 1966 (the start of the Cultural Revolution) and 1976 (the end of the Cultural Revolution) as the breakpoints, the Chow tests show that the variances of the residuals are also statistically different for the corresponding periods at the 1 per cent, 5 per cent and 10 per cent significance levels, respectively. This leads to the conclusion that there are several structural breaks in the residuals. The implication is that although a co-integration relationship may exist between consumption and income, the long-run equilibrium is unlikely to be stable.

The alternative test for co-integration is to apply the ADF-test to examine the residuals of the TVP co-integration regression. (15.11) and (15.12) are estimated using the Kalman filter approach (for a detailed explanation of the approach, see, for example, Harvey, 1987; Engle and Watson, 1987) and the ADF(2) statistic of −4.85 from the TVP regression (15.11) is obtained. This suggests that TVP co-integration may exist. However, since there is a possibility of spurious TVP co-integration, the Granger and Lee-test procedure is employed. We compare the one-period-ahead forecasting performance of the TVP co-integration model with alternative constant-parameter models. After some experimentation, the following three best specifications of the constant parameter models in terms of forecasting performance are chosen for the comparisons:

$$ECM^2 : \Delta c_t = \beta_0 + \beta_1 \Delta y_{t-1} - \gamma(c - y)_{t-1} + e_t$$
$$OLS : \Delta c_t = \beta_0 + \beta_1 \Delta c_{t-1} + \beta_2 \Delta y_t + e_t$$
$$VAR^3 : \Delta c_t = \beta_0 + \beta_1 \Delta c_{t-1} + \beta_2 \Delta c_{t-2} + \beta_3 \Delta y_{t-1} + \beta_4 \Delta y_{t-2} + e_t$$

The above models, together with the TVP co-integration regression, are estimated initially over the period 1952–79 and the rest of the observations are recursively estimated to produce the one-period-ahead forecasts for the purpose of forecasting evaluation. The one-period-ahead forecasting errors from the ECM, OLS and VAR models are easily obtained from the estimation.

Table 15.2 t statistics from (15.8)

Model	t-statistics
ECM	1.541
OLS	1.537
VAR	2.880

On the other hand, the one-period-ahead forecasts of the TVP co-integration model are generated from:

$$\hat{e}_t^t = \Delta c_t - (\hat{c}_t^t - \hat{c}_{t-1}^t)$$

where $\hat{c}_t^t$ is the Kalman filter estimate of c_t in (15.11).

The forecasting performance t-statistics of (15.8) are then calculated for each constant-parameter model in relation to the TVP co-integration model, and the results are presented in Table 15.2.

The positive values of the t-statistics suggest that the forecasting performance of the TVP co-integration model is better than all the alternative constant-parameter models. This confirms that TVP co-integration exists between aggregate consumption and income. The constant parameter models developed by Chow (1987) and Qin (1991) may thus not be appropriate in the explanation of consumption behaviour in China.

The TVP consumption propensities

Unlike the constant parameter estimation in which a single value for each parameter is estimated, the Kalman filter approach provides a series of recursive estimates for each parameter corresponding to the sample periods. This allows us to examine the changing pattern of the parameter over time and analyze the effects of political and economic changes.

Estimation of the co-integration regression via the Kalman filter gives us rich information about how the co-integration relationship between consumption and income evolves over time. Figure 15.1 plots the co-integration vector $(\alpha_{1t}, \alpha_{2t})$. It shows clearly that the values of the co-integration parameters have been increasing steadily since the early 1950s.

Based on the estimates of the time-varying co-integration vector, one can also examine the time-varying average propensity to consume (TVAPC) and the time-varying marginal propensity to consume (TVMPC)[4]:

$$MPC_t = \exp[\hat{\alpha}_{1t} + \ln \hat{\alpha}_{2t} + (\hat{\alpha}_{2t} - 1)y_t] \tag{15.13}$$

$$APC_t = \exp[\hat{\alpha}_{1t} + (\hat{\alpha}_{2t-1})y_t] \tag{15.14}$$

where $\hat{\alpha}_{1t}$ and $\hat{\alpha}_{2t}$ are the Kalman filter estimates of the parameters, α_{1t} and α_{2t}, in (15.11).

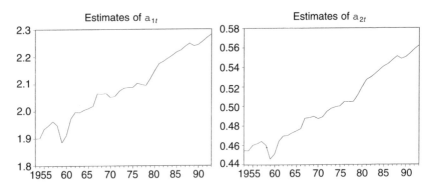

Figure 15.1   Kalman filter estimates of the TVP co-integration parameters

The plots of the estimated long-run TVAPC and TVMPC are presented in Figure 15.2

Figure 15.2 shows that the long-run APC and MPC have experienced several distinct shifts which are closely associated with the following political, economic and social changes.

In line with the Soviet-type economic development model, China's first 'Five-Year Plan' (1953–8) gave priority to heavy industry. Not much attention was given to the development of agriculture and light industry which actually provided consumers with basic necessities. This resulted in a persistent shortage of food and clothing. The 'Great Leap Forward' programme in 1958 and poor harvests from 1959 and 1961 caused a further deterioration in the economic situation. Since expenditure on basic necessities accounted for a major part of Chinese consumers' total income, a decline in their supplies combined with the government's development policy on heavy industry caused both the APC and MPC to fall. The long-run APC dropped from about

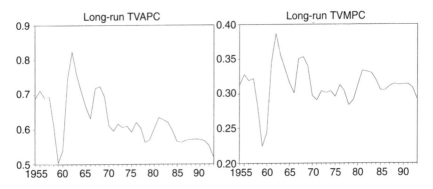

Figure 15.2   Estimated long-run TVAPC and TVMPC

0.7 in 1954 to 0.5 in 1959 while the MPC fell from 0.33 to 0.22 during the same period.

As a result of the 'Great Leap Forward' movement and the natural disaster in 1960, agricultural production fell drastically. This led to a similar decrease in the production of the light industries which depend on the agricultural sector. The government had to shift its policy in favour of consumption by increasing agricultural procurement prices and reducing agricultural taxes. With an improvement of the supply of agricultural products and other basic necessities, the long-run APC rose as high as 0.82 in 1962. It then fell to, and fluctuated around, 0.6 during the 'Cultural Revolution'. The low and stable APC during the period 1969–78 is associated with the continued consumer-goods rationing and stable price controls.

The transformation of the CPE into a market-oriented economy commenced in 1979 when China adopted the policy of economic reform and opening to the outside world. Reform began with agriculture where rural households were allowed to manage production in response to market signals within the system of individual farm plots and rural free markets. This led to a very quick increase in the supply of basic necessities and other non-durable goods in the early post-reform period, and the APC went up from about 0.56 to 0.62.

The reforms gradually spread to enterprise, price and wage systems, labour markets, external policies and banking. During this process total factor productivity (TFP) increased and *per capita* income rose substantially. With further increases in income, the share of consumer spending on basic consumer goods in total household expenditure fell. Although disposable income increased, there was limited scope for consumers to invest in housing and the financial markets. Household savings in the form of bank deposits increased dramatically and the long-run APC gradually declined in the post-reform period.

As can be seen in Figure 15.2, the long-run MPC follows a similar pattern to the long-run APC. This reinforces our argument that consumer behaviour in China has been changing. These changes are closely associated with various changes in the political, economic and social conditions throughout the history of the People's Republic of China (PRC), among which the 'Great Leap Forward' and the succeeding poor harvests, the 1960–2 economic readjustment and the economic reforms seem to have very significant effects on Chinese consumers' behaviour.

Although applications of the TVP approach to the analysis of consumers' behaviour in LDCs are limited in number, the method has been used by many researchers in the examination of the relationship between consumption and income in industrialized countries (such as Gausden and Brice, 1995; Hall and Scott, 1990; Harvey and Scott, 1994). Using Japanese data, Hall, Psaradakis and Sola (1997) develop a TVP co-integration consumption function in which the long-run parameters are allowed to switch between several regimes following a finite-state Markov process with an unknown transition mechanism. Their findings suggest that the long-run co-integration relationship changes over time as a result of changes in the economic environment. Fielding (1996) develops a robust time-series model of consumer expenditure in South Africa for the period 1962–91, and his empirical results suggest that consumption is highly sensitive to measures of political and economic uncertainty, and that higher uncertainty increases APC. An important policy implication of the empirical results of this paper together with the findings of other studies outlined above, is that consumers adjust their behaviour in response to policy changes. This suggests that any regime shift in government policy in relation to the total income level of households in an economy has an irreversible impact on consumers' APC and MPC, and therefore aggregate demand is also affected through the multiplier effect.

Conclusions

Both traditional and time-varying parameter (TVP) co-integration techniques are employed in this chapter to examine the nature of the long-run relationship between consumption and income in China. Although the standard co-integration test apparently shows that there is a long-run equilibrium relationship between the two macroeconomic variables, the Chow statistics demonstrate that the relationship is unstable. Structural breaks can be identified not only for 1979, but also for 1963, 1966 and 1976. In addition, the effects of major political, economic and social changes are seldom once-and-for-all. Rather, they tend to persist over time. To treat the year of 1979 as the only switching point when modelling Chinese aggregate consumption behaviour is not sufficient to capture the effects of all those changes on Chinese consumers' behaviour.

The Granger and Lee (1991) TVP co-integration test suggests that there is a gradually evolving long-run equilibrium relationship between consumption and income in China. However, this conclusion should be treated with some caution because Granger and Lee state in their paper that the distribution property of the t-statistic calculated from (15.8) is not the same as that of the standard t-statistic, and the power of the test is therefore in need of further investigation through simulation. The Kalman filter algorithm provides us with a series of estimates for the long-run APC and MPC. This enables us to investigate in detail the variation over time of the parameters of the Chinese consumption function, and examine how this variation is related to changes in China's political, economic and social conditions.

Appendix

The long-run TVP consumption function may be written as:

$$C_t = K_t Y_t^{\eta_t} \varepsilon_t \tag{15A.1}$$

The expected value of ε_t is unity – i.e. $E(\varepsilon_t) = 1$. Taking logs of (15A.1), we obtain the long-run co-integration regression:

$$c_t = \alpha_{1t} + \alpha_{2t} y_t + u_t \tag{15A.2}$$

The time-varying marginal propensity to consume (TVMPC) based on (15A.1) is:

$$MPC_t = \frac{\partial C_t}{\partial Y_t} = \frac{\partial (K_t Y_t^{\eta_t} \varepsilon_t)}{\partial Y_t} = K_t \eta_t Y_t^{\eta_t - 1} \varepsilon_t \tag{15A.3}$$

and the time-varying average propensity to consume (TVAPC) is:

$$APC_t = \frac{C_t}{Y_t} = \frac{K_t Y_t^{\eta_t} \varepsilon_t}{Y_t} = K_t Y_t^{\eta_t - 1} \varepsilon_t \tag{15A.4}$$

(15A.4) and (15A.5) can be transformed into:

$$\ln(MPC_t) = \ln K_t + \ln \eta_t + (\eta_t - 1)\ln Y_t \tag{15A.5}$$

$$\ln(APC_t) = \ln K_t + (\eta_t - 1)\ln Y_t \tag{15A.6}$$

From the long-run co-integration regression (15A.2), we know that $\alpha_{1t} = \ln K_t$, $\alpha_{2t} = \eta_t$ and $\ln Y_t = y_t$. Therefore, from the estimated results of (15A.2) together with the expressions in (15A.5) and (15A.6), we obtain:

$$MPC_t = \exp[\hat{\alpha}_{1t} + \ln \hat{\alpha}_{2t} + (\hat{\alpha}_{2t} - 1)y_t] \tag{15A.7}$$

$$APC_t = \exp[\hat{\alpha}_{1t} + (\hat{\alpha}_{2t-1})y_t] \tag{15A.8}$$

Notes

* We would like to thank Dr J. Zhuang for his valuable comments and suggestions on earlier drafts of this chapter.
1. The 5% critical value of -0.72 was generated from a simulation by Granger and Lee (1991, p. 151, Table 10.4).
2. In the ECM model we impose a unity restriction on the coefficient of y_t. The forecasting performance of this specification is better than that of the unrestricted ECM model.
3. The second equation in the VAR model is omitted for convenience.
4. See the Appendix above for the derivation of the TVAPC and TVMPC.

Bibliography

Chow, G. C. (1960) 'Tests of Equality between Sets of Coefficients in Two Linear Regressions', *Econometrica*, 28, pp. 591–605.

Chow, G. C. (1985) 'A Model of Chinese National Income Determination', *Journal of Political Economy*, 93, pp. 782–92.

Chow, G. C. (1987) 'Development of Control Theory in Macroeconomics' in C. Carraro and D. Sartore (eds) *'Developments of Control Theory for Economic Analysis' Advanced Studies in Theoretical and Applied Econometrics Series, vol. 7* (Amsterdam: Kluwer Academic): 3–19.

Engle, R. and C. W. J. Granger (1987) 'Co-integration and Error Correction: Representation, Estimation and Testing', *Econometrica*, 55, pp. 251–67.

Engle, R. and M. Watson (1987) 'Kalman Filter Applications to Forecasting and Rational Expectations Models', in T. F. Bewley (ed.), *Advances in Econometrics*, Fifth World Congress, 1, (Cambridge: Cambridge University Press) pp. 245–81.

Fielding, D. (1996) 'Consumer Expenditure in South Africa: A Time-series Model', *Applied Economic Letters*, 3, pp. 385–9.

Gausden, R. and S. J. Brice (1995) 'Forecasting Aggregate Consumers' Expenditure in the UK Using the DHSY Model', *Applied Economics*, 27, pp. 1059–67.

Granger, C. W. J. (1991) 'Developments in the Study of Co-integrated Economic Variables', in R. F. Engle and C. W. J. Granger (eds), *Long-run Economic Relationships: Readings in Co-integration* (Oxford: Oxford University Press).

Granger, C. W. J. and S. H. Lee (1991) 'An Introduction to Time-varying Parameter Co-integration', in P. Hackl and A. Westlund (eds), *Economic Structural Change* (Berlin: Springer-Verlag).

Hall, S. and A. Scott (1990) 'Seasonal Unit Roots, Structural Breaks and Co-integration', London Business School, Centre for Economic Forecasting, *Discussion Paper*, 24–90.

Hall, S., Z. Psaradakis and M. Sola (1997) 'Co-integration and Changes in Regime: The Japanese Consumption Function', *Journal of Applied Econometrics*, 12, pp. 151–68.

Harvey, A. C. (1987) 'Applications of the Kalman Filter in Econometrics', in T. F. Bewley (ed), *Advances in Econometrics*, Fifth World Congress, 1 (Cambridge: Cambridge University Press).

Harvey, A. C and A. Scott (1994) 'Seasonality in Dynamic Regression Models', *Economic Journal*, 104, pp. 1324–45.

Lucas Jr, R. E. (1976) 'Econometric Policy Evaluation: A Critique', *Journal of Monetary Economics*, Supplement, pp. 19–46.

Portes, R. and A. Santorum (1987) 'Money and the ELES Consumption Function: An Application to China', *Journal of Comparative Economics*, 15, pp. 132–41.

Qian, Y. (1988) 'Urban and Rural Household Saving in China', *International Monetary Fund Staff Papers*, 35, pp. 592–627.

Qin, D. (1991) 'Aggregate Consumption and Income in China – An Econometric Study', *Journal of Comparative Economics*, 15, pp. 132–41.

Song, H., X. Liu and P. Romilly (1996) A Time Varying Parameter Approach to the Chinese Aggregate Consumption Function, *Economics of Planning*, 29, pp. 185–203.

State Information Centre of China (1995) *Macroeconomic Analysis System* (MEAS) (Beijing).

Index

Note: page numbers in **bold** type refer to illustrative figures or tables.